Recipes for Life

from God's Garden

by Rhonda J. Malkmus

Recipes for Life ... from God's Garden

Recipes for Life ... from God's Garden

The nutritional and health information in this book is based on the teachings of God's Holy Word, the Bible, as well as research and personal experiences by the author and many others. The purpose of this book is to provide information and education about health. The author and publisher do not offer medical advice or prescribe the use of diet as a form of treatment for sickness without the approval of a health professional.

Because there is always some risk involved when changing diet and lifestyles, the author and publisher are not responsible for any adverse effects or consequences that might result. Please do not apply the teachings of this book if you are not willing to assume the risk.

If you do use the information contained in this book without the approval of a health professional, you are prescribing for yourself, which is your constitutional right, but the author and publisher assume no responsibility.

*However, you are encouraged to quote this book liberally, so that as many people as possible may hear about these ideas and Biblical truths to the ultimate end that somehow, some day, in some way, the whole world may be reached with the knowledge and message, "YOU DON'T HAVE TO BE SICK!!!" You are also encouraged to read this book out loud to your family, friends, acquaintances and even total strangers. May pastors proclaim it from their pulpits. May doctors share it with their patients. Take this book to foreign lands and share it. In fact, please do anything you can to make the world a better place to live, and the people in it happier, healthier and more loving. *It is the goal of Hallelujah Acres to try to bring the people of today back to the simple lifestyle and natural diet that God originally planned for mankind ... a peaceful, happy life, free from stress and sickness.*

Library of Congress Cataloging in Publication Data
Malkmus, Rhonda J.
  Recipes for Life ... from God's Garden
    1. Christian, 2. Recipes, 3. Health, 4. Food, Raw - Therapeutic use.

Library of Congress Catalog Card No. 97-95318
ISBN 0-929619-03-X

First Printing 1998
Thirteenth Printing 2007

Printed in the United States of America
All Bible quotations are taken from the authorized **King James Version**
Cover art by Lorna Spring. Inside art work by Tata Andres, except pages 19, 103 and 223 by Lorna Spring.

Published and Distributed by:

Hallelujah Acres Publishing
PO Box 2388
Shelby, NC 28151
704.481.1700

Visit our web site at www.hacres.com

What Others Are Saying About "The Hallelujah Diet^{sm}" and the Teachings of Dr. George & Rhonda Malkmus

"I have received your teaching series on Back to the Garden and the success that you have had with your modified raw diet. The tape lectures that I have reviewed were inspiring to me. I am a research scientist retired from the FDA/NIH. I am currently working on nutrition and oxygen therapy. Our research has shown that when we eat natural nutrients (at least 65% raw fruits and vegetables) there is an energy explosion within our body. This gives the body the necessary tools it needs to rebuild strong cells that it takes to gain control of the body... We have had great success with our program... This we believe is or will be the beginning road map to return to the Garden of Eden... I would like very much to meet with you."
　　John H. Norris, Ph.D., Maryland

"For the past 15 years, I suffered from acute colitis with constant pain and much bleeding. It drained me physically – I was always tired. A year ago I got desperate before the Lord, praying, *Lord, I can't minister to this huge congregation and keep all these ministries to the needy going unless You heal my bowels. I am at my wits end; I'm too weary to go on.* The Holy Spirit directed me to nutrition for healing. I always made fun of **health nuts** and all the claims being made for alternative health plans. The Holy Spirit taught me what to do: I got off sugar. I drink the juice of carrots and apples daily. I have been completely healed! I have more energy than I had at thirty years of age, and I have never felt better in my life..."
　　David Wilkerson, President, World Challenge

"I was diagnosed with fibromyalgia in 1995 and was on several different medicines. None of the drugs helped me and I spent most of 18 months in bed. Through our church I heard about a seminar on 'Diet for Healing' and was introduced to the book *God's Way to Ultimate Health*. I started on The Hallelujah Diet full force and within three weeks I knew I was getting better. I made a complete life change and now I am able to exercise. I have more energy and walk six miles a day plus bicycle riding. I didn't have a severe weight problem but in the last 14 months I have lost 25 lbs. and I feel wonderful. My family is as happy as I am and have made diet changes also. My 84-year old father is taking Barleygreen and juicing carrots. HALLELUJAH!"
　　Judy Boling, Florida

"We are so glad we found your book. We started on The Hallelujah Diet and have lost nearly 70 lbs. between the two of us in two months. Not to mention how much better we feel. We are ordering more books to pass around to the people in our church. Some have already started the diet without reading the book but want to read it when we can get more copies..."
　　Pastor Mike and Cathy Hoover, Arizona

"... we have more good news for you. We went to the doctor for a check up. The blood profile was beautiful. Blood pressure for George was 127/70. EKG good, urine good, etc. Then we asked the doctor for an extra test for the bladder cancer without going into the bladder and poking around. He said yes. He sent George to the cancer lab... They sent this to a special cancer testing place... it came back – no cancer! Praise the Lord!!"
　　Erna and George Rizzotto, Florida

"I gave a set of your books to my doctor and told him that I wanted to try eating this way. He said it looks good to me, so go ahead and try it. In six weeks I was off Zocor and the chol/tg were way down from the last two years. Thank God and you."
　　Bossie Carlsen, Florida

"It was my dad who gave me your video a year and a half ago and when I started the raw diet my sinus (chronic) problems completely went away as well as the colon problem. I had (still do) fibroid tumors, but they are reduced 50%. And my cholesterol got back down to normal. So I know it works."

     Yvonne Williams, Alabama

"Three months ago I saw your video and read your book *God's Way to Ultimate Health* and it changed my life. Praise God! I was crippled with arthritis in my knees, right shoulder, and degenerative joint disease in my right ankle due to an auto accident in 1989 which broke my ankle in eleven different places. I thought I was headed for a wheelchair. The pain was so severe... God heard my cry and through your ministry I have lost 32 lbs, walk a mile a day or ride my stationary bike for 30 minutes. We had a foot washing service at church Saturday and praise God I was able to kneel and wash my partners feet. Haven't been able to do that since the accident in 1989. I also can walk on the sole of my feet instead of my toes. I am so excited and telling everyone. Haven't had this much excitement since I was saved in 1977. I will keep you in my prayers as I am a believer in your teachings. Thank you."

     Marian Duffield, Kentucky

"When I heard Dr. George H. Malkmus on the 700 Club I sent for a copy of the *Back to the Garden* magazine. After reading it, I ordered all the back issues, plus *Why Christians Get Sick* and *God's Way to Ultimate Health*... We bought a juicer and went cold turkey on The Hallelujah Diet. It has been six months and I have lost 31 lbs. which I needed to lose... As a child of God I cannot sit down to food that I know to be poison to my body and ask God's blessing on it... I am 76 years old."

     Dorothy Johnson, Minnesota

"... I am a great fan of George Malkmus, and about a year ago I went on his diet and changed my life... a year ago, I was crippled to the point of pulling myself out of bed each morning on a wire after hurting my back two years prior... Then I learned of George's diet. After starting George's diet, only three weeks later I was bouncing out of bed like a 16-year old. I am a professional Christian Country Singer from Nashville..."

     Steve Hamby, Tennessee

"Today I thought I would write to let you know I have been working on the new way of eating (Hallelujah Diet) and living. Overweight, I have had high blood pressure for over 30 years and taking medication every day. I went to the doctor the fifth of this month after making the (diet) change only two months ago and for the first time my blood pressure went from 140/80 to 120/60. He couldn't believe this and was almost angry when I told him how I changed my food intake. He told me it will never go down and stay down. He told me I would always have high blood pressure. Besides this, here are the other changes that have taken place. Smooth as silk skin; no more pain in legs and feet and arms; rest better; lost 17 lbs. Thank you."

     Carrie Leiphart, Pennsylvania

"I read your Hallelujah Acres story with much interest. You have discovered that the diet given in Genesis is the key to good health. It is truly amazing that medical science is just catching on to this. I just want to say congratulations and that I hope and pray that your vital message will reach many, many thousands."

     Ken McHenry, Ilinois

"Dear Dr. Malkmus: I would like to formally thank you for all that you have done for my family, myself, and all of God's people... I am a graduate student in the Department of Cell and Molecular Pharmacology and Experimental Therapeutics at a medical university... I have been doing what you refer to as the Hallelujah Diet for over a year now – to the extreme – totally raw... I have realized the power and full potential of this truth. This is the cure to cancer, heart disease, diabetes, and almost every disease..."

     Tobiah Pettus, California

"Thank you so much! I've lost 50 pounds (on The Hallelujah Diet) and no longer take thyroid medication. Hallelujah!"

     Pat Frost, New Mexico

Dedication

This book is dedicated to my wonderful husband, Dr. George H. Malkmus. At a time when all hopes and dreams had been shattered, George came into my life, picked up the broken pieces and gently mended my shattered heart and spirit. He has lovingly taught me a new and better way of living, including eating to live rather than living to eat. George is my hero; he gives of his life and time every day to reach the world with the message, "You Don't Have to be Sick." He never tires of helping others and is such an inspiration to me and to many thousands of people whose lives he has touched.

This book is also dedicated to my parents, Gene and Eleanor Brandow, who have always supported my dreams and taught me, "that with God all things are possible." Their constant love and support have kept me focused. It has given me the burning desire to be a living testimony for our Lord Jesus Christ and a servant to my fellow man even during the trials of my life. Of all the parents in the world, I'm thankful to have been given two of the best!

In addition, I dedicate this work of love to my brothers and sisters who are all very precious, and I feel so honored to be a part of such a special family. Even though we live many miles apart, I carry their love and support in my heart and I want the whole world to know just how special each one is to me. They are Terry Brandow, Cindy King, Tom Brandow, Julie Zumach and Jolene Trickle.

Without the love, encouragement and faith in me by these important people in my life, this book would not have become a reality. Thank you for being such a positive influence, not only to me, but to everyone who has contact with you.

Last, but certainly not least, this book is dedicated to our Lord and Saviour, Jesus Christ, that He might be lifted up, and that you may know Him as your personal Saviour.

"Grace be unto you, and peace, from God our Father,
and from the Lord Jesus Christ.
I thank my God upon every remembrance of you."
– Philippians 1: 2 - 3

Acknowledgements

I would like to thank all of the very special people who have given tirelessly to assist in making my dream of having a recipe book for the Hallelujah Diet and Lifestyle a reality.

First, I would like to thank my sweetheart, George, who has tasted many recipes and was sometimes painfully honest in his evaluations. He has given me ideas, assisted in proofreading and rewriting and encouraged me when the task seemed impossible. George is such a blessing to me; he is truly God's man and I feel so blessed to be able to share his life!

I would also like to thank Michael Dye, who spent countless hours sharing ideas, editing and upgrading my efforts. His work has assisted in making this dream a reality.

Thanks also to Lorna Spring, a former employee of Hallelujah Acres, who spent many hours of her "spare time" creating for me the beautiful painting on the cover of this book.

A special thank you, too, goes to Tata Andres, whose excitement is contagious and who spent a great deal of time creating the art work on the inside pages.

To Carolyn Cocks, my lovely sister-in-law, who volunteered to proofread along with Sharon Whittle and Jean Stoltzfus of our staff at Hallelujah Acres.

To the rest of our staff at Hallelujah Acres who gave me ideas and encouragement, and who shared recipes and covered for me on many occasions so I could take the extra time necessary to make this book a reality. Each one is special and we feel indeed blessed to have them as part of our team!

"The Lord bless thee, and keep thee:
The Lord make his face shine upon thee, and be gracious unto thee;
The Lord lift up his countenance upon thee:
and give thee peace."
– Numbers 6: 24 - 26

Recipes for Life
... from God's Garden

Contents

Testimonies 3
Dedication 5
Acknowledgements 6
Forewords. 11

Part I: Why The Hallelujah Diet^{sm}?

Introduction 19
Chapter 1: Man Has Corrupted God's Way 23
Chapter 2: Back to the Garden 26
    Proper Nutrition 28
    Pure Air 29
    Pure Water 30
    Vigorous Exercise. 32
    Sunshine. 33
    Rest 33
    Postive Thinking (Faith) 34
Chapter 3: Why the Standard American Diet is So SAD 36
    Dangers of Meat. 38
    Dairy Products 42
    Eggs 43
    Food Additives 43
    How to Read Labels 45
    Pesticides 46
    Cholesterol 47
    Sugar and Other Sweeteners 48
    Sodium Chloride and Table Salt 49

Chlorine 50

Fluoride 50

Colas and Other Carbonated Beverages 51

Chapter 4: Unlearning the Reasons You Shouldn't be a Vegetarian . . . 54

Protein 55

Calcium 58

Iron. 60

Vitamin B12 60

Fat 60

Heat Destroys Nutrition 61

My Goal 63

Hallelujah Acres Healthy Foods Pyramid 65

The Hallelujah Diet^sm 66

The Hallelujah Diet...Explained 67

Food Combining Charts 68,69

Chapter 5: Cell-Building Salads 70

Chapter 6: Juicing. 76

Juicing Machines 80

Chapter 7: Enzymes – The Key to Life 82

Chapter 8: Vitamin, Mineral & Protein Supplements – Do We Need Them? . . . 85

Chapter 9: The Healing Crisis 91

Chapter 10: What Are We Feeding Our Children? 94

Raising Health Children Begins with a Healthy Pregnancy and Nursing 94

Children Have Special Needs 101

Tips for Moms and Dads 103

Hallelujah Acres Suggested Program for Children 105

Examples of Meals 108

Breakfast Recipes for Children 109

Chapter 11: Setting Up Your Hallelujah Kitchen 115

Juicing is the Key to Gaining and Maintaining Optimal Health 115

Champion Juicer 116

Green Star Juicer 116

Water Distillers 117

Food Dehydrator 117

Vita-Mix Machine 118

Other Items You Will Find Valuable in Your Kitchen 119

Aluminum Cookware 120

Microwave Oven 120

Replace Cans, Jars, Bottle Food. 122
Revising Recipes. 122
Steps to Prepare a Recipe 122
Setting Up Your Pantry 122
Substitutions 123
Conversions. 123
Recipe Measurements 124
Liquid and Dry Measurement Conversions 124
Chapter 12: Grocery Shopping 125
Produce. 125
Vegetables 126
Fruits. 127
Melons 129
Pantry Items 130
Pasta 130
Grains 130
Condiments 132
Sea Vegetables. 133
Thickeners. 134
Oils 134
Dried Fruits 136
Sweeteners 136
Seasonings. 137
Baking Needs 137
Soy Products 137
Legumes 138
Herbs. 138

Part II: Recipes for Life

The Five-Star System.. 142
Abbreviations and Using a juicer, blender, food processor or Vita Mix 143
Chapter 13: Fruit Salads 144
Chapter 14: Vegetable Salads 151
Chapter 15: Salads and Grain Combinations. 169
Chapter 16: Delightful Dressings 175
Chapter 17: Fresh Vegetable Juices ... The Healers 184
Chapter 18: Fruit Juices ... The Cleansers 191
Chapter 19: Raw Soups. 199
Chapter 20: Delicious Cooked Soups & Stews 207
Chapter 21: Live Food Delicacies 220
Chapter 22: Tempting Cooked Foods 245
Chapter 23: Tasty Breads, Snacks & Sandwiches 274
Chapter 24: Healthy Condiments, Sauces, Dips & Spreads 283
Chapter 25: Dehydrated Foods 296
          Delightful Dehydrates 305
Chapter 26: Special Occasion Treats 314
Fourteen Days of Menu Suggestions 331
Conclusion 337
The Most Important Decision of Life 338
Bibliography. 339
Index of Recipes — by Chapter 342
Index of Recipes — by Alphabet 346
Glossary of Ingredients. 350
Improve Your Health with our Books, Tapes and Videos 354
The Hallelujah Acres story 355
Recipes for Life ... from God's Garden ORDER FORM 356, 357

Foreword by Dr. George H. Malkmus

The first time I met Rhonda in 1990, her body was racked with arthritis and pain. She was taking as many as six to eight Ibuprofen an hour for that pain, she wore a size 20 dress, and she had no hope of ever living without her pain and suffering or physical problems.

This first meeting with Rhonda came only a few months after I started holding seminars on nutrition in the small mountain town of Rogersville, in East Tennessee. The very first time we met, after she shared her physical problems with me, my heart went out to her. I felt I could help her and that the Hallelujah Diet that had restored my body to wellness in 1976 could help alleviate her physical problems also. And so I invited her to one of my very first "How to Eliminate Sickness" seminars.

Well, to make a long story short, Rhonda went on the Hallelujah Diet. When she first started the program, she was severely overweight and couldn't even walk a block without pain. Within one year after adopting the Hallelujah Diet and program, she had dropped from a dress size of 20 to 12, she had lost over 80 pounds in weight, all her arthritic pain had disappeared, and she could walk four miles every morning, without suffering, in less than an hour. Read her own testimony on page 19 for more details.

During this time of restoring her body to wellness, Rhonda worked right across the street from where I had my store, and she would come over almost daily to give me a progress report and to ask questions. All of her problems did not go away immediately, and so she sought encouragement and support. These almost daily contacts led to a friendship and then to a romance and ultimately to a beautiful wedding in the spring of 1992 on an island in the middle of a small lake on our former property in Tennessee.

Before Rhonda came into my life, I had struggled for years to get the message "You don't have to be sick" out to the public and especially to the churches. But during those years I met with very little success. After Rhonda came on the scene, however, the ministry started to grow in leaps and bounds, and soon she was experimenting on me with various concoctions and recipes that fit the guidelines of the Hallelujah Diet I was teaching. She would try the recipes on me, and if I raved about them or even thought they were good, she would try them on the folks who visited our restaurant. If I got excited about a particular recipe and the restaurant customers liked it too, she would put it in her Hallelujah Acres recipe file.

As time went by, more and more people started asking for "Rhonda's Recipes" and that ultimately led her to start writing this book, *Recipes for Life... From God's Garden*. For the past two years Rhonda has spent almost every waking hour (when she wasn't busy in the office at Hallelujah Acres) working on this recipe book. It has been a passion of hers to put recipes into print that support the diet and lifestyle we teach. I believe this book will ultimately be an encouragement and motivation to literally millions of people as they realize that eating God's Way can not only build health but that it actually tastes good too!

For those who don't know Rhonda, she is a very special person who has a heart for helping people. I believe her love and concern for others and her ability to help others has only begun. Through the contents of this book, her influence on others will multiply greatly as her recipes and teachings circle the globe.

Rhonda, God bless you and your new book. I love you and appreciate you and can honestly say that without you and your daily support and encouragement, especially in those early years, I do not believe Hallelujah Acres would even exist today.

Dr. George H. Malkmus
Hallelujah Acres

Foreword by Joel R. Robbins, M.D., D.C.

Recipes for Life ... from God's Garden is a tremendous teaching manual on how to eat a diet that promotes our body's God-given ability of self-healing. Rhonda Malkmus has written an incredibly practical guide that offers **both the information on "how-to" and the inspiration on "why-to" implement a diet that glorifies God as we purify His temple.**

Most people have a diet that contributes to their disease and deterioration rather than healing and glorification of God. We all have a choice when it comes to our health and we will be held accountable for all our choices.

The problem is that usually even when people see the need to improve their health, they simply do not know how. If you are one of the many people who want a healthier diet and lifestyle, but don't know where to begin, this book is for you.

Recipes for Life ... from God's Garden is a very practical and inspirational guide on how to implement a healthy lifestyle and glorify God with a revitalized temple.

Joel R. Robbins, M.D., D.C.

Foreword by Chaplain Graeme D. Coad

George and Rhonda Malkmus came into my life when I was desperate for help. Diagnosed with step 3 prostate carcinoma with a Gleason reading of seven, I was given no hope of a cure and a 20-percent chance to survive for five years. Well wishers bombarded me with alternate remedies and cures … and I tried as many as I could, but it was confusing and discouraging. I did not know what I was trying to achieve.

Then the books *Why Christians Get Sick, God's Way to Ultimate Health* and the tape series, *How to Eliminate Sickness,* came my way. At last I saw light and grasped the simplicity of the remedy. This I could do without great expense and with understanding. By eating raw vegetables and fruit, using barley juice powder as a supplement and fiber supplement as a bowel cleanser, I could get the toxins out of my system and build healthy cells. Add to this exercise, rest, sunshine, faith in God and the basis for healing would be right there.

So I began, and it worked. My body is responding wonderfully. My wife Beverly and I did the training at Hallelujah Acres to become Health Ministers, and have seen many people helped by adopting The Hallelujah Diet and lifestyle.

However, we had questions which were not answered completely by the books or other publications that were available. People wanted recipes and they wanted to know about the special needs of babies and children. They wanted a woman's point of view on this "Diet." After all, they prepare most of the food … and even more so now since eating out is not a great option with the changes. Rhonda Malkmus has answered these questions and much more. *Recipes for Life … from God's Garden* offers the most detailed information yet on how to put the healing power of the Genesis 1:29 diet to work in your life.

Parents, grandparents and mothers-to-be should read, study and practice all of this book, especially Chapter 10, "What Are We Feeding Our Children?" As surely as we are responsible for the care of our own bodies, which are the "temple of the Holy Spirit," so are we responsible for the care of the bodies of our dependents. With this book we have the information needed to honor God in this way.

Rev. Graeme D. Coad
C.B.N. Corporate Chaplain

Foreword by Ron Price

Who says eating fresh, raw fruits and vegetables is boring? In *Recipes for Life ... from God's Garden,* Rhonda Malkmus proves otherwise! A quick glance through the pages of this book stirs the appetite! A little deeper review will uncover a wealth of information about diet, exercise, nutrition, deep breathing, pure water and a myriad of ideas that can make a tremendous difference in your health. Whether you are fighting a debilitating disease or just looking for optimal wellness, this book is for you.

For many years, Rhonda has worked side by side with her husband, George, to teach thousands of people around the world about The Hallelujah Diet. People can come up with lots of arguments to discount this Biblical approach to nutrition, but they cannot argue with the results experienced over and over by those who follow the Malkmus' program. Plain and simple – it works!

The concepts Rhonda teaches in this book have served our family well. For over 10 years, we have followed many of her suggestions. As a result, our family of eight has enjoyed good health, not requiring a single drug for medication (with the exception of two minor injuries) over the entire 10-year period. Imagine that ... 10 years with no medication amongst six children and two adults! If that's the kind of lifestyle you want to enjoy, read this book carefully. It offers fantastic secrets that will help you enjoy a quality of life greater than you may have ever thought possible!

Ron Price, President
AIM International

Foreword by Dr. Mary Ruth Swope

You've heard it said, "The proof of the pudding is in the eating." Maybe that was true in past generations, but not in the 20th century. We have proven that our choices of "good tasting" foods, selected primarily to please the palate and provide healthy profits for food purveyors, have only proven tragic for the health of our society.

When "man's diet" was exchanged for "God's diet," it brought unprecedented degenerative results in the quality of people's health. No doubt about it!

Rhonda and George Malkmus in their new book *Recipes for Life ... from God's Garden* are making a gigantic contribution toward a solution to all of that. They are in the forefront of providing people with a new option for preventing and/or reversing our poor-health syndrome. They are clearly showing us how to return to God's Farmacy (as opposed to man's PHARMACY) to get what we need for optimal health. Truly, as the Malkmus' say, ***"We do not have to be sick!"***

Part I of this new book contains a wide range of reliable nutritional information, along with "how-to's" on a wide variety of subjects, i.e., meal planning, buying household equipment, juicing, diets for children, etc. This book will prove invaluable to those people who are serious about wanting the truth regarding ways to improve their food preparation and eating habits.

Part II of the book consists of nearly 200 pages of recipes which the author has ranked on a scale of 1 to 5, with 5 stars for the all-raw and properly combined foods. These foods are believed to have the greatest positive effect on the health of anyone who consumes them on a regular basis. Foods ranked with 4 stars are also all-raw, but are not properly combined. The other three ratings are applied to various cooked food recipes, as explained on page 142 of the text.

This book will make an outstanding contribution to the health and longevity of all its readers who ***commit*** to its teachings. My prayer is that millions of people world-wide will quickly get on The Hallelujah Diet Bandwagon.

Dr. Mary Ruth Swope
Nutrition Educator

Foreword by Francisco Contreras, M.D.

Health is the perfect balance between God and His creation. In the beginning, God created all things and He saw that they were good. He put the universe into motion and with His love and blessing inititiated natural laws to sustain His masterpiece forever. Each time I hear my infant son giggle or see perfect snowflakes adorn a Colorado mountainside, I am moved to praise God for His omnipotence. When I bite into a crisp apple and am blessed with the sweet juice of life it has to offer, I thank God for His provision.

Once, when I went to a city to lecture, smog began to burn my eyes and my concern for humanity was heightened. After I talked to hundreds of people with illnesses, almost got hit by a taxi, heard gunshots in the background and saw a billboard using cartoon characters to convince children to start smoking, it became clear to me that we had abandoned God's laws. Jesus taught that we reap what we sow. Isn't it true? For decades we have been self-serving creatures of comfort. Today, we are an emotionally, spiritually and physically sick world. The medical industry has offered no salvation. What can we do to get back to the balance we once enjoyed?

I believe we must turn to God for wisdom. The more we get to know God and His way, the more we will receive knowledge and understanding. As we arm ourselves with God's knowledge, we will increase our longevity, joy and productivity. Reading God's Word will encourage you to find His original design amidst the chaos of our existence. You will begin to see that He designed us to breathe fresh air, drink pure water and eat wholesome foods. The original lifestyle is in sharp contrast to the way we are living these days. Government health agencies have completely overlooked what is good and natural. They do not show us the way to health. They have been approving medicines and non-foods for consumption that have been devastating to our health. Was the Apostle Paul referring to our healthcare officials when he wrote, "But their understanding was futile and their foolish hearts were darkened. Professing themselves to be wise they became fools?" We must be wiser than the world's sages.

The human race has upset the natural balance God had set up. After years of abusing natural laws, it has finally caught up with us. We are reaping unnatural illnesses such as cancer, diabetes and heart disease. Thousands of people look to me to find cures to disease. After working for 15 years, side by side with my father, I have come to the conclusion that the only general cure to disease is prevention. The most important part of a good prevention program is diet. Hippocrates, the father of medicine, shared wisdom when he said, "Let your food be your medicine and your medicine be your food." This concept is so basic, yet I have found it to be a profound truth.

Think of your body as a machine. Imagine that you purchased the machine for $50,000 and you expect it to last 10 years. The owner's manual tells you to use only pure top-grade fuel, free of oxidizing by-products that lead to malfunction and breakdown. You have $50,000 invested. Do you risk all by disregarding the owner's manual? Probably not. Does the human body come with an owner's manual? Yes – the Bible.

This "owner's manual" suggests fueling the body with fruits and plants, and has warning labels against gluttony and drunkenness. Jesus said that His Word is living water and that He is the bread of life. Sure, many people disregard the owner's manuel and survive to age 70. Unfortunately, their last 20 years of life are plagued with illness and suffering. I want to live 80 or more healthy and happy years.

In Galatians 5, the Bible teaches us about the fruits of the Spirit. One of the fruits, found in verse 23, is self-control. Only through the Spirit are we able to gain dominion over our bodies and resist the temptation that the food industry presents to us.

Food is one of the most addictive agents I know. It can be easier to give up cigarettes and alcohol than junk food. Fast food has re-educated our taste buds to the point of dependence. Most of us are probably guilty of food worship (idolatry). But Jesus did not come to accuse us. He came to give us abundant life. He came to liberate us from slavery.

I believe that God has sent a love letter to each of us in this wonderful book written by Rhonda Malkmus. I have worked with thousands of patients and tried to help them transition into healthy eating habits. So many have been unable to make that transition. They explain that they do not know how to prepare good and natural food. They complain that the flavor of natural food is not appealing. Rhonda's book will enable these people to overcome these obstacles and free themselves from the bondage of non-nutritious food products.

I thank God for the lives of Rhonda and Dr. George Malkmus. God has used them greatly to save thousands of people from the wages of poor nutrition. I will be recommending this book to all of my patients because Rhonda has made vegetarian food preparation easy, delicious and fun. We will be using her recipes at the Oasis of Hope to the delight of many. As I go out to educate people, I will share *Recipes for Life … from God's Garden* with everyone. It will be an important tool for people to use in their prevention program.

I especially like the recipe for vegetarian taco salad, and that's not just because I'm Mexican! I have been enjoying my meals more and *Recipes for Life* makes it easier for me to promote a raw food diet to the people I meet.

Remember that the beginning of wisdom is the fear of the Lord, the fear of the Lord is the respect of what He stands for, and God stands for order. This order is maintained through natural laws. I consider *Recipes for Life* a message of wisdom, because it provides us with easy tools to comply with natural eating laws established by God. May *Recipes for Life* add many healthy and productive years to your life.

My congratulations to you Rhonda, and my appreciation.

Francisco Contreras, M.D.
Oasis of Hope Hospital

Part I

Why The Hallelujah Diet?sm

Introduction

*"Finally, brethren, whatsoever things are true,
whatsoever things are honest, whatsoever things are just,
whatsoever things are pure, whatsoever things are lovely, whatsoever things
are of good report; if there be any virtue, and if there be any praise,
think on these things."*
– Philippians 4:8

Growing up on a farm in Iowa, I learned early in life the joys of working in the garden. Little plants would appear, as if by magic, a few weeks after planting the seed. If properly cared for, these seedlings would develop into big, strong, healthy plants. Later, I learned it wasn't magic at all, but God's beautiful plan for His creation. How exciting it is to know that He designed all forms of life, even the most simple and basic ones.

Those early years were wonderful as I learned to work with my Mom tending the garden, caring for baby animals and learning how to be a homemaker. It was a very precious time in my life and, as the years passed, brothers and sisters joined our family until there were six of us "little ones."

Being second-eldest, I had the opportunity to help my mother prepare meals, and I soon learned that I loved to cook. My mother is a wonderful cook, and I always admired her ability to take the ordinary and create something wonderful and delicious. Mother shared with me everything she had learned over the years, and I have always been grateful that she was so patient!

When I was in Junior High School, a very important event occurred in my life … one that I shall never forget. I was attending a church youth camp with a very special friend – when I was introduced to John 3:16:

**"For God so loved the world, that he gave his only begotten Son,
that whosoever believeth in him
should not perish,
but have everlasting life."**

Recipes for Life … from God's Garden

At that camp, I also learned that Jesus had taken my place on the cross, paid my sin debt on that old rugged cross with His own precious blood, and all that I had to do was to believe that He had done that for me, and, in simple faith, receive Him into my heart through prayer. I didn't have to buy anything, or earn anything. God gave me a gift, and He offers that same gift today to whomever will accept Jesus Christ as their personal Lord and Saviour. My life has never been the same, and I am so thankful that Jesus loves even me!

After graduation from high school, I ventured out on my own. I lived in various cities in the Midwest and finally settled in Prairie du Chien, Wisconsin. Because of my "lack of knowledge," I spent many years eating the "Standard American Diet" and fighting many bouts with walking pneumonia, ear-aches, sinus infections, colds, flu, headaches, decreasing eyesight that required thicker and thicker glasses, etc.

In 1981, a car accident occurred that would transform my life from a carefree young lady to one of constant pain. Meeting a freight train at a rural Iowa railroad crossing was to make me realize how precious and fragile life can be. It taught me to be thankful for the "little things" and to praise God in the midst of my trials.

There were two impacts that dark October night in Iowa. First when the train hit my little Renault LeCar and the second when the car landed. The car landed nose first, then rolled onto its top. Before the car finally stopped tumbling, my knee went through the dash, the steering wheel was bent in two and the rearview mirror was broken off by my head. The impact was so great it pushed the car engine back four inches and shattered not only every filling in my mouth, but cracked several teeth! Neither I nor my passenger were wearing seatbelts, and I ended up on the passenger side with my passenger on my lap. By the grace of God we walked away with no broken bones!

The very first thought I had when the car stopped rolling was *"In everything give thanks: for this is the will of God in Christ Jesus concerning you."* (I Thessalonians 5:18) With fear and trembling I thanked the Lord as my hand landed on the window crank. The train engineer had already run to my car, and I called to him to open the door, but he apparently thought we were dead and just stood there. Imagine his shock when I rolled down the window and climbed out of the car and opened the door to help my passenger out to safety.

My friend and I were rushed to the hospital where we received many X-rays. The doctors were amazed when they could not find a single broken bone in either of us. What they did find in me, however, was a great deal of deterioration along my spinal column which they attributed to the spinal meningitis I had suffered with as a child. (Spinal meningitis is the inflammation of the meninges and can often be fatal. The miracle drug at that time was penicillin, which was administered to me. As a result, I developed an allergic reaction and lapsed into a coma. The doctor wasn't sure I would live, and if I did live, he was sure I would be physically handicapped the rest of my life. God, however, had a much greater plan for me. My doctor always called me his "miracle girl." He had no other explanation for my recovery.)

In the days and weeks following the car/train accident, I suffered terrible pain. A brain concussion caused short-term memory loss, and I had black and blue eyes for six months. The medical doctors could offer me no relief except for pain killers, telling me, "You will just have to learn to live with it!"

At times, the pain was so intense I would take as many as six to eight Ibuprofen an hour. The only other option I was aware of for possible relief was to try going to a chiropractor. I was very fortunate to find a Christian chiropractor who encouraged me not to take any pain medication, which was all the medical doctors had to offer, because he was afraid I would become dependent on them. It took many, many painful months and extensive treatments to even start to undo what the train had done in a few short seconds.

But even with the chiropractic treatments, the end result of the car/train collision was arthritis in every joint in my body with pain often so intense I thought going home to heaven would be easier. Many times I asked the Lord, "Why?" I couldn't see the big picture. So I clung to the scripture, *"There hath no temptation taken you but such as is common to man: but God is faithful, who will not suffer you to be tempted above that ye are able; but will with the temptation also make a way to escape, that ye may be able to bear it."* (I Corinthians 10:13) I knew in my heart there must be a way to escape the almost constant pain, but I didn't know the answer, and thus I suffered excruciating pain accompanied by severe physical limitations.

By 1986 the arthritis was causing such severe pain and frustration that my physician suggested a move to a milder climate. I placed my home on the market, prayed seeking God's wisdom and waited. No offers materialized. Finally, four years later, a friend who had moved to Northeast Tennessee invited me to come for a visit. When I arrived in Rogersville, Tennessee, located in the beautiful foothills of the Smokey Mountains, I was impressed and immediately felt at home.

Heading back to Prairie du Chien, Wisconsin, after a wonderful visit to Tennessee, I began to seek God's will regarding relocating. I put a fleece before the Lord and said: "Lord, if I'm to move to Tennessee, my home has been on the market for four years, I'll need to have a buyer, and I need a certain amount of money."

The day I arrived home, there was a note on my door from the realtor which read, "Call me; I have an offer on your home." When I called the realtor, I told her, "You don't even have to tell me, I already know the amount of the offer." When I shared with the realtor the dollar amount, she was stunned as the offer was the exact amount, to the penny, I had talked to the Lord about. Within a week, the house was sold and I was on my way to Tennessee. I could hardly wait to see what God had planned for the rest of my life. Little did I know my life was about to change completely.

In October of 1990, shortly after moving to Rogersville from Wisconsin, I happened to stop in a craft mall to see about selling my handmade porcelain dolls. Working behind the counter was a very energetic, enthusiastic man with a beautiful heart-warming smile. His name? George Malkmus, who soon became a friend, later my pastor, and finally my best friend and beloved husband.

George invited me to attend a seminar on health and nutrition that he was conducting. Due to the arthritis, which by this time was causing problems in every phase of my life, I was only too happy to attend. Listening and learning from George was incredible. Could it be that I could be free from the awful pain that racked my body every day? Could what he had to say about diet and lifestyle work for me? The information he shared was all new to me, but it made sense and so I decided to do as he suggested... seek God's Word, pray, and give his program a 90-day trial.

At first, I could only walk about one block due to the excruciating pain. My mind remembered as a child when my mother would tell me, "Rhonda, never give up. Try, try again." Another of her favorite sayings was, "Behind every cloud there is a silver lining – keep searching." These thoughts helped keep me going. So even though my parents were over 1,000 miles away in Iowa, I carried their love and courage in my heart, and it helped me to never give up! Soon I was able to walk a quarter-mile, then a half-mile, and eventually four miles in one hour. What a victory. To God be the glory!

George's health and nutrition seminar had brought me to the threshold of a whole new and exciting world. I realized I would need to abandon my Standard American Diet (SAD) but how to fully adapt this change presented a challenge. What kind of meals can one prepare without meat? How can anyone live on only vegetables, fruits and a small amounts of grains, nuts and seeds? The challenge was before me, and I knew that the Lord wouldn't bring me this far to abandon me now. And so I began a quest to find good nutritious foods. I visited health food stores for the first time in my life. What an adventure! I discovered a wonderful machine called a juicer that extracted the juice from carrots and other vegetables and fruits. I was intrigued; I had to know more!

I began to seek George out, ask questions, and learn from this wonderful teacher that the Lord had put in my path. George kept encouraging me and finally I could not only walk a 15-minute mile, but I had lost 60 pounds and was down to a size 12. My life was beginning to return. I was learning what it means to eat to live, rather than living to eat.

As George and I spent more and more time together, a beautiful and wonderful romantic interest kindled ... a special gift God had been saving for me through all of those years of pain and suffering. Finally, after my physical body had been restored and the pain was gone, God allowed me to become the wife, friend and partner of my best friend. What an exciting day April 11, 1992 was for me as the pastor said, "I now pronounce you man and wife." Finally, I began to see and understand God's plan for my life.

John 10:10 tells us, ***"The thief cometh not, but for to steal, and to kill, and to destroy: I am come that they might have life, and that they may have it more abundantly."*** My prayer is that as I accepted the challenge George presented to me in my time of pain and great need, that you also will accept the challenge before you and give this lifestyle a chance so you too can experience the abundant life I have come to know.

Let me also encourage you with the thought that it is never too late to accept our Lord and Saviour Jesus Christ as your own personal Saviour. He came, lived and died so that you might have eternal life. If you have never accepted Him as your personal Saviour and would like to know more about how to become a Christian, please don't hesitate to contact me.

"For the wages of sin is death;
but the gift of God
is eternal life through Jesus Christ our Lord."
– Romans 6:23

Chapter One:

Man Has Corrupted God's Way

"Be not deceived; God is not mocked:
for whatsoever a man soweth,
that shall he also reap."
– Galatians 6:7

If you could come to Hallelujah Acres and listen in on our telephone conversations for just one day, you would be utterly amazed and in awe of what you would hear. The most frequently asked question is, "Do you think there is any hope?" The word "hope," according to Webster's Dictionary, is defined as "desire accompanied by expectation of or belief in fulfillment." At Hallelujah Acres, we believe as long as there is life and breath, there is always hope. Without hope we are defeated, and the potential for a positive outcome quickly disappears. Following is a sampling of the types of calls we receive:

A dear little lady, crying because she is losing her husband to cancer. The doctors have said, "There is no hope. Put your affairs in order."

A young mother weeping because she is too tired to take care of her family. She has Chronic Fatigue and nothing the doctors are doing seems to be helping.

A young married couple who cannot conceive and the doctor has no explanation. Can anything be done?

A pastor has high blood pressure and hypoglycemia, and the doctors have told him that he will have to be on medication the rest of his life.

A missionary has had to come home from the field because he is too sick to return to the work to which God has called him. The medical doctors have said, "You have contracted some disease in the jungle for which we have no cure."

Recipes for Life … from God's Garden

"And as ye go, preach, saying,
The kingdom of heaven is at hand.
Heal the sick, cleanse the lepers, raise the dead, cast out devils:
freely ye have received, freely give."
– Matthew 10:7-8

A person has contracted AIDS. Is there any hope? Medical science is offering none.

A woman has problems with menopause. The only help the medical profession can offer are drugs. These drugs are causing side effects and she is seeking an alternative. Can anything else be done?

An Evangelist is losing his health. After extensive testing, the medical community cannot tell him the cause or offer him any hope for a cure. Is there any help for him?

A gentleman calls and says, "I've been in an accident which left me with a lot of terrible arthritic pain. Nothing helps, and the pain is so great I just want to die! Can The Hallelujah Diet help me?"

A missionary with a brain tumor the size of an orange calls. The Mayo Clinic says there is no hope – prepare to die! Is there hope? What can we do in addition to prayer?

These are just a sample of the cries for help that come to us everyday. Our response is: "God gave us a truly beautiful self-healing body, and when we apply His teachings on health as found in the Bible, the body will almost always restore itself to wholeness. Hallelujah!"

Within a relatively short period of time we often receive a follow-up call, and on the telephone we may hear:

From a cancer patient: "I just came back from the doctor and the test results were negative. There is no sign of the cancer in my body! The doctor can't believe it and told me that he doesn't know what I'm doing, just keep it up! May God Bless your ministry; what can I do to help?"

From a Chronic Fatigue sufferer: "I'm finally beginning to feel like myself again. For months, I've just been so tired. Thank you for giving me back my life. My family can't believe what's happening, but they love it. When I get totally well, I'm going to tell the whole world."

From the young couple unable to conceive: "You're not going to believe this, but we have just come from the doctor and we are going to have a baby! We are telling everyone we know about The Hallelujah Diet."

From the pastor with high blood pressure and hypoglycemia: "My congregation can't believe what is happening to their pastor. I had not told anyone about my changed diet, but now they are asking questions that I don't know how to answer. Can you please come and give a seminar in my church? I want you to preach the Sunday School Hour, the Morning and Evening Service. My people need to hear what you have to say."

From the missionary sent home from the field: "Mrs. Malkmus, you would not believe what God has done! I'm getting well and we are making plans to go back to the field! You must find a way to get this message into the hands of all of the missionaries doing work for the Lord. They need it desperately!"

From the person with AIDS: "I have a hard time sometimes staying on The Hallelujah Diet, but when I do my energy level is much better. I had blood work done recently and slowly it is improving. I think I'm going to live. I will keep you posted on my progress. Thanks for giving me hope."

From the menopausal woman: "My husband was about to leave me because my mood swings were so severe. No one can imagine how embarrassing and frustrating the acute hot flashes were. Since I have been on The Hallelujah Diet, exercising every day and trying to think positive, some wonderful things are happening. I have gradually cut back on my medication and will be off of it shortly. My mood swings have all but disappeared and the other symptoms have almost gone away as well. I'm telling all of the other ladies I know about this program, and they want me to start teaching them classes on health. Please send me information on how to become a Health Minister!"

From the evangelist: "This program works. After going through the detoxification, which was a little difficult, I'm feeling much better. My voice is stronger, and I don't get as weary. I'm so excited over what I have personally experienced in my own body that I am going to start incorporating what you teach at Hallelujah Acres into my evangelistic message!"

"What do ye imagine against the Lord? he will make an utter end:
affliction shall not rise up the second time."
– Nahum 1:9

The gentleman with arthritis calls and says, "Within a month from the time I changed my diet, I began to see some improvement. Now most of the pain is gone. It's incredible. I have suffered with this pain for years! My family is so impressed they have gone on the program with me, and they are seeing improvement in their health also. My wife likes the fact she doesn't have to cook all of the time."

Less than three months on The Hallelujah Diet, the missionary calls to advise they are preparing to go back to the field, the brain tumor is completely gone, and the doctors are baffled.

All of these results have been accomplished when people simply switched their diet from the Sad American Diet as practiced by the world to God's simple diet as given to mankind by God in Genesis 1:29 shortly after creation! We teach that the only way to eliminate sickness and reach our ultimate level of health is to quit consuming harmful substances – such as meat, dairy, sugar, salt, white flour and other processed foods – which caused or contribute to the sickness, and begin nourishing our body's living cells with the nutrients by which our Creator intended us to be sustained.

"Bless the Lord, O my soul:
and all that is within me, bless his holy name.
Bless the Lord, O my soul, and forget not all his benefits:
Who forgiveth all thine inequities; who healeth all thy diseases;
Who redeemeth thy life from destruction;
who crowneth thee with lovingkindness and tender mercies;
Who satisfieth thy mouth with good things;
so that thy youth
is renewed like the eagle's."
– Psalms 103: 1 – 5

Chapter Two:

Back to the Garden

"The thief cometh not, but for to steal,
and to kill, and to destroy:
I am come that they might have life, and that they might
have it more abundantly."
– John 10:10

Just as our Lord and Saviour Jesus Christ came to offer us eternal life with our Father in Heaven in the next life, He also offers us abundant physical life while we serve Him here on earth in this present life. However, if we want to experience this abundant physical life here on earth, we must choose to follow the guidelines He has given us in the Bible.

After we purchase a new vehicle, the prudent car owner studies the owner's manual thoroughly and follows the instructions precisely in the care and maintenance of that vehicle. Most realize that if they do not, their investment will not last nor perform up to their expectations. For instance, we would never consider taking our expensive automobile to an unqualified mechanic. Or we wouldn't fill its gas tank with low-grade fuel or additives not recommended by the manufacturer. Should we be any less conscientious in the care and maintenance of our body/temple?

Our Heavenly Father has given us a blueprint to follow for the proper care and maintenance of our bodies. That owner's manual for health and well being is, of course, the Bible. Often, it lays on the shelf growing dusty until a time of crisis. Only then do we dust off the cover and search its pages for answers.

Sickness is a problem that plagues both Christians and non-Christians today, as doctors, nutritionists and scientists search everywhere for answers. Everywhere, that is, but the one place where the answers are to be found. The brilliant scientists are looking for genes, viruses, germs or bacteria and yet the answers escape them. The doctors are looking for that miracle drug but never seem to be able to find it. Nutritionists tell us how many milligrams and international units we need of each vitamin and mineral, yet our national health continues to deteriorate. The government puts billions of dollars into research, and the more they spend the poorer our health becomes. Why are they not finding solutions? The answer is they have neglected to look for the *cause*. Unless and until the cause of disease is recognized, understood and removed, the illnesses we suffer will never be eliminated.

It is imperative that we learn to recognize that our lifestyle and eating habits pollute our beautiful bodies, break down our immune systems and *cause* us to be sick. Sickness is simply the body reacting to us putting something into it that God never intended. Until steps are taken to recognize and remove the cause of disease and suffering, only degeneration and early death will result. The Bible puts it this way: We must learn, ***"Be not deceived; God is not mocked: for whatsoever a man soweth, that shall he also reap"*** (Galatians 6:7). We cannot eat the diet of this world and enjoy perfect health and vitality. The choices we make determine whether we live in sickness or in health.

Our Heavenly Father is able to heal sick bodies and minds, and He wants His children to be made whole. But it appears in these days that He is not doing a lot of healing because the percentage of various physical problems of Christians and non-Christians is almost identical. This is because their diets and lifestyles are almost identical. Yes, God wants his children to be made whole, but He usually will not work contrary to His natural laws. For example, if a person is dying of cancer while smoking cigarettes and eating junk food, a prayer asking that their health be restored without them giving up cigarettes or junk food must evidently not be too convincing to God. This is not to underestimate or belittle the power of God; it is only to recognize that God has already offered us a perfect plan for sustaining our health, but His plan has largely been ignored.

We must realize that what we do has consequences that not only affect us personally, but our family members and friends as well. So if we *choose* to have abundant life, it will be necessary to change the diet and lifestyle to which we have become accustomed or addicted. Although it initially may sound difficult and restrictive, if we are to obtain optimum health it is the only wise choice we have.

Our Heavenly Father set these laws in motion for our infinite good to preserve life and to allow His children to attain their highest possible achievements. He set no boundaries on what we may attain, but our diet and lifestyle choices often limit us when we knowingly or unknowingly violate His natural laws. When we bring our lifestyles into alignment with God's laws, most physical problems just simply vanish. Usually we will never get sick anymore. Occasionally, through wrong diet and lifestyle, we do such great harm to our bodies that we take them beyond the point where complete restoration is possible. However, even then, by making simple diet and lifestyle changes set forth in this book, health and quality of life will usually improve.

Yes, God wants His children to be well, and He is able to heal our broken bodies just like when He walked among us. However, He very seldom will overrule His natural laws! When natural laws are violated, we reap the consequences of our actions. Many Christians want to live the way they like, eat what they want, and then when they get sick expect God to bail them out. My friend, it just doesn't work that way. As we humble ourselves to become obedient to our Creator and the natural physical laws He established, we will realize that it is a privilege and indeed an honor to serve such an awesome God!

"And if it seem evil unto you to serve the Lord,
choose you this day whom ye will serve;
... but as for me and my house,
we will serve the Lord."
– Joshua 24:15

Recipes for Life … from God's Garden

The Choice is Yours

In America today most have strayed far from the guidelines we have been given in the Bible. We have violated all of the natural laws God provided at the time of creation, and we have become complacent about our health. We accept illness as a normal part of life. So, let's consider some of the reasons why it is imperative for us to get "back to the garden," and to the diet and lifestyle God originally planned for us.

Too often we feel the need to seek out the physician, whom we have been taught has the cure for all of our ills. However, prevention and maintenance are much easier and certainly more cost effective and will produce superior results. It is important for everyone to learn how to more effectively implement these natural laws God has given us.

When God set before us life and death and admonished us to "choose life," He did not leave us without some guidelines to follow. These guidelines are quite simple and are found in the Bible, and in nature all around us. These guidelines do not stress the body nor will they tax the emotions, even though they contain tremendous powers. The guidelines God gave us are ***proper nutrition, pure air, pure water, vigorous exercise, sunshine, rest and positive thinking (faith).***

"In the beginning God created the heaven and the earth" (Genesis 1:1). This recipe book is based on the evidence that we are, indeed, the creation of God, that He created this planet and all that live upon it and that He laid down for us the principles of correct diet and health.

1. Proper Nutrition

> *"And God said, behold, I have given you every herb bearing seed,*
> *which is upon the face of the earth.*
> *And every tree, in the which is the fruit of a tree yielding seed;*
> *to you it shall be for meat."*
> *– Genesis 1:29*

Come with me, if you will, on a journey back to the beginning, "Back to the Garden." Look at the bountiful fruit and abundant herbs (vegetables) God has provided in nature – perfect food in a perfect setting. Only Almighty God could create such a complete garden. Can you close your eyes and imagine the lovely garden He created for mankind? The birds are singing their lovely songs; the butterflies and bees flutter about; the animals scurry along unharmed by man. It is faultless, with total harmony and love. No anger or violence here. No need to kill another living thing for food. God provides everything we need!

While food only comprises 4 percent of the body's nutritional need (air provides 96 percent), food seems to be the one requirement most of us are concerned about. God's diet provides all the nutrients the body requires to produce healthy blood, calm nerves, a keen mind and abundant health.

In our ignorance and unbelief, we have totally changed and adulterated His plan. We are eating the wrong foods, prepared by methods that destroy rather than nourish our bodies. And then we wonder why our health deteriorates? Even our young people are afflicted with diseases that were once common only among the aged. Why? Have you ever considered the cause?

Although our meals should be lovely and enticing, it is important that they be comprised of the nutrients that our bodies require. They should provide the building blocks of life, not death. It is imperative to learn what are nutritious meals for our families so that we are not creating physical problems and premature deaths by the meals we prepare and serve.

Meals should always be a time of fellowship with one another, a joyful happy time where love abounds. Some of my favorite memories with my family are when the whole family gathered together to share the bounties God has provided for us.

2. Pure Air

"And the Lord God formed man of the dust of the ground,
and breathed into his nostrils the breath of life;
and man became a living soul."
– Genesis 2:7

The air and atmosphere are pure – no pollution here. The garden is filled with beautiful life-giving plants that purify the air. Take a deep breath, smell the flowers and the clean, pure air. Isn't it refreshing? Oxygen is the breath of life, and we find it in abundance in its purest form here in the Garden.

Oxygen is the very source of our life. When each of us were born, the very first need we had to meet was to have our lungs filled with God's life-sustaining breath that He gives us, the breath of life. Ninety-six percent of the nutritional need of the body is in the air we breathe. Every cell in the body depends upon oxygen for fuel, yea for our very life! The human body can't survive even four minutes without oxygen. To provide this invaluable nutrient, it is necessary to breathe. Breathing deeply provides the oxygen needed to purify the blood and help to soothe the nerves. Fresh air not only stimulates the appetite, it also aids in complete digestion of food.

By being conscious of your breathing you can begin to take in deep breaths and then slowly exhale. When you begin inhaling deeper breaths, you may notice that you feel light-headed. However, as your body becomes adjusted to the wonderful nourishment you are providing, these feelings will dissipate. When exercising, it is best to work out in fresh air. It has been estimated that outdoor air is 10 times more beneficial to the body than indoor air.

Outdoor air provides an electrical charge required by the body for optimum health. In the past when our homes were less airtight there was no problem getting sufficient air. Today, our homes are so well-built and insulated that regular indoor air is nutritionally deficient. Unless the windows are open on a regular basis, fresh air is not available. Recently, however, ozone machines have been introduced to provide a means of improving indoor air.

3. Pure Water

"And a river went out of Eden to water the garden:"
— Genesis 2:10

God also provided that first family with pure water in the Garden. No pollution in the streams; only pure, fresh water. Look, you can see clear to the bottom of the stream! Look at the beautiful fish swimming by. Isn't it amazing? No water purifier needed in this perfect atmosphere.

Yes, man cannot live without water! Our bodies need pure, fresh water to function properly. Unfortunately, our rivers, streams and almost all groundwater sources have been contaminated by mankind and are no longer safe for drinking.

Water is needed to build cells, cleanse the body of waste and prevent diseases. We wouldn't consider doing laundry with only a small amount of dirty water to remove the debris. If insufficient water is consumed, the body will utilize what liquids it has available. It will recirculate water from the colon for instance. When this occurs, the body can become constipated since the fecal matter becomes dry and adhesive.

Pure water is vital to vibrant health, and, after the naturally distilled water found in raw fruits and vegetables, steam distillation provides the purest water possible. Steam distilled water is merely the condensed steam from boiling water. The process of distillation leaves the impurities in water behind.

Dr. Norman W. Walker, who lived to be 119 years old, wrote: "To help retard the process of premature and decrepit old age, it is essential that you drink plenty of distilled water daily." In *Your Body's Many Cries for Water,* F Batmanghelidj, M.D. advises, "You can save yourself much money and the anxiety of falling ill by paying attention to your body's constant need for water."

Water should never be consumed with a meal. At least 30 minutes prior to eating or at least one hour after a meal is best. When water is consumed with a meal, it dilutes the digestive juices. When drinking water, it is best to drink water at room temperature.

Just as the water we drink should be pure, it is also important to remember that the water used on the exterior of the body is important as well. Our skin is an organ that eliminates many impurities. If the skin is not properly cleansed, these impurities can be reabsorbed. Chlorine and fluoride in our water systems are extremely toxic to the body, both inside and out. There are filters available which can filter out most of these impurities, and they should be used if pure water is not available.

When we consider the importance of pure water, fresh air and soil nutrients in regard to our health, this should serve as a reminder of the need for us to maintain good stewardship of the Earth. One of the ways to instill this principle in our children is to teach them to never litter. The things people throw out on the land stay there for a long time. To give you an idea of how long litter lasts:

cigarette butts	1 - 5 years
aluminum cans	500 years
glass bottles	1,000 years
plastic bags	10 - 20 years
plastic coated paper	5 years
plastic film containers	20 -30 years
nylon fabric	30 - 40 years
leather	up to 50 years
wool socks	1 - 5 years
tin cans	50 years
plastic six-pack holders	100 years
plastic bottles & styrofoam	indefinitely

4. Vigorous Exercise

"And the Lord God took the man
and put him into a garden of Eden to dress and keep it" – Genesis 2:15
and told him "In the sweat of thy face shalt thou eat bread ..." – Genesis 3:19

Exercise is the order of the day. No time to watch TV or play computer games; there is abundant work to be done. Toil is required in order to live and it is done gladly. Anxiety and frustration are not a part of this pristine setting. The fruit is ripe unto harvest; the animals need tending to; the gardens need to be gleaned.

God placed Adam and Eve in a garden where exercise was required on a daily basis. They were to dress and keep the garden for a very good reason. Exercise is required for the organs of the body to develop and function properly. Beyond that, it is a known fact that exercise reduces stress, strengthens muscles, improves oxygen intake, helps the body to rid itself of impurities, enhances a person's positive outlook on life, aids in digestion, improves circulation, increases our vitality, and much more.

The reverse is true when the body does not receive sufficient exercise. Inactivity invites disease. Without exercise, the lymph system cannot eliminate toxins properly because it does not have a pump like the heart does. And without exercise, the heart, the most important muscle in our body, cannot work at peak efficiency to circulate life-giving nutrients throughout our body. Fresh air, so vital to health, is not available in sufficient quantities when a body is inactive. Without proper exercise, muscles and lungs wither in a state of atrophy, and the body's lymphatic system fails to work properly. The lymphatic system, a vital part of the body's waste-elimination system, is used to transport toxins out of the body through sweat glands in the skin. But, unlike the circulatory system, the lymphatic system has no pump, and is reliant on exercise to move waste from cells and vital organs out of the body. Without exercise, these toxins back up in the system and pores in the skin clog up, giving every cell and organ in the body excess toxicity to deal with.

Vigorous aerobic exercise is vital to life; it speeds up the metabolism, which helps burn up excess acidity. In America today, life has become too easy and we are suffering the consequences!

Of all forms of exercise, ***brisk walking*** is the one that brings most of the body into action. In no other exercise do you get the same harmony of coordinating sinews, the same perfect circulation of blood. ***"Brisk walking is 'the King of Exercise,' ideal for you ... and your heart."***
– Paul Bragg

5. Sunshine

"Truly the light is sweet,
and a pleasant thing it is for the
eyes to behold the sun:"
– Ecclesiastes 11:7

Here in the garden we have bountiful sunshine. It provides warmth and allows the plants and us to grow strong, vibrant and healthy. Sunshine also provides daylight, and we bask in its warmth, not even realizing God is supplying our bodies with the vitamin D we need.

Without vitamin D, our bodies cannot utilize the calcium it so desperately needs. Also, sunshine contains healing properties that are not available elsewhere. Studies have shown that **proper and not excessive** exposure to the sun lowers blood pressure, reduces the resting heart rate, balances the production of hormones, strengthens the immune system, lowers blood sugar, increases cardiac output, and increases stress tolerance levels. Unfortunately, the depletion of the ozone layer does cause concern when too much sun is absorbed. Therefore, it is best to spend time in the sun during the cooler parts of the day. Sunburn can be painful, as well as harmful to our health, and should be avoided.

Studies have shown that families living in crowded cities have more problems with rickets due to air pollution, skyscrapers and narrow streets. These conditions do not allow sufficient sunshine to penetrate the skin. Sunlight is a tremendous gift that has been provided for our good and we need to make time in our hectic schedules to enjoy it.

6. Rest

"And on the seventh day God ended his work
which he had made;
and he rested on the seventh day
from all his work which he had made."
– Genesis 2:2

God rested. He took time out from all that He had created to rest. We too must learn to rest. Rest according to Webster is to refrain from labor or exertion, to cease from action or motion, to be quiet and in repose, free from anxiety.

In generations past, when physical exercise was the order of the day, rest came easy. Today, rest sometimes escapes us as the turmoil of life takes its toll on our tranquility. In order to regain composure, one should take a walk in a park or spend time in the woods, observing nature that God has provided for us.

Perhaps one of the most relaxing and most important things people can do for their body/temple is to turn their cares over to the Lord and allow Him to carry the burdens for us. We are told, **"Come unto me, all ye that labour and are heavy laden, and I will give you rest."** (Matthew 11:28)

A person's physical, mental and emotional well-being are dependent upon the quality of sleep they are able to attain. It is often stated that two hours of sleep prior to midnight are worth four hours after, thus bringing new meaning to the old phrase, "Early to bed, early to rise, makes a man healthy, wealthy and wise." We must realize that the body requires rest in order to function at its optimal level, and most people require an average of eight hours of uninterrupted sleep. This may vary with each individual and most people find they need less sleep as they improve their diet and follow a daily vigorous exercise routine.

While the body is resting, it is able to purify itself, removing toxins that have accumulated during the day. It is a time of restoration and revitalization of the cells and it gives the muscles time to relax and restore. Fresh air aids the body during the cleansing process, and it is advisable to sleep with open windows, if possible.

7. Positive Thinking (Faith)

"If you realized how powerful your thoughts are,
you would never think a defeatist or negative thought.
Since we create through thought, we need to concentrate very strongly
on positive thoughts. If you think you can't do something, you can't.
But if you think you can, you may be surprised to discover
that you can. It is important that our thoughts
be constantly for the best that could happen in a situation
— for the good things we would like to see happen."
— Peace Pilgrim, 1983

"All the days of the afflicted are evil:
but he that is of a merry heart hath a continual feast. "
— Proverbs 15:15

As we continue our journey through the Garden, we find that every good and perfect thing comes from the Lord. He would have us to be joyful and positive about life. Positive thoughts such as hope, happiness, love, gratefulness and joy actually increase the immune system's ability to fight disease.

So often in this world, outside forces play a part in our well-being. When we heed the urgings of others rather than follow what we know to be right, we often get into all kinds of trouble. The thoughts that we have do make a difference. They produce hormones within the body. These hormones may have a positive or negative effect on the body, depending upon the thoughts our minds entertain.

Many studies have been done that prove when a person is negative, that the poor attitude robs the body of energy and saps strength from the immune system, inviting disease to take control. Negative emotions include fear, worry, envy, guilt, hatred and jealously. These powerful emotions, if left unchecked, can even cause death!

On the other hand, while negative thoughts and emotions destroy, positive emotions build and enhance not only our outward appearance but also our inner being. It is vitally important that we provide a happy, positive environment where there is hope, joy, peace, gratefulness and love. These precious gifts can make the difference in not only our lives but in every life that we touch.

Perhaps we can all learn a lesson from Dr. Robert Schuller, who said, "All the while I'm working to change my attitudes: I let go of revenge. *I want to 'get well,' instead of 'get even.'* I no longer wallow in resentment. I still have wounds, but no longer nurse them; instead I immerse them in helping others; I reverse them by changing my negatives into positives. I am on my way to becoming weller than well!" We literally become what we think!

34

"A merry heart doeth good like a medicine:
but a broken spirit drieth the bones."
– Proverbs 17:22

As we leave the Garden, it is important to take with us all of the knowledge that we have gained on how to take care of our precious body/temple. Our heavenly Father did not want His children to suffer and be in ill health. Quite the contrary, for He tells us in III John 2: ***"Beloved, I wish above all things that thou mayest prosper and be in health, even as thy soul prospereth."***

We, in our ignorance and unbelief, have totally changed and adulterated God's plan, and the result is sickness, disease and unhappiness. But we can't serve the Lord in a sick body, so it is time to take responsibility for our own body and health and not leave it up to anyone else nor blame other people or outside causes (germs, heredity, etc.) for our ill health.

God has not failed us. He is the same yesterday, today and forever. We, my friends, are the ones who have gone astray. It is far beyond time for us to get "Back to the Garden."

"The longer I live,
the more I realize the impact of attitude on life.
Attitude, to me, is more important than facts.
It is more important than the past, than education, than money,
than circumstances, than failures, than successes, than what other people
think or say or do. It is more important than appearance, giftedness, or skill.
It will make or break a company … a church … a home.
The remarkable thing is we have a choice every day
regarding the attitude we will embrace for that day. We cannot change
our past … we cannot change the fact that people
will act in a certain way. We cannot change the inevitable.
The only thing we can do is play on the one string we have,
and that is our attitude … I am convinced that
life is 10% what happens to me and 90% how I react to it.
And so it is with you …
we are in charge of our Attitudes."
– Charles Swindoll

Chapter Three:

Why the Standard American Diet is So SAD

"I beseech you therefore, brethren,
by the mercies of God,
that ye present your bodies a living sacrifice,
holy, acceptable unto God, which is your reasonable service.
And be not conformed to this world…"
— Romans 12:1-2

The primary motivation that has led many people to find an alternative to the Standard American Diet (SAD) is that this way of eating and lifestyle has caused them or their loved ones to suffer a heart attack, cancer, diabetes, arthritis or some other major disease. So often, people fail to see the need to change their diet and lifestyle until a crisis arises. I acknowledge that change is often difficult unless we understand the reasons **why**, and so it is my prayer that as you study these pages, you will allow the Holy Spirit to guide you and show you **why** the Standard American Diet is doing such great harm to you and those you love.

At Hallelujah Acres, we have seen thousands of people's experiences with degenerative disease turn into a tremendous motivating force for them and others around them to adopt The Hallelujah Diet as a new way of living. For many of these people, this transformation has become a wonderful experience, giving them a whole new lease on life, along with a powerful testimony that has led dozens or hundreds of their friends, relatives and church members to make similar changes.

This is good, but the needless suffering is also often very sad. Our prayer is that you will use the information in this book to make necessary changes in your diet without this type of suffering and negative factors that force some people into a dietary change. There are many very positive reasons for returning to a diet based on the fresh fruits and vegetables offered to mankind in Genesis 1:29.

"Know ye not that ye are the temple of God, and that the Spirit of God dwelleth in you?
If any man defile the temple of God, him shall God destroy;
for the temple of God is holy,
which temple ye are."
– I Corinthians 3:16 & 17

As I have already stated, our bodies are the temples of the Holy Spirit, and we are the keepers of the temples. Thus, it is our responsibility to not put harmful and unnatural products into our bodies, and to honor our bodies literally as temples of God. If church members put loads of garbage in the sanctuary and consistently damaged the walls and foundation of their church building, perhaps you might question whether they had much reverence for the church and what it stood for. Well, our bodies are no less Holy than the lumber, bricks, mortar, plaster, glass and carpet that make up a church building. Truly, it is time for Christians to begin honoring the temples of God in which they live! No one else can do that for us. Now, we can choose to ignore the evidence set before us and suffer the consequences or we can accept the diet and lifestyle God planned for mankind and experience the abundant life He promised in His Word. And remember, God told us we were to glorify Him in our bodies!

In the United States of America, we seem to feel that it is the responsibility of the government to provide health care for the American people. And yet approximately 50 percent of the American people die from heart attacks and strokes, while 33 percent die from cancer, and 8 percent die from diabetes. Obviously, the government doesn't have the answer and isn't taking very good care of its people.

Neither can we depend upon the medical establishment to maintain our health. Medical doctors are trained to look at the symptoms and give drugs that mask or hide these symptoms rather than teaching us how to change our diets and lifestyles so that the physical problem will go away. Every drug is liver toxic and for every drug given there are side effects. Is that God's way? Unfortunately, most medical doctors receive less than three hours of nutritional training in all their years of study to become a doctor. Therefore, how can they teach us to eat properly so that we can stay well?

The failure of our medical system to adequately deal with cancer has become apparent to practically everyone, even the medical establishment. Writing in the June 1997 issue of the *New England Journal of Medicine,* Drs. John Bailar and Heather Gornick assert: "The effect of new treatments for cancer on mortality has been largely disappointing. The most promising approach to the control of cancer is a national commitment to prevention, with a rebalancing of the focus and funding of the research."

Obviously the reason billions of dollars have been spent researching and implementing technologies such as radiation, chemotherapy, drugs and surgery is that these procedures are where the profit comes from.

"The doctor of the future will give no medicine
but will interest his patients in the care of the human frame,
in diet and in the cause and prevention of disease."
– Thomas A. Edison, 1900

37

Recipes for Life ... from God's Garden

This is not a game we are playing. Your life is on the line not only physically but spiritually as well. The abundant life can only be achieved by setting a higher standard than the world and seeking the Lord in all that we say and do. *"What? know ye not that your body is the temple of the Holy Ghost which is in you, which ye have of God, and ye are not your own? For ye are bought with a price: therefore, glorify God in your body, and in your spirit, which are God's."* (I Corinthians 6:19 & 20)

Over the past several decades, the health of the people in the United States has been on a steady decline. If we were to compare today's diet to the way our ancestors ate, we would find that today we consume 280 percent more poultry, 50 percent more beef and 33 percent more dairy products. As a direct result of these dietary changes, in the years since World War II, the health of the American people has plummeted. Perhaps it is time to take a hard look at what we eat to see if we can discover the reason why we are getting sicker and sicker with each passing year. You may be shocked to learn that since 1945:

1. The dietary intake of pastry has *risen 70 percent.*
2. The consumption of snack foods has *increased 85 percent.*
3. Soda and soft drink intake has *gone up over 200 percent.*
4. The daily intake of vegetables has *decreased by 23 percent.*
5. The use of fruit has *declined by 25 percent.*

FACT: <u>Most of the physical problems plaguing our country today can be directly attributed to the diet we eat.</u>

> *"Today, a large part of our foods can rightfully be called foodless (produced totally in our big labs), drugged, embalmed, dead, coal-tarred, artificial, skeletonized, polished, processed, refined, sterilized, oiled, sprayed, waxed, degenerated, unclean, frozen, canned, dried, impure junk and now the threat of irradiated food.*
> *(Is it logical to believe humans can tolerate food treated with atomic waste?! My answer is no!) All of the above foods can be put down the esophagus with varying degrees of ease and pleasure, but they do not feed the cells with the nutrients required to create and sustain healthful bodies.*
> *Those come only from a 'natural' food supply."*
> – Dr. Mary Ruth Swope from <u>Green Leaves of Barley</u>

The Dangers of Meat

"The Department of Agriculture's promotional poster used to list milk as the first group and meat as the second. Grains got a group, and fruits and vegetables had to share a group. Because livestock products were assigned two of the four groups, menus developed under this plan were often loaded with fat and cholesterol. This is how an entire generation learned to eat, and how they, in turn, raised their children. The results are tragic. There are 4,000 heart attacks every single day in this country. The traditional four food groups and the eating patterns they prescribed have led to cancer and heart disease in epidemic numbers, and they have killed more people than any other factor in America. More than automobile accidents, more than tobacco, more than all the wars of this country combined." – Neal Barnard, M.D.

Dr. Paavo Airola, a Nutritionist, warns that excessive protein contributes to toxemia, excessive acidity, nutritional deficiencies, uric acid accumulations and putrefaction in the intestines. An over-abundance of protein also contributes to arthritis, kidney disease, atherosclerosis, cancer, osteoporosis, heart disease, schizophrenia and even pyorrhea, which is the inflammation of the sockets of the teeth leading to loose teeth and eventually tooth loss. Heavy consumption of protein lowers life expectancy and leads to premature aging of the body.

"Although we think we are one, and we act as if we are one,
human beings are not natural carnivores ...
When we kill animals to eat them, they end up killing us
because their flesh ... was never intended
for human beings,
who are naturally herbivores."
– William Roberts, editor in chief
of the American Journal of Cardiology,
1991 editorial

Although animal protein is the most devastating to the body, too much vegetable protein can also cause problems. Many vegetarians have gone heavy into the soybean-based meat analogs only to discover that the high protein in the analogs cause many of the same problems as the meat! The body does need protein, but it needs to be in a form that the body can assimilate and in much lower quantities than previously thought. Recent studies have shown that less than 20 grams of protein daily is sufficient for the human body while the average American consumes over 100 grams per day. A diet too high in protein, especially animal protein, actually causes calcium loss from the body. Consumption of animal products makes the body too acidic, so the body robs the bones of calcium (an alkaline mineral) to help neutralize this excess acidity. We are told to drink milk (cow's milk, of course) for calcium, but numerous studies have consistently shown that cultures with the highest consumption of meat and dairy products have the highest occurrence of osteoporosis, which is loss of calcium from our bones. Consumption of animal products is the primary cause of osteoporosis!

Protein is composed of many small components called amino acids. There are 22 known amino acids and of these, eight are considered essential (meaning that these eight amino acids are not produced by the body and must be obtained through our diet). The body must have all 22 amino acids in order to function properly.

The body utilizes protein for maintenance and repair. What is left over may be stored as fat; however, excess protein also gives off toxic waste which causes burdens for the kidneys, liver and all other waste-removal organs. What few people realize is that when meat is cooked (heated above 160 degrees), the protein molecules are altered, thus rendering the protein basically unusable by the body. Because the body cannot use the now-altered protein properly, it rots in the digestive system. This creates many problems for the body's defense mechanism. As the body tries to deal with it, the colon often becomes irritated and infected as it tries to eliminate the dead animal flesh and the toxins it contains.

Recipes for Life ... from God's Garden

*"It takes sixteen pounds of grain to produce a pound of feedlot beef.
It takes only one pound of grain to
produce a pound of bread."
– John Robbins from May all be Fed*

When we look at the way God created man, we find the anatomy of man was not designed to consume flesh foods. Carnivores (meat eaters) have teeth and claws designed by God to rip and tear animal flesh. The human body has teeth designed for grinding, not tearing. Our jaws move up and down as well as side to side which a flesh-eater's jaw cannot do. Flesh-eaters also have a high hydrochloric acid content in their stomachs to break down and digest flesh, while humans do not. The digestive tract of the flesh-eater is short and designed to get the flesh out of the system before it has a chance to putrefy. The digestive tract of the humans is long (about 26' long or about four times longer than that of flesh-eaters) with many twists and bends, which produce monumental problems for the colon when flesh foods are consumed.

The flavor in meat is derived from the blood and uric acid (nitrogenous waste) within its flesh and other tissues. The uric acid causes tremendous problems for the body, burdening the liver and kidneys as these organs try to deal with all of the toxins contained in meat. The increased consumption of flesh foods can be directly related to the deterioration of the health of the American people. Sadly, we in America have been taught that eating flesh foods is required to receive our protein and for proper nourishment.

For a Biblical account of the benefits of a vegetarian diet, see Daniel 1:11-20.

Contrary to popular opinion, a vegetarian diet provides sufficient and complete protein. As Dr. Malkmus often asks in his lectures, "If man has to eat the flesh of the cow for protein, what does the cow eat to produce that protein?" And of course, the answer is grass! The protein by which God designed our bodies to be sustained is the living protein found in plants. Protein is found in all green leafy vegetables and, in fact, in all living plants. At one time it was thought that to obtain complete protein, foods would have to be carefully combined. Frances Moore Lappé, the woman who helped popularize the myth that vegetables must be properly combined in order to obtain complete protein in her 1971 book, *Diet for a Small Planet,* has admitted this premise was incorrect. Even the American Dietetic Association now says you get more than enough protein by simply eating a variety of plant foods. Although public opinion may take a long time to change, there is practically no controversy on this subject among the experts with the most up-to-date information. Nearly all of these experts now agree it is not necessary to "complement your proteins," neither do you have to consume foods from all the food groups at each meal, and you certainly don't have to eat meat to obtain sufficient amounts of protein.

Not only is meat consumption **unnecessary for protein,** this meat-eating habit is killing us! It should be noted that animal products are the only source of bad cholesterol (LDL) in the diet. The main reason approximately 50 percent of all Americans die of heart disease and strokes is that their arteries are clogged up with cholesterol. People who do not eat animal products practically never have a cholesterol problem.

Neal Barnard, M.D., President of the Physicians Committee for Responsible Medicine, reports: *"The beef industry has contributed to more American deaths than all the wars of this century, all natural disasters and all automobile accidents combined."*

And consider the unclean nature of dead animals. When meat is butchered at the slaughterhouse, meat inspectors only have 12 seconds to check inside the dead animal for grubs, parasites, abscesses and disease. A meat inspector is required to check approximately 300 carcasses per hour!

Many people are unaware of the cancer growths in animals which must be cut out prior to being sold to the consumer in the supermarket. As these diseases in cattle and poultry become immune to the drugs being used to control them, it is necessary to develop ever stronger and more deadly poisons.

Some who have been convinced of the need to avoid red meat unfortunately believe poultry and fish are a healthier choice. Not so! Chicken contains the same cholesterol pound for pound as beef. Plus, it is often contaminated with salmonella and loaded with growth hormones. Is this what we want to feed our precious families?

Recent tests have shown that over 50 percent of marketable cod fish have been found to have cancer. Fish has been shown to have twice the cholesterol of pork or beef. To say nothing of the pollution in our lakes, ponds, streams, rivers and oceans where they swim.

Another serious problem with all animal products is that they contain zero fiber. The lack of fiber in meat, dairy and eggs leads them to rot in the colon, causing constipation, body odor and colon problems. It is the fiber, which can only be found in plant life, that acts as an "intestinal broom" to keep our colons clean.

Green leafy vegetables and succulent fruits are the primary foods needed to feed the human body. They are also the most healing foods God has given us. Watch an animal when it is sick and you will find that the only thing it will eat is grass. Why? The grass contains enzymes, vitamins, proteins, organic minerals, chlorophyll, anti-oxidants, and much more. Dr. Malkmus and I use a product called Barleygreen with amazing and exciting results. (I personally think it tastes a lot better than grass.)

The original diet God handed down to mankind in Genesis 1:29 was raw fruits and vegetables only! This is the diet that allowed man to live an average of 912 years prior to the flood without a single incidence of recorded sickness. And this is the same diet we are finding today that will restore us to health if we are sick and give us wellness like we have never experienced before in our lives.

It is important to note here that even after Adam and Eve sinned by eating the forbidden fruit and were banished from the Garden, the Scriptures indicate that even after the fall, man continued on this raw fruit and vegetable diet and lived an average of 912 years without a single recorded incident of sickness. It was not until after the Flood, when meat and cooked food were added to his diet that man started to experience physical problems.

Following the flood in Genesis, Chapters 7 and 8, meat was added to the diet of mankind. In Genesis 9:3, man began eating flesh and cooking his food. As a result of this dietary change, sickness entered the human race and man's lifespan drastically declined from an average of 912 years before the flood to 100 years by the end of the Book of Genesis! Dr. Malkmus' theory on this subject, which makes perfect sense, is that meat was added to the diet of mankind at that time because God was very displeased with the wickedness of man and felt that it was not good for man to live on the earth for 900 years. For example, Genesis 6:5-6 states: ***"And God saw that the wickedness of man was great in the earth, and that every imagination of the thoughts of his heart was only evil continually. And it repented the Lord that he had made man on the earth, and it grieved him at his heart."***

"And by the river upon the bank thereof, on this side and on that side,
shall grow all trees for meat, whose leaf shall not fade,
neither shall the fruit thereof be consumed:
it shall bring forth new fruit according to his months, because
their waters they issued out of the sanctuary:
and the fruit thereof shall be for meat,
and the leaf thereof for medicine."
Ezekiel 47:12

Recipes for Life … from God's Garden

We must also understand that meat eaten in Biblical times was literally a different animal than the meat being eaten today. Wild animals eaten during Biblical times were only about 3 percent fat. Beef, the way it is grown today is 20 to 30 percent fat, while pork is 40 to 60 percent fat. And the meat of our Biblical forefathers was not full of cancer, antibiotics, growth hormones, preservatives and chemical toxins from feed.

It is also interesting to realize that in most cases, the word "meat" in the Bible does not have the same meaning as the word "meat" does today. In 1947 Rev. V. A. Holmes-Gore took on the task of looking up the original Greek Text that referenced the word "meat" in the King James Version of the Bible. The following is what he discovered:

Greek	number of references	translation
Broma	4	"food"
Brosis	4	"the act of eating"
Phago	3	"to eat"
Brosimos	1	"that which may be eaten"
Trophe	6	"nourishment"
Prosphagen	1	"anything to eat"

Not one of these 19 references translates to the common usage of the word "meat" as we have been taught.

Dairy Products

God never intended cow milk to be consumed by humans. We are the only species that drinks the milk of another animal. And cow milk is never even mentioned in the Bible. Cow milk was designed by God to nourish an 80 to 100-pound calf at birth, a calf that would ultimately reach 1,500 pounds at maturity. Cow milk *was not* designed by God to nourish a 7 to 8-pound human baby! The milk of each species of mammal was designed by God as nourishment for the young of that particular species only. Most physical problems babies and young children experience can be linked to cow's milk, including colds, runny noses, ear infections, swollen glands, allergies, etc. In fact, almost all mucous membrane problems are caused by the consumption of dairy products. Furthermore, studies have shown that dairy products can be linked to skin rashes, arteriosclerosis, acne, rheumatoid arthritis, tooth decay and many other diseases.

"Cow milk has no valid claim as the perfect food.
As nutrition, it produces allergies in infants, diarrhea and cramps
in the older child and adult, and may be a factor in the development of heart attacks
and strokes. Perhaps when the public is educated as to the hazards of milk,
only calves will be left to drink the real thing.
Only calves should drink the real thing."
– Frank A. Oski, M.D., Head of Pediatrics,
Johns Hopkins University School of Medicine,
from his book, Don't Drink Your Milk

There is also a bovine virus that causes tumors in cattle, and this virus is not destroyed in the pasteurization process. This virus has been proven to introduce leukemia in the cattle and in chimpanzees. Most infections that can be transmitted to chimpanzees can also be transmitted to humans, according to Dr. Frank Oski, M.D.

Americans, it seems, are hooked on cheese, another dairy product. Cheese is available in over 800 different varieties and is made almost exclusively from cow milk. The United States alone produces over one billion pounds of cheese annually. Approximately one tenth of the milk we produce is used in making cheese.

Cheese contains bacteria and molds which can be hazardous to our health. The fermentation process breaks down the proteins and fats and that process produces amines, ammonia, irritating fats and lactic acid. When these toxic substances are ingested, they have to be processed and broken down by the body. It is not uncommon for cheese to cause stomach irritation and migraine headaches, to say nothing of overworking the kidneys and liver.

Eggs

Eggs are not good food! One egg yolk contains 80-percent fat and more than twice as much cholesterol as four ounces of beef. In addition, just as chickens are often contaminated with salmonella and other bacteria, so are their eggs.

In 1971 the American Heart Association took on the National Commission on Egg Nutrition in court over ads placed in the *Wall Street Journal,* which were stating among other claims that "There is absolutely no scientific evidence that eating eggs, even in small quantities, will increase the risk of a heart attack." After a lengthy court battle Judge Ernest G. Barnes ruled: "There exists a substantial body of competent and reliable scientific evidence that eating eggs increases the risk of heart attacks or heart disease ... This evidence is systematic, consistent, strong and congruent."

Dr. John McDougal, clinical nutritionist, reported the following findings when reviewing information regarding the "egg studies" used by the National Commission on Egg Nutrition to try to prove eggs are harmless: "Of the six studies in the medical literature that fail to demonstrate a significant rise in blood cholesterol level with the consumption of whole eggs, three were paid for by the American Egg Board, one by the Missouri Egg Merchandising Council, and one by the Egg Program of the California Department of Agriculture. Support for the sixth paper was not identified ... The trick is knowing how to design your experiment so you will get the results you are looking for. To get little or no increase in cholesterol results, you first saturate the subjects with cholesterol from other sources, because studies show that once people consume more than 400 to 800 milligrams of cholesterol per day, additional cholesterol has only a minor effect on blood cholesterol levels ... Well-designed studies by investigators independent of the food industry clearly demonstrate the detrimental effects of eggs on blood cholesterol levels."

A study conducted at the University of Minnesota found that 380 milligrams of egg yolk cholesterol per day caused an average blood cholesterol level 16 milligrams higher than a diet with only 50 milligrams of cholesterol. This translates to a 32-percent increase in the risk of a heart attack if a person consumes one-and-one-half eggs per day.

Food Additives

Another problem with the Standard American Diet involves the chemicals and additives food manufacturers put into the food stuffs they sell. A food additive is any substance added to the food itself. Currently there are approximately 3,000 additives used in the food industry with an additional 100 new food and color additives being submitted to the Food and Drug Administration for approval each year. Flavorings from natural and artificial sources average about 1,700 annually and comprise the largest food additive group.

There may be a few that are harmless; however, the majority are toxic to the body. When these additives enter the human body, they upset the delicate system created by God. The body struggles to excrete them as wastes, but many remain behind as accumulative toxins within the cells.

"What we put in our mouths strongly determines
the daily and long-term quality of our lives"
— Rita Romano, author of Dining in the Raw, Cooking in the Buff

In their book *Prescription for Nutritional Healing,* James F. Balch, M.D., and Phyllis A. Balch, C.N.C., write: "The history of (food) additive use includes a number of products that were once deemed safe but later were banned or allowed to be used only if accompanied by warnings. The artificial sweeteners cyclamate and saccharin are just two examples of such products. Other additives, like monosodium glutamate (MSG) and aspartame, are used without warnings, but have been known to cause problems ranging from headaches and diarrhea to confusion, memory loss, and seizures."

In the processed food industry, additives have over 40 different uses. Here are just a few common additives that pose great threat to humans:

1. Acesulfame-K is a sugar substitute. During initial test trials, acesulfame failed to meet the FDA's standards. The tests concluded that this sweetener produced cancer in laboratory animals. The FDA recently *approved* Acesulfame-K for use as a sugar substitute in chewing gums, powdered beverages, instant coffee and tea, pudding mixes, non-dairy creamers and in gelatins.

2. Artificial colorings are often added to give the illusion of fruit or other genuine ingredients. Studies have shown that Yellow Dye # 5, Red Dye # 3 and other artificial coloring agents may cause cancer, allergic reactions and even behavioral problems. These dyes are used in breakfast cereals, ice cream, candy, soft drinks and a multitude of other products.

3. Aspartame is probably the most widely-used sugar substitute. It is sold as Equal and Nutra-Sweet. One study linked Aspartame to a slightly higher incidence of brain tumors. There have been reports by consumers of headaches and dizziness after consuming this artificial sweetener found in diet soft drinks and other diet foods.

4. BHA and BHT are preservatives that prevent oils from going rancid. Some lab tests suggest that both of these additives may cause cancer. These two products are added by the manufacturers to increase shelf life of hundreds of processed foods. You will find BHA and BHT listed on the ingredients labels of shortenings, potato chips, dry cereals, bouillon cubes, etc.

5. Sodium nitrate and sodium nitrite are meat preservatives which can react with other chemicals in food or in the body to form carcinogens. This chemical reaction also occurs when meats that contain them are cooked at high temperatures. During the 1970s, the USDA lowered the level of sodium nitrate and sodium nitrite allowed in animal products, which has alleviated some of the problems. Sodium nitrate and/or sodium nitrite are found in most brands of bacon, bolognas, hot dogs and other processed meats.

6. Monosodium glutamate (MSG) is a flavor enhancer found in many manufactured products and should be avoided. It can cause burning sensations, tightness of the chest, headaches and other symptoms. MSG is used in many Chinese restaurants.

7. Propyl gallate is an additive similar to BHA and BHT found in vegetable oils, meat products,

potato sticks, chicken soup base, chewing gums and many other manufactured food items. It has produced cancer in laboratory animals.

8. Saccharin, an artificial sweetener, was banned in the 1970s, because of the cancer it caused in laboratory animals. Recently, it has been allowed back on the market. Now products using this sugar substitute carry warning labels which read: "Use of this product may be hazardous to your health. This product contains saccharin which has been determined to cause cancer in laboratory animals." Saccharin can often be found in restaurants as a sweetener in packets on the tables.

9. Sulfites are preservatives which are especially dangerous to some asthmatics who are sulfite sensitive. Death can result when sulfite is eaten by a person who is sulfite sensitive. The FDA has banned the use of sulfite on most fresh fruits and vegetables; however, sulfite is still being used in dehydrated potatoes, dried fruits and sea food.

Another very hazardous means of preserving food is irradiation. Although irradiation is not a food additive, the Food and Drug Administration has given approval to this procedure, which submits fruits and vegetables to radiation to give them a longer shelf life. This process destroys the enzymes that are the life force within the food. The fact that the food is now dead doesn't seem to bother the food merchants or government agencies. Irradiation levels can be as high as 100,000 rads, which is equal to 4 million chest X-rays. When irradiation was first introduced, the food had to be labeled as having been irradiated, but the problem was that most people did not want to buy food that has been submitted to radiation, so food processors successfully lobbied to have these labels removed. So now, consumers buy fresh-looking strawberries and other produce without knowing that they have been irradiated.

Studies have shown that there are over 150 chemical residues found in the foods we consume. Many crops are sprayed dozens of times in a single season. Foreign imports may be sprayed as many as 50 times with poisons that are *outlawed* in the USA. In the food industry, thousands of pesticides, antibiotics, additives, and other chemicals are used in growing and preparing for storage the foodstuffs we consume. It is imperative that we learn to read labels when searching for food for our families.

Ideally, every family in America should have a garden and orchard from which they could pick and prepare their meals. Obviously this is not always an option. However, you can see the need for organic produce to feed your family. It is encouraging to note that because of consumer awareness, the production of organic produce is increasing every year.

> *"If mankind would at once discard all refined, sprayed, and unnatural foods,*
> *it would be the beginning of a race of people that would live long happy lives*
> *and be free of disease."*
> – Paul C. Bragg

How to Read Labels

It is imperative that we become familiar with these food additives and learn what damage they can do. That is why we must learn to read labels and demand better from our food suppliers. Labels list ingredients in *descending order of predominance or weight.* If the first ingredients on the label are sugar, white flour, fat or water, it isn't something you will want to feed your family. Always be on the lookout for harmful additives that may be hiding in the product. It is common for products to have claims such as "All Natural Ingredients," etc. on the package in large, bold print, but don't let that mislead you. Look at the fine print, which actually lists the ingredients. Many products claiming to be "all natural" have white flour, sugar and other harmful substances among their primary ingredients.

It is also important to realize that the labels on processed food provide nutritional information for a "serving." Sometimes a "serving" is defined as an unrealistically small amount (such as a half-cup of cereal) to bolster claims such as "low in fat," "low-sodium," etc. That means in order to accurately determine how much fat, sodium, etc. you are getting from this food, you must determine whether the serving size listed is what you are actually consuming. If not, be sure to adjust all of the nutritional information accordingly. Every label should list the fat, sodium, sugar and ingredients of the contents of the item you are purchasing.

Fat – Labels will tell you the amount of total fat grams along with the "percent daily value" which is the maximum amount of fat one should eat in a 2,000-calorie diet. Saturated fat as well as total fat should be listed. Remember that saturated fat goes right into the arteries, leading to many health problems.

Sodium – Labels also list the amount of sodium per serving. This sodium is almost always in the form of sodium chloride and thus harmful to the body (as opposed to the sodium in celery, which is beneficial).

Sugar – Sugar on labels is listed in grams. To convert the grams to teaspoons, divide the number of grams listed by four. Remember that sugar also can be listed by using other words for sugar – such as glucose, sucrose, maltose, dextrose, etc. Some breakfast cereals have as many as six different names for sugar listed on the ingredients label in an effort to prevent the public from realizing how much sugar is contained in their cereal.

> *"In my mind the greatest mistake a person can make*
> *is to remain ignorant when he is surrounded, every day of his life,*
> *by the knowledge he needs to grow and be healthy*
> *and successful. It's all there.*
> *We need only to observe, read, learn ... and apply."*
> *– Paul C. Bragg*

Pesticides

The National Research Council (NRC) stated recently: "The average consumer is exposed to pesticide residues, although in minute quantities, in nearly every food, including meat, dairy products, fruits, vegetables, sugar, coffee, oils, dried goods, and most processed foods."

Imported produce items have often been treated with pesticides which are banned in the USA, according to the FDA. These imported fruits and vegetables should be avoided.

A report by Donald Reed of the FDA states that in the United States, farmers apply approximately 700 million pounds of more than 300 different pesticides to their crops to destroy weeds, insects, fungi, bacteria and rodents.

According to the National Research Council, fruits and vegetables may be sprayed dozens of times with six or more different active ingredients, some of which are systemic (can't be washed or peeled off). The FDA insists that small amounts of pesticides pose no health threat. By contrast, the Environmental Protection Agency rates pesticides as the third-highest risk for causing cancer. In a February 1987 EPA report, they estimated that pesticides caused cancer in 6,000 Americans each year. At a subcommittee hearing on health in June 1991, concern was also voiced that pesticides are contributing to suppressed immune systems and neurotic behavior.

According to the "Residue Monitoring 1992" FDA report, only about half of the pesticides applied to food can be detected by routine tests, and only a small fraction of the nation's food supply is actually tested for pesticide levels. This report indicates that in 1992 only 413 samples of apples across the entire country were tested. Only 21 samples of raspberries, 90 samples of watermelon, 78 samples of tomatoes, and 37 samples of eggplant were tested.

To protect the body from cellular damage, it is vitally important to scrub all non-organic produce, which is not peeled, with a brush, and a non-toxic biodegradable cleaner. Scrubbing with water alone will not remove many pesticide residues. Some veetables like cabbages can have their outer leaves removed and discarded. Apples, peaches, pears and potatoes as well as other fruits and vegetables with skins can be peeled.

Buy organic produce (grown without pesticides or chemical fertilizers) whenever possible. If this is not an option, check for a local farmers' market. Area farmers usually don't use the waxes or pesticides required when produce will be sitting in warehouses.

Cholesterol

There are two types of cholesterol. The low-density lipoproteins (LDL), commonly called "bad cholesterol," is found in all animal products. In addition to animal products, saturated fats such as those found in coconut oil, cause the body to manufacture LDL. The LDL molecules carry cholesterol from the liver to all of the cells in the body. The high-density lipoproteins (HDL) commonly referred to as "good cholesterol" carry very little cholesterol and circulate in the bloodstream removing excess cholesterol from the blood and tissues. If there is too much cholesterol for the HDL to handle or if there is insufficient HDL to accomplish removal of the LDL cholesterol, plaque can form, which sticks to the artery walls and may eventually cause heart disease.

An ongoing medical study since 1948 conducted in Framingham, Mass., has identified a direct correlation between high LDL cholesterol and heart disease. Amazingly, during the study it has been discovered that no person who consistently maintained a cholesterol level below 150 has ever suffered a heart attack.

The current death rate in the United States runs around 923,000 due to heart disease. A cholesterol reading of 205 is being taught as an acceptable level; however, if that number were reduced to a reading of 190, nearly 200,000 lives could be saved annually! To go one step further, if the cholesterol level of the general population were reduced to 167, approximately 500,000 families could remain whole and healthy. At Hallelujah Acres, we teach a safe cholesterol level is 100 plus your age.

LDL cholesterol and saturated fat are found in all animal products. Since the human body also manufactures cholesterol, when animal products are consumed, the cholesterol level increases. In *Food for Life,* Dr. Neal Barnard, M.D., writes: "Cholesterol is something animals produce in their bodies, and all animal products contain cholesterol. If you eat part of an animal or a glandular secretion like milk, you will get a dose of cholesterol. In turn, this will increase the amount of cholesterol in your blood. Every 100 mg of cholesterol you eat in your daily routine adds roughly 5 points to your cholesterol level. (Everyone is different, and this number is an average.) In practical terms, 100 mg of cholesterol is four ounces of beef, or four ounces of chicken, or one-half of an egg, or three cups of milk." A single egg yolk contains 213 mg of cholesterol. Fish also has high amounts of cholesterol and some species of fish contain even higher amounts than beef!

As stated earlier, when large amounts of refined (saturated) fats are consumed, cholesterol sticks to the blood vessel walls. It causes the red blood cells to stick together, clogging the blood vessels, and leading to heart attacks and strokes.

Sugar and Other Sweeteners

Sugar is the word used by chemists to describe over 100 substances. Most of us think of sugar as the granular white substance made from sugar cane or sugar beets. It is used in our society to sweeten desserts, salad dressings, beverages, canned and frozen fruits and vegetables, cereals and even table salt.

These unnatural, processed forms of sugar are among the most dangerous of substances in the American diet and one of the most important ingredients for a health-conscious person to avoid. When reading labels, it is important to know that *any word that ends in "ose" or "rose" is probably a sugar.* For instance, *sucrose, lactose, maltose and dextrose.* One reason that several forms of sugar are listed in the ingredients of some processed foods is to help disguise the fact that some products, including breakfast cereals, are more than 50-percent sugar.

Processed sugar has become the scourge of our children's health, causing dental decay, obesity, hyperactivity, weakened bones and diminished immune systems. Not only does white sugar have zero nutritional value, it actually robs nutrients from the body, particularly the teeth and bones. Processed sugar is also harmful to the stomach lining and can interfere with digestion of nutrients from other food. Sugar becomes even more harmful when consumed with starch (a common mix), because this combination leads to a fermentation in the digestive process that breaks down to alcohol (a drug) and other toxins.

Sugar is addictive like a drug, can cause mood swings like a drug (from hyperactivity to depression), and has withdrawal symptoms like a drug. Considering all its adverse effects on human health, and the fact that it has zero nutrition, it is difficult to defend the perception of processed sugar as a food rather than a dangerous poison and addictive drug. And it is even more difficult to defend the common practice of giving this harmful and addictive substance to our children.

But with all this said, it must also be understood that sugar – in its natural form as glucose – is an essential nutrient for children and adults. The central nervous system of the body needs glucose to function properly and the best source can be found in the raw fruits and vegetables supplied by nature as God provided. When natural sugars are refined and processed, our bodies have a difficult time handling the altered, unnatural product.

The sugar found in almost every manufactured product on the market shelf is very different in quality and quantity from the sugar we were intended to consume in the form of raw fruits and vegetables. For example, one candy bar contains the amount of sugar that would be found in *3 pounds* of apples! It looks innocent and pure, but processed sugar is one of the most deadly substances we put into these beautiful body temples God has given us.

According to Frances Moore Lappé in *Diet for a Small Planet,* the average American consumes a third of a pound of sugar per day. The main reason American sugar consumption has increased over the decades is that more processed foods are being consumed and practically all processed foods have sugar added. About 25 percent of America's total sugar consumption comes in the form of colas, which can contain up to 11 teaspoons of sugar.

Nancy Appleton, M.D, and author of *Lick the Sugar Habit,* reveals that "sugar can: suppress the immune system (3 pops will wipe out the immune system for the day); upset the minerals in the body; cause hyperactivity, anxiety, difficulty concentrating; produce a significant rise in triglycerides; cause reduction in defense against bacterial infection; cause kidney damage; reduce high density lipopoteins; lead to chromium deficiency; lead to cancer of the breast, ovaries, intestines, prostate, and rectum; increase fasting levels of glucose and insulin; cause copper deficiency; interfere with absorption of calcium and magnesium; weaken eyesight; raise the level of neurotransmitters called serotonin; cause hypoglycemia; produce an acidic stomach; cause aging, arthritis, asthma, candida, gallstones, appendicitis, heart disease, multiple sclerosis, hemorrhoids, varicose veins, and periodontal disease; increase cholesterol, migraine headaches, interfere with the absorption of protein; cause toxemia during pregnancy, impair the structure of DNA; cause cataracts, emphysema, atherosclerosis; can cause free radicals in the blood stream; and it can cause hunger pains and overeating."

It is equally important to avoid "sugar substitutes" such as NutraSweet and Equal. Reports of serious physical problems have been made by large numbers of people following the use of these sugar substitutes. Dr. Mary Ruth Swope listed seven symptoms that she said have been "experienced in epidemic proportion in those who use Nutrasweet and Equal." These include loss of memory, loss of eyesight, epileptic seizures in those whose families do not have a genetic history of seizures, heart palpitations that lead to fibrillations and can lead to death, deep depression, small multiple tumors on the brain and migraine headaches.

In *Food for Life,* Neal Barnard, M.D., writes, "It is hard to find anything good to say about synthetic sweeteners. Their main benefit is to their stockholders, not to the consumer. … Chemical sweeteners also pose potential health risks. Cyclamates and saccharin have both been under suspicion for their cancer-causing potential. Some have suggested that NutraSweet may cause headaches and seizures. There are also case reports of children whose behavior has become extraordinarily disturbed after drinking aspartame-flavored beverages. Others have concluded that, for most people, aspartame is safe."

Although honey and maple syrup are natural sugars, they should be consumed very sparingly. It takes 40 gallons of maple tree sap to make one gallon of maple syrup.

Raw honey contains natural enzymes and is about 40 percent fruit sugar (fructose), 35 percent glucose, 2 percent or more sucrose, 3 to 23 percent water, maltose and other sugars. Diabetics seem to handle honey better because it is about 40 percent fruit sugar. Honey should *not* be given to infants because their systems are not developed enough to handle it and it may cause a toxic side effect.

Fruits and vegetables contain natural sugar and their sweetness is often enough to satisfy the sweet tooth. Dried fruits are high in concentrated sugar, and can be used as natural sweeteners. Dried fruits can be eaten alone, as snacks, or in food preparation.

Sodium Chloride or Table Salt

"The greatest harm done by the presence of salt in the body is to the cardiovascular system. A severe enough potassium deficiency caused by excessive salt intake will shrink, calcify, scar and destroy the muscles, valves and arteries along the entire coronary route. This finally culminates in congestive heart failure. It is no wonder succumbing to heart disease is the leading cause of death in the United States today." – Andrew & Cheryl Zuppo, from "The Hazards of Salt," in the May/June 1984 issue of *Healthful Living.*

Sodium is a required ingredient in our body chemistry. It is natural for a 154-pound (70 kilogram) person to contain 83 to 97 grams of sodium. A normal saline solution is 0.9 to 1 teaspoon per quart of liquid. It is important to remember that sodium and refined table salt (salt as herein used is in reference to refined table salt) are not synonymous, as there are many sources of sodium. For instance, according to James Percival, in his article "Salt and Your Health," refined table salt and most refined sea salts are 99 percent sodium chloride with chemical anti-caking agents added to prevent absorption of moisture and keep it free flowing. Eighty-two of the natural occurring 84 minerals have been extracted.

Just as most commercial products include sugar, they also contain table salt, and Americans are consuming far too much of it. Diets high in sodium chloride result in kidney, liver and heart problems, and tumors. Salt can also cause elevated blood pressure (hypertension), distorted vision, arthritis, ulcers and edema.

Sodium is one of the nutritional needs of the human body, and we can obtain all the sodium we need on a diet of raw fruits and vegetables. For example, celery is an excellent source of sodium in a form the body can utilize. When table salt is eliminated from the diet, the body's sodium level will usually normalize and excess fluid will be released.

Americans consume far more salt than they realize because salt is added to most processed foods. The body struggles constantly to remove this toxic substance. The body deposits salt in the tissue fluids in an attempt to dilute this toxicity. When a person goes on a juice fast, the body immediately starts releasing the excess fluid it has retained to neutralize the salt.

Salt is used as a preservative because it kills bacteria. Salt also kills the life force in foods, which is bad news for the consumer of the food, but good news for the manufacturer and retailer, because killing this life force is the only way to keep foods on a grocery shelf for months or years at a time without decay. In the body, salt destroys the living cells and wreaks havoc with our immune system. Salt is an addictive substance that most people have become "hooked on," and it should be removed from the diet as quickly as possible.

Chlorine

Chlorine is a heavy greenish-yellow gas with a pungent odor used to disinfect water. This same poisonous chlorine gas was used as a weapon during World War I. Later, it was decided it should be used in our drinking water to kill bacteria. Chlorine has been shown to suppress the immune system.

Paul Bragg states that if the chlorine in the water is "sufficient to produce an offensive smell, enough chlorine may enter the intestinal tract to destroy helpful and friendly bacteria and thereby deprive us of the important vitamins which they make for us."

Dr. Herbert Schwartz of Cumberland County College in Vineland, New Jersey, states: "Chlorine has so many dangers it should be banned. Putting chlorine in the water supply is like starting a time bomb. Cancer, heart trouble, premature senility – both mental and physical – are conditions attributable to chlorine-treated water supplies. It is making us grow old before our time by producing symptoms of aging such as hardening of the arteries."

Fluoride

Fluorine, according to Webster is, "a nonmetallic univalent halogen element that is normally a pale yellowish flammable irritating toxic gas." Fluoride is formulated from fluorine. Fluoride, the same toxic chemical used in our water supplies, is also used in a stronger concentration to make roach and rat killer. It has also been found to suppress the immune system. Paul Bragg states that fluoride was first added to the drinking water in about 1939, approximately the same time when large industries needed a "dumping ground" for the toxic flurried waste they were producing in the manufacture of aluminum products.

We are told fluoridation is an additive that is put into the drinking water "to prevent tooth decay" in small children. If these people sincerely wanted to prevent tooth decay, they would be campaigning against sugar instead of for fluoride. Studies have shown that fluoride causes many disorders, some of which are allergies, heart and kidney problems, cancer, deficiency in growth and development and birth defects, while not reducing cavities by one iota.

Recently the *Journal of the American Medical Association* reported that hip fracture rates are higher in both women and men who reside in communities with fluoridated water supplies. The study notes all cancer incidents increased by 5 percent and that bone cancer in young men is dramatically increased. It went on to say that there is virtually no difference in decay rates between those children who drink fluoridated water and those who do not. It is interesting to note that Europe banned fluoride in the water years ago, and the rate of tooth decay has remained similar to that in the U.S.

In October 1944 the American Dental Association issued the following statement: "We do know that the use of drinking water containing as little as 1.2 to 3.0 parts per million of fluorine will cause such developmental disturbances in bones as osteoporosis, as well as goiter, and we cannot afford to run the risk of producing such systemic disturbances in applying what is at present a doubtful procedure intended to prevent development of dental disfigurements among children."

Colas and Other Carbonated Beverages

Caffeine is an addictive drug found in coffee, tea, chocolate, most soft drinks and even in some over-the-counter and prescription drugs. This dangerous, but socially accepted, stimulant causes many problems for the body. Americans drink 137 billion cups of coffee annually. That is over 50 tons of caffeine per day! Even more caffeine is consumed in the form of soda pops. These products with caffeine artificially stimulate the body and increase the heart rate. While this artificial stimulation temporarily arouses the intellect and fatigue seems to disappear, it is short-lived. The excess stimulation depletes the body of vital energy as it struggles to deal with this poison which has entered its system. There are many effects from the consumption of caffeine, including increased incidence of bladder and stomach cancer, raised blood pressure, increased heart rate, and it aggravates diabetes and damages the lining of the stomach. Caffeine contributes to or causes birth defects in children, at least six kinds of cancer and provides the body with zero nutrition.

Family Size

Cola

Vending machines allowing children to purchase colas can be found in most schools, shopping malls, grocery stores, and even in some churches. Soft drinks are being sold and marketed to even the youngest children and their unsuspecting parents. In 1980, the U. S. Department of Agriculture attempted to limit the sale of soft drinks and other junk foods in schools. The department adopted a regulation that prohibited schools from selling soft drinks, gum and hard candy before the last lunch period ended.

In 1984, the National Softdrink Association filed suit challenging the regulation. A federal appeals court sided with the Association. It ruled that the USDA did not have the legal authority to ban competitive foods from the cafeteria during lunch. This ruling opened the door for vending machines to invade school lunch rooms and challenged the local school systems to control the sale of competitive foods.

For an idea of how much caffeine is found in coffee, colas and some over-the-counter prescriptions: Maxwell House coffee (electric perk) has 97 mg. of caffeine per 6 oz. serving, one ounce of chocolate has 35 mg., "decaffeinated" coffee has 2 to 5 mg., and colas range between 34 and 49 mg. per 12 ounces. Comparing the colas, Mountain Dew topped out at 49 mg. per 12 ounces, while the lowest was Diet Pepsi and Pepsi Light at 34 mg. Coca-Cola has 42 mg. while regular Pepsi-Cola has 35 mg. As for over-the-counter drugs, there is 100 mg. of caffeine per tablet of Nodoz, 200 mg. in Vivarin, 64.8 mg. in Excedrin, 30 mg. in Sinarest, 200 mg. in Dexatrim and 100 mg. in Pre-Mens Forte.

But caffeine is not the only dangerous ingredient in cola. Soda pops contain caffeine, sugar or artificial sweeteners, carbonated water, and artificial coloring, including Amaranth (red), Bordeaux (brown) Orange I (yellow) and Ponceau (scarlet) dyes, all of which are unfit for human consumption. In his book, *Water Can Undermine Your Health,* Dr. N. W. Walker writes, "Supposing you knew that Soft Drinks could cause your brain to disintegrate, would you drink them? More than a million children today are afflicted with cerebral lesions (injury to the brain that causes sudden discharge of excessive nervous energy) and other afflictions caused by Soft Drinks!"

In a speech at Loma Linda, Hans Diehl, M.D., made the following statement: " All kinds of soft drinks are very acidic, especially colas. In order to neutralize a glass of cola, it takes 32 glasses of high pH alkaline water. It is well known by the medical profession that disease loves acid. In fact, a physician from Loma Linda University said in a speech that if we could get our cells to maintain a normal pH (slightly alkaline), cancer could not grow in our bodies."

Francisco Contreras, M.D. of the Oasis of Hope Contreras Cancer Care Center in Tijuana, Mexico, said at an AIM Convention in 1990 that cancer "can't live in an oxygen-rich environment. Cola drinks make our bodies poor in oxygen."

Beatrice Hunter in her book, *Consumer Beware* (1971), states: "Nutritionally, soft drinks are low in value. Their food energy comes solely from refined sugar. Every element of nutritional importance, except calories is **zero.** Soft drinks have much in common with hard liquor, claimed the co-discoverer of insulin, Dr. Charles Best. Cirrhosis of the liver has been found among teenagers who drink large quantities of soft drinks, as well as among chronic alcoholics."

In a report found in the *FDA Consumer,* October 1980, we read, "Most soft drinks, including the cola and pepper-type drinks contain caffeine and are the number one beverage in the United States today, with coffee second. Caffeine is a drug which stimulates the central nervous system. In the amounts presently being consumed, it can cause insomnia, nervousness, irritability, anxiety and disturbances in the heart rate and rhythm. Cola and pepper-like drinks account for 80 to 90 percent of the caffeine added to foods today. Its long-term effects on people are not clearly known."

In making a public announcement regarding caffeine's possible dangers to unborn children, past FDA Commissioner Dr. Jere E. Goyan urged pregnant women to avoid the use of caffeine products. He stated, "So while further evidence is being gathered on the possible relationship between caffeine and birth defects, a prudent and protective mother-to-be will want to put caffeine on her list of unnecessary substances which she should avoid." Goyan goes on to say, "that as a general rule, pregnant women should avoid all substances that have drug-like effects."

Dr. Mary Ruth Swope in her article titled, *Why I Don't Drink Soft Drinks and I Wish You Didn't,* makes the following statement: "Cola drinks contain caramel coloring, which, according to some researchers, has genetic effects and is a cancer-causing suspect. Polyethylene glycol is used as an ingredient sometimes. Glycol is used in anti-freeze in automobiles and as an oil solvent. Perhaps you have noticed that pouring cola drinks on your windshield in a snow or ice storm will keep the windshield from freezing over with ice." She also comments that, "Soft drinks use predominately three types of sweeteners - saccharin or aspartame in the diet type and sugar, cane syrup or corn syrup in the regular drinks. These substances enhance taste appeal and come touted as 'refreshing' and 'high energy.' The truth is that saccharin has been shown to cause cancer in laboratory animals and Nutra-sweet and Equal are linked to convulsions, depression, insomnia, irritability, weakness, dizziness, migraine headaches, mood changes and mental retardation. (Which of these, I ask, is something you really want in your life?)" She goes on to say, " A government warning was once issued the manufacturer of a certain world-famous refreshing soft drink for its suspected effect on the bones of children because of the large amount of phosphoric acid in it. Pour coke over an extracted baby tooth or a 10-penny nail and see it totally dissolve in a few days!"

Dr. Swope's article also states: "Diet sodas that are low in calories are high in sodium. **Six ounces** of regular Pepsi-Cola have 5 mg. of sodium; Diet Pepsi has 31 mg. (But who only drinks 6 oz. at a time now?) Classic Coke has 19 mg. of sodium. High blood pressure is a very common ailment in our society; I wonder why!"

"And who shouldn't have high sodium in their diets? My personal answer to that question, is that any condition which causes a person to have high blood pressure should be considered a condition where limiting sodium intake would be helpful. Here are a few of those: certain tumors, kidney disease, adrenal or thyroid or pituitary gland malfunctioning – even diabetes and arteriosclerosis or hardening of the arteries. Soft drinks, in my estimation, should be off-limits to persons with these conditions."

An article titled *Confessions of a Soft Drink* makes the following statement about soft drinks "The bubbles and fizz in soft drinks can potentially burn human insides: this is caused by the phosphoric acid and carbon dioxide. The phosphorus in the acid upsets the body's calcium-phosphorus ratio and dissolves calcium out of the bones. This can eventually result in **osteoporosis,** a weakening of the skeletal structure, which can make one susceptible to broken bones. Also, the phosphorus fights with the hydrochloric acid in human stomachs and renders it ineffective. This promotes indigestion, bloating and gassiness in many individuals. Carbon dioxide is a waste product exhaled by humans, but they ingest it when they drink cola drinks."

Dr. George M. Halpern, Division of Allergy at the University of California Davis School of Medicine, reports that diet soft drinks may cause allergies. "The potential problem may be due to toxicity because of the increase in consumption of diet drinks. Acute or chronic hives may be symptoms caused by this low-calorie, artificial sweetener."

In her 1971 book, *Consumer Beware,* Beatrice Hunter writes, "Dr. Clive McCay, working at the Naval Research Institute, placed extracted human teeth in cola drinks. Within two days, the teeth became very soft, and the enamel surface lost much of its calcium. Rats, well fed but given nothing to drink except cola beverages, after six months had their molar teeth dissolved down to the gum line. When Dr. McCay reported years ago the rat experiments before the Delaney hearings on chemicals in foods, a lawmaker reminded him that the soft drink industry represented huge economic investments. He suggested that these alarming findings be soft-pedaled to avoid disrupting the industry and the economy as a whole. Dr. McCay countered by stating that the health of the nation's children might be as important as the welfare of the soft-drink industry."

The research is abundant and I believe the case is clear; colas and other soft drinks are detrimental to all of God's children no matter what their age and should be eliminated from the diet immediately.

James Beasley, M.D., of the Ford Foundation Project stated that "If Americans do not change their eating and drinking habits within twenty years we will have nutritional obliteration." Reviewing the facts of the decreased health in our country, one would think Dr. Beasley is right on track.

One of our intentions in writing this book is to collect and present the evidence, as clearly as possible, to show the harmful effects these products are having on our people. But we, at Hallelujah Acres, are just one voice among many in this world. In your lifetime, you and your family will be exposed to countless advertisements, commercials and "scientific" studies designed to promote meat, dairy products, sugar, white flour and other processed foods, as well as drugs such as coffee, cigarettes, alcohol, etc. We hope you will carefully consider your response to these issues as you plan meals for yourself and your family. Make these decisions as if your life – and the lives of your family members – are at stake, because this is truly the case. People are dying every day because of what they eat, and these premature deaths can be prevented by making the right decisions about diet and lifestyle.

"I call heaven and earth to record this day against you,
that I have set before you life and death, blessing and cursing:
therefore choose life, that both thou and thy seed may live:"
– Deuteronomy 30:19

Chapter 4:

Unlearning the Reasons
You Shouldn't be a Vegetarian

"Whether therefore ye eat, or drink,
or whatsoever ye do,
do all to
the glory of God"
– I Corinthians 10:31

In addition to informing readers about the potential dangers of the SAD American Diet, another one of our intentions in writing this book is to show how wise – and easy – it is to switch to a mostly-raw vegetarian diet that avoids all the harmful processed foods and drugs cited in the previous chapter. There is considerable scientific evidence supporting the wisdom of eating fruits and vegetables for the purpose of preventing or healing disease. For example, the National Cancer Institute and most nutritional experts advise us to eat plenty of fruits and vegetables to prevent cancer and other life-threatening diseases. Much of the information that is coming from the scientific community today is reminiscent of what we were told several decades ago by our mother or grandmother, encouraging us to eat our green vegetables. And we all remember the old adage, "An apple a day keeps the doctor away."

That sounds simple enough, but then there are all the other voices out there causing people to wonder: "If I become a complete vegetarian, where will I get my protein?" "If I don't drink milk, how can I get enough calcium?" "How would I get vitamin B-12 if I don't consume animal products?"

These are all legitimate questions. But unfortunately, the reason so many people are asking these questions is because of the misinformation and propaganda distributed by those who profit from the sale of meat, dairy products and processed foods. *If you research proper diet and nutrition, one of the first things you will learn is that the average American must first "un-learn" most of what we have been taught about nutrition, including the four food groups, half of which are animal products.* Once this propaganda is unlearned, we will realize that every element of nutrition needed by the human body can be provided by a diet of raw fruits and vegetables. For example:

Unlearning the Reasons You Shouldn't be a Vegetarian

Protein

Protein has been the most widely-publicized of all human nutrional needs, and this has led many people to be obsessed with making sure they get enough protein. The problem is that the average American consumes over 100 grams of protein a day, which is three to five times the amount experts now say is necessary. This excessive amount of protein is harmful, and more physical problems are being caused by people consuming too much protein than are caused by people not getting enough protein.

Several generations of school children and doctors were taught incorrectly that we need meat, dairy and eggs for protein. The meat, dairy and egg industries funded this "nutritional education" and it became official U.S. government policy. Much of the evidence used to support the claim that animal products are ideal for meeting human protein needs was based on a now-discredited experiment on rats conducted in 1914.

Nutritionists have drastically altered their thinking about human protein needs since that infamous rat study. But this updated knowledge has been very slow to reach the public. Most adults will remember being told repeatedly (and incorrectly) in school about how important it is to get lots of protein.

Official U.S. policy on human protein needs has changed so drastically that there is no longer even a minimum daily requirement for protein listed on the latest nutrition labels. Modern research has shown that most people have more reason to be concerned about medical problems caused by consuming too much protein, rather than not getting enough. Protein is an extremely important nutrient, but when we get too much protein, or protein that we cannot digest, it causes problems. In his book, *Your Health, Your Choice,* Dr. Ted Morter, Jr. warns, "In our society, one of the principle sources of physiological toxins is ***too much protein.***"

It may come as quite a shock to people trying to consume as much protein as possible to read in major medical journals and scientific reports that excess protein has been found to promote the growth of cancer cells and can cause liver and kidney disorders, digestive problems, gout, arthritis, calcium deficiencies (including osteoporosis) and other harmful mineral imbalances.

It has been known for decades that populations consuming high-protein, meat-based diets have higher cancer rates and lower life-spans (averaging as low as 30 to 40 years), compared to cultures subsisting on low-protein vegetarian diets (some with average life-spans of more than 90 years).

Numerous studies have found that animals and humans subjected to high-protein diets have a consistently higher rate of cancer development. As for humans, T. Colin Campbell, a Professor of Nutritional Sciences at Cornell University and the senior science advisor to the American Institute for Cancer Research, says there is "a strong correlation between dietary protein intake and cancer of the breast, prostate, pancreas and colon." Likewise, Myron Winick, director of Columbia University's Institute of Human Nutrition, has found strong evidence of "a relationship between high-protein diets and cancer of the colon."

In *Your Health, Your Choice,* Dr. Morter writes, "The paradox of protein is that it is not only essential but also potentially health-destroying. Adequate amounts are vital to keeping your cells hale and hearty and on the job; but unrelenting consumption of excess dietary protein congests your cells and forces the pH of your life-sustaining fluids down to cell-stifling, disease-producing levels. Cells overburdened with protein become toxic."

Writing in the Sept. 3, 1982 issue of the *New England Journal of Medicine,* researchers Dr. Barry Branner and Timothy Meyer state that "undigested protein must be eliminated by the kidneys. This unnecessary work stresses out the kidneys so much that gradually lesions are developed and tissues begin to harden." In the colon, this excess protein waste putrefies into toxic substances, some of which are absorbed into the bloodstream. Dr. Willard Visek, Professor of Clinical Sciences at the University of Illinois Medical School, warns, "A high protein diet also breaks down the pancreas and lowers resistance to cancer as well as contributes to the development of diabetes."

In his 1976 book, *How to Get Well,* Dr. Paavo Airola, Ph.D., N.D., notes we "have been brought to believe that a high protein diet is a must if you wish to attain a high level of health and prevent disease. Health writers and 'experts' who advocated high protein diets were misled by slanted research, which was financed by dairy and meat industries, or by insufficient and outdated information. Most recent research, worldwide, both scientific and empirical, shows more and more convincingly that our past beliefs in regard to high requirements of protein are out-dated and incorrect, and that the actual daily need for protein in human nutrition is far below that which has long been considered necessary. Researchers, working independently in many parts of the world, arrived at the conclusion that our actual daily need of protein is only 25 to 35 grams (raw proteins being utilized twice as well as cooked) ... But what is even more important, the world-wide research brings almost daily confirmation of the scientific premise ... that proteins, essential and important as they are, ***can be extremely harmful when consumed in excess of your actual need.***"

Dr. Airola continues: "The metabolism of proteins consumed in excess of the actual need leaves toxic residues of metabolic waste in tissues, causes autotoxemia, overacidity and nutritional deficiencies, accumulation of uric acid and purines in the tissues, intestinal putrefaction, and contributes to the development of many of our most common and serious diseases, such as arthritis, kidney damage, pyorrhea, schizophrenia, osteoporosis, arteriosclerosis, heart disease, and cancer. A high protein diet also causes premature aging and lowers life expectancy."

The good news about protein, however, is that ***it is much easier to meet our minimum daily protein requirements than most people would imagine ... with just fruits and vegetables.*** Because much of what experts once believed about protein has been proven incorrect, U.S. government recommendations on daily protein consumption have been reduced from 118 grams to 46 to 56 grams in the 1980's to the present level of 25 to 35 grams. In fact, the most recent (1994) nutrition labels for food do not even include a minimum daily requirement for protein because nutritionists know it would be very unusual for a person to not meet his or her protein requirements. Many nutritionists now feel that 20 grams of protein a day is more than enough, and warn about the potential dangers of consistently consuming much more than this amount. The average American consumes a little over 100 grams of protein per day.

Drastically reduced recommendations for protein consumption are an obvious indication that official information about protein taught not so long ago to everyone from school children to doctors was incorrect, but there has been no major effort to inform the public that what we were taught has been proven wrong. So there are large numbers of people with medical problems caused by eating more than four or five times as much protein as necessary, yet their misguided obsession is still to ensure that they get enough protein.

A good way of determining which foods provide sufficient protein is to consider recommendations on the percentage of our total calorie intake that should be made up of protein, and then determine which foods meet these recommendations. These recommendations range from 2 1/2 to 8 percent. Reports in the *American Journal of Clinical Nutrition* say we should receive 2 1/2 percent of our daily caloric intake from protein, and that many populations have lived in excellent health on that amount. The World Health Organization established a figure of 4 1/2 percent. The Food and Nutrition Board recommends 6 percent, while the National Research Council recommends 8 percent of our calories should come from protein.

The 6 and 8 percent figures are more than what most people need, and these higher percentages are intended as a margin of safety. But still, these recommendations are met by many fruits and greatly exceeded by most all vegetables. For example, the percentage of calories provided by protein in spinach is 49%; broccoli 45%; cauliflower 40%; lettuce 34%; peas 30%; green beans 26%; cucumbers 24%; celery 21%; potatoes 11%; sweet potatoes 6%; honeydew 10%; cantaloupe 9%; strawberry 8%; orange 8%; watermelon 8%; peach 6%; pear 5%; banana 5%; pineapple 3%; and apple 1%. Considering these figures, any nutritionist would have to agree it is very easy for a vegetarian to get sufficient protein.

Two reasons we have such a low protein requirement, as noted by Harvey and Marilyn Diamond in *Fit for Life,* are that, "the human body recycles 70 percent of its proteinaceous waste," and our bodies lose only about 23 grams of protein a day.

Another important lesson to "unlearn" is that the need to consume foods or meals containing "complete protein" is based on an erroneous and out-dated myth. Due to lingering misinformation from that 1914 rat study, many people still believe they must eat animal products to obtain "complete protein." And for other people, this fallacy was replaced by a second inaccurate theory that proper food combining is necessary to obtain "complete protein" from vegetables. Both of these theories have been unquestionably disproved, because we now know people can completely satisfy their protein needs and all other nutritional requirements from a good variety of raw fruits and vegetables without worrying about proper food combining or adding protein supplements or animal products to their diets.

In fact, the whole theory behind the need to consume "complete protein" – a belief once accepted as fact by medical and nutritional experts – is now disregarded. For example, Dr. Alfred Harper, Chairman of Nutritional Sciences at the University of Wisconsin, Madison, and of the Food and Nutrition Board of the National Research Council, states, "One of the biggest fallacies ever perpetuated is that there is any need for so-called complete protein."

Protein is composed of amino acids, and these amino acids are literally the building blocks of our body. There are eight essential amino acids we need from food for our body to build "complete protein," and every one of these amino acids can be found in fruits and vegetables. (There is a total of 23 amino acids we need, but our body is able to produce 15 of these, leaving eight "essential" amino acids that must be obtained from food.) There are many vegetables and some fruits that contain all eight essential amino acids, including carrots, brussels sprouts, cabbage, cauliflower, corn, cucumbers, eggplant, kale, okra, peas, potatoes, summer squash, sweet potatoes, tomatoes and bananas.

But the reason we do not necessarily need all eight essential amino acids from one food or from one meal is that our body stores amino acids for future use. From the digestion of food and from recycling of proteinaceous wastes, our body maintains an amino acid pool, which is circulated to cells throughout the body by our blood and lymph systems. These cells and our liver are constantly making deposits and withdrawals from this pool, based on the supply and demand of specific amino acids.

The belief that animal protein is superior to vegetable protein dates back to 1914 when two researchers named Osborn and Mendel found that rats grew faster on animal protein than plant protein. From these findings, meat, dairy and eggs were termed as "Class A" proteins, and vegetable proteins were classified as an inferior "Class B." In the mid-1940s, researchers found that ten essential amino acids are required for a rat's diet, and that meat, dairy and eggs supplied all ten of these amino acids, whereas wheat, rice and corn did not. The meat, dairy and egg industries capitalized on both of these findings, with little regard for the fact that nutritional requirements for rats are very different than for humans.

It was discovered in 1952 that humans required only eight essential amino acids, and that fruits and vegetables are an excellent source of all of these. Later experiments also found that although animal protein does speed the growth of rats, animal protein also leads to a shorter life-span and higher rates of cancer and other diseases. There are also major differences in the protein needs of humans and rats. For example, human breast milk is composed of 5 percent protein, compared to 49 percent protein in rat milk. And a human infant requires an average of 180 days to double its birth weight, compared to only four days for rats.

To illustrate how ignorant "experts" can be, during the time that high-protein diets were thought to be healthy, many experts felt it was a "mistake of nature" that human females produced breast milk of only 5 percent protein. Instead of assuming that God made a mistake, perhaps it would be wiser to realize that the promoters of meat, dairy and eggs have made a mistake by encouraging us to consume dangerously high amounts of protein. If a human infant can be perfectly nourished during the most rapid period of growth with nothing but 5-percent protein from breast milk, there is no reason to believe that older humans need more protein.

The "complete protein" myth was given another boost in 1971 when Frances Moore Lappé wrote *Diet for a Small Planet.* Lappé discouraged meat eating, but promoted food combining with vegetable proteins, such as beans and rice, to obtain all eight essential amino acids in one meal. But by 1981, Lappé conducted additional research and realized that combining vegetarian foods was not necessary to get proper protein. In her tenth-anniversary edition of *Diet for a Small Planet,* Lappé admitted her blunder and acknowledged that food combining is not necessary to obtain sufficient protein from a vegetarian diet. In fact, Dr. John McDougall warns that efforts to combine foods for complete protein are not only unnecessary, but dangerous, because "one who follows the advice for protein combining can unintentionally design a diet containing an excessive and therefore harmful amount of protein."

Another myth that needs to be dispelled about protein is its relationship to strength, energy and athletes.

As pointed out by John Robbins in *Diet for a New America,* many studies have shown that protein consumption is no higher during hard work and exercise than during rest. Robbins writes, "True, we need protein to replace enzymes, rebuild blood cells, grow hair, produce antibodies, and to fulfill certain other specific tasks ... (But) study after study has found that protein combustion is no higher during exercise than under resting conditions."

A 1978 issue of the *Journal of the American Medical Association* warns athletes against taking protein supplements, noting, "Athletes need the same amount of protein foods as nonathletes. Protein does not increase strength. Indeed, it often takes greater energy to digest and metabolize the excess of protein."

Most athletes are not aware of this information on protein, but there have been attempts to make this warning known. For example, George Beinhorn wrote in the April 1975 issue of *Bike World,* "Excess protein saps energy from working muscles ... It has also been discovered that too much protein is actually toxic. In layman's terms, it is poisonous ... Protein has enjoyed a wonderful reputation among athletes. Phrases like 'protein power,' 'protein for energy,' 'protein pills for the training athlete' . . . are all false and misleading."

Robbins gives additional evidence for this claim in *Realities for the 90's* by naming some of the world's greatest athletes, all holders of world records in their field, *who all happen to be vegetarians:* Dave Scott, six-time winner of the Ironman Triathlon (and the only man to win it more than twice); Sixto Linares, world record holder in the 24-hour triathlon; Paavo Nurmi, 20 world records and nine Olympic medals in distance running; Robert Sweetgall, world's premier ultra-distance walker; Murray Rose, world records in the 400 and 1500-meter freestyle; Estelle Gray and Cheryl Marek, world record in cross-country tandem cycling; Henry Aaron, all-time major league home run champion; Stan Price, world record holder in the bench press; Andreas Cahling, Mr. International body building champion; Roy Hilligan, Mr. America body building champion; Ridgely Abele, eight national championships in karate; and Dan Millman, world champion gymnast ... all vegetarians.

That's a list that would surprise the average American, based on what we have been taught to believe about protein and meat.

Calcium

Calcium intake is another subject many vegetarians are concerned about. We are told we must consume milk and other dairy products to get calcium, but, actually, the best source of calcium is from green leafy vegetables. The trace mineral boron is essential for calcium to be properly absorbed, and the best source of boron is leafy vegetables and fruits.

Neal Barnard, M. D., states "that green leafy vegetables provide generous amounts of calcium without the animal protein of meat diets. In fact, green vegetables such as broccoli, collard greens, and kale are loaded with calcium." The reason Dr. Barnard emphasizes the importance of obtaining calcium without animal protein is that the acidity of animal protein robs calcium from the bones. Calcium is one of the most alkaline minerals in the body, and when our blood stream becomes too acidic because of meat, dairy and other acidic foods, the only way for the body to balance this acidity is to rob calcium from the bones.

The incredible lesson to learn here is that calcium deficiencies are not caused by insufficient intake of dietary calcium. Calcium deficiencies are actually caused by excessive acidity, primarily animal protein. Dr. Barnard notes that when volunteers eat a high-protein meal, they lose calcium in their urine.

John McDougall, M.D., also writes: "An important fact to remember is that all natural diets, including purely vegetarian diets without a hint of dairy products, contain amounts of calcium that are above the threshold for meeting your nutritional needs.....In fact, calcium deficiency caused by an insufficient amount of calcium in the diet is not known to occur in humans."

But many people, especially elderly women have a very serious problem with calcium deficiencies, which cause brittle bones. One of the most serious problems caused by loss of calcium is osteoporosis, which is characterized by the loss of 50 to 75 percent of a person's original bone material. The orthodox approach of medical doctors and nutritionists in dealing with osteoporosis and other calcium deficiencies is to tell the person to consume more dairy products or even calcium supplements. This approach has not been successful, because in the United States, 25 percent of women over the age of 65 suffer from osteoporosis. Their bones become brittle and are easily broken. Something as minor as a sneeze can lead to a cracked rib.

For people wanting to prevent or heal osteoporosis, their primary goal should be to minimize calcium loss by avoiding animal products and other acidic foods. A diet of raw green vegetables will supply plenty of dietary calcium, without any need for harmful products such as dairy or calcium supplements. There is an incredible amount of evidence from all around the world to substantiate this claim.

Anyone successfully indoctrinated by the meat and dairy industry's nutritional education would be baffled by the numerous studies finding osteoporosis, a calcium deficiency that makes the bones porous and brittle, is very prominent among people with high consumption of both protein and calcium. For example, the March 1983 *Journal of Clinical Nutrition* found that by age 65, the measurable bone loss of meat-eaters was five to six times worse than of vegetarians. The August 22, 1984 issue of the *Medical Tribune* also found that vegetarians have "significantly stronger bones."

African Bantu women average only 350 mg. of calcium per day (far below the National Dairy Council recommendation of 1,200 mg.), but seldom break a bone, and osteoporosis is practically non-existent, because they have a low-protein diet. At the other extreme, Eskimos have the highest calcium intake in the world (more than 2,000 mg. a day), but they suffer from one of the highest rates of osteoporosis because their diet is also the highest in protein.

The explanation for these findings is that meat consumption leaves an acidic residue, and a diet of acid-forming foods requires the body to balance its pH by withdrawing calcium (an alkaline mineral) from the bones and teeth. So even if we consume sufficient calcium, a high-protein, meat-based diet will cause calcium to be leached from our bones. Dr. John McDougall reports on one long-term study finding that even with calcium intake as high as 1,400 mgs. a day, if the subjects consumed 75 grams of protein daily, there was more calcium lost in their urine than absorbed into their body. These results show that to avoid a calcium deficiency, it is more important to reduce protein intake than to increase calcium consumption.

Recipes for Life ... from God's Garden

Iron

Another concern frequently expressed about vegetarian diets is the possibility of developing an iron deficiency. This should not be a problem for anyone eating a healthy vegetarian diet because the plant kingdom provides all the iron the body needs, and in an organic form that is usable by the body. The iron found in cooked flesh is in an inorganic, toxic form that cannot be used as nutrition by our bodies. Neal Barnard, MD., says, "According to research studies, populations that consume little or no animal products actually have equal or greater iron intake than meat eaters."

Vitamin B-12

Vitamin B_{12} is another concern of many vegetarians because there is negligible B_{12} in plant life. But likewise, animals do not make Vitamin B_{12} either. B_{12} is made by bacteria in the soil, and can be synthesized by bacteria within the body.

Vitamin B_{12} plays a role in many important functions including folate metabolism, red blood cell formation, synthesis of DNA and RNA, maintenance of the myelin sheath of nerves, and digestion and absorption of food.

The RDA for vitamin B_{12} is 2.4 micrograms for adults, 2.6 micrograms during pregnancy, and proportionally less for children. Victor Herbert, M.D., a research expert on B_{12}, believes nobody needs more than 1 microgram/day, with 0.3 micrograms/day being adequate for most people. The liver stores B_{12}, so daily intake is not required. However, our research found signs of impaired metabolism within two years of stopping dietary intake.

Contrary to previous beliefs, our current research has shown that people following the Hallelujah diet, including generous use of Barleygreen, are at high risk (~50%) for metabolic B_{12} deficiency. While serum B_{12} levels may remain normal for several years, the body, especially the central nervous system, can be suffering a deficiency at the cellular level, as measured by elevated methylmalonic concentration.

There are bacteria in the small intestine of the human body that can make B_{12}, but our research shows that intestianl flora is not a sufficient source for everybody. Probiotic supplementation did not fully alleviate metabolic deficiency, with wide differences in tested brands.

Many plant foods which claim to contain B_{12} only contain analogs of B_{12}, which interfere with the body's metabolism of true cobalamin. Sea vegetation such as chlorella, spirulina, blue-green algae, nori, and dulse contain almost exclusively analogs of B_{12}. Also, supplementation experiments with spirulina and nori failed to improve deficient subjects' B_{12} status.

Nutritional yeast, such as Red Star Vegetarian Support Formula, which is grown in a B_{12} enriched medium, is a good vegetarian source of B_{12}. Our research shows that a sublingual B_{12} supplement effectively restored people's deficient B_{12} metabolism to normal. One should verify that their body makes B_{12}, identify a reliable and sufficient source of B_{12} in their diet, or take a sublingual supplement.

Fat

Fat is essential for the human body to function properly. The two essential fatty acids (and the most important) are linoleic and linolenic acids. Over the years our diets have become deficient in these two very important nutrients. The highly processed fats we consume compete with and replace these essential fatty acids within our bodies. As a result, there has been an increase of immune-related diseases in our society. Some of these are multiple sclerosis, diabetes, lupus, and arthritis, just to name a few.

Raw flaxseed oil contains both of these essential fatty acids, along with vitamins A, E, and D, and the water-soluble vitamins B1, B2 and C, as well as many minerals, including iron, zinc and potassium.

Flaxseed oil should be purchased in dark containers since exposure to the light destroys some of the nutrients. It should be "cold pressed," stored in the refrigerator and consumed within three months of the date of purchase. In the beginning, a person may notice some loosening of the stool; however, this usually stops within one or two weeks. After approximately three to four weeks a person should notice healthier skin and hair, increased vitality, and some have reported a lessening of arthritic pain.

Fats cannot be broken down in the mouth, and only a minute amount can be broken down in the stomach. It is not until it reaches the bile and pancreatic juices that fats can be broken down.

Saturated fat is any fat that is solid at room temperature, like margarine, lard and creamed cooking oils. Since saturated fat becomes rancid when exposed to air for even a short period of time, various chemical techniques are used to alter their chemical makeup so that the fat-containing products will have an extended shelf life. When these unnatural oils are heated, they become very dangerous for the body, causing the blood platelets to become sticky, increasing the possibility of heart attack, stroke, cancer or high blood pressure. Look for the words "hydrogenated" or "partially hydrogenated" on the label and avoid them like the plague! Saturated fat is linked to over 50 percent of all deaths in America. If a person eliminates saturated fat and meat from their diet, they will reduce their chances of having a heart attack by 96 percent. Most Americans consume 42 to 45 percent of their calories from fat, while people in the Orient consume only 10 percent of their calories from fat! As a result, the rate of heart disease is 17 times higher in the United States than in China, and breast cancer is five times more prevalent.

Several well-documented studies have shown that in cultures and countries where fat is consumed in higher quantities, especially animal fats, there is a higher incidence of heart disease, certain types of cancer, and other diseases. Even within Japan, affluent women who eat meat daily have 8.5 times higher risk of breast cancer compared to poorer women who rarely or never eat meat.

Unsaturated fats are those that remain liquid at room temperature. There are two types of unsaturated fat: monounsaturated which is found in olive oil, almonds and almond oil and polyunsaturated fat found in corn, safflower and cotton seed oils. The monounsaturated fats found in natural foods do not cause increased levels of cholesterol. However, unsaturated fats should be eaten very sparingly!

As God designed, our body can only digest 2 teaspoons of fat per hour. Due to the slow digestion of fat, a high-fat meal can stay in the digestive system for up to 19 hours! During this time the food ferments, which produces toxic waste that travels through the bloodstream causing headaches, bursitis, irritation of the stomach and intestines, along with other body pain and physical problems.

The National Academy of Sciences has reported that bowel, breast and prostate cancer incidence are highest among those Americans who consume a high-fat diet. The Academy has recommended that the American people decrease their intake of meat, fried foods and high-fat dairy products. In addition, they have determined that an increase in the consumption of foods high in carotene decreases the incidence of cancer of the bladder and larynx. To improve circulation and to reduce triglyceride and cholesterol levels, one should avoid fats found in meat, dairy products, oils, margarine, shortenings and most store-bought salad dressings. Heart attacks, strokes, diabetes, many types of cancer and other diseases are the end result of a high-fat intake.

Heat Destroys Nutrition

When food is heated above 107 degrees, the enzymes start to die. By 122 degrees, they are completely destroyed. Heating not only destroys enzymes, but alters the chemical make-up, rendering the food nutritionally-deficient for the human body. The body then has to work overtime to move this dead, unnatural substance through the digestive system, causing great stress for the colon and robbing the bones and other organs of their enzymes to complete the process. (Enzymes are required for all bodily functions. Vitamins, minerals, hormones and protein all require enzymes to perform their functions.) Processed foods are not only cooked, but are also full of chemicals and other toxins our bodies were never designed to have to deal with.

Consequently, over 65 percent of our adult population and over 20 percent of our youth (those under 17) already have chronic diseases and are on medication. If that doesn't make you angry, it should! We need to wake up and take back the control of our bodies before the foods of this world destroy us! I know it is not easy, but thousands are doing it each day and so can you. My Bible says: ***"I can do all things through Christ which strengtheneth."*** (Philippians 4:13)

By God's design, we were meant to eat our food raw, just like all of the rest of the animal kingdom that God created. Raw food is digested very quickly, usually within 30 to 60 minutes – rather than the hours or even days required by many of the cooked food or cooked flesh products. Raw fruits and vegetables also are a wonderful source of fiber.

Raw foods are certainly more economical than flesh and processed foods, and require much less time to prepare. In fact, if a person has an area where they can garden, they can produce their own food for pennies while enjoying healthy exercise. When it comes to cleanup, it is much easier to simply rinse off a plate that has contained a raw meal than to clean up grease on dishes, pots and pans after a meal based on the SAD American Diet.

Raw foods help the body's weight to normalize and keep the body's appetite in check. It is almost impossible to overeat on a raw, whole-foods diet. Amazingly, when we eat foods the way God designed them to be eaten, degenerative diseases do not occur; in fact, if we are already experiencing these diseases, they will usually reverse and disappear quite quickly. People often report having more energy, being better rested at night and do not require as much sleep. Mood swings usually disappear and even the need for a deodorant or breath deodorizers often vanishes. Problems with PMS and menopause usually become nonexistent and often the mind becomes clearer while memory and concentration improve.

Dr. James B. Sumner, a 1946 Nobel Prize winner, states: "Raw foods contain health-giving rejuvenating enzymes. Cooking, pasteurization, smoking, pickling, air pollution, pesticides, drugs, antibiotics, chlorination and fluoridation of water and many other interferences in nature's processing will denature enzymes, thus making the nutrients in food not readily available."

Cooking food has a devastating effect on nutrition. All enzymes and most vitamins are destroyed by heat, while minerals and protein are converted by heat to a form that is not usable by the body. According to John Michael Douglas, M.D., Ph.D., Dr.P.H., F.A.C.P.: "When we treat food with thermal fire, we lose up to 97 percent of the water soluble vitamins (Vitamins B and C) and up to 40 percent of the lipid soluble vitamins (Vitamins A, D, E, and K)."

The composition of protein is drastically changed by heat. If you have ever fried an egg, this is obvious. Once the egg hits the hot frying pan, the clear, runny "albumen" (protein) of the egg instantly changes to a white, rubbery texture. Protein is obviously not the same substance before and after it hits the heat. And the form of protein that mankind was created to be sustained by is raw protein from living plants.

Minerals undergo a somewhat similar transformation when exposed to heat, as they lose their life and vitality, and revert back to an inorganic form. The difference between a mineral in a plant versus a mineral in the ground is that the plant has taken this inorganic mineral from the ground and (by photosynthesis and help from lots of micro-organisms in the soil) transformed it into a vital, living, organic mineral in the body of the plant, which we are able to eat and use to build new, living, vital cells that become a part of our body. A mineral in the ground – calcium for example – is the same as the mineral in the plant, but the difference is that our bodies can use calcium from plants, such as green vegetables, but our bodies can't use calcium straight from the ground. The difference is directly related to the very life of the plant, because in a raw fruit or vegetable, the minerals have been transformed into a living substance. The molecules of a living substance, such as a plant, vibrate at a different level than a dead substance, such as a rock or piece of soil. The minerals in a plant are alive and vibrant, but the heat of cooking takes that life away.

Enzymes are the very first nutrient to be lost to heat, as they begin to die at 107 degrees. This is bad news because enzymes are necessary for the functioning of every other nutrient, so nothing works the same without the benefit of the enzymes from the food you consume.

So this means that by cooking food, you have killed all its enzymes, destroyed most vitamins, and transformed protein and minerals into a form the body can no longer use to build new, vital, living cells. This is not good. Considering the dead-food diets of most Americans, it is no wonder that we are a sick nation in the middle of a health care crisis that no vitamin supplements, medical drugs, surgeries, radiation or chemotherapy will ever solve.

We must acknowledge that there is a difference between food that is alive and food that is dead, and we must ensure that the majority of what we put into our body is material which we can use to build healthy new living cells. This is why The Hallelujah Diet is at least 75 to 85 percent raw fruits and vegetables. And if and when we do eat cooked foods, we must ensure that this 15 to 25 percent portion of our diet does not contain toxic chemicals, animal products, white flour, white sugar and other processed foods that are very hazardous and difficult for the body to eliminate. Foods such as steamed vegetables, baked potatoes, brown rice and other cooked food recipes found in this book are not health-producing and cell-building in the way that raw foods are, but these cooked foods do not have the same negative impact as consuming hamburgers, hot dogs, colas, sugar desserts and other processed foods.

Another category of food that should be eaten raw rather than cooked is spinach and other green leafy vegetables, such as Swiss chard, beet greens, turnip and mustard greens, kale and collards. The reason is that these green, leafy foods contain oxalic acid, which is a very healthy substance in its raw form, but causes several problems when it is cooked. In his book, *Fresh Vegetable and Fruit Juices,* Dr. Norman W. Walker writes: "Spinach should never be eaten when cooked unless we are particularly anxious to accumulate oxalic acid crystals in our kidneys with the consequent pain and kidney trouble. When spinach is cooked or canned, the oxalic acid atoms become inorganic as a result of excessive heat and may form oxalic acid crystals in the kidneys."

Dr. Walker explains that oxalic acid – in its raw, organic form – is one of the elements that contribute to the wave-like movement, known as peristaltic motion, that moves food and its waste products through our digestive and eliminative systems. Dr. Walker writes: "Organic oxalic acid is one of the important elements needed to maintain the tone of, and to stimulate peristalsis. It is perfectly obvious, of course, that any motion of the body which takes place by the 'involuntary' action of its organs is predicated on there being life in the cells and tissues of such organs. Life is active, magnetic; whereas there is no action in death nor in dead matter, and this applies definitely to cells and tissues of our anatomy. If the important organs comprising the alimentary and eliminative departments of our system, or any parts of them, are moribund or dead, the efficiency of their function is impaired, to say the least. This condition can result only from a lack or deficiency of live atoms in the food nourishing the cells and tissues concerned. Live food means that food which contains live organic atoms and enzymes found only in our raw foods."

Dr. Walker further explains that oxalic acid readily combines with calcium, and if both of these elements are in their raw, organic state, "the result is a beneficial constructive combination." But he warns: "When the oxalic acid has become inorganic by cooking or processing the foods that contain it, then this acid forms an interlocking compound with the calcium, even combining with the calcium in other foods eaten during the same meal, destroying the nourishing value of both. This results in such a serious deficiency of calcium that it has been known to cause decomposition of the bones. This is the reason I never eat cooked or canned spinach."

Recipes for Life ... from God's Garden

My Goal

My goal in writing this book is to set before you a simpler, healthier lifestyle. A lifestyle that will enable you to so eat that you might live! At Hallelujah Acres, we do not teach an all-raw diet (although that is the ideal). Many find an all-raw diet too difficult and thus will not stick with it. We strive to maintain a diet of at least 75 to 85 percent raw foods, with the cooked food portion making up no more than 15 to 25 percent of our diet. In this book you will find some transitional recipes for those just beginning The Hallelujah Diet, some recipes for that 15 to 25-percent of cooked food intake, and some recipes for special occasions, as well as many all-raw recipes.

Dr. Malkmus became a vegetarian in 1976 due to a potentially life-threatening physical problem in a desperate attempt to save his life. My problems were not life-threatening, although they certainly did affect my quality of life. My prayer is that you will not have to have a serious physical problem before you are ready and willing to make changes in your diet and lifestyle.

Prior to changing our diet and lifestyle, Dr. Malkmus and I had both been, in ignorance, on the SAD American Diet for all our lives. We had to learn the hard way that animal products, dairy products, sugar, salt, and white flour products are harmful and potentially deadly.

A trip through the supermarket should make one realize that the American people are in trouble physically. How much space is given to live, fresh foods in comparison to manufactured, dead, devitalized, chemically-altered foods? This manufactured food keeps for a long time on the supermarket shelf and makes the food manufacturer a lot of money, but at the expense of the health of the people who eat these devitalized foods.

The SAD American Diet of today is lacking in nutrition! The nutrients our body needs cannot be found in the dead, unnatural, manufactured products we buy in cans, bottles, jars, boxes and packages found on the supermarket shelves. As Dr. Malkmus so often says, "Once you leave the fresh produce department in your supermarket, you are literally in the non-food section of the store and there is practically zero nutrition in any product found outside of the fresh produce department."

In America, we live in a fast-paced world where we don't take time to prepare healthy meals. It is so much "easier" to stop by the fast-food restaurant on the way home. Have you ever stopped to realize that fast-food restaurants are slowly destroying the health of those who patronize them? The "foods" found in these establishments are full of fat, salt, sugar, white flour and harmful additives that cause most of the physical problems being experienced by our people and contribute to the heart attacks, strokes and cancers suffered by a large percentage of the American population.

But even after people purchase raw foods from their produce markets, most Americans cook that food by some method prior to consuming it. In the Bible, we find that God gave mankind the Ideal Diet in Genesis 1:29. Here God is telling us that He has supplied all the nutrients we need in the fresh, raw fruits and vegetables without cooking our food or consuming the flesh of another animal. No doubt about it, there was no stove, grill or microwave in the garden!

May our Lord guide you, bless you, strengthen you and help you to do that which you know in your heart is right for your own body and those you love. My prayers are with you!

"Trust in the Lord with all thine heart;
and lean not unto thine own understanding.
In all thy ways acknowledge him, and
he shall direct thy paths."
– Proverbs 3: 5 - 6

Hallelujah Acres Healthy Foods Pyramid

The original Basic 4 Food Groups that most of us were raised on has produced massive physical problems. Two of the four food groups were animal products. These animal products are producing heart attacks, which are the cause of 50 percent of all deaths in America today. Animal products are also the primary cause of most cancers and adult-onset diabetes, not to mention acid stomach, most allergies, etc. The Hallelujah Acres Healthy Foods Pyramid, by comparison, produces abundant health and a long life.

High-fat, high-protein & concentrated foods should be kept to a minimum. Extra-Virgin Olive Oil or raw Flax Seed Oil can be used on raw vegetable salads. Beans (including tofu and other soybean products) should not be relied upon as a regular staple of the diet because they are cooked and too high in protein. Small amounts of butter and honey can be used occasionally.

Minimize grains because most are acid-forming. Fruits and vegetables, by comparison, are alkaline. Cancer cells cannot survive in an alkaline environment. Limit cooked veggies to the evening meal. Remember, cooking destroys most nutritients.

Nuts & seeds are too high in fat & protein to eat regularly.

With the fiber removed, fresh vegetable juices are the most efficient way of getting nutrition to the cellular level.

In addition to great nutrition, eating raw vegetables & fruits are the best source of fiber.

If one eats a diet of at least 75 to 85 percent raw foods, this leaves 15 to 25 percent of the diet for cooked food. This 15-25 percent should not be junk! No meat, dairy, white flour, white sugar, salt, chemical preservatives or processed foods. If one avoids these harmful processed foods and animal products, the cooked food portion of the diet can satisfy cravings and offer a variation at the end of the day, with very little harmful effect on overall health. A cooked meal at the end of the day can be very satisfying, but remember, the only food that is cell food is raw food.

We recommend that at least 75 to 85 percent of one's diet be living (raw) food. This provides our living cells with the nutrition they need to function properly and to build healthy new cells. Living food is the key to a healthy life!

Pyramid

High-Fat and High-Protein Concentrated Foods, Oils, etc
flax seed & olive oil, butter, beans, honey, etc. **eat very sparingly**

Bread and Cooked Grains
whole-grain bread, brown rice, millet, etc. **eat moderately**

Cooked Vegetables
steamed vegetables and baked potatoes or sweet potatoes, vegetable soups and stews. **eat moderately and only at the evening meal**

Raw Nuts and Seeds
High Protein & Fat – Consume Sparingly

Fresh Vegetable Juices And, no, that does not include frozen, bottled or canned juice
Two to eight 8-oz. servings a day. Carrot juice should comprise at least 50% of any vegetable juice mix. Drink fruit juices sparingly.

BarleyMax
Minimum of 2 teaspoons daily. For optimal nutrition, take 3 - 4 teaspoons daily. BarleyMax is a (convenient) form of vegetable juice. Take 30 min. before each meal.

Raw Fruits
Fruits are a cleansing food, and are very easy to digest, so they are ideal for the first meal of the day. Do not mix fruits with other foods, and do not mix different types of fruit improperly. (See pages 66-67 for more on food combining.) Generally one should eat more raw vegetables than fruits. Too much fruit can create hypoglycemic problems for some people due to its high content of natural sugars.

Raw Vegetables
You may eat **unlimited quantities** of raw vegetables. Raw vegetables are your best source of nutrition, and one should strive to eat a good variety of vegetables, especially greens and deeply-colored vegetables such as broccoli, spinach, carrots, beets, squash, etc. The deep colors indicate high quantities of beta-carotene and other vital nutrients. Eating a raw vegetable salad before a meal of cooked vegetables or grains will provide your body with living enzymes necessary to help digest the cooked food.

The Hallelujah Diet[sm]

by Rev. George H. Malkmus

People often ask me, "What do you eat?" Here is my answer:

Breakfast: Upon rising, one teaspoon of BarleyMax powder – either dry and let it dissolve in the mouth, or in a couple ounces of distilled water at room temperature, but never in fruit juice. No cooked food, or food containing fiber at this meal, so as not to stop or hinder the cleansing process, as the body eliminates accumulated toxins.

Mid–Morning: An eight–ounce glass of carrot juice. If juice is not available, a piece of juicy fruit would be second best.

Lunch: Before lunch, another teaspoon of BarleyMax powder as at breakfast. Thirty minutes later, it's either a raw vegetable salad or raw fruit. This also is an all–raw meal, as cooked food is limited to the evening meal. Fruit should be limited to no more than 15% of total daily food intake.

Mid–Afternoon: An eight–ounce glass of carrot juice. If juice is not available, some carrot or celery sticks would be second best.

Supper: Before dinner, another teaspoon of BarleyMax powder as at breakfast and lunch. Thirty minutes later, a LARGE green salad comprised of leaf lettuce (never head lettuce as it has very little nutritional value) along with a variety of vegetables. After the salad, comes the only cooked food of the day – the 15% cooked food portion allowed on The Hallelujah Diet. This could be a baked potato, brown rice, steamed veggies, whole grain pasta, or a veggie sandwich on whole grain bread, baked sweet potato or squash. (If desired, Lunch and Supper can be switched, but only one meal should contain cooked food on any given day.)

Evening: If desired, a piece of juicy fruit or a glass of freshly extracted apple or pear juice may be consumed.

In Addition To The Above, The Following Is Also A Part Of The Hallelujah Diet

A Good Psyllium-based Fiber product: Serving recommended on container according to weight, either before leaving for work, or late morning. (Not recommended for pregnant or lactating mothers, or for long-term use.) An alternative would be 2 to 3 tablespoons of organic flax seed, freshly ground in a coffee mill, mixed into 8 ounces of distilled water or juice.

Flax seed oil or Udo's Choice Perfected Oil Blend: One to two tablespoons. Can be taken straight, or used on salad. Not recommended for cooking.

Vitamin B12: To insure adequate B–12 intake, 1/2 tablet of a vegetarian, sublingual, methylcoballamin tablet three times a week. Vitally important for pregnant women.

Sunshine: Each day the sun is shining, some (15 minutes) sunshine on as much of the skin as possible, as sun is so important in the production of vitamin D.

Exercise: Physically exercising every day for a minimum of 30 minutes is extremely important. Half the time should be in aerobic activity and the remainder in resistance exercises. A stretching and fast walking program is a good place to begin.

Carrot Juice: Freshly extracted carrot juice made from large California juicing carrots is extremely important in meeting daily nutritional needs. The carrot juice, along with BarleyMax makes a dynamic duo in providing the body with high–octane fuel. As a maintenance program, consume at least two 8oz glasses of carrot juice along with two to three teaspoons of BarleyMax daily. When I had my colon cancer in 1976, I consumed 32 to 64 ounces of carrot juice mixed with freshly juiced vegetable greens daily. BarleyMax powder did not exist back in 1976. If I had a serious physical problem today, I would increase my carrot juice to six to eight 8oz glasses along with four or more teaspoons of BarleyMax powder daily.

BarleyMax: The reason I supplement my diet with BarleyMax is that, for the most part, food produced today is grown in soil that often lacks the nutrients my body needs for building new, strong, healthy, vital, and vibrant cells. BarleyMax is grown organically and contains the widest spectrum of nutrients from a single source (that I am aware of). I always consume at least three teaspoons daily. When starting, one teaspoon per day may be a good starting point, and then building up to two to three teaspoons to prevent too rapid of a cleansing reactions.

The Hallelujah Diet^{sm} . . . Explained

The Hallelujah Diet, once understood, is very simple to prepare and apply. Breakfast is simply BarleyMax powder! Lunch is a vegetable salad or some fruit, while dinner consists of a raw vegetable salad followed by some cooked food.

Carrot Juice is the in between meal snack. We try to follow a ratio of 85% raw and 15% cooked food each day, with the cooked food usually coming only at the end of the evening meal.

The 85% Portion

This is the "Hallelujah" portion of The Hallelujah Diet! An abundance of God's natural foods, uncooked (raw), and unprocessed. The dense living nutrients found in raw foods and their juices are what meets and satisfies the cells nutritional needs, so that a person no longer needs to struggle with uncontrollable hunger. Live foods are also what produce abundant energy and vibrant health.

Following are items from each category that fit into the 85% portion of each day's food intake:

Beverages: Freshly extracted vegetable juices, BarleyMax, and distilled water.

Dairy Alternatives: Fresh almond milk, creamy banana milk, as well as frozen banana, strawberry or blueberry "fruit creams."

Fruit: All fresh, as well as unsulfured organic dried fruit. Limited to no more than 15% of daily food intake. (Fruit juice would be included in this 15%, while fruit juice is never recommended in large quantities.)

Grains: Soaked oats, millet, raw muesli, dehydrated granola, dehydrated crackers, and raw ground flax seed.

Nuts And Seeds: Raw almonds, sun-flower seeds, macadamia nuts, walnuts, and raw almond butter or tahini. Consume sparingly.

Oils And Fats: Extra virgin olive oil, Udo's Choice Perfected Oil Blend, Flax seed oil (the oil of choice for people with cancer), and avocados.

Seasonings: Fresh or dehydrated herbs, garlic, sweet onions, parsley and salt free seasonings.

Soups: Raw soups.

Sweets: Fruit smoothies, raw fruit pies with nut/date crusts, date–nut squares, etc.

Vegetables: All raw vegetables.

The 15% Portion

The following foods make up the 15% portion of The Hallelujah Diet. These are the cooked foods that follow the raw salad at the evening meal. This cooked food portion can be very delicious, and actually proves beneficial for those trying to maintain body weight.

Beverages: Caffeine free herb teas and cereal coffees, along with bottled organic juices.

Dairy: Non–dairy cheese, rice milk, and organic butter, all sparingly.

Fruit: Stewed and unsweetened frozen fruits.

Grains: Whole–grain cereals, breads, muffins, pasta, brown rice, millet, etc.

Oils: Mayonnaise made from cold–pressed oils.

Seasonings: Light Gray Celtic Sea Salt (Use sparingly)

Soups: Soups made from scratch with-out fat, dairy, or table salt.

Sweeteners: Raw, unfiltered honey, rice syrup, unsulfured molasses, stevia, carob, pure maple syrup, date sugar. (Use very sparingly.)

Vegetables: Steamed or wok cooked fresh or frozen vegetables, baked white or sweet potatoes, squash, etc.

Foods To Be Avoided

These foods are what create most of the physical problems we experience, and are not a part of The Hallelujah Diet. They should be eliminated from the diet as quickly as possible.

Beverages: Alcohol, coffee, tea, cocoa, carbonated beverages and soft drinks, all artificial fruit drinks, including sports drinks, and all commercial juices containing preservatives, salt, and sweeteners.

Dairy: All milk, cheese, eggs, ice cream, whipped toppings, and non–dairy creamers.

Fruit: Canned and sweetened fruits, along with non–organic dried fruits.

Grains: Refined, bleached flour products, cold breakfast cereals, and white rice.

Meats: Beef, pork, fish, chicken, turkey, hamburgers, hot dogs, bacon, sausage etc. All meats are harmful to the body and the cause of up to 90% of all physical problems.

Nuts And Seeds: All roasted and/or salted seeds and nuts. Peanuts are not a nut, but a legume and very difficult to digest.

Oils: All lard, margarine, and shortenings. Anything containing hydrogenated oils.

Seasonings: Table salt, black pepper, and any seasonings containing them.

Soups: All canned, packaged or creamed soups containing dairy products.

Sweets: All refined white or brown sugar, sugar syrups, chocolate, candy, gum, cookies, donuts, cakes, pies, or other products containing refined sugars or artificial sweeteners.

Vegetable: All canned vegetables, or vegetables fried in oil.

Food Combining – Fruits

Acid Fruits

Cranberries
Gooseberries
Grapefruit
Kiwi
Kumquat
Lemons*
Limes
Oranges
Pineapple
Pomegranates
Raspberries
Sour Plums
Strawberries
Tangelos
Tangerines
Tomatoes

* Lemons combine well with all plant foods and can be used to replace vinegar in recipes.

Sweet Fruits

Bananas
Dates
Figs
Muscat Grapes
Papaya
Persimmon
Prunes
Raisins
Thompson Grapes
Other Dried Fruits

Do Not Combine –

digests poorly together

Sub-Acid Fruits

Apples
Apricots
Blackberries
Blueberries
Cherries
Guava
Kiwi
Mangos
Most Grapes
Nectarines
Papaya
Passion Fruit
Peaches
Pears
Plums

Combine –
digests well together

Combine –
digests well together

Do Not Combine Fruits with Vegetables or Grains

An exception to this rule is that you may combine leaf lettuce or celery with fruits to help deal with the excessive sugar.

Melons

Cantalope   Crenshaw   Persian
Casaba   Honey Dew   Watermelon

Eat melons alone or leave them alone, as they do not digest well with other foods. Any of the melons can be combined with each other, however.

Food Combining – Vegetables & Grains

Starches

All Grains
Bread
Brown & Wild Rice
Coconut
Corn
Lima Beans
Most Legumes
Parsnips
Pasta
Potatoes
Pumpkin
Whole-Grain Cereals
Winter Squash
Yams

Do Not Combine –

⟷

digests poorly together

Proteins

All other bean products
Dairy**
Dried Peas & Beans
Flesh Foods**
Lentils
Nuts*
Seeds*
Soybean Analogs (fake meat)**
Sprouted Legumes

* Best soaked 24 hours in distilled water before use.

** Included for clarity ONLY. Not recommended.

Vegetables

Asparagus
Beets
Bok Choy
Broccoli
Cabbage
Carrots
Cauliflower
Celery
Cucumbers
Eggplant
Kale
Kohlrabi
Leaf Lettuce & Endive
Okra
Onions
Parsley
Radish
Red, Yellow, Green Bell Peppers
Rutabaga
Snow Peas
Spinach
String Beans
Summer Squash
Sweet Potatoes
Turnips
Zucchini

Tomatoes (a fruit) may be eaten with non-starchy vegetables

Combine – digests well together

Combine – digests well together

Fresh Vegetable Juice

Drink at least 30 minutes before a meal, and not with a meal. Barley Green is in the Vegetable Juice category.

Oils and Fats

Almonds
Avocados**
Butter*
Coconut
Flax Seed Oil
Olive Oil
Pecans
Pumpkin Seeds
Sunflower Seeds

* Use very sparingly. Never use margarine or other hydrogenated oils.

** Avocado is best mixed with green vegetables or sub-acid fruits.

A Note on Food Combining:

Various foods require different digestive juices and enzymes, and require different lengths of time for digestion. So, for optimal digestion and assimilation, it is best when foods are consumed in simple and compatible combinations. These food combining charts are included as a helpful guide, but are not absolute, and are not intended to be a set of unbending rules. Some recipes in this book do violate ideal food combining guidelines, which is one reason we implemented the five-star rating system. For people on the Hallelujah Diet who are not fighting a serious illness, less than perfect combinations can be eaten on occasion.

Chapter Five:

Cell-Building Salads

"I will praise thee; for I am fearfully and wonderfully made:
marvelous are thy works;
and that my soul knoweth right well."
– Psalms 139:14

Many people consider a salad to be an optional or less important part of their evening meal … somewhat of an appetizer before the "main course." This popular belief is wrong because a good salad has all the nutritional components required by our body, and that is a claim that can't be made for the cooked "main course" or any other food group.

When planning your evening meal, there are a lot of things you could – and should – skip, but a salad isn't one of them. For example, you could omit the bread and the cooked food without creating any nutritional deficiency. You could *– and should –* skip the meat and dairy products (even though these are two of the four traditional basic food groups), and your health will benefit greatly from their absence. The same is true for dessert. But if you want all the essential nutrients needed by your body, you cannot omit a good, raw salad full of fresh, living vegetables.

<u>**Vitamins, minerals, amino acids (protein), enzymes, carbohydrates, fats, water**</u> and <u>**fiber**</u> are all essential components of a healthy diet, *and every one of these essential components can be found in raw fruits and vegetables. This is a claim that can be made for no other type of food other than raw fruit and vegetables.* The bottom line is that, based on everything known by modern medical science and nutritionists, not one single substance has been found, manufactured, synthesized or advertised that can even come close to the nutritional value for mankind as the original diet handed down by God in the first chapter of Genesis. As our world suffers painfully and needlessly from disease, malnutrition and premature degeneration, let us not lose sight of the significance of this realization.

As we begin to nourish our bodies with the foods God intended, many people enjoy coming to learn and appreciate more about the way our body uses the nutrients we consume to carry out several zillion functions and actually build a new body, cell by cell, all at the same time. This appreciation and reverence for

God's wonderful plan for nourishing and creating our bodies can be understood and expressed on a simple, child-like level, or a more complex, scientific level. On a simple level, we can understand that our bodies are made up of living cells that need to be nourished by living (raw) foods, which God has provided for us in abundance in the form of raw fruits and vegetables. Child-like faith can be used to give thanks for this wonderful provision and accept the fact that these delicious fruits and vegetables offered by our Creator in Genesis 1:29 are exactly what is needed to nourish and sustain us in perfect health. A pre-schooler can understand the difference between a fresh, living, raw carrot or apple made by God and a tin can full of dead, devitalized food and chemical preservatives manufactured by man.

If you want to go beyond this simple understanding, we can take a more scientific approach to understanding the complexities of how nutrients work in our body. But despite everything modern science knows about how dozens of vitamins, minerals and amino acids, thousands of enzymes, along with carbohydrates, fats, water and fiber all work together in our body, there is much still to be learned and even more that will never be known about the marvelous and intricate workings of our body/temple. For example, scientists have concluded that just one strand of DNA in just one of our hundred trillion microscopic cells contains so much information that, if it were decoded, this information would not begin to fit in an entire volume of encyclopedias.

With this understanding, it is fun to learn more about what makes our body work, but all the more important to realize that we must combine this knowledge with a child-like faith in the wisdom of God's plans … including his plans for nourishing our body/temple.

More and more studies are concluding that processed foods and vitamin supplementation do not offer the same nutritional value as raw foods (see Chapter 14 in *God's Way to Ultimate Health*). Somehow it is

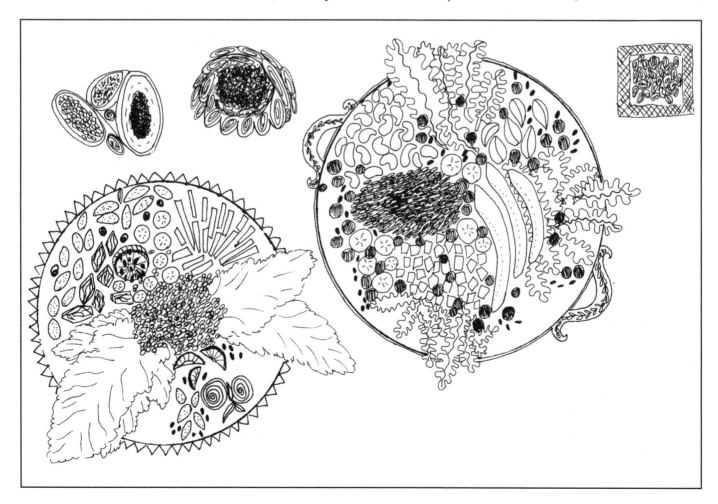

not too surprising that what man would manufacture would fall woefully short of the nutritional value of what God has created, in the form that he created it, which is raw. The more you learn, the more you will see the nutritional advantage of raw fruits and vegetables over cooked and processed foods. Heat from cooking destroys all enzymes and most vitamins, while protein and minerals are altered by heat to a form that is not usable by the human body.

Raw fruits and vegetables are also a good source of water, considering that they are composed of between 70 and 90-percent water. (Our bodies lose almost a gallon of water a day which must be replaced, and the water from raw fruits and vegetables should account for a large part of this replacement.)

Raw vegetables are an ideal source of protein, partly because this protein has not been altered by heat, and also because this protein is not in an excessive amount. Heat from cooking alters amino acids (protein) into a non-living form, unusable by our body. You have seen this immediate change with your own eyes if you have ever fried an egg. The instant that the protein in the clear, runny (albumen) portion of the egg hits the hot frying pan, its form is immediately changed from clear and runny to white and rubbery.

When protein is heated or consumed in excess, it is harmful to the body and must be eliminated. Excess protein feeds cancer cells, burdens the liver, is stored as fat, and causes numerous other problems. Many Americans consume in excess of 100 grams of protein a day, even though nutritional experts now agree that only 20 to 25 grams a day are necessary. In the past, the amount of protein we need has been greatly exaggerated in "nutritional education" funded by the meat and dairy industries to encourage the myth that consumption of animal products is necessary for protein. The truth is that the calorie content of human breast milk is only about 5 percent protein, and this is the perfect food designed by God to meet all nutritional needs during the fastest stage of human growth. Most fruits have approximately the same protein content as human breast milk, and this level is exceeded by vegetables. Modern nutritional experts are in near unanimous agreement that a person with a healthy vegetarian diet should have no reason to be concerned about a protein deficiency, despite what we have been told in the past about needing meat for protein. And there is no need to worry about "proper combining" of amino acids for "complete protein." (Even Frances Moore Lappé, who helped to popularize the idea of proper combining for complete protein in her book *Diet for a Small Planet,* now acknowledges this combining is completely unnecessary. The body stores amino acids from food to manufacture its own "complete protein.")

According to Dr. N. W. Walker in his book, *Diet and Salad,* "All vegetables and fruits contain the necessary atoms from which amino acids are formed in the system. The human body cannot utilize for constructive purposes flesh products of any kind in the form of 'complete proteins' but it can gather from the fresh vegetables and their juices, when they are fresh and properly made, the finest atoms from which to construct its own vital amino acids and protein."

Historically, protein has been America's number one nutritional concern, but most Americans are much more likely to have a deficiency of vitamins, minerals and enzymes than they are to have a protein deficiency.

The reason for an enzyme deficiency is simply that enzymes are only in living (raw) food and most Americans eat very little living food.

As for vitamins and minerals, there are three major obstacles we must overcome to avoid a deficiency in these areas:

1) There are over 100 different essential vitamins, minerals and trace minerals, and you have to obtain sufficient amounts of every single one of them in your diet to avoid having a vitamin or mineral deficiency of some kind;

2) Most vitamins and minerals consumed by Americans are not in a form that can be used by our bodies to build vital, healthy, new, living cells; and

3) Trace minerals are especially scarce in the American diet because they are scarce in American

topsoil, much of which has eroded into the ocean.

These three obstacles can make it difficult to avoid some vitamin or mineral deficiency, even for people who try to eat what they believe to be a healthy diet.

The solution to avoiding any of these deficiencies is to consume a broad variety of raw fruits, vegetables and fresh vegetable juices, especially dark green and deeply-colored vegetables, organic whenever possible, and some sea vegetable, such as kelp. With this type of diet, not only will you get every vitamin, mineral and trace mineral you need, but you will also be well-supplied with amino acids (protein), enzymes, carbohydrates, fats, water and fiber.

By eating several servings of the following foods daily, you can ensure that your family is receiving all of the vitamins, minerals and trace minerals required: Barleygreen powder with kelp, raw carrots (including plenty of carrot juice), raw green veggies such as broccoli, spinach and leaf lettuce, raw beets, raw cabbage, cucumbers, sunflower seeds, pumpkin seeds, watercress and fruit with a high water content.

The reason Barleygreen with kelp is so important is that when all of the sources of nutrition are compared, green vegetables rank the highest, and the young leaves of barley contain the highest amount and broadest spectrum of all the vitamins, minerals, enzymes and amino acids needed by the human body. And with kelp added, we are assured of getting a substantial dose of all the trace minerals that have eroded from our topsoil into the ocean, because kelp is grown in the ocean. And because Barleygreen is not processed with heat higher than body temperature, we know that its nutrients are in a raw, living form.

Certain trace elements are also available in many other foods, but in smaller quantities. Trace minerals are so minute they are invisible except when extremely powerful microscopes are used; however, the body cannot function without them. The body requires at least 59 trace minerals to function properly. Maintaining a diet of fresh raw vegetables, fruits, freshly-extracted juices and Barleygreen with kelp assures a person that they are doing everything they can to receive the full complement of all nutrients (in a natural form) required to maintain optimum health.

Enzymes are another extremely important element of nutrition … perhaps the most fragile and least understood of all. The reason I say enzymes are perhaps the most fragile of all nutrients is that they are the first to be destroyed by heat or lengthy time of storage. Enzymes can be lost even in raw foods that lose their freshness after several weeks or months elapse from the time the food is harvested and transported to various warehouses, trucking companies, then to your local grocer, then to your house before it is served.

Enzymes are the first nutrients to be lost in the cooking process because they begin to die at 107°, and are completely destroyed at 122°. Water boils at 212° and baking begins at about 250°, so that means all enzymes are lost almost immediately from the start of any cooking process, even in steaming vegetables.

But that's worse than you may realize. Because when you lose all the enzymes in a food that has been cooked, you are losing more than just enzymes. Among the seemingly infinite roles played by enzymes, they are involved in a synergistic sort of way in helping all vitamins, minerals and amino acids (protein) to be absorbed – as living, vital nutrients – into our living cells in a way that allows these nutrients to be used to build new living cells in our body. Loss of enzymes in food will have an impact on the vitality and absorbability of all other major nutrients in that food.

"It is my view that the vegetarian manner of living
by its purely physical effect
on the human temperament would
most beneficially influence the lot of mankind."
– Albert Einstein, 1940

Recipes for Life ... from God's Garden

The importance of enzymes cannot be over-emphasized because enzymes are the life-energy of everything that is living. Every living thing – plant or animal – has enzymes, and if it didn't, it wouldn't be alive. In his book, *Food Enzymes: The Missing Link to Radiant Health,* Humbart Santillo compares enzymes to electrical energy in a light bulb, writing, " The current is the life force of the bulb. Without electricity we would have no light, just a light bulb, a physical object without light. ... The same situation exists when trying to describe what an enzyme is within our body structure. A protein molecule is a carrier of the enzyme activity, much like the light bulb is the carrier for an electrical current. ..."

Enzymes are found in every live atom and cell in our body. Every bodily function from moving a muscle to thinking a thought requires enzymes. Most people would be amazed at the number (like I said, "seemingly infinite") of everyday life processes that would not be possible without enzymes. For example, the endocrine glands manufacture hormones that seep directly into the bloodstream through osmosis, which would not be possible if it weren't for enzymes. These hormones are not only comprised of enzymes, but also dozens of other invaluable trace elements that are required for life.

Enzymes are also required to digest food, and if you eat dead (cooked) food without enzymes, this means that because the food you are eating does not have enzymes, the process of digestion robs your body of its collected pool of enzymes. In other words, you are robbing your body of enzymes – its vital life energy – by eating cooked food. This makes it all the more important to make sure you eat a fresh, raw salad before eating any cooked meal. A raw salad will supply enzymes necessary to help with the body's more difficult task of digesting the cooked portion of the meal.

Fiber is another essential ingredient to health that will be lacking in the diet of anyone who relies on processed foods and vitamin supplements for nutrition. There are no nutrients in fiber that can be assimilated by the human body, yet fiber is an essential element of a healthy diet. All of the other elements of nutrition discussed in the chapter are absorbed and metabolized by the body, but the importance of fiber is that it is *not* absorbed or metabolized. Instead of being absorbed by the body, fiber acts as an intestinal broom to help move food and waste through the small and large intestines and out of the body. Fiber increases the water content of waste passing through the intestines, making stools softer, better formed and faster moving. A soft, moist, steady-moving stool is better able to absorb toxins and waste from the entire body for more efficient removal. On the other hand, a stool that is hard, dry and slow-moving through the intestines creates more toxins for the body to deal with. So, although fiber itself provides no nutrients, it maximizes our absorption of nutrients, prevents fermentation and infection in the digestive tract, and helps to improve detoxification with more effective waste removal.

And, like all the other elements of nutrition, the best place to get fiber is from raw fruits and vegetables. The reason that most Americans have problems with constipation, digestion and toxicity is that they do not eat enough fiber. There is *zero fiber* in all animal products – including meat, dairy and eggs – and practically no fiber in any processed foods. White flour has had all fiber removed, and the fiber in cooked vegetables is mushy and lifeless, without the electromagnetic current that exists in living food.

With this understanding, it becomes more and more apparent that the importance of daily consumption of raw fruits and vegetables cannot be overstated. Not only does the Genesis 1:29 diet of raw fruits and vegetables provide every single type of nutrient needed by your body, but it also helps with assimilation of these nutrients and with the smooth flow of waste through and out of your body for healthy detoxification.

This has been an incredibly brief summary of the way vital nutrients are used by our body to function and re-create a new body. This is all very complex, yet it is also incredibly simple. It is complex because the nutrients we consume are necessary to help our body perform such a wide variety of functions that these could not be thoroughly listed and explained even in a full volume of encyclopedias. Yet this is all so incredibly simple because eating a good variety of fresh, raw fruits and vegetables – as provided by God in Genesis 1:29 – furnishes our body with everything it needs to do everything it does ... without the unnecessary sickness, degeneration, pain and premature death that has become so prevalent in our world.

Learning more about the complexities of the human body and the rest of God's creation is made all the sweeter when we return to our child-like faith and say thanks to the Lord for the delicious assortment of fruits and vegetables He has offered for our nutrition.

"Then said Daniel to Melzar, whom the prince of the eunuchs
had set over Daniel, Hananiah, Mishael, and Azariah, prove thy servants,
I beseech thee, ten days; and let them give us pulse (vegetables) to eat, and water to drink.
Then let our countenances be looked upon before thee, and the countenance
of the children that eat of the portion of the king's meat:
and as thou seest, deal with thy servants.
So he consented to them in this matter,
and proved them ten days. And at the end of ten days
their countenances appeared fairer and fatter in flesh than all the
children which did eat the portion of the king's meat.
Thus Melzar took away the portion of their meat,
and the wine that they should drink;
and gave them pulse (vegetables). As for these four children,
God gave them knowledge and skill in all learning and wisdom:
and Daniel had understanding in all visions and dreams.
Now at the end of the days that the king had said he should bring them in,
then the prince of the eunuchs brought them in before Nebuchadnezzar.
And the king communed with them; and among them all
was found none like Daniel, Hananiah, Mishael and Azariah:
therefore stood they before the king. And in all matters of wisdom
and understanding, that the king inquired of them,
he found them ten times better than all the magicians
and astrologers that were in his realm."
Daniel 1:11-20

Chapter Six:

Juicing

"Nature's medicines are locked in the cells of growing plants
and released in their juices … These juices, subtle in their action, yet more potent
than any medicine, and without the toxic effect of drugs, can eliminate
or prevent many of the chronic and degenerative diseases
with which human beings are afflicted.
Fresh fruit juices are the cleansers of the human system.
Vegetable juices are the regenerators and builders of the body. … When we
consider that vegetables and fruits have been naturally cooked by solar energy;
that they contain all the elements the sun and earth have buried deep in their fibre cells;
that they are nature's live-cell foods – then it follows as logical that if we crush
the juices from the cells of these fresh fruits and vegetables and put
their health-giving fluid into our blood stream, we will
receive a share of their vital energy."
– John Lust, from Drink Your Troubles Away

The fresh fruits and vegetables created by God in the Garden of Eden offered mankind the best of all possible sources of nutrition for sustaining and healing our bodies. Since that time, we have polluted the Earth and eroded many of the precious minerals from our topsoil, but we must understand that the best of all possible sources of nutrition for sustaining and healing our bodies is *still* the fresh fruits and vegetables created by God.

The nutritional composition of fresh, raw fruits and vegetables is unique because on the cellular level these raw fruits and vegetables are composed of vitamins, minerals, amino acids (protein) and enzymes, all in their natural form and proper combination, that are exactly what your body needs to become the building blocks and fuel to build and rebuild vital, new living human cells of every kind – blood cells, hair cells, brain cells, heart muscle cells, lung cells, etc. These essential nutrients offer what we need not just to sustain, but to literally rebuild our vital organs, immune system, and every cell in our body.

John H. Norris, Ph.D., a biochemist and microbiologist who is a research scientist retired from the U.S. Food & Drug Administration and the National Institute of Health, has determined the Hallelujah Diet to be a very potent form of nutrition. Writing to Hallelujah Acres, in a letter published in Issue #15 of *Back to the Garden,* Dr. Norris states, "Our research has shown that when we eat natural nutrients (at least 65-percent raw fruits and vegetables) there is an energy explosion within our body. This gives the body the necessary tools it needs to rebuild strong cells that it takes to gain control of the body. … This we believe is or will be the beginning road map to return to the Garden of Eden."

There is nothing created by man – no processed food, no miracle drug, procedure, or whatever – that can offer the same healing benefits of raw fruits and vegetables because none of these man-made substances can be used by our cells to actually rebuild vibrantly healthy new cells and organs.

All this is even more significant when we understand that the Lord gave us a self-healing body. We can witness our body's self-healing ability with our own eyes. If we get a cut or scratch on our skin, we can actually see it heal before our very eyes. Every organ in our body has that same self-healing ability and the best way to promote this ability is to build a strong immune system with raw foods created by God, rather than weaken that immune system with hazardous foods, drugs, radiation, chemotherapy and other unnatural substances the world has to offer.

Raw fruits are the best cleansers of the human body, and raw vegetables are the best feeders and healers. The reason raw vegetables are the best healers is that vegetables are higher in most nutritional content than fruit, especially mineral content. Raw fruits are great cleansers because they are quickly digested and their fiber is able to flush out our system. Fiber acts as an intestinal broom to clear out our colon. Although fiber has no nutritional value itself, it is an essential part of our diet and the best form of fiber we can consume is in the form of raw fruits and vegetables.

So where does juicing fit in? It's true that, in the Garden of Eden, there were no juicing machines. And it's also true that juicing removes the fiber, which is essential to keep our colon clean. So, what is the advantage of juicing?

Well, the need for juicing arises because neither our world nor our bodies are as pure and perfect as they were at the time of the original Garden.

A person trying to heal or prevent disease needs to offer his or her body's cells as much high-quality, usable nutrition as possible so those cells can revitalize weakened organs by creating new cells that are healthier than the ones being replaced. The best way of doing this is with the consumption of fresh vegetable juice because the nutrients in this juice offer the very components – vitamins, minerals, amino acids and enzymes – that are needed to rebuild our cells. The advantage in drinking fresh vegetable juice rather than eating the whole vegetable is that the fiber has been removed, and thus we can get much more nutrition to the cellular level of our bodies much quicker, and with much less energy expended in assimilating it.

For example, we can consume the nutrition from a whole pound (16 ounces) of carrots by drinking just one 8-ounce glass of carrot juice, and get that nutrition into our bloodstream and on the way to our cells in a matter of minutes. And then in another hour, we can drink another 8-ounce glass. *Always strain juice before drinking it.*

Compare this to eating raw carrots: First of all, the amount of nutrients from *eating* carrots would be much less because a person would not eat anywhere near 16 ounces of raw carrots in one meal. Eating and digesting carrots also would take more time and would require much more energy to be expended by the body in the process of digestion, which would take at least an hour (or longer if improper food combinations occur). Eating whole raw fruits and vegetables is a very important part of The Hallelujah Diet, but juicing vegetables (and taking Barleygreen) is the ***most efficient*** means of getting large quantities of high-quality nutrition into the body without the time-consuming and energy-depleting process of digestion.

A person should eat enough raw fruits and vegetables each day to provide all the fiber necessary to maintain a clean and healthy colon, which will have an impact on the waste elimination and cleansing of every cell and organ in the body. It must be remembered that when food is cooked, heat destroys the fiber's magnetism, and leaves a mushy coating on the intestinal walls, which putrefies, leading to disease, according to Dr. N.W. Walker. So we see that fiber is like all the other major nutritional needs of the body in that it is either destroyed or altered by cooking, so the nutritional advantages to maintaining a diet of at least 75 to 85 percent raw food are obvious.

But the question is sometimes asked, "If I just eat raw food, can I get the same results as juicing?" The answer is unfortunately, "NO!" When we eat raw foods, most people do not chew (masticate) their food properly. And then, solid food requires an hour or more in the digestive system before it can be broken down and assimilated at the cellular level in liquid form. And, of course, the amount of food that can be eaten is much less than can be juiced. Therefore, the quality and quantity of nutrients made available at the cellular level from freshly-extracted vegetable juices are much higher than what can be obtained by eating solid food.

Juicing vegetables allows us to take in much more nutrients, much faster and without expending energy in the process of digestion. In his book, *Live Food Juices,* H. E. Kirschner, M.D., notes, "The juice of the plant, like the blood of the body, contains all the elements that build and nourish. It is a well-known fact that all foods must become liquid before they can be assimilated."

Juicing enables the body to flush toxins that have been stored in cells and vital organs, giving you energy and leaving you feeling refreshed and alive! Live foods make your hair shine, your skin becomes soft and glowing, your breath becomes fresh and your whole being has more vitality than you ever imagined possible. All of the body systems begin to function better as they receive the live, fresh nutrients – vitamins, minerals, proteins, enzymes, etc. – they so desperately need.

The beta carotene found in live plants is a known antioxidant that neutralizes harmful free radicals before they can damage the "genetic blueprint" within each cell. Beta carotene is found not only in carrots, but also in cabbage, broccoli, kale, cauliflower, brussels sprouts, spinach, rutabagas, kohlrabi, watercress and other greens. According to the American Cancer Society, three or four of these vegetables should be consumed every day. In articles published by the American Cancer Society, they state "that any plant of the Cruciferae family might reduce the incidence of colon, stomach and esophageal cancers. In animals, these vegetables have inhibited the effects of carcinogens."

Chlorophyll is another component the human body desperately needs. Man cannot make chlorophyll – it can only be found in plants. Current research indicates that chlorophyll appears to fight tumor growth, especially in the lungs. The chlorophyll works on the adrenal glands and cleans the lymph nodes, improving the blood and removing debris that clog the arteries. Chlorophyll is also a deodorizer.

When we were born, God built into each one of us an enzyme supply that is required to digest food. Although many are able to maintain life on a cooked-food diet, their bodies break down quickly. People on a mostly cooked diet become lethargic since the body does not receive the nutrients it needs to regenerate the life force. Disease can invade a weakened and depleted immune system because the body is using all of its reserves just to stay alive!

It is important to remember that enzymes are the life force within the plants. When food or juice is heated over 107 degrees, the live enzymes begin to be destroyed and other vital nutrients are changed into a form that the body can no longer use. Therefore, juices that are canned, frozen or bottled lack any nutritional value and should not be used.

Hint: Beets and beet greens are very cleansing to the body and help to build strong blood cells as well as cleanse the kidneys. Dr. N.W. Walker advocated that beet juice is very beneficial during the menstrual cycle. Beets are such powerful cleansers that it is best to use only a couple of ounces at one time and always in combination with another juice.

What to Juice

An important rule of thumb in juicing is to "juice your vegetables and eat your fruits." Vegetable juices are the healers while fruit and fruit juices are the cleansers. Raw vegetables require more time and energy to digest when eaten whole since they break down much slower than fruit.

Vegetables contain the "building blocks" that develop powerful, healthy muscles, tissues, glands and organs. While all fruits and vegetables are important to maintain good health, some are exceptionally beneficial. Carrot juice is the vital key and should be the base of all vegetable juices. Carrot and celery juice are a favorite at Hallelujah Acres. (When juicing celery in a Champion Juicer, cut stalks in half-inch pieces to prevent the strings from winding around the blade, which causes the motor to overheat.) Add an apple and the taste treat is sensational. Apples are the only fruit that can be used with either fruits or vegetables.

Fruit juices are too high in natural sugar to be consumed on a regular basis. However, raw fruit, when thoroughly chewed, digests very rapidly and provides the body with fiber. Fruits that contain pectin, such as apples and pears, contain a digestive aid that helps to regulate the body. Pectin is more easily obtained when the fruit is eaten rather than juiced. Drink citrus juice in moderation, because excess acidity can leach calcium from the body, leading to softened bones and teeth. Vigorous daily exercise speeds up the metabolism, which helps to burn up excess acidity.

Dark leafy greens – such as spinach, (Raw spinach is a rich source of vitamins A and E as well as a wonderful source of iron. Spinach is also higher in usable protein than many of its other counterparts. However, spinach should never be juiced alone) parsley, kale and leaf lettuce – are extremely high in nutrients, and taste great when juiced with carrots. Barleygreen is also a dark, leafy green food, and since the barley has had the fiber removed, Barleygreen is in the same category as vegetable juice.

Melon juices are also extremely beneficial. If the melons are organically grown, the entire melon can be juiced, including the rind and seeds, to provide maximum nutrition. Melons of different varieties can be juiced together, but melons should not be mixed with any other juice.

Note: Dr. N.W. Walker states that cucumber juice is a natural diuretic, is beneficial for those with rheumatic ailments, is high in potassium, promotes hair and fingernail growth and helps to eliminate skin eruptions.

Note: Bell peppers have a very hearty flavor which can be dominant in juice. Peppers are rich in vitamin C and also beta carotene.

Note: Broccoli contains a copious amount of beta carotene as well as many other valuable nutrients that make it a powerful cancer-fighting food.

Celery juice also contains organic sodium combined with many minerals the body requires.

Parsley juice is also nutritionally dense and is very concentrated, which is why it is mixed in combination with other vegetables.

Recipes for Life ... from God's Garden

Juicing Machines

A blender is not a juicer. Blenders are wonderful and a great help in the kitchen; however, they are not designed to make juice as they leave the pulp or fiber in with the juice. (The very purpose of juicing is to remove the fiber.) A blender operates at a high speed, producing only a small amount of liquid that is mixed with the fibers of the plant. In order to drink it as a juice, water must be added, which creates a mushy, grainy and unpleasant beverage that must go through the digestive system in order to be assimilated.

A juicer, on the other hand, is designed to extract the juice from the fibers of the plant, separating the pulp from the juice. It is important to remember that the fiber needed for good health is received by eating fresh fruits and vegetables; however, you do not want any fiber in the juice that you drink. The pulp that is left behind has little nutritional value, it is hard to digest and Dr. N. W. Walker says it contains the toxins that a chemically-grown fruit or vegetable may have contained. Therefore, the pulp is usually discarded into a compost pile for use in the garden.

It is important to remember when using any juicing machine to use the plastic or wooden pusher (tamper) to help push the vegetables through the machine to ensure no harm comes to the fingers. Always follow the manufacturer's directions when assembling, taking down or cleaning your juicer.

Centrifugal Juicers have a spinning basket that rotates at a very high rate of speed (usually 5,000 to 6,000 revolutions per minute), shredding the food and flinging the juice through the air causing oxidation to take place. Dr. Max Gerson, originator of the Gerson Therapy, claimed that juice from centrifugal juicers would not cure cancer. A centrifugal juicer should be used only if it is the sole option available, and it should be replaced with a masticating juicer as soon as possible. Why? Because the shredding action is not very efficient in breaking open the cells to extract the nutrients from the pulp, and then the juice is flung through the air, causing oxidation and nutritional loss. At Hallelujah Acres, we do not recommend centrifugal juicers.

Masticating Juicers operate at much slower speeds. We are aware of only three juicers on the market that would fit into this category at the present time. Masticating juicers also have the capability to be used as a grinder for nuts, seeds, sprouted grains or dried fruits. Nut butters, breads, crackers and other tasty treats such as frozen banana ice cream can also be made with this type of juicer. These juicers are:

1. The **Champion Juicer sells** for approximately $300 and has hundreds of little teeth that revolve at 1725 revolutions per minute. This juicer, after it has shredded the carrot, presses the pulp against a stainless steel screen, thus forcing out more nutrients. This juicer will yield about the same amount of juice as the centrifugal juicers, but laboratory tests show that this machine will yield three to four times more nutrients than centrifugal juicers. This is a good low-end juicer that has served many people well.

2. The **Green Star Juicer** currently sells for around $500 and is the only juicer that does not use knife blades to extract the juice. Rather, it uses twin gears that revolve at only 110 rpm. These twin gears draw the food down between the gears and press out the juice in an airtight chamber, without pumping oxygen into the juice. Laboratory reports show that this juicer yields approximately 10 more ounces of juice from a 5 lb. bag of carrots than a centrifugal or Champion juicer while doubling the nutrients of the Champion. Because oxygen is not pumped into the juice, juice made with this juicer will keep for much longer periods without breaking down. The Green Star Juicer is the juicer we recommend here at Hallelujah Acres if a person can afford it. For more information, see page 116.

3. The **Norwalk Press** sells for around $2,000. It has large, heavy-duty knife blades that run at 3,500 rpm and force the pulp and juice through a fine strainer. The shredded pulp and juice then drops into a cloth bag. The bag is then placed onto a hydraulic press (which is part of the same juicer) and the bag of shredded pulp is pressed under great pressure. This type of processing yields approximately 16 ounces more than juice from a 5 lb. bag of carrots than does the Champion Juicer and about 6 ounces more than the Green Star. This

juicer was developed by the father of carrot juice, Dr. N.W. Walker, and is a good machine, but because of the high cost and rapidly spinning knife blades, we prefer the Green Power.

Juicing is very personal and you can adjust any of the juice recipes to suit your taste buds. They are offered here to give you ideas and as a place to start. As you learn more, you will easily develop your own personal favorites.

When purchasing carrots for juicing, look for large California juicing carrots. They are usually much sweeter than those grown in other parts of the country because of the high trace mineral content of the soil. If your first encounter with carrot juice is bitter, you may miss the joy of juicing! *It is important to remember that to obtain the optimum nutrients, fresh juice should be consumed as quickly as possible after juicing.* **Also, all juice should be run through a fine screen strainer before consuming!** If any pulp is left in the juice, it will hinder assimilation.

Although some chemical poisons are systemic (stay in the plant), it is important to remove as much of the chemical sprays and pesticides as possible prior to juicing. One of the recommended ways to accomplish this is to fill the sink about half full of cold water, and add soap for cleaning fresh fruits and vegetables that is available in most health food stores. Another option is to peel the fruits and vegetables prior to juicing. We always peel our carrots prior to juicing. We also remove any blemishes or cracks which can contain bacteria.

Other Juicing Hints

* - Beets and beet greens are very cleansing to the body and help to build strong blodd cells as well as cleanse the kidneys. Dr. N. W. Walker advocated that beet juice is very beneficial during the menstrual cycle. Beets are such powerful cleansers that it is best to use only a couple of ounces at one time and always in combination with another juice.

* - Apples are the only fruits that should be mixed with carrot juice. Vegetable and fruit juices otherwise do not combine well and should not be mixed.

* - Raw spinach is a rich source of vitamins A and E as well as a wonderful source of iron. Spinach is also higher in usable protein than many of its other counterparts. However, spinach should never be juiced alone.

* - Broccoli contains a copious amount of beta carotene as well as many other valuable nutrients that make it a powerful cancer-fighting food.

* - Although tomatoes are a fruit, most people think of them as a vegetable so this juice is listed here. Fresh, raw tomato juice will taste and look quite different from those found in bottles and cans. Never use hot house tomatoes, since they are picked green and gassed to make them turn color.

* - If you are using a Champion juicer, cut celery into half-inch pieces to prevent the strings from wrapping around the blade, which causes the motor to overheat.

Chapter Seven:

Enzymes – The Key to Life

"Enzymes are the body's labor force,
the active construction-and-demolition teams that constantly build
and rebuild the body. Approximately 1,000 different enzymes are known.
At any one time there will be millions of enzymes working in every living body.
Without enzymes a human would be a lifeless pile of unusable chemicals.
Outside the human body, enzymes are found in all living things,
including food in its raw, uncooked state. ...
Fresh juices are excellent sources of important food enzymes,
as are all raw foods."
– Stephen Blauer, from The Juicing Book

When we are born, God builds into each one of us a supply of enzymes which are involved in some way in every body function. Each enzyme performs a specific duty, such as digesting food, repairing the immune system, building protein in the bones, regenerating skin and assisting the body to detoxify. The enzymes produced by the body are needed for daily repair and rebuilding and are depleted during the digestion process when cooked foods are consumed. There is a direct correlation between the enzymatic content in our bodies and the quality of our health. In fact, without enzymes life cannot exist and we die!

The importance of enzymes cannot be overstated! There are three types of enzymes and they are:

• Metabolic enzymes, which make the body organs function and are found in every cell and tissue in the human body. Their jobs are to boost the immune system, prevent disease, slow the aging process, repair damage to the body, build healthy tissue, and many other functions. A shortage of these enzymes can cause serious health problems.

• Digestive enzymes are produced by the body and are responsible for breaking down the food we eat so that it may be assimilated. Live foods enable the body to work more efficiently without having to rob organs of the enzymes required to break down food.

• Food source enzymes may be found in all freshly extracted juices and raw food, raw marinaded foods, as well as soaked nuts and seeds. Some examples of foods high in enzymatic activity are raw figs, dates, pineapple, grapes, avocado, banana, raw sauerkraut and raw nut and seed loaves.

The four types of enzymes found in food are:

1. Lipase - which breaks down the fat
2. Protease - which assists to break down protein
3. Cellulase - which works on breaking down cellulose
4. Amylase - which breaks down starch

Enzymes start to die at 107 degrees Fahrenheit! By 122 degrees Fahrenheit, the enzymes or life force are destroyed. This statement can easily be proven by a simple experiment: Take two raw carrots; cut the top off one and place it in water. Take the second carrot and cook it; then after it has been cooked, cut its top off and place it in a saucer of water. The raw carrot top will grow while the cooked carrot will not. The raw carrot is alive, with enzymes, and the cooked carrot is dead, with no enzymes.

Another example of what heat does to enzymes is the heating or pasteurization of cow's milk. A calf nursing at a mother cow will grow up into a healthy animal. But if the calf is removed from the mother and cow's milk is pasteurized (heated to 160 degrees) and then that pasteurized milk is fed to the calf as its exclusive diet, the calf will be dead in 30 to 60 days. Heat destroys the life in any form of food!

Our bodies are living organisms, comprised of living cells, and living cells require living food to be properly nourished. All cooked food is dead food and thus not proper nourishment for humans or animals.

Furthermore, cooked and highly processed foods that contain high protein, fat and refined carbohydrates generate acidity and poison within the body. Food that has been cooked and is devoid of enzymes takes much longer to pass through the digestive system, creating monumental problems for the body. With a lifetime of processed, overcooked and improperly combined meals, gourmet foods and sugary desserts, it is no wonder we are a sick nation.

Although most people are able to maintain life on a cooked food diet, their bodies break down over the course of time. Humans with all of their intellect are the only species on earth that attempts to live on a mostly cooked diet without the benefit of raw food and living enzymes. People on a mostly cooked diet become lethargic since the body does not receive the nutrients it needs to regenerate the enzyme supply. Unfortunately, we have become addicted to fast food, toxic chemicals and life in the fast lane – all of which breed disease. Disease is allowed to invade a weakened and depleted immune system because the body is using all of its reserves just to stay alive!

When a person is young, the body can handle a lot of abuse. However, as a person grows older, the enzyme reserve starts to become depleted, fewer enzymes are produced and the build-up of toxins begins. A cooked-food diet rich in fat leads to high cholesterol and unwanted pounds, while inorganic calcium intake leads to arthritis, and too much fat and sugar contributes to diabetes. When starch remains undigested, it puts stress on the liver, kidneys and even the skin. Excess protein that the body cannot remove rots in the digestive system, creating acid and waste for the body to dispose of. This process of decay may contribute to allergy problems and degeneration of the heart, kidney, blood vessels, and even the joints can become affected. The end result of a high-fat, high-protein diet high in refined carbohydrates is a body destined to disease.

White blood cells are part of the body's defense system. Their job is to devour foreign matter and to destroy any disease-causing organisms which enter the body. During the 1930s, a study was conducted which showed that when cooked food was consumed, the white blood cell count increased immediately. This indicates that when cooked food is eaten, the white blood cells have to stop their work protecting the body and must help with the digestion of the non-food poisons that have entered the system. When the same foods were eaten in their raw state, there was no change in the blood chemistry.

Recipes for Life ... from God's Garden

Undigested proteins, bacteria and yeast that enter the bloodstream through the intestinal wall have toxic effects on the body. Once they have entered the bloodstream, they spread quickly and can cause many symptoms. An example would be Candida Albicans, which lives almost everywhere in the body. If a body's immune system is in a compromised condition, Candida can take over the whole body. If the body has an adequate supply of enzymes, the yeasts, which are protein bodies, can be easily digested by the body.

For more information on enzymes, read chapter 17 in *God's Way to Ultimate Health*.

"Thou shalt come to thy grave in a full age,
like as a shock of corn
cometh in in his season."
– Job 5:26

Chapter Eight:

Vitamin, Mineral and Protein Supplements – Do we need them

"There is no business more profitable than the sale of vitamins, and money is the reason behind the hoopla about vitamins. Take the money out of vitamins, and they would practically disappear overnight. Imagine a product that has a long shelf life, that requires no refrigeration, that can be easily stored and transported, that can be marked up by more than 100%, that promises to do everything, but that can be held to do practically nothing, and you will have a pretty good picture of what vitamin sales are all about."
– Ralph C. Cinque, D.C., from Quit for Good

Today we hear many "experts" say that we need to take vitamins, minerals and protein supplements because we cannot obtain sufficient nutrients from the food we eat. The two most familiar arguments used to support the need for nutritional supplements are, *number one, that the American diet has become too reliant on nutritionally-deficient processed foods,* and, *number two, that our soil has been depleted of many of the nutrients required for optimal health.* Therefore – these "experts" say – vitamins, minerals and protein supplements must be added to our diet to ensure that proper nourishment is obtained.

Argument number one can be negated simply by avoiding processed foods and relying on fresh fruits and vegetables rather than frozen TV dinners, potato chips and Twinkies for nourishment.

But argument number two goes a bit deeper. Many studies have shown that soil erosion and unwise farming practices have indeed depleted our soil of many of the minerals and trace minerals we need for optimal health. If these minerals are lacking in the soil, they will likewise be lacking in the food grown from that soil. That means even people who eat a diet of fresh fruits and vegetables can be lacking in some nutrients if those fruits and vegetables were grown in nutritionally-deficient soil.

This dilemma could be minimized if every family were to organically grow their own food in ideal soil, or buy nothing but organic produce grown from ideal soil. But both of these options are difficult to attain, and neither would provide an absolute guarantee against the existence of some nutritional deficiency.

So, the question is, how can we ensure that our diet is not nutritionally deficient if the soil from which our food is grown has had a portion of its minerals depleted and eroded away into the ocean? This is an extraordinarily important question and, unfortunately, modern nutritional scientists have come up with what is absolutely the wrong answer! First, let's look at the solution provided by the mainstream nutrition industry, and then we'll consider the merits of a more natural answer.

Mainstream nutritionists – with the help of the multi-billion dollar vitamin supplement industry and media advertising – have convinced millions of Americans that their nutritional deficiencies can be met simply by taking an assortment of pills and powders such as vitamin C, multi-vitamins, calcium tablets, iron, mineral supplements, protein powders, etc.

The reason these types of supplements do not provide significant benefit is that the "nutrients" they contain are not in a form that can be utilized by our bodies. God created our *living* bodies to be nourished by *living* nutrients from *living* fruits and vegetables rather than from mega-doses of heat-processed vitamins in the form of a pill. God created the plant kingdom to provide us with every vitamin, amino acid, enzyme, mineral and fatty acid we need, even the oxygen (a very vital element) that we breathe. And as an added bonus, these plants are even pretty to look at. What more could we ask for?

Most vitamin and mineral supplements may be lumped into three categories. Some vitamin supplements are synthetic; some minerals are derived from rocks instead of plants; while many other supplements claim to be made from a natural vegetable-based source. Let us consider the shortcomings of these three approaches to nutrition.

First of all, anything from a synthetic source is totally useless because no scientist will ever be able to create a synthetic pill, powder or potion that can even come close to duplicating the nutritional benefit of the vitamins, minerals, amino acids, enzymes and other nutrients found in live fruits and vegetables.

Secondly, minerals derived directly from the earth, rocks or ancient mineral deposits are also not in a form that can be utilized by humans or any other animal. These minerals from the earth are essential because they nourish our soil and the plants that grow in that soil. But these minerals are of no nutritional benefit to humans until plants – with the help of micro-organisms from the soil and the process of photosynthesis – transform them into a living, organic form. Calcium, for example, from a raw head of broccoli or a raw leaf of spinach is in a living form and can be taken in and utilized by your living cells to help your body grow and maintain strong bones. But calcium from rocks and mineral deposits cannot be utilized by your living cells, and causes many problems for the body, such as hardening of arteries, kidney stones, gallstones and arthritis in joints. (This is also why we drink distilled water rather than spring water, well water or other forms of ground water; the minerals in ground water have been absorbed from rocks and soil and cannot be utilized by your body.)

The third category, perhaps the largest, is supplements that are claimed to be derived from a natural, vegetable-based source. Some of the ingredients in these supplements are indeed very nutritional in their initial raw state, but these ingredients have usually been extracted from their naturally-occurring form and then cooked and processed into a pill or powder. The only advantage to this pill or powder is that it is in a marketable form, with a shelf "life" that could last for years, or even decades. This is an advantage for those who profit from the sale of these supplements, but it's not very helpful to anyone in need of nutrition. From the perspective of an exhausted cell in need of nourishment, these processed nutritional supplements have no resemblance to the natural, raw nutrients from which they were derived.

Two serious problems exist with nutrients in this processed form. First, the isolation of a specific nutrient – such as vitamin C – from its naturally-occurring source gives us a substance that was intended to work in conjunction with other nutrients in whole food, but not all by itself. For example, if you eat a fresh, raw apple, your body will benefit from vitamin C – along with dozens of other vitamins and minerals, hundreds of enzymes, etc. – in a totally natural configuration formulated and designed into that apple by our Creator. You will not obtain the same benefit by consuming one isolated ingredient from that apple, such as vitamin C.

A second and more serious problem with this form of supplementation is the cooking and processing with heat, which destroys the life force in what was once a natural substance. The vitamin makers and processed foods industry realize that destruction of the life force in foods is necessary in order to give these products a long shelf "life." Actually, the phrase "shelf death" would be more appropriate here.

Any person knowledgeable on the subject of nutrition should know that an apple or carrot that has been steamed, boiled, baked, microwaved, canned or frozen does not provide the same nutritional benefit as a raw apple or carrot. Live fruits and vegetables provide the nutrients to help your body build new, live cells, but dead foods cannot. So, a "natural" vitamin that has been killed by the heat of cooking and processing cannot be used by your body to create new, living cells.

Any substance you consume that cannot be used to build new living cells must be eliminated by the body as waste. For a nutrient to help you create new living cells in your body, it must pass through two barriers: First it must be absorbed through the intestinal wall, and then it must pass through the microscopic cell wall, where it is used by that cell to carry out its functions and ultimately create a new living cell. If your vitamin, mineral and protein supplements cannot be used to build new living cells, these supplements must be eliminated as waste, and they are burdening your body by providing this extra waste for it to deal with.

There have been many people in the business of cleaning septic tanks and porta-toilets who have said they routinely find hundreds of vitamin pills, completely intact, in the human waste from these tanks and toilets. As Dr. Malkmus often notes in his seminars, "The net effect of taking megavitamins is to produce an expensive and exotic urine, and to overwork the kidneys."

Dr. Ralph C. Cinque writes in his book, *Quit for Good:* "Don't be tempted to join the vitamin brigade. Notwithstanding the hundreds, if not thousands, of books available, urging you to 'boost your energy,' 'enhance your immune system,' 'heighten your sexuality,' and 'extend your life span' by taking supplements, there is virtually no evidence to support these exorbitant claims made for vitamins. Not a single human life has ever been 'extended' by taking vitamins (except where there have been frank deficiencies to begin with). Vitamin therapy is just another pie-in-the sky promotion, designed to separate you from your money. In fact, the sale of vitamin pills is the biggest commercial health racket of all time."

One of the greatest cover-ups of our time is the refusal of most scientists in the nutrition industry, medical community and government to acknowledge that there is any difference between the nutrients in a fresh, raw fruit or vegetable versus the so-called "nutrients" in cooked, processed foods and nutritional supplements. The government has established a "recommended daily allowance" (R.D.A.) of certain vitamins and minerals, and we are told that a "milligram" (mg) of vitamin C from a synthetic pill counts just as much as a milligram (mg) of vitamin C from a fresh, juicy apple or stalk of broccoli. How could we ever comprehend or explain the reasoning behind such a harmful and illogical lie if we didn't consider the fact that there is more money to be made from selling vitamin pills than from fruits and vegetables that can be grown in a backyard garden?

With all this in mind, let us now go back to the topic of how we can best ensure that our diet is not nutritionally deficient, considering that the soil in which our food is grown has been depleted of a portion of its mineral content.

First of all, we should get as much nutrition (and as few toxins) as possible from the food we eat, which means putting an emphasis on raw fruits and vegetables and avoiding processed foods, animal products, drugs and other junk that give the body more toxic waste to deal with and eliminate. The reason for emphasizing raw fruits and vegetables is that the human body was created by God to be nourished with vitamins, minerals, amino acids and enzymes in a living form as they exist in raw foods. After nutrients have been altered by cooking, microwaving or other forms of food processing, they do not provide the same benefits as you will receive by consuming these nutrients in the form that God created them. Eating a diet of at least 75 to 85 percent raw food, as we recommend at Hallelujah Acres, provides a good supply of nutrients, along with the fiber needed to keep the digestive and eliminative systems flowing smoothly.

Even though raw fruits and vegetables are the ideal food for humans, research has shown that due to soil erosion and unwise farming practices, these raw fruits and vegetables do not have the same mineral content as they did several decades ago. Some minerals are found in a much lower quantity and some trace minerals are not found at all.

Therefore, in order to obtain optimal nutrition, it is now necessary to do more than just eat raw fruits and vegetables.

The first logical step is to drink freshly-extracted vegetable juice on a daily basis. The advantage to juicing vegetables is that we get a much higher concentration of all nutrients, including minerals, in fresh vegetable juice than we do from eating these vegetables, because we can consume the nutrients from an entire pound of carrots in one eight-ounce glass of carrot juice. The other big advantage to fresh juice is that because the pulp (fiber) has been removed, all these nutrients can be in the bloodstream and on their way to feeding the cells in just a few minutes, without the time-consuming and energy-depleting process of digestion.

The reason fresh vegetable juice makes such a difference in our body's health and self-healing ability is that we are taking nutrients in the form in which we were intended to consume them (as raw vegetables), and producing a liquid that offers more of these nutrients than we would otherwise be able to consume by eating the whole vegetable. And this is without cooking, freeze-drying or any other process that changes the basic structure of the nutrients.

Anyone who has ever given fresh vegetable juice (from a good quality juicer) a serious try knows that it *will* produce healthful results. The man who developed the process of juicing, Dr. Norman W. Walker, lived to be 119 years old and wrote his last book at the age of 115. This is even more impressive when you consider that Dr. Walker was seriously ill and dying in his early 50s when he was persuaded to try natural healing rather than the medical route.

Fresh vegetable juice could be categorized as a nutritional supplement, because it is a means of supplementing the nutrition we receive from the food we eat. We would be equally justified in categorizing fresh vegetable juice as a natural food because its essential nutrients (vitamins, minerals, protein and enzymes) are in the same form as they were in the raw vegetables created by God for our sustenance. Just as a whole raw carrot, fresh carrot juice is actually alive as it enters your body, bringing living nutrition to your living cells. The only part of the carrot that is removed to make carrot juice is the pulp or fiber. Fiber has no nutritional value per se, so its removal does not take away from the nutritional value of the food. The value of fiber is that it acts as an intestinal broom to cleanse the colon, so we do need to consume plenty of fiber (the best of which comes from eating raw fruits and vegetables). But drinking fresh vegetable juice without fiber is an excellent means of assimilating much more nutritional value than could be obtained from eating that same food.

And the reason we recommend drinking carrot juice on an empty stomach at least 30 minutes before a meal is that food should not be digesting in your stomach at the time your body is assimilating the juice. If solid food and carrot juice is in your stomach at the same time, this will require the juice to go through the same time-consuming and energy-consuming process of digestion as your food.

If you contrast juicing with conventional forms of nutritional supplements, you will see the clear advantage to juicing. The problem with conventional vitamins, minerals, protein powders, enzymes, etc., is that they either start with a substance never intended as food for humans (such as vitamins from coal tar or minerals derived from rock), or else they start with a natural food and ruin it by an unnatural process such as cooking or freeze-drying, so that its nutrients are no longer in their original, natural, raw form that we can utilize. On the other hand, fresh vegetable juice starts with a natural source of nutrition, and no heating, freeze-drying, microwaving, etc. is involved to alter the structure of these nutrients.

So, fresh carrot juice is clearly superior to run-of-the-mill vitamin pills, mineral supplements, protein powders, enzymes, etc. In this comparison, the number of milligrams or international units of a vitamin or mineral is irrelevant because one milligram of a nutrient in its natural form is better than ten pounds of that nutrient in an unnatural, processed form that must be eliminated by the body as a foreign substance. It takes more time and effort to juice carrots than it does to open a bottle of vitamin pills, but the benefit is well worth the extra effort.

We teach that fresh vegetable juice is the fastest way of nourishing the body's cells and immune system, which boosts the body's self-healing capabilities to enable the body to heal diseases and disorders. With this understanding, it should come as no surprise when we see people healing all types of cancer, heart disease, diabetes, arthritis and many other diseases after switching to a vegetarian diet with an emphasis on raw foods and fresh vegetable juices.

When you consider that God created fruits and vegetables to meet our nutritional needs, just think of juicing as a means of getting an extra dose of these nutrients in pre-digested (liquid) form. This is true especially for freshly-extracted vegetable juice, since vegetables contain the highest amount of nutrients that build our new living cells. (Raw vegetables are the best builders of new cells, while raw fruits are the best cleansers.) And we specifically recommend drinking freshly-extracted juice from California juicing carrots.

Juicing vegetables gives us an extra dose of all the nutrients that are in these vegetables, but remember, there are some trace minerals that are said to be totally eroded from most American topsoil. That is where the importance of sea vegetables comes in. If some of the trace minerals have eroded from our soil, the only way to obtain them is from plants grown in the ocean (which is where the minerals have eroded to). Examples of very nutritious sea vegetables include kelp, nori, dulse and kombu, but our favorite is kelp. Kelp powder can be consumed as a seasoning on vegetables and grains (but don't cook it, because it should be consumed raw).

As a nutritional supplement, BarleyMax has some of the same advantages as vegetable juice, because BarleyMax is a powder derived primarily from the *juice* of young barley plants. But there is a wider spectrum of all the nutrients needed by humans in BarleyMax than in any vegetable juice, which is part of the incredible benefits from consuming BarleyMax. This is because young leaves of barley have been determined to have a wider spectrum of all the vitamins, minerals, protein and enzymes necessary for human nutrition than any other single food. And with alfalfa, we have the addition of trace minerals, not found in barley.

This juice is spray-dried into a powder in a patented process, taking two to three seconds, in which no heat above body temperature is used. This spray-drying process dries the juice and keeps it safe until it comes into contact with water or saliva. Because of this juicing process, BarleyMax has the same advantage as fresh vegetable juice in that its nutrients can go directly into the bloodstream and to the cells without digesting fiber. And because no heat or freeze-drying is involved in the processing, the nutrients in

Recipes for Life ... from God's Garden

BarleyMax are still in their live, raw, natural form.

Green leafy vegetables have the highest concentration of nutrients of all categories of food, and young leaves of barley have been determined to have the widest spectrum of all the necessary vitamins, minerals, enzymes, proteins and chlorophyll of any source on Earth. That is why young leaves of barley are the main ingredient in BarleyMax. The grain of barley has been used as a staple of human nutrition for thousands of years, but the peak of nutritional value of the barley plant is reached when the young plant's leaves are about 10 to 12 inches tall, the stage at which it is harvested to produce BarleyMax.

The fact that BarleyMax begins with such nutritional ingredients and then maintains the value of those nutrients by avoiding heat in its patented processing makes it a product beyond comparison with other packaged nutritional supplements of any kind. BarleyMax is a living food while other vitamin supplements are dead chemicals! Our bodies recognize only living food as nourishment while they recognize dead chemicals as poison that must be eliminated.

With this in mind, it is clear that the quality of a nutritional supplement is much more important than its quantity. Too many people put too much emphasis on how many milligrams or international units of some isolated nutrient they consume, without any determination of whether any of that can actually be utilized by our body. The U.S.R.D.A. is seriously flawed, partly because it does not even recognize the difference between nutrients from real food versus synthetic vitamins.

For proof, compare the health of the average American who takes standard vitamins with the health of a person who takes barley powder, drinks fresh vegetable juice and maintains a vegetarian diet of primarily raw fruits and vegetables. Then read the testimonies in our free newsletter, *Back to the Garden,* and note the incredible results people are receiving on The Hallelujah Diet.

"One pint of carrot juice, daily, has more constructive body value
than 25 pounds of calcium tablets."
– Dr. Norman W. Walker

Chapter Nine:

The Healing Crisis

"Letdowns can be caused
by the dumping of too much disease, dead cells and poisons too quickly.
You are healing too fast; your treatment is really working – too well.
You may feel worse, but you are not worse."
– Leo Roy, M.D., N.D.

Some people are surprised to find that shortly after they change to a healthier diet, they often experience generally brief but unpleasant reactions such as headaches, pimples, nausea, flu-like symptoms or loss of energy.

When people give up things like meat and coffee and switch to raw vegetable salads and carrot juice – *and then feel sick* – it may be enough to make them wonder if this natural food is really good for them!

If this happens to you, don't be alarmed and don't turn back. You have just entered the first phase of your healing.

This unpleasant little episode is known as "The Healing Crisis," "Detoxification" or a "Cleansing Reaction," and it is fairly common. Dr. Norman W. Walker refers to this as our body's way of "housecleaning." At Hallelujah Acres, Dr. George Malkmus estimates that about 40 percent of the people who make a major dietary change to natural foods go through some form of healing crisis. About 60 percent of people who convert to a natural diet have no such reaction; about 30 percent will have a mild healing crisis; and about 10 percent will have a more severe reaction, he said.

The healing crisis can be a very discouraging setback to some people if they don't understand what is happening with their body. When we start eating a healthier diet, we expect to feel better, not worse. Some people are so discouraged that they are tempted to abandon their newly-improved diet and return to their old ways at the first sign of unpleasant symptoms. This is unfortunate, because the healing crisis is a classic example of the darkest hour being right before the dawn. This temporary discomfort can be the first sign that our body's natural process of self-healing is kicking into high gear.

As our healing begins, we must remember that our body is dealing with toxins that are deep within our cells and vital organs. As our body strives to eliminate these deep-seated toxins, it is very easy to understand how we may feel nauseous or get a headache as these toxins – on their way out of our body – first get circulated a bit in our bloodstream. Or if these toxins are eliminated through the skin in the form of pimples or a skin rash, we should feel relieved to have these impurities exiting at the surface level rather than remaining and accumulating deep in our body.

When the body has accumulated many years of toxic wastes and poisons, this has a degenerative effect, to one extent or another, on every cell and every vital organ in our body. The very first step in our healing process must be eliminating these toxic wastes from the cellular level of our body, and from our vital organs, as we begin to bring in the vital nutrients that our body needs to rebuild its immune system, its 100 trillion living cells and its organs. As we switch to a diet that brings in fresh, living, high-quality nutrients, our body will use these nutrients as building blocks to regenerate new living cells. Because our body now has this new high-quality building material to work with, it will start to discard the old, lower-quality material, including toxins that may have been slowly degenerating our vital organs for years.

So are we happy and relieved to know that these deep-seated toxic wastes are on the way out of our body? Or are we disappointed when these impurities circulate in our blood long enough to let us feel a headache or nausea? Or do we grimace when these poisons are eliminated through the skin in the form of pimples or a rash?

The main thing to remember is that regardless of how bad we dislike these pimples, nausea, fatigue or headaches, we should realize that it is better for our body to deal temporarily with these symptoms on the surface level rather than to continue holding these toxins deep within our cells and vital organs where they will have a more gradual degenerative effect that could eventually culminate in a serious, life-threatening disease.

Now I realize that pimples, nausea and headaches are difficult things to feel good about, but if we can comprehend the wisdom of our body's process of self-healing during the healing crisis, we really would appreciate these symptoms of minor discomfort.

Specific symptoms of the healing crisis will vary according to the type and quantity of toxins that need to be eliminated, the health of the organs involved in this elimination, and how abruptly the dietary transition is being made. Other possible symptoms of the healing crisis include diarrhea, constipation, frequent urination, nervousness, irritability, fevers, or pain in an area where we previously had a physical problem.

Diarrhea and cold-like symptoms are good examples of reactions you may think are bad, but are actually doing good things for your body. The cleansing aspect of fruit can help clean out old, impacted fecal matter from your intestinal walls and flush out this toxic fecal matter in the form of loose stools. This may seem uncomfortable or inconvenient, but it is very beneficial to your body. Another example of something good that may seem bad is a large discharge of mucus from your nasal passages. This may seem like a bad cold or a sinus attack, but a more accurate explanation is that the dietary change is allowing your body to eliminate excess toxins that have been built up in your mucous membranes.

Since these reactions are part of our body's healing process, experts in natural health recommend against taking pain-relievers or other drugs to mask these symptoms. If we want to learn how to eliminate the cause of our sickness, rather than just continuing to mask its symptoms, we will be willing to tolerate the temporary discomfort of a healing crisis.

But there are some things we can do to minimize these symptoms. Dr. George Malkmus recommends slowing down on the Barleygreen and raw foods, while eating more cooked food (such as lightly-steamed vegetables), which will make your body's transition more gradual. Increased quantities of freshly-extracted carrot juice is another means of speeding up the body's process of flushing out these toxins. Dr. Malkmus notes the advantage to using fresh juice, rather than water, is that juice also contains the vital nutrients to help regenerate our body's cells while it is flushing out the toxins. It is also good during a healing crisis to give your body plenty of rest, including your digestive system. This means eating less than normal so you are not overworking your digestive tract while your body is trying to eliminate toxins.

Dr. Leo Roy, M.D., N.D., advises, "If you are worried or confused, call the doctor who helped design your program. Anxiety can drastically slow down healing. Don't get discouraged. Don't quit. If you have not gone back to doing anything detrimental to your health, then you are not going back to being sick … Letdowns can be caused by the dumping of too much disease, dead cells and poisons too quickly. You are healing too fast; your treatment is really working – too well. You may feel worse, but you are not worse."

For most people, a healing crisis does not last more than two or three days. And when it is over, many people report feeling better than they have ever felt in their lives, and have described tremendous bursts of energy. In more extreme cases, symptoms could last a week or so, but they rarely continue for more than 30 days. Sometimes a few days of healing crisis will be followed by feeling great, and then another healing crisis and then feeling better again. With this pattern, generally the extent of each healing crisis gets shorter and less severe, while the periods of feeling good get progressively better and last longer.

Another way of understanding the healing crisis is to remember that certain toxic substances such as cigarettes, coffee, tea, refined sugar, chocolate, soft drinks, alcohol and prescription drugs can be addictive; and when we stop consuming any addictive substance, it is common to have headaches or a "let-down" feeling. Most long-term users ("addicts") of nicotine or caffeine will feel terrible during the transitory period in which they are withdrawing from cigarettes or coffee. Keep in mind, this terrible feeling is only temporary. In the long run, you'll feel much better. (After all, how could quitting nicotine or caffeine be bad for you?) Withdrawal from meat can also cause a "let-down" feeling in some people, because the large amount of protein in meat has a stimulating effect on the body, even though this type and quantity of protein is unnecessary and not usable by our bodies. Again, experts in natural health recommend against taking any painkillers or stimulants to offset the symptoms of withdrawal from these addictive drugs or meat. Part of the withdrawal symptoms people may feel from giving up these addictive substances is caused by the cells of the body beginning to discard toxins such as caffeine, nicotine, chemical preservatives and excess bile and fat that clogs the arteries. The sooner a person can rid their body of these substances, the better off they will be; and any drugs they take to relieve the symptoms will just dump more toxins into their body.

If you consider your overall health to be more important than your brief, short-term discomfort, you won't let the healing crisis tempt you to turn back to your old diet. It may be necessary to remind yourself that, although the discomfort of a healing crisis is being felt as you quit consuming harmful substances, the root of the cause of this discomfort was putting these substances into your body in the first place.

"Watch ye and pray, lest ye enter into temptation. The spirit truly is ready, but the flesh is weak."
– Mark 14:38

Chapter Ten:

What Are We Feeding Our Children?

"Lo, children are an heritage of the LORD:
and the fruit of the womb
is his reward."
– Psalm 127:3

Raising Healthy Children Begins with a Healthy Pregnancy & Nursing

Children are a gift from God that we are to treasure and nurture even before conception! Prior to a husband and wife becoming one to produce a child, they must realize that with that innocent gift comes awesome responsibility … a responsibility that lasts a lifetime! Think about the impact a new child will have on your home, your work schedule and your freedom. A baby needs love, security, warmth and understanding and these things can only be provided by parents who know the meaning of love and are willing and able to share that love unselfishly. Children born for the wrong reasons suffer problems and complications and often do not receive the nurturing God intended, which is so necessary to develop into healthy adults.

Several months or even years prior to becoming pregnant, the parents should share with one another what their desires and expectations are. Their thoughts and actions should be aimed toward a goal of serving the Lord, and their diets should be composed of foods that contain and produce life – the living foods that God has given us. Live plants have abundant oxygen and chlorophyll so essential for the healthy environment of a growing infant. Improper diet and bad lifestyle choices (drug use, lack of exercise, etc.) can cause a wide range of problems, including miscarriage, excessive weight gain and retention of fluids by the mother, low birth weights, or insufficient nutrients for proper cell growth and brain development.

At Hallelujah Acres we recommend, whenever possible, that a young couple get on the Hallelujah Diet at least six months prior to conception. The reason? We have found that this diet of living foods can actually repair damaged DNA. By giving both parents living food, they develop the strongest sperm and egg possible so the child produced by this union will have the very best start in life.

During pregnancy the body requires high-quality nutrients, which can best be found in organically-grown fresh vegetables and fruits. A few nuts and seeds can be eaten as well, but they are very high in fat and difficult to digest, and thus should be eaten sparingly. Some "experts" teach that expectant mothers require approximately 300 extra calories per day. These 300 extra calories could be obtained by consuming about one and one half cups of a starchy food like brown rice or millet, or half an avocado, or three to four apples in addition to their regular food intake. However, during pregnancy, be sure that fruit is no more than 15 percent of the total food intake, because fruit is very high in natural sugar and can cause cleansing problems.

Positive mental attitudes and exercise are vitally important in maintaining a healthy, vibrant body and are especially important during pregnancy. Walking and swimming are two exercises that can easily be done, and both provide a release for tension while building a healthy environment for the child. An expectant mother also needs to get adequate rest and should not push herself to exhaustion.

There are seven components required for a healthy diet: carbohydrates, fats, proteins, vitamins, minerals, enzymes and water, all provided by God in the living plants. Women who are expecting a little one also can use some extra iron, especially during the latter half of pregnancy. Recent reports have indicated that iron supplements can be toxic to the body and can cause an increase in the length of the pregnancy and potential complications. Barleygreen, carrot juice, raw spinach, raisins and other dried fruits are tremendous natural sources of iron in a form the body can easily assimilate and utilize.

An expecting or nursing mother also needs to have an abundant supply of calcium which can be found in the green leafy vegetables such as raw broccoli, kale and Barleygreen. These sources of calcium are easily absorbed by the body, with no harm to the mother or developing child. Calcium supplementation as found in pill form or dairy products can be harmful to both mother and baby.

The B-complex group of vitamins help the baby's nerve development and can also help prevent the mother's sugar cravings. B-complex vitamins are found in green vegetables, grains and whole-grain breads.

Fats are also necessary for proper brain development for the child and the hormones of the mother. But it must be the right type of fat. Most of you already know the Standard American Diet is much too high in fat, and that there is a direct relationship between diets rich in fat and cancer, heart disease and other killers. But even though Americans eat too much fat, most are deficient in the two essential fatty acids, linoleic and alpha-linolenic acids. Part of the reason for this deficiency is that Americans eat too much saturated fats from animal products and partially-hydrogenated fats from foods such as margarine, both of which block the body's utilization of essential fatty acids. All fruits and vegetables have some of these essential fatty acids, while nuts, seeds and avocados provide even more.

Flax seed oil is an especially good source of fat because it is extremely rich in omega-3 fatty acids and lignans. Lignans are best known for their anti-cancer effect. Another vital key to health is consuming more omega-3 and less omega-6 fatty acids. Most people consume too much omega-6 fatty acids (mainly from processed foods) and not enough omega-3 fatty acids. A diet low in saturated fat and high in omega-3 fatty acids has been shown to prevent many of the same diseases caused by a diet high in saturated fats.

A 1995 pharmaceutical bulletin noted that omega-3 fatty acids are essential for establishing and maintaining proper brain function, especially in infants and children. The pharmaceutical bulletin noted that breast-feeding supplies a substantial amount of omega-3 fatty acids, while almost all infant formulas are limited in omega-3 fatty acids, which can hinder brain and eye development of the child.

Protein should not be a problem during pregnancy for anyone with a good diet. Complete protein is constructed in the human body from amino acids obtained from the food we eat. All vegetables and most fruit provide sufficient amounts of amino acids to meet our protein needs, while higher amounts are found in nuts, seeds and avocados. Mothers that eat too much protein are increasing their chances of complications, according to Dr. M.T. Mortor, Jr. He states: "Some are going to advise you to eat more protein, but if you do, you are increasing the chances of a complicated pregnancy and delivery."

He adds, "A mother's diet should be mostly vegetables with some fruit, nuts, seeds and whole grains. If hunger in the morning is a problem, some fruit or fresh juice is a good solution. For lunch, eat fruit or a raw green salad that can include either nuts and seeds or an avocado. For supper, eat a large green salad and steamed vegetables, along with something starchy such as a baked potato, whole grain bread, brown rice or pasta. For dealing with hunger between meals, ideal snacks include fruit or vegetable sticks, especially celery and broccoli, since they are high in iron and calcium. Fresh vegetable juices are also an ideal in-between-meal "snack." All vegetable juices should include a base of at least 60-percent carrot juice, giving you the option of adding an apple, celery, broccoli, cucumber, beet, bell pepper, parsley, spinach or most any other vegetable. Fruit juices may be consumed occasionally, but should be limited to one serving per day."

These dietary recommendations for expectant mothers are similar to those being recommended by some nutritionally-educated medical doctors, such as Joel Robbins, M.D. As Dr. Robbins says in his tape, *Pregnancy, Childbirth and Children's Diet*, "By juicing fresh fruits and vegetables and by having at least two 8-oz. glasses of fresh juices daily along with a healthy diet is the best vitamin and mineral supplement there is to insure mother and baby get all the nutrients they need."

Also, Neal Barnard, M.D. states, *"Plant-based diets provide a good balance of nutrients to support a healthy pregnancy and are superior to diets containing milk or other animal products. Whole grains, vegetables, beans and fruits give both mother and baby the nutrients they need. Support for a vegan diet during pregnancy comes from a study of 1,700 pregnancies at The Farm, a large community in Tennessee. The study showed a record of safety that would delight obstetricians. Only one in a hundred delivered by cesarean section. And in twenty years, there was only one case of preeclampsia, a syndrome of hypertension, fluid retention, urinary protein loss, and excessive weight gain, that occurs in at least 2% of pregnancies in the United States overall. Other studies have found similar results."*

> *"Most of the mentally retarded babies born in America are due to the mother's drug, cigarette or alcohol addiction or their poor eating habits where they lacked the basic vitamins and minerals needed to produce a healthy baby."*
> *– Dr. Roger Williams, noted scientist and nutritionist*

Pregnant and nursing mothers should avoid junk foods, foods high in sugar and fat, and they should never consume alcohol, caffeine or smoke cigarettes. Women who drink during pregnancy are shown to have babies with decreased birth rates, smaller heads, mental retardation, and can even have abnormal face, heart and appendages. Caffeine and cigarettes can cause birth defects as well as many other complications.

Fish that swim in polluted waters carry in their flesh PCBs, mercury contamination and many other toxins that appear in a much higher concentration in their flesh than in the waters. According to John Robbins in *Diet for a New America,* the E.P.A. estimates that fish can accumulate up to 9 million times the level of PCB's in the waters in which they live. Extremely high levels of PCB's accumulate in the bodies of fish (and animals that eat the fish) because this toxic material is very difficult to eliminate once it is inside the body. When ingested into the human body, PCB's can remain for decades. A study done at Wayne State University showed that women who ate fish regularly – even years prior to conception – had higher incidence of babies who were slow to respond at birth, smaller head circumference and other problems as well.

Another serious problem with fish is bacteria. In his book, *Food for Life,* Neal Barnard, M.D., writes, "Unlike cows and chickens, fish are cold-blooded. So the bacteria that live in them are quite comfortable – and even grow – at the temperature in your refrigerator. *Consumer Reports* found that bacterial contamination is so common in fish that at least 40 percent have begun to spoil before they leave the grocery case. And a slightly higher percentage contain fecal bacteria from human or animal waste. Fish pick up these bacteria in polluted waters and (from human hands) in the ironically named process of 'cleaning' and handling."

It is unfortunate that some people who have quit eating meat still believe that fish is a healthy alternative. The reasons for not consuming meat (high cholesterol, zero fiber, excessive chemical toxins, high fat and undigestable protein) are equally true for fish.

The human body is made up of 70 percent water and the baby is suspended in a sac of specially formulated water. In order to ensure a healthy environment for the baby, six to eight glasses of distilled drinking water daily is vital, along with the naturally distilled water found in plants.

One of the common discomforts of the beginning stages of pregnancy is a form of early-morning nausea known as morning sickness. Morning sickness usually subsides after the first couple months of pregnancy, but can be experienced in some cases for as long as three to five months. There is more than one medical theory on the cause of morning sickness, but this is usually not a problem for women with an ideal diet.

Joel Robbins, M.D., D.C., N.D., explains that morning sickness is an "extraordinary cleaning" to rid the mother's body of any toxins for the sake of the unborn baby living inside her body. He writes "when a mother conceives, her body wants to prepare the best environment possible for the unborn child. So the mother's body will do some extraordinary cleaning to rid itself of toxins. While the mother sleeps, her body is dumping all kinds of poisons into the bloodstream to be removed through the kidneys and the liver. A mother who has not been eating well has backed up kidneys and liver, her body is congested and toxic. Through the night the toxins are dumped into the bloodstream which carries them to the kidneys and liver, causing them to be overloaded and extremely toxic first thing in the morning. The sensation of morning sickness is the body's way of saying don't put anything else in here, I'm just barely keeping my nose above water right now trying to deal with the toxins which are being eliminated."

Dr. M.T. Mortor, Jr. writes, "When you experience morning sickness, your doctor may recommend a pill to eliminate the symptoms, and it may work. However, I want to remind you that years ago they recommended thalidomide and it made the expectant mothers feel fantastic in the morning and totally eliminated morning sickness. Therefore, it was widely used in this country and everyone was happy. What happened, however, was that the babies were born without arms and legs. What a tremendous price the mothers paid to eliminate a little bit of morning sickness. Covering up the symptoms is not the answer, we have to find the cause … Morning sickness can be prevented if mothers follow the diet program before pregnancy. In any case, no medication should be taken for morning sickness."

"My file is full of examples of Americans with soft bones (dissolved, I believe, by their phosphoric acid consumption) and my heart-felt concern for fetuses is now a reality - many are being born without face bones, with missing ribs, with fewer than normal carpal bones, and so forth. Do we really care? Do we care enough to change our lifestyle? I sincerely hope so."

– Dr. Mary Ruth Swope
from her article, "Why I Don't Drink Soft Drinks and I wish You Didn't" (see page 102)

Recipes for Life ... from God's Garden

For nursing mothers, a plant-based diet reduces levels of environmental contaminants found in their breast milk, compared to mothers who consume flesh. As stated earlier, the flesh tissue concentrates the chemical contaminants eaten by the animal during its lifetime. It is also important to avoid dairy products because the high protein in the cow's milk can travel through the placenta and even combine with breast milk. If a nursing mother consumes the flesh or milk from a cow, the hormones, antibodies and other drugs administered to that cow can be passed on to the infant in the mother's breast milk. These antibodies can cause colic as well as other problems in the child.

Breast-feeding is the method God designed for the baby's complete nourishment and meets all of their nutritional needs for the first 18 to 24 months of life. Many parents incorrectly think that starting an infant on solid foods earlier than recommended will make their child healthier and stronger. This is a false assumption that will have the opposite effect because breast-feeding provides a natural immunity to many diseases and provides nurturing that cannot be obtained elsewhere. If a mother is eating a proper diet, breast milk contains 100 percent of the nutrients needed for proper growth of the infant. As the baby requires different nutrients, these nutrients are formulated in the mother's body, meeting all of the child's needs, which often varies from day to day. Baby cereals were never meant by God to be a source of nourishment for infants and can produce many problems within the child's body.

"A nursing mother in close contact with her infant can make antibodies on demand to pathogens that challenge him (or her) and transfer them in milk."

H. Marano, <u>Breast Feeding: New Evidence It's Far More Than Nutrition</u>

If breast-feeding is not an option, the next-best thing is expressed mother's milk which has been stored in the refrigerator. If expressed human breast milk is not available, then try to find a source for raw, unpasteurized goat's milk. Goat's milk is similar to human milk in composition and many children have been successfully raised on it. Goat's milk will keep approximately four days in the refrigerator. Formulas that contain rice or soy products are not recommended as they can produce allergies and are difficult for the child to digest. Goat's milk is a little richer than human milk and should be diluted 50-50 with distilled water. Another recommended mixture is one-third goat's milk, one-third fresh carrot juice and one-third distilled water.

If nursing is not an option and goat's milk is not available, raw almond milk combined with a green drink (raw, freshly-juiced vegetable greens or Barleygreen) and/or diluted carrot juice might be used. Be sure these are **well strained.**

Commercially-available infant formulas are never recommended! These formulas cause mucous membrane problems such as chronic colds, ear infections, bronchitis and allergies.

If colic is a problem (which shouldn't occur if mother is eating properly), diluted, freshly-extracted, carrot/apple juice can be given as early as three weeks of age. Start with one ounce carrot/apple juice in three ounces of distilled water in a four-ounce glass bottle. (Never use plastic bottles or nipples containing nitrates.) At four months, this mix can be strengthened to 50 percent carrot/apple and 50 percent distilled water and after eight months the pure juice can be given. Always strain juice through a very fine strainer. Organic produce is always preferred.

One of the causes of colic can be dairy consumption by the mother. According to the August 1991 issue of *Lady's Home Journal,* "If your breast-fed newborn has colic, you may want to eliminate dairy products from your own diet. Colic may be caused by a protein in cow's milk that can be passed from mothers to babies, say researchers at the Washington University School of Medicine in St. Louis. Associate Professor of Medicine Anthony Kulczycki, M.D., and Patrick Kline, M.D., recently studied milk samples from 59 mothers and found that protein (bovine) ran about 30-percent higher in mothers with colicky babies than whose infants didn't have colic."

If cow's milk consumed by a breastfeeding mother can have this type of effect on a baby, consider the potential problems that can be caused by a young child directly consuming this product. Infants should never be reared on cow's milk! In addition to the colic cow's milk can cause, it can also produce all kinds of mucous membrane problems, diaper rash, allergies, ear infections, etc. It is thought that the proteins in cow's milk (which are very different from the proteins in human breast milk) can ignite the production of antibodies that can produce insulin-dependent diabetes in mothers as well as unborn children.

Approximately 100 vital nutrients are missing in cow's milk and cannot be duplicated in formulas. Actually, formulas are probably the single most dangerous substance that you can feed an infant. For proof of this statement, watch the frequent mucous membrane problems that formula-fed infants experience. If an infant with mucous membrane problems is switched from cow's milk or formula to raw goat's milk, the problems almost always disappear.

A very authoritative book on the subject is *Don't Drink Your Milk!* by Dr. Frank A. Oski, M.D., who is Director of the Department of Pediatrics at the Johns Hopkins University School of Medicine. Dr. Oski writes, "… allergy to cow milk is far more common than is generally appreciated. Dr. Joyce Gryboski, who directs the Pediatric Gastrointestinal Clinic at Yale University School of Medicine, states that they see at least one child a week who is referred for evaluation of chronic diarrhea and proves to have nothing more than an allergy to cow milk."

Dr. Oski's book includes an account of one child who had developed an extreme case of iron-deficiency anemia at six months of age. "He had diarrhea, he was very pale and he developed a swelling in his hands and feet and a bloating of his abdomen. His iron-deficiency anemia was treated for months with iron supplements, but with no improvement. The child was eventually taken to a large medical center, where it was determined that he had an allergy to the protein in cow's milk and beef. Once all cow's milk and beef were removed from the child's diet, he completely recovered. In this case, the diarrhea was preventing the child from retaining nutrients from his feedings, and the allergic reaction caused "seepage of the child's own blood into the gut. This loss of plasma and red cells leads to a lowering of the infant's blood protein level and to the development of anemia. The lowering of serum proteins, if profound, results in swelling of the abdomen, hands, and feet. Most infants with this condition respond promptly to the elimination of cow milk from the diet."

Dr. Oski adds, "A less dramatic form of gastrointestinal sensitivity to cow milk is also being recognized with increasing frequency. This form of sensitivity rarely produces dramatic symptoms but results in slow and steady bleeding. Infants with this form of milk sensitivity may lose 1 to 5 milliliters of blood per day in their stool. Eventually they become anemic from the steady hemorrhage. The volumes of blood lost each day are too small for detection by simple visual examination. The stools appear to be of normal color and the blood can only be detected by chemical tests."

Normally a newborn has a rather high iron level, which it maintains during the first three months of life. However, as a baby grows the body does need iron, which can be found in a variety of fruits. The vitamin C found in fresh fruit enhances iron absorption. Cow's milk is very low in iron and can cause a chronic blood loss through the digestive system.

A child can develop allergic reactions if whole foods are introduced too early in life; therefore, add new foods slowly. As teeth start to appear, some ripe, raw fruit like a little mashed banana or avocado can be added to the diet, but acid fruits should be avoided. Noted author, Elizabeth Baker writes, "The baby, when breast fed by an optimally nourished mother, will develop more quickly than average. He/she will be active, curious, happy, good natured and strong. It is well not to introduce solid foods for five or six months (until front teeth appear), and then only mashed or strained raw fruits such as banana, avocado, scraped apple, peach, apricot, sweet plum, etc. Cooked cereals introduced at a few weeks, or meat purees, puddings and sugar sweetened cooked fruits will almost assuredly cause baby to be allergy-proned because a baby cannot digest cooked carbohydrate and animal proteins before approximately one year of age. Infants lack the digestive enzymes for assimilation. These undigested foods become toxins, the beginning of problems for the tiny body."

"The brain gets bigger right after birth.
By the age of two, it's close to adult size.
Man's future depends on what his food is as an infant."
– Quoted in Liebman, B.,
"Baby Formulas: Missing key Fats?"
<u>Nutrition</u> <u>Action</u>, October 1990

Raw foods can be pureed in a Champion Juicer, Green Star Juicer or Vita Mix very easily. Over a period of months, add more fruit until the child's diet consists of up to 40 percent fruit. Never use jarred baby foods as they have been cooked, thus destroying the nutrients, and often they have had salt and/or sugar or other harmful ingredients added to them.

Until a child's molars start to appear about the age of 18 to 24 months, the child's jaws are not fully formed, nor is the digestive system developed enough to handle solids. Therefore a child should not be weaned until his system is ready for a more diverse diet. After molars appear, raw vegetables can be pureed and added to the diet and as the child begins to chew, these raw vegetables can be ground less and less finely in a food processor or blender. As the child begins to chew food, some cooked food – such as baked potatoes, baked sweet potatoes, steamed vegetables and perhaps some brown rice can also be added to the diet.

When a child starts to eat solids, it is imperative to teach them to take small bites and to chew (masticate) their food well. All foods should reach a creamy consistency before being swallowed. Otherwise they reach the stomach in a form which takes much longer to break down.

When introducing new foods in your child's diet, it is important to remember that children are often reluctant to try new things. New foods should be served along with foods the child is familiar with to lessen the shock. Just because a child rejects a particular food one time, don't get discouraged and never try it again. Often with repeated exposure children will accept foods they initially rejected. A good rule of thumb is to require the child to try one bite of a new food and not force them to eat more, since it takes time to adjust taste buds. Don't limit a child's food intake to only the foods you like. There are many taste treats out there. Remember, meals should be a positive, enjoyable time and your attitude about new foods will go a long way in developing a positive attitude in your child.

Because it is very difficult to change a behavior that has become a "part of you," any foods that are addictive or harmful should always be avoided. This would include anything that comes from an animal source (meat, dairy, eggs, etc.), refined sugars, salt, white flour products, coffee, colas, heated oils, peanuts, cashews or any manufactured product containing the above.

When children reach school age, they should be on the same nutritional program as their parents, with some slight modification. Breakfast is recommended for children.

What Are We Feeding Our Children?

Children Have Special Needs

Some people may be concerned about raising children without the "benefits" of meat and dairy products. Studies have shown that vegetarian children are more slender, healthier and live longer than do their meat-eating companions. Remember a child should not be pudgy! Overfeeding leads to obesity, lethargy and an unhealthy lifestyle that produces many physical problems.

Ralph Cinque, D.C., states in a recent article, ***"Feed your children fresh fruits and vegetables, but also make sure that they consume a sufficient amount and variety of concentrated foods. By concentrated foods, I am referring primarily to whole grains, legumes, and nuts. These are the foods that have the most calories per unit volume in a vegetarian diet. ...Caloric undernutrition is a distinct possibility if too many watery foods are eaten, especially with children. The results may include: being underweight, have low energy, having low resistance to infection, and being hungry all the time. Being hungry all the time is a tell tale sign. Children usually have hearty appetites, but it is not normal for them to be constantly preoccupied with food. A child who always wants to eat rather than play may not be getting a balanced diet."***

Calcium is supplied by fruits, vegetables, beans and grains. Animal products rob the body of calcium and should not be a part of the diet.

Just as children require raw juices and raw food for enzymes and live nutrients, children also require protein for growth and maintenance, but not high-protein foods. A varied vegan diet provides plenty of protein when protein-rich foods like almonds, sunflower seeds, lentils, quinoa, brown rice, split peas, etc. are included in the diet. Barleygreen is an excellent source of protein. The "protein deficiencies" that caused concern for our parents were because of reports from poor countries where starvation or severely restricted diets of a few food items were the norm. A protein deficiency is highly unlikely on a diet comprised of a variety of plant foods. (For more information on protein, see Chapter 15, "Protein and Propaganda," in *God's Way to Ultimate Health.*)

The fat intake required by very young children is greater than that of an adult. Modest amounts of nuts, seeds and avocados should be included in the diets of children. However, it is important not to allow children to over-indulge. Many children in the United States, as early as age 3, are well on their way to heart disease before they ever enter school. Fat from animal products and hydrogenated oil sources begin to layer on artery walls, and this continues through the teen years and on into mid-life. Between 1963 and 1980, obesity among 6 to 11-year-olds increased 54 percent in a study conducted by Dr. Dietz and his associates. In this same age group extreme obesity rose 98 percent! Other studies have shown that Japanese children who were brought up on diets which contain only about 10 percent fat are much healthier than their American counterparts whose diets are much higher in fat.

"The average 12-ounce cola
has about 150 calories and over an ounce (9 teaspoons)
of refined sugar: a 12-ounce un-cola has 7 ½ teaspoons of sugar."
(Dr. Agatha Thrash, M.D., reports that 24 teaspoons of sugar
in one day destroys 92% of the body's ability to destroy bacteria).
– Home Remedies, Yuchi Pines Institute, Seale, Alabama, 1981

God created fruits and vegetables that contain natural sugar, which is accompanied by vitamins, minerals, fiber and phytochemicals. Children do not need the added sugar and salt found in most manufactured products. They are very destructive to a child's body.

Sugar provides quick energy; however, each calorie that children ingest from sugar is one less they can spend consuming nutrient-dense foods that are required for proper growth and development.

In a recent report from the Sugar Task Force, the U.S. Food and Drug Administration found that children between the ages of 1 and 18 are consuming about one quarter of their calories from sugar. The annual sugar consumption in America has risen from an average of seven pounds per person per year in 1900 to 150 pounds per person today - that's over 50 teaspoons per day!

Refined sugar contributes nothing but empty calories. Soft drinks are one of the biggest culprits in adding sugar to children's diets. For example, in a 12-ounce can of Coke you will find over *9 teaspoons of sugar,* flavorings, water and *caffeine* along with its 144 empty calories. Children who consume a lot of sugar often have trouble getting enough nutrients.

A nutritionist at the U.S. Department of Agriculture, Patricia Guenther, reports that, *"soft drinks have the greatest impact on the adequacy of calcium intake."* Her findings note that children who consume one or more soft drinks per day have about one fifth less calcium absorption than those who drink no soft drinks.

Sodium chloride or table salt increases the risk of high blood pressure in children just as it does in adults. Children, like adults, need sodium, but the amount is minimal compared to what is being ingested through the Sad American Diet. A one-year-old child requires 225 milligrams of sodium per day, while an 18-year-old requires 500 milligrams a day. The results of a study in Louisiana by the Bogalusa Heart Study found that after two years of age, the average child consumed 2,670 milligrams of sodium chloride daily. The sodium intake increased with age with the average 17-year-old consuming 3,670 milligrams of sodium per day. *What are we feeding our children?*

Like adults, children need sunlight, which allows their bodies to produce vitamin D and provides other nutrients necessary for proper growth.

" A government warning was once issued to the manufacturer
of a certain world-famous refreshing soft drink for its suspected effect
on the bones of children because of the large amount of phosphoric acid in it.
Pour coke over an extracted baby tooth or a 10-penny nail
and see it totally dissolve in a few days!"
Dr. Mary Ruth Swope from Why I Don't Drink Soft Drinks and Wish You Didn't

Research testing was done to test the IQ of children on vegan diets versus the typical American diet. It was found that the average IQ of the vegan child was 116. This should ease the minds of parents who are concerned that the vegetarian diet may not provide enough nutrition for proper brain development.

Many children brought up on the vegan diet are a little smaller than those brought up on the Standard American Diet, but adult heights and weights are similar to those eating a meat-based diet. It is interesting to note that breast-fed babies grow slower than bottle-fed babies, perhaps just as God intended! Studies also have found that young girls raised without the consumption of animal products reach puberty at approximately age 16, compared to about age 12 or less for girls who consume meat, dairy and eggs. Do you think God had it all figured out when He planned for children to grow up gradually, reach puberty later and to live a longer, more productive life?

Perhaps the most important aspect of raising children that we need to remember is those habits that are learned as a child will follow them into adulthood. Children who acquire a taste for meat and junk food today will be the patients found in the hospitals and clinics tomorrow.

Tips for Moms & Dads

Perhaps one of the most difficult challenges for parents of children who have been accustomed to the Standard American Diet is to make a change in lifestyle. It is important for children to understand, so be sure to teach them *why* you are making the changes. Share with them your concerns about their health as well as your own.

1. Set a positive example. Children learn by what they see and hear! It is impossible to teach good eating habits to children if the parents eat poorly. Start teaching healthy eating habits as early as possible. The task becomes increasingly difficult once poor eating habits become established.

"Habits of rapid eating are most harmful, and must be overcome.
Quietness and cheerfulness at meals is most essential."
– Oliver Wendell Holmes

2. Maintain authority over the food in your home. Parents should decide and make children aware of what foods are acceptable and available in the home. If you take the time to plan ahead, you can save many hours and lots of frustration. For instance, have fresh vegetables and fruits easily accessible for the children to snack on.

3. Plan your meals ahead, too. There are some tasks that can be done ahead of time to make meal preparation much easier. As you plan your meals make note of things like soaking beans, preparing fruits or vegetables for a salad, or other tasks that need to be done ahead of time.

4. Involve the children in grocery shopping. Have them assist with making a grocery list, and allow them to choose which fresh vegetables they would like to try. Take them on an outing to a farmer's market or to a local orchard that does not use chemicals. Take the time to teach the children about the choices you are making and why. Be sure to feed the children prior to going shopping so they will not become demanding at the super-

103

Recipes for Life ... from God's Garden

market.

5. Include the children when making some of the meal selections. Make up menus ahead of time and post them so the children know what to expect. Children can be involved in preparing for the meal; setting the table, helping with the salad, helping with the juicing, and even clean-up chores. For instance, each child could be responsible to rinse his or her plate after the meal.

6. Make mealtimes an enjoyable occasion for the whole family – a place to share the positive things that happened during the day, tell stories and laugh together. Teach children to slowly chew their food and savor the flavor, to not rush through the meal and hurry off to the TV or some other activity. It may take some extra effort, but it will be worth it in the long run. Parents should also establish a firm rule that the dining room table will never become a battleground.

7. For school lunches, include a vegetarian sandwich on whole-grain bread, some veggie sticks, vegetable grain crisps (page 305) and fruit for dessert. Children don't like to be different. Their sandwiches could include lettuce, tomato and avocado, or almond butter (page 284) with bananas or an all-fruit jam or a pita pocket stuffed with salad or left over veggie pizza or spaghetti. There are lots of wonderful ideas. With each new day look for something unique to make the lunches an event the children look forward to.

8. Perhaps **occasionally** take children to restaurants for an opportunity to guide them in learning how to choose healthy foods. Later allow the children an opportunity to eat a school lunch to give them the opportunity to exercise what they have learned about healthy choices.

9. Plant a small garden that is easy to manage and allow the children to take part in the care of the vegetables. It gives them a sense of belonging. As a child watches the plants grow and mature they become excited about eating what they have helped produce. If you live in an area where you can't plant a garden, window box gardens are a wonderful option. For instance tomatoes, carrots and lettuce can all be planted in one-gallon containers with holes for proper drainage. You could even plant squash if you use a large enough container, like a half barrel. Push six or eight seeds into the soil, water them on a regular basis. After the plants come up, thin them to two, otherwise you will have a jungle!

Children are very smart and learn quickly. Remember, you are their teacher and the way you react to a changed diet and lifestyle will be seen by your children. When a child begins to ask "why," it is important to take the time to explain the health benefits of Genesis 1:29 diet. **Education is the key**! It may take some time, but be patient, loving and understanding. The rewards will be worth it!

"Train up a child in the way he should go;
and when he is old,
he will not depart from it."
– Proverbs 22:6

Hallelujah Acres Suggested Program for Children

Birth Through 24 Months

Mother's breast milk is God's plan for nourishing infants and is always preferred. It should be the primary source of nourishment for the child for at least 18 to 24 months. Human breast milk contains all the nutrients a baby needs – including vitamins, minerals, amino acids, hormones, enzymes, essential fatty acids, carbohydrates and immune system factors. Expressed milk can be refrigerated up to 24 hours.

If breast-feeding is not an option, raw goat's milk is an acceptable substitute. Goat's milk is similar to human breast milk in composition. However, goat's milk should be diluted 50-50 with distilled water as the protein content is slightly higher than that in mother's milk. Goat's milk keeps about four days in the refrigerator.

If neither of the above are available, well-strained raw almond milk, diluted BarleyMax and/or well strained, diluted carrot juice may be used.

Birth until the Front Teeth Begin to Appear

As early as one or two months, raw, freshly-extracted carrot juice, diluted with one part carrot juice to 3 parts distilled water can be introduced in small quantities ($1/4$ tsp.) at first, and then slowly increased. Juices need to be well-strained through a very fine stainless steel strainer. By age 6 months, serving amount can be increased to as much as 4 ounces. BarleyMax ($1/4$ tsp.) diluted in distilled water, can also be introduced, along with the carrot juice. As the child grows and develops, the amount of Barleygreen can gradually be increased.

If the child develops loose stools, the juices may be too strong and should be diluted with more distilled water. For best assimilation, schedule the juices at least 30 minutes before breast-feeding or two hours after.

Remember, mother's milk is still the primary food, and it is important to note that if large volumes of juices are given, the child may not wish to nurse as often, which will eventually decrease mother's milk supply and short-change the child's nutritional intake.

Cow's milk and soy products are not recommended. Babies cannot digest them and they often cause allergic reactions.

After Front Teeth Begin To Appear

Breast feeding, carrot juice and BarleyMax should still be the main sources of food!

Children are, however, born with God-given instincts and they will let you know when it is time to add some solid foods. If a child is not satisfied with breast milk alone, if the baby cries after feeding for no apparent reason, or if the child begins to chew on mother's breast, it is a signal that fresh (organic when possible) ripe fruit, can now be added. It is important to remember, however, that solid foods introduced too early will *decrease* the babies desire to nurse.

When introducing babies to solid food, it is vitally important to teach them to take small bites and chew (masticate) their food well. As a child begins to chew, fresh fruit helps develop brain and neurological systems. Offer small ($1/4$ tsp.) portions once a day of raw apple sauce. Or you may mash *freshly prepared,* very ripe bananas. Mashed peaches, pears, papaya and avocados are also excellent choices.

It is important to remember that when introducing a baby to one of these fruits, only one kind should be introduced at a time. No other new food should then be introduced for at least a week to allow the child's system a chance to adapt. These fruits can be grated or pureed in your Champion or Green Star juicer. Over a period of months, work up to as much as 40 percent raw fruits. Mother's milk should continue to be the largest percentage of nutritional intake.

Note: When a child is cutting teeth, dry whole grain toast may be given for them to "chew" on. Never leave a child unattended while food is within reach, as they may take too big of a bite and choke.

When Molars Appear

Mother's milk is still the primary source of nutrition.

As the molars start coming in, vegetables may be slowly introduced in a pureed form to the baby's diet. A blended salad may be made in a blender, Vita Mix, Green Star or Champion Juicer with avocado, a small amount of fresh carrot juice or distilled water, fresh greens, and a small amount of fresh, organic apple may be added for sweetness. To add variety, different greens and vegetables may be used, which will provide additional essential nutrients necessary for healthy babies.

Finger foods should continue to be soft, such as very ripe peeled fruit or soaked dehydrated fruit cut into a bite-sized piece (one piece is usually sufficient). Organic raisins, dates and figs are very high in sugar, which promotes tooth decay; therefore, use sparingly until a child is old enough to brush and floss their teeth with a little help!

Acid fruits such as tomatoes, oranges, grapefruit and other citrus and berries should not be given to children for at least the first 12 to 14 months, and then only sparingly. Large amounts of citrus fruits can actually eat into the enamel that coats their teeth.

When All Teeth Are In

After all the teeth are in, you can slowly start weaning the child from breast milk; however, it is important to continue carrot juice and BarleyMax. Now that all their teeth are in, cooked foods can slowly be introduced into the child's diet. However, we never want to reach a higher percentage of cooked food vs raw food in their diet than 25 percent.

When a child is being weaned, start adding new semi-solid foods to the diet. Start with small portions of the new food, at no more than one meal per day. Add one new food at a time with no other new food being introduced for at least one week. Puree vegetables at first, later blended or those processed in food processor can be used for a more coarse consistency. Serve food at room or warm temperatures – never hot or cold. As the child is able to handle new foods, vegetables like sweet potatoes, squash and beets can be added, as well as grains like brown rice, millet, quinoa, barley and oatmeal.

Baby foods should never be seasoned with salt, spices, sugar, oil or butter. The cooked portion should never exceed 25 percent of the daily diet.

Uncooked grain cereals made in a blender or food processor can be slowly introduced into the diet. To prepare, grind grain in a blender, coffee mill or Vita Mix, place raw cereal in a bowl, add enough distilled water to cover and allow to soak overnight. The next morning, place the raw cereal in a blender. Start machine, adding nut or banana milk, distilled water or fruit juice to thin, if necessary, and serve at room temperature. Additional nut milk, banana milk or fruit juice may be added when serving.

If a child does not accept a new food, don't force it. Simply wait a few weeks and try it again. Stomach pain after eating indicates the food was not properly chewed or the digestive system is not yet ready to handle this new food. If you notice that food is passing through the system whole, go back to pureeing the baby's food for a few weeks and then try again. Remember, it takes time for a baby's digestive system to develop.

Hint: To prevent accidental choking, children should also be taught never to run or play with food in their mouth.

After the Age of Weaning

A child can be given a modified Hallelujah Diet three meals per day, if required. Gradually include whole grain cereals and breads, almond butter, legumes and whole grain pastas. Food may still need to be cut into small pieces to make the child's transition to whole foods easier. If snacks are given, they should be natural foods (eg. apples, pears, grapes, celery and carrot sticks, etc.) and should contain no added sugar. If the child is not given "junk food," there will be no need to worry about "spoiling a child's appetite."

After the age of weaning, a child's diet should include the following:

BarleyMax: As the child continues to grow, the vital nutrients found in BarleyMax are essential.

Freshly extracted carrot juice: At least two or three servings per day. As the child grows, slowly increase the amount to four to six ounces per serving.

Vegetables: Three or more servings a day. At least one of the servings should be raw, dark green, leafy vegetables.

Note: Spinach, New Zealand Spinach, Swiss chard, collard greens, beet greens, mustard greens and kale should always be served raw. When cooked, the oxalic acid contained in them is converted to a harmful form that causes the body to lose calcium and can also cause inorganic oxalic acid crystals to form in the kidneys, according to Dr. N.W. Walker.

Also, beets are cleansers and should be used sparingly during early childhood.

Fruits: Two to four pieces of raw fruit per day. Dehydrated fruits, preferably soaked in distilled water, without sulphur may be used sparingly.

Select one of the following groups: Legumes, whole grains and starches or nuts and seeds, and provide one or two servings per day:

Legumes (anything that grows in a pod): Serving size should be no more than four ounces.

Whole Grains and Starches: This category includes whole-grain breads and whole-grain cereals, except wheat. Serving size should be no more than four ounces.

Nuts and seeds: Almonds and sunflower seeds are most preferred. Other nuts and seeds should be used sparingly. Serving size should be no more than one ounce.

Never serve liquid with meals. Fruit, vegetable and green drinks can be given between meals. All juices should be freshly-extracted so all nutrients will be alive. All juices found in containers in your supermarket have been pasteurized (enzymes destroyed) so they will have a long shelf life.

FOODS TO BE AVOIDED: All animal products (flesh foods, dairy products, eggs), salt, refined sugars, artificial sweeteners and coloring agents, heated oils, cashews and all nuts except almonds. Wheat products should be used sparingly as they are acid-forming and leave an acid ash rather than the desired alkaline ash.

"He sent his word, and healed them,
and delivered them from their destructions.
Oh that men would praise the LORD for his goodness,
and for his wonderful works to the
children of men!"
– Psalms 107:20 - 21

Recipes for Life ... from God's Garden

Four Examples of Raw Breakfast Meals After Weaning:

¼ cup brown rice cereal
¼ fresh pear
creamy banana milk (page 108)

¼ cup barley cereal
1 or 2 pitted, cut up dates
sweet almond milk (page 108)

apple juice
grated fresh apple
¼ cup rolled oat cereal (not instant)

¼ cup quinoa & millet cereal
3 or 4 rehydrated peach slices
sweet almond milk (page 108)

See page 225 for directions on preparing raw whole-grain cereals

Four Examples of Raw Lunches After Weaning:

peeled raw apple cut into ¼-inch cubes
4 or 5 ground raw almonds
¼ ripe banana

¼ cup raw summer squash, peeled & grated
¼ cup raw carrot, grated
1 Tbsp. grated broccoli

Blended salad made with spinach,
leaf lettuce, avocado, small amount
of carrot juice, vegetables of choice.
No seasoning required

¼ cup pear, peeled & diced
¼ ripe banana
1 Tbsp. ground sunflower seeds

Four Examples of Dinners After Weaning:

2 tsp. cooked brown rice
2 tsp. cooked lentils
¼ cup raw grated carrot

1 Tbsp. cooked millet
1 stalk raw asparagus, cut fine
2 tsp. steamed cauliflower

2 tsp. grated raw beet
1 Tbsp. mashed potato
2 tsp. of raw sweet potato,
cubed or shredded

½ stalk celery, sliced fine
1 Tbsp. cooked barley
1 Tbsp. grated raw broccoli

Hint: Adjust amounts to meet your baby's hunger needs.

Breakfast Recipes for Children

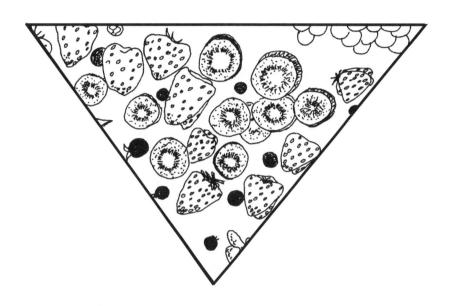

Strawberries, Kiwis and More

½ peach or nectarine
½ kiwi

4 whole strawberries
¼ cup raspberries

Peel peach or nectarine and kiwi, hull strawberries and wash raspberries. Cut into bite-size pieces and serve. Option: blend one third of the fruit to make a sauce.

Blueberries, Peaches & Cream

1 peach
1 tsp. organic maple syrup

½ cup blueberries
sweet almond milk (page 111)

Cut peach into slices or cubes, add blueberries and maple syrup. Top with Sweet Almond Milk and serve.

muesli

Apple Blueberry Cereal

2 apples of a sweet variety   1 cup of blueberries
3/4 cup rolled oats   1/2 cup almonds
1 cup distilled water   1 cup organic apple juice

Soak the rolled oats and almonds placed in separate bowls in the distilled water overnight, and drain. Chop or grind the almonds, chop the apples and combine with the almonds, and add the blueberries. Top with a sprinkle of nutmeg, cinnamon and organic apple juice. No milk required.

Melon Balls

1/2 cup watermelon balls   1/2 cup honey dew melon balls
1/2 cup cantaloupe

Cut and seed melons. Use a melon ball tool to make balls of each type of melon. Combine and enjoy. Use melon varieties such as crenshaw or casabas.

Mixed Fruit Combo

1/2 apple   1/2 ripe banana
1/2 pear

Soak 1/4 cup organic raisins and 1/4 cup chopped dates in distilled water over night. Drain and save soaking water. Slice or dice fruit. Make the following sauce to pour over fruit: In a food processor or blender, place one or two ripe, peeled bananas, raisins and dates with as much of the raisin water as required to blend to a creamy consistency. Add a pinch of nutmeg and cinnamon, if desired.

Note: For variation, use nectarine and peaches instead of apple and pear.

Creamy Banana Milk
☆ ☆ ☆ ☆

1 quart distilled water	$1/2$ - 1 cup sunflower seeds
$1/2$ ripe banana	3 Tbsp. raisins or 4 - 5 dates

Soak sunflower seeds overnight, and drain. Place all ingredients in blender and blend for 2 minutes. For a thicker milk, add more banana.

Sweet Almond Milk
☆ ☆ ☆ ☆

1 cup almonds	6 cups distilled water
3 – 4 dates	

Soak almonds 18 to 24 hours, drain and rinse. Pit dates. Blend half the almonds, half the dates and 3 cups of the distilled water until very creamy. Repeat with remaining ingredients.

Pour through a very fine strainer to remove the pulp. If being used for an infant, strain through cheese cloth also.

Serve at room temperature, and refrigerate any remaining. Almond milk will keep 3 to 4 days.

Peaches & Cream Cereal
Muesli! Good!

☆ ☆ ☆ ☆

1 peach	$1/4$ cup almonds - *less*
$1/4$ tsp. vanilla	1 tsp. maple syrup
$1/4$ cup sweet almond milk	$3/4$ cup organic cereal *1/2 C*
1 cup organic apple juice *-less*	

Soak the cereal in distilled water overnight, and drain off excess juice the following morning. Slice peach, grind or sliver almonds, add vanilla and maple syrup, and mix to combine. Top with a small amount of Sweet Almond Milk (above).

Raw Whole-Grain Cereal
☆ ☆ ☆ ☆

2 Tbsp. whole grain(s) of choice *
2 or 3 pieces of dried fruit **
5 Tbsp. distilled water (enough to cover the cereal)

The evening before, grind grain to a coarse powder consistency. Add liquid, cover and allow to sit overnight. May be refrigerated. Before serving, drain excess water, prepare and add fruit, fruit juice or almond milk, rice milk or banana milk, if desired.

* Any number of grains may be ground and used together or separately; some which might be included are: brown rice, buckwheat, rye, barley, millet, quinoa, oat groats (never use instant oatmeal), flax seeds, or almonds.

Grind the grains in a food mill, coffee grinder, blender or Vita Mix. Store in tightly covered container. For each serving use two to four Tbsp. of ground grains.

** Use one or more properly combined fruits (See chart on page 68). If using fresh fruit, add it just prior to serving.

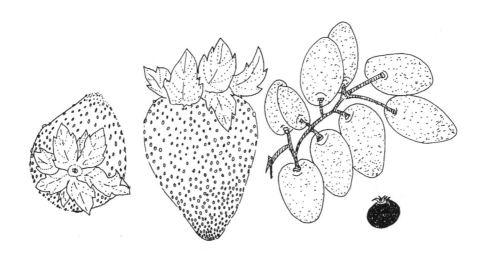

Fruit Plate
☆ ☆ ☆ ☆ ☆

½ sweet apple   ½ pear
2 or 3 dates   ½ ripe banana
1 fig   ¼ cup organic raisins

Note: Many different types of in-season fruits can be substituted. For best digestion, mix fruits according to the food combining chart on page 68.

try

Granola
☆ ☆ ☆

4 cups rolled oats	1 cup sunflower seeds
1 cup crushed almonds	½ cup wheat germ or other whole grain bran
½ cup whole grain flour	1 cup honey, sorghum, molasses or maple syrup
1 tsp. cinnamon	1 tsp. vanilla
¼ cup shredded coconut	1 cup pumpkin seeds

To dehydrate your granola, rather than baking it: Grind pumpkin and sunflower seeds to a finer texture. In a large bowl combine with all of the other dry ingredients. In a separate bowl combine the wet ingredients. Combine and mix well. Place on solid dehydrator sheets and dehydrate until dry.

or

Spread evenly on a non-stick cookie sheet. Bake 20 minutes in a preheated 250 degree oven, stir and continue to bake another 20 minutes, stirring periodically to prevent burning. The granola should be lightly browned. Remove from oven and serve warm or cool thoroughly and store in tightly sealed container or plastic bags.

Option: After the granola has cooled, add organic raisins or other organic, unsulphured dehydrated fruit.

Raw Apple Sauce
☆ ☆ ☆ ☆ ☆

almonds ground into small pieces
½ raw peeled apple cut into small pieces
½ ripe banana

This combination can be served as is or put through the Champion or Green Power Juicer (use solid "blank" instead of screen) to make a wonderful apple sauce. Serve with ½ ripe banana, cut into rounds.

For variety add a date and/or a few almonds while putting apples through the juicing machine.

Lunch Examples for Children

Any of these soups and/or salads with any of these sandwiches

1 cup Asparagus Soup
(see recipe on page 199)

1 Broccoli/Red Pepper Pita Pocket
(see recipe on page 275)

1 cup Tomato Soup
(see recipe on page 203)

1 Tomato and Avocado Pita Pocket
(see recipe on page 278)

1 cup Green Pea Soup
(see recipe on page 204)

1 Hummus in a Pita
(see recipe on page 276)

2 cups Hallelujah Acres Vegetable Salad
(put dressing in separate container)
(see recipe on page 152)

1 Eggless Salad on whole-grain bread or pita
(see recipe on page 295)

1 cup Hallelujah Acres Cabbage Salad
(see recipe on page 155)

1 Cucumber Sandwich on whole-grain bread or pita
(see recipe page 276)

Include with all lunches a variety of raw vegetables and/or dehydrated crackers. (page 305)

Use your imagination to come up with other exciting lunches for your children. Raw or cooked soups, salads and other sandwiches can be created for a great deal of variety. If sending fruit for lunch, do not send vegetables, because fruits and vegetables do not digest well together.

A combination of these suggestions and a healthy imagination will ensure your growing children are well-nourished, whether they are eating at home or school. The evening meal should be with the entire family, with children eating the same food as the adults.

"Every man is the builder of a temple called his body....
We are all sculptors and painters, and our material is our own flesh,
blood and bones. Any nobleness begins at once to refine a man's features,
any meanness or sensuality to imbue them."
– Henry David Thoreau

Chapter Eleven:

Setting up Your Hallelujah Kitchen

Questions I am often asked include, "How do I begin changing my kitchen so that I can prepare the foods I will be feeding my family with this new lifestyle? What do I need to eliminate and what shall I keep? What about my cookbooks and canned and frozen food?" Sound familiar?

Let me begin by quoting Dr. Dean Ornish, M.D.: ***"When people make only moderate changes in diet and lifestyle, they have the worst of both worlds. They have the sense of deprivation because they're not able to eat and do everything that they want, but they're not making changes big enough to make them feel much better or to have much effect on their weight, their cholesterol, or their health. On the other hand, when people make comprehensive changes in their diet and lifestyle, they begin to feel so much better so quickly that the choices become clear and, for many people, worth making."***

Dr. Ornish reflects my personal experience also. The easiest way to change your diet and lifestyle is to jump right in and make it happen. And don't look back!

There are some very basic essentials to setting up a natural foods kitchen and they are as follows:

Juicing is the Key to Gaining and Maintaining Optimal Health

As finances allow, we recommend the purchase of a Champion or Green Star juicer, which we consider the most valuable appliance in the kitchen. These juicers, in addition to making fresh vegetable and fruit juices, can be used for making baby food, nut butters, soft banana/fruit ice cream, and applesauce. They also can be used to grind nuts or shred cabbage, beets, carrots, etc. for salads.

We recommend only two juicers: The Champion, which currently retails for under $300, and the Green Star, which retails at $515. Both of these juicers break open the cell structure of the vegetables or fruits being juiced to release the nutrients.

Recipes for Life ... from God's Garden

The most common type of juicer on the market today is a "centrifugal" juicer, which has a spinning basket that cuts and shreds the fruit or vegetable as it is spinning at a high speed. We do not recommend any centrifugal juicers because this method is not a sufficient means of breaking open the cell to extract vital nutrients into the juice. Because fewer nutrients are provided in the juice from a centrifugal juicer, it does not produce the same results.

The Champion yields up to four times more vitamins, enzymes and trace minerals than a "centrifugal" (spinning basket) type juicer, and juice from a Green Star approximately doubles the nutritional value of that from a Champion.

Both the Champion and the Green Star also come with a variety of attachments that enable them to be used as a grinder for grain and nut butters, and include options for making treats such as fresh applesauce or frozen banana "ice cream." Juicers with a spinning basket cannot be used to make baby foods, soft frozen fruit creams, nut butters, etc.

The Champion Juicer

For the money, the Champion is a dependable, easy to use machine that is easy to care for. It has a 1/3-horse power, heavy duty motor so you need not worry about putting it to heavy use. Many have told us of using their Champion juicers daily for over 20 years. A commercial model is available with an even heavier motor.

The Champion is a masticating juicer that has been on the market for many years. It has a rotating cutter with stainless steel teeth that cut and grind the fruit or vegetable, which is forced up against a fine screen, which separates the juice from the pulp. The Champion weighs 25 pounds and is 13 inches high and 17 inches long.

The Green Star Juicer

If a person can afford the Green Star machine, we would highly recommend it. We consider it to be the very best juicer on the market.

The Green Star has a patented twin-gear triturating action featuring gears that spin at the low speed of 110 r.p.m. to reduce heat and friction so that enzymes and other nutrients are maintained, plus a revolutionary magnetic and far-infrared technology that prolongs the freshness and shelf life of freshly-extracted juices. This allows freshly-extracted juice from a Green Star to be stored in the refrigerator in single-serving, 8-ounce jars (filled to overflowing, to minimize oxygen and oxidation) for up to 48 hours, according to Green Star literature.

Today we are seeing magnetic technology used in several ways, such as magnetic bed mattresses, innersoles for shoes, tooth brushes and even devices that generate pulsating magnetic fields for the purpose of relaxation or energizing. With the Green Star, this technology entered into the field of raw food processing. At the core of each of the two gears is a series of in-line magnets equalling 2,600 gauss, surrounded by a bioceramic material that generates far-infrared frequencies, known as life force frequencies, because they are similar to the frequencies emitted by the human body and by water.

According to the Green Star manufacturers, far-infrared "is the natural resonant frequency range of water and organic substances, including man. We call it the life force frequency. Infrared wave lengths range from 7 to 1,000 microns, just beyond visible light. Far-infrared is a part of this wave length family we use in infrared photography, mapping the earth's surface and guiding missiles to their target. Our skin radiates 9.36 microns far-infrared wave, which is very close to the resonant frequency of a water molecule, and rightly so since our bodies are about 70 percent water. Far-infrared waves are the safest and most beneficial energy source available."

The combination of this magnetic and far-infrared technology stabilizes the fragile structure of the juice. When fruits and vegetables are juiced, oxidation causes minerals and other nutrients in the juice to lose their freshness and vitality for the same reason that an apple oxidizes and turns brown when it is cut in half. What is happening here on the molecular level could be compared to the spinning of a child's "top." For a while, the top will spin rapidly and upright, but eventually will start to slow down and wobble, and ultimately stop spinning. On the molecular level, this is comparable to the electron spin of the minerals in the juice, which have been destabilized during the juicing process. As the electrons start to "wobble" and slow down, the minerals lose their vitality and start to oxidize. The spinning magnets and bio-ceramic material in the twin gears of the Green Power add vitality to the minerals by giving their electrons a little extra spin.

The bottom line is that after 24 to 48 hours, carrot juice from a Green Star is still bright orange in color and it still smells and tastes fresh. (The juice does tend to separate because it is not homogenized, but this can be remedied by shaking or stirring.) Carrot juice from most other juicers begins to turn brown after about 15 minutes, and after an hour or so it does not taste or smell like fresh juice, which is an indication that its nutritional value has been greatly deteriorated. Because of its ability to keep juice fresher longer, the Green Star is particularly beneficial for people who find it convenient to make a full day's supply of juice at one time, or for those who like to drink juice at work, etc.

The Green Star weighs 32 pounds and is 13 inches high and 20 inches long. For more information on juicing, see Chapter 6 (pages 76-81)

Hint: A juicer makes a great wedding gift for a new family.

Water Distiller

We also highly recommend that a water distiller be a part of your new kitchen. We believe that distilled water is the only water that should ever be consumed. Our bodies need minerals but not in powdered rock form as found in all ground water sources (spring, river, well, etc.). These minerals cause many problems for the body such as arthritis, gallstones, kidney stones, hardening of the arteries, etc. For more information on this subject, see Chapter 22 in *God's Way to Ultimate Health*.

A distiller is filled with ordinary tap water, which is heated to 212 degrees. This heating process kills bacteria, germs and viruses that the water may contain. Light gases are removed by a gaseous vent. As the water turns into steam the minerals, salts, etc. are left behind. Unlike other forms of water purification, a distiller separates water from pollutants by evaporation rather than trying to separate pollutants from water.

Distilled water can also be purchased in plastic containers in most grocery stores, but you have less knowledge about and control over the purity of store-bought water than water you distill in your own home. If you buy distilled water in plastic jugs at a store, make sure the label says "Distilled Water," rather than Spring Water, Mineral Water, Drinking Water, etc. If the water tastes like plastic, don't drink it. Plastic can leach into the water if the container is stored in the sun. Also, it is best when you open a new container of distilled water from the store that you immediately pour it into a glass container with a lid.

Food Dehydrator

A food dehydrator is a wonderful machine that allows food to be preserved using a *low heat* process, thus leaving the enzymes (the life force) and other nutrients intact. When purchasing a dehydrator, it is of vital importance that it have a thermostat that can be set at 107 degrees or lower. Some models come with a fan and this is preferred. Any dehydrator lacking a thermostat will probably reach temperatures high enough to kill the enzymes and destroy many other nutrients.

Food drying is one of the oldest methods of preservation there is, dating back many centuries. Fruits and vegetables were dried by being laid in the sun in the 15th century. Many dehydrated foods were found in the ancient Egyptian tombs recently when they were excavated. The first dehydrator arrived on the scene in 1795 and was developed in France. In the United States, dehydrated food became a necessity during World War I when troops and supplies were being sent to Europe on a daily basis.

During the spring, summer and fall, when fruits and vegetables are in abundance, dehydrating is a wonderful way to preserve surplus foods for future use. When a low-heat dehydrator is used, most of the enzymes and nutrients are retained. No chemicals or additives are needed to preserve these foods.

The flavors of dried foods are enhanced and improved because the natural sugars are concentrated, making sweet, natural snacks. Dried vegetables can be ground into a wonderful seasoning, which can be added to soups and stews or used as salad toppings. Dehydrators can also be used to preserve fresh herbs, make vegetable grain crisps (raw crackers) page 305 and seed patties and other treats for your family. Dehydrated foods are easy to store. Approximately 60 tomatoes will fit in a quart jar after they are dehydrated. Dehydrated foods have a long shelf life, if dried properly, and can be used when traveling, hiking, camping, etc.

To rehydrate (restore the liquid) simply soak them in distilled water or in freshly extracted fruit juice. For instance, blueberries are wonderful soaked in fresh apple juice. Vegetables may be rehydrated in distilled water or vegetable soup stock. It is not necessary to rehydrate herbs, banana chips or vegetable chips before serving. A rule of thumb is that it takes about 30 minutes to an hour to rehydrate dried fruits and vegetables.

On an annual basis, dehydrating is probably cheaper than either freezing or canning, and the space saved is considerable.

Remember, there is a difference between what you dehydrate at home and what you buy in the store. When purchasing dehydrated foods commercially, it is important to make sure to read the label. Most have had poisons added in the form of color enhancers, additives and preservatives.

Vita-Mix Machine

The Vita Mix Machine is a great machine in the kitchen. It can be used for pureeing baby food, making batters, grinding flour from whole grains, coarse grinding grain for cereals, making frozen smoothies, dips, spreads, nut butters, raw sauces, dressings and raw soups that are out of this world! ***But we do not recommend the use of a Vita Mix for making juices because it leaves the pulp in the juice!***

Remember, the primary purpose of a juicer is to **remove** the pulp. With the pulp removed, the nutrients are literally pre-digested and can enter almost immediately into the bloodstream. Thus, the nutrients reach the cellular level in a matter of minutes. Anyone who is interested in exploring the tremendous health benefits of juicing should know that a Vita-Mix is not a juicer. A Vita-Mix is a very good blender, but it does not make juice because it does not separate the juice from the pulp. The Vita-Mix blends food into a mushy mix, similar to the texture of applesauce. Water must be added to this mixture if you want to drink it. This does not produce the same benefits as drinking fresh juice from a masticating juicer, because the fiber or pulp has not been separated from the juice. Even after the fruit or vegetable has been blended and mixed by this machine, the pulp is still in it and thus it still must go through the digestive system. This requires much energy and time, and many of the nutrients will be lost during the digestive process. This defeats the prime purpose of juicing, which is to get large amounts of nutrition to the cellular level quickly without going through the process of digestion. For more information on juicing, see Chapter 6.

Other Items You Will Find Valuable In Your Kitchen Include:

A. **A large cutting board.** Because wood is natural, a wooden cutting board has certain advantages over a plastic cutting board. Plastic was once considered a better material for use as a cutting board, but recent findings have found plastic to be a more fertile environment for bacteria and germs than wood. A wooden cutting board should be cleaned periodically with a solution of lemon juice and baking soda.

B. **A good blender** or Vita Mix used for making blended salads, sauces and dressings.

C. **A food processor** saves time when chopping, shredding, grating, making bread dough.

D. **Set of sharp knives,** including a chopping knife and hand steel for sharpening.

E. **Stainless steel or glass saucepans**, skillets, kettles and a stainless steel wok if you can afford one.

F. **Measuring cups,** including 2 and 4-cup glass measurers and a set of $1/4$, $1/3$, $1/2$ and 1-cup measurers.

G. **Scissors** for snipping fresh herbs as well as other uses.

H. **Hand juicer** for extracting citrus juices used in dressings and sauces.

I. **Oven-proof casserole dishes** made of glass, stainless steel, earthenware or ceramic for lasagna, braising vegetables, etc.

J. **Stainless steel steamer** for vegetables.

K. **Peeler** for carrots, potatoes, broccoli stalks, etc.

L. **Miscellaneous Items** - Spatulas, measuring spoons, garlic press, hand grater, potato masher (which works great for avocados), melon ball tool, colander, and a funnel are a few items that you will find useful.

Recipes for Life ... from God's Garden

Remove Aluminum Cookware

"I have been a medical man for forty years and because of the work I have done in relation to the aluminum question I can state, without a shadow of a doubt, and with all the urgency of my command, that the use of aluminum in the preparation of food and food products is one of the most harmful factors in modern civilization." – H. Tomlinson, M.B., Ch.B, M.R.C.S., L.R.C.P., London, England

As early as 1913, *Lancet,* a British medical journal, reported that aluminum cookware could be injurious to health. Since that time, medical studies have been done in Germany, Canada, the United States and France, all finding the same results. Aluminum cookware causes disease and has been banned in most of the aforementioned countries. Aluminum is a soft metal and is easily pitted and dissolved. Unfortunately, in the United States the aluminum cookware industry is a multi-million dollar business.

Remove all aluminum cooking utensils or any items on your shelves that contain aluminum. In spite of the industry's claims to the contrary, aluminum leaches or is dissolved into food and has been linked to Alzheimer's disease and cancers. It has also been known to cause intestinal disorders, migraine headaches and other serious health problems. Aluminum is also found in under-arm deodorants and colas served in aluminum cans. Aluminum is leached from the can into the cola, which makes the drink even more hazardous than without the can.

For pots and pans, stainless steel, glass, ceramic or earthenware are the best replacements for aluminum. This is an investment that should be made for the sake of the health of all your family. Also, be sure your vegetable steamer is stainless steel instead of aluminum.

Remove Microwave Oven

Remove the microwave oven from your kitchen, because it can be hazardous to your health. The microwave oven is an appliance that many have become dependent upon due to the fast pace in which we live. Have you ever wondered about the consequences of long-term use? What effect does it have on the food with which you are trying to nourish your body/temple? Do the molecules remain unchanged or are they rearranged and even destroyed in the process? Microwaves are high-frequency electromagnetic waves that alternate in positive and negative directions. These high-frequency electromagnetic waves reverse polarity of food molecules up to 100 billion times per second, vibrating these molecules and causing them to collide at destructive speeds, which creates friction and heat. The living cells in raw food are torn apart and destroyed and molecules are deformed by friction from the inside out. Of all heating methods, microwaving results in more lost nutrients than any other method, as protein, vitamins and minerals are made useless. There is also considerable scientific evidence of health risks associated with even standing near a microwave oven while it is in use.

After extensive research by scientists in the former Soviet Union, the use of microwave ovens was banned in that nation in 1976.

In 1989 the Minnesota Extension Service of the University of Minnesota put out the following warning to parents of young families: *"Although microwaves heat food quickly, they are not recommended for heating a baby's bottle. The bottle may seem cool to the touch, but the liquid inside may become extremely hot and could burn the baby's mouth and throat. Also, the buildup of steam in a closed container such as a baby bottle in a microwave can cause slight change in the milk. In infant formulas, there may be loss of some vitamins. In expressed breast milk, some protective properties may be destroyed. Warming a bottle by holding it under tap water or by setting it in a bowl of warm water and then testing it on your wrist before feeding, may take a few minutes longer, but it is much safer."*

In 1991, a lawsuit was filed in Oklahoma when a woman went into the hospital for hip surgery and died because of a blood transfusion she was given. The nurse simply "warmed the blood for the transfusion in a microwave oven." Although blood is normally warmed before a transfusion, it is not warmed in a microwave! Warming the blood in the microwave altered the blood molecules and the woman died due to this effect.

In the April 1992 issue of the *Journal of Pediatrics,* a similar case was reported. This study states that researchers at Stanford University Medical Center found that microwaving breast milk just to warm it destroyed 98 percent of the immunoglobulin A antibodies which are necessary for the immunization properties to be passed along to infants. Researchers also found that 96 percent of the liposome activity that inhibits bacterial growth was also destroyed by just warming the milk "a little." Stanford University no longer uses microwaves to warm breast milk.

According to an article in *Acres, USA,* "Hans Hertel of Switzerland is the first to conceive and carry out a quality study on the effects of microwaved nutrients on the blood and physiology of human beings. This small, but well-controlled, study pointed the firm finger of a degenerative force to microwave ovens and the food produced in them. The conclusion was clear: microwave cooking changed the nutrients so that changes took place in the participants' blood, and these were not healthy changes, but changes that cause deterioration in the human systems."

Hertel further states: "There is extensive scientific literature concerning the hazardous effects of direct microwave radiation of living systems. Technically produced microwaves are based on the principal of altering current. Atoms, molecules, and cells hit by this hard electromagnetic radiation are forced to reverse polarity 1 to 100 billion times per second. There are no atoms, molecules or cells of any organic system able to withstand such a violent destructive power for any extended period of time, not even in the low energy range of milliwatts."

In another study conducted in Germany last year, eight people were given a morning meal that consisted of milk or lightly-cooked vegetables. Some were given food that had been microwaved. During the two-month study, each person had his or her blood drawn three times per day to test nutrient and bacteria levels.

The blood measurements from those who ate the microwaved food were quite alarming because they indicated molecular changes in the food which cannot be detected until after the food is consumed. Some of the findings include:

• Decrease in the hemoglobin levels in the blood of those people that ingested the microwaved food. These reductions in the hemoglobin can indicate anemia which could lead to rheumatism, fever and thyroid insufficiency.

• When microwaved food was eaten, the lymphocyte levels dropped dramatically and the leukocyte counts sky-rocketed. This indicates that the body is treating the microwaved food as a toxic substance.

• Lipoprotein levels (both high and low) rose significantly after vegetables that were microwaved were consumed. Lipoprotein levels are used to measure cholesterol in the body.

• The radiation levels of light-emitting bacteria were highest in those who ate microwaved food, which indicates that microwave energy may be transferred from the food to the person who consumed it.

It is a known fact that heating destroys nutrients; however, ***the most frightening discovery of all was that the blood of those who ingested the microwaved food showed pathological changes in the body's cells!***

The microwave oven is an example of a 20th Century "convenience" invented by mankind that is a very unnatural and harmful means of food preparation. God never intended for us to submit our food molecules to such a destructive force before putting them into our body/temple, but many people today are convinced this is a convenience they cannot live without. The choice is yours – man's way, or God's Way!

Recipes for Life … from God's Garden

Replace Cans, Jars and Bottled Food

As you are able, replace all items which have been purchased in cans with fresh produce or that which has been prepared by you. Most all supermarket items contain chemical additives and preservatives. If you read the label, you will find they contain refined sugars, dyes, MSG and other additives. Many of these products also come in aluminum cans and should be avoided.

If you cannot prepare your own fruits and vegetables and must buy products in a supermarket, buy things in glass or make sure the cans are lined. Look for those that are whole food items rather than refined. Refined means that more of the essential nutrients have been destroyed in the processing. Home canned and frozen items are much preferred to those purchased at a supermarket. They have reduced nutritional value, but you know there are no chemicals added. Home-canned and frozen products can be used in the 15 to 25 percent cooked food portion of your diet.

Revising Recipes

Go through your favorite recipes and see if the harmful ingredients can be replaced by those less harmful. For example, replace white sugar with honey or maple syrup, white flour with whole grain flours and unbleached white, white pastas with whole grain pastas, etc. If you are unable to figure out revisions at this time, set them aside until you have learned more.

Steps to Prepare a Recipe

A. Assemble ingredients
B. Preheat oven, if required
C. Do chopping
D. Measure carefully
E. Follow directions
F. Cook as directed, if cooking is required

When increasing the size of a recipe, do not increase the seasoning automatically. Taste after adding the regular amount of seasoning to see if more is required.

Setting Up Your Vegetarian Pantry

Just as it is important to have the proper tools for your new lifestyle, it is equally vital to have a pantry that will provide you with items required to prepare appealing and nourishing vegetarian meals for your family to enjoy. As you review your pantry, bear in mind you are switching from a Standard American Diet to the Hallelujah Diet. You will want to remove the ancient bottles of seasonings, beef bouillon and other items no longer needed and replace them with ingredients to make healthy meals for your family. Although the Hallelujah Diet is predominately raw, herbs play an important role.

Substitutions

Try some of the following substitutions to convert traditional recipes to healthier recipes. Replace all animal products, including poultry, fish, eggs and cheese with something less harmful.

Meat stock can be replaced with vegetable soup stock.

In yeast breads, try leaving out the eggs.

Use crumbled tofu instead of cottage cheese.

Replace traditional pork and beans with vegetarian baked beans.

Replace eggs when used for liquid in recipes by adding one of the following substitutions: 2 tablespoons of another liquid such as lemon juice or water, 1/2 of a banana, 1/4 cup of raw applesauce or ground zucchini.

To replace eggs when used as a binder, try using mashed potatoes, oatmeal, or fine bread crumbs. Or 1/2 cup flax seeds and 1 1/2 cups distilled water. Grind the flax seeds to a fine powder, add water and blend on high for 2 to 3 minutes. Chill for 1 hour. This will keep up to 2 days refrigerated. To replace one egg, use 1/4 cup of the flax seed mixture. One cup of the flax seed mixture equals 4 eggs.

To make cream soups, add rice that has been cooked and then pureed, or add some potatoes and allow them to cook down or mash.

Replace buttermilk with rice milk to which 1 tablespoon apple cider vinegar has been added.

Replace ground meats with lots of cut-up vegetables or try TVP (texturized vegetable protein) if you are in the transition stage and feel you still need something that looks like ground beef.

In baked goods, replace fat (butter, margarine or shortening) with applesauce, mashed bananas, pumpkin or ground zucchini. Bananas, applesauce and pumpkin will add flavor; zucchini will not.

Use whole grains with a portion of the mix being **unbleached** white flour instead of white flour.

Sauté without oil. Use lemon juice (or other citrus juices), vegetable broth, or water. Celtic Sea Salt, minced garlic, finely chopped onions and/or your favorite herbs will add lots of flavor. This method is preferred to using oil.

Replace salt and pepper with herbs and juices to put a whole new taste sensation together. For example, with broccoli try lemon juice, nutmeg, basil, curry, oregano or garlic. With steamed carrots, try adding parsley, lemon juice, cinnamon, mace, thyme, honey or allspice.

Remove black pepper from the kitchen. It contains two carcinogens, peperine and safrole. Dr. Douglas Graham, D.C., states, "If you wouldn't feed it to a baby, don't consume it yourself." Our body/temple deserves the best!

Replace sugar with 1/2 to 2/3 cup honey, molasses or maple syrup, or a combination of these for each cup of sugar called for in a recipe. Add 1 tsp. to 1 Tbsp. of the replacements listed above in any cake recipe that does not call for it, as it will make the cake lighter.

Conversions

1/4 tsp. dried powdered herbs = 3/4 to 1 tsp. dried crumbled herbs = 1 1/2 to 2 tsp. freshly chopped herbs.

1 Tbsp. dried onion flakes = 1 medium raw onion

1/2 tsp. garlic powder = 1 clove fresh garlic

1 tsp. dried dill = 1 stalk fresh dill

1 Tbsp. flour for thickening = 1/2 Tbsp. Arrow Root powder

1 large lemon = approximately 1/4 cup of lemon juice

Rind of one lemon = 1 Tbsp. grated lemon

1 whole orange = approximately 1/2 cup of orange juice

Recipes for Life ... from God's Garden

Recipe Measurements

For best results when preparing recipes, it is imperative that proper measurements are used.
To measure liquids, use glass measuring cups for a more accurate measure.
To measure dry ingredients, use dry measuring cups.
To measure spices, use measuring spoons.
For less than 1/4 cup, use standard measuring spoons.
The term "dash" means less than 1/8 tsp.
1 tbsp. equals 3 tsp.

Liquid and Dry Measurement Conversions

1 cup = 8 fluid ounces	3 tsp. = 1 Tbsp.
2 cups = 16 fluid ounces	4 Tbsp. = 1/4 cup
4 cups = 32 fluid ounces	16 Tbsp. = 1 cup
2 cups = 1 pint	2 Tbsp. = 1 ounce
2 pints = 1 quart	4 ounces = 1/4 pound
1 quart = 4 cups	16 ounces = 1 pound
4 quarts = 1 gallon	1 pound = 454 grams

1/2 to 2/3 cup dehydrated vegetables = 1 cup fresh vegetables

When Planning Your Menus, Ask Yourself the Following Questions:

1. What can I serve my family that is raw and delicious?
2. What new taste treat can we try?
3. What is easy to prepare for the cooked food portion of the family meals?

Plan ahead, and make your meals attractive. Eye appeal is very important.

"While in a period of transition to living foods,
it is best to allow your body to accept new food materials into the system,
to incorporate new eating patterns so thoroughly that they become lifetime habits,
rather than being discarded as soon as the weight is lost
or physical problems overcome."
– Ann Wigmore, from Recipes for Longer Life

Chapter Twelve:

Grocery Shopping

"The average supermarket is a mausoleum where dead foods lie in state."
– Evangelist Lester Roloff

When grocery shopping, try to avoid all refined foods. Select natural foods which provide you and your family an adequate intake of vitamins, minerals, amino acids and trace elements. Remember that once you leave the produce department of your supermarket, there is practically no nutrition to be found in any item in the rest of the store.

Be adventuresome! Try adding new and unusual items to your diet. If you aren't sure how to prepare them, ask a clerk who works in the produce department. Add fresh, raw greens to your diet. Try collards, spinach and leaf lettuce.

Choose fresh vegetables when available. If you must buy frozen when some produce is out of season, select only those frozen foods with no salt or sugar added. Vegetables should always be cleaned with a non-toxic, biodegradable soap and rinsed well before using.

Produce

Fresh, organic fruits and vegetables are the most important items in The Hallelujah Diet. It is not unusual for a family on The Hallelujah Diet to purchase a second refrigerator to store the necessary produce to maintain a healthy diet and lifestyle for their family. Fresh, organic fruits and vegetables are the most nutritious foods and an absolute necessity to maintain optimum health.

In order to provide the maximum benefit from your produce purchases, it is important to know how to select them. The following guidelines should prove beneficial to you.

Recipes for Life ... from God's Garden

Vegetables

Artichokes - An unusual looking vegetable with spiked, calloused looking leaves. The best flavor comes from artichokes that are firm, plump and bright green in the spring or olive green in the fall. Occasionally they will be streaked with purple, which is fine; however, do not buy those with black blotches. Squeeze them to see if they squeak; if so, they are fresh. If they rattle, they have sat too long on the shelf and should be avoided. There are two peak seasons: spring and fall. Store uncooked, wrapped in plastic and keep refrigerated up to one week.

Asparagus - One of the first signs of spring, tender asparagus shoots are firm, slender and tight with compact tips. Their peak season is early spring through summer, depending upon the area of the country it's grown in. Asparagus does not store well and becomes tougher the longer it sits. For the best flavor consume within a few hours of picking. Store in the refrigerator wrapped in plastic until ready for use.

Avocado - Really, a very versatile fruit which can be used in sandwiches, salads, dips and spreads. See fruit section for more information.

Broccoli - When picking broccoli, the greener the better. Yellow indicates maturity. The heads should be wide with buds that are tight and firm (not rubbery). The stalks should be short and a dark even color. The leaves of the broccoli plant may be eaten and are nutritious. Stems can be peeled and eaten raw or frozen for use in soups or stews. Broccoli was first cultivated in the United States in the early 1900s.

Carrots - For juicing, California juicing carrots are recommended because of their sweetness and nutritional content. The sweeter a carrot, the higher its nutritional content. Carrots grown in warm climates have a tendency to be bitter and are not recommended for juicing. For salad use, smaller carrots are easier to use, but the juicing carrots can be substituted. Organic carrots are always preferred, when available. Carrots are native to Afghanistan and were used by the Greeks and Romans for medicinal purposes.

Cauliflower - When looking for a head of cauliflower, look for a head that is white and firm, without any brown spots. The leaves should be green and soft, not brown and brittle. Cauliflower has been grown in North America since the 17th Century. As with other members of the cruciferous family (broccoli, cabbage, collards, horse radish, mustard greens, cresses, Chinese cabbage, kohlrabi, kale, turnips, brussels sprouts, rutabaga and radishes), cauliflower is known for its cancer-fighting properties.

Celery - Celery stalks that are thick, stout and succulent are less likely to be stringy. When celery is too green, it tends to be bitter; when too white, the nutrient value is low. Try to pick stalks that are in between. Celery should be kept in an airtight container to protect it from exposure to air. If kept in an airtight container, celery will remain fresh for two weeks. If celery is left exposed to the elements, it will become limp in two days.

Cucumbers - Cucumbers are technically a fruit, but most commonly used in salads. Look for the short, slender cucumbers which are more favorable and have fewer seeds. Look for the pickling cucumbers because they are not waxed or oiled. However, they do not have a long shelf life.

Lettuce - Avoid head lettuce, since it has very little nutritional value, very little fiber and tends to plug up the colon. There are a number of leaf lettuces available- the darker the color the more food value it has. Choose heads that are crisp, dense and heavy. Do not pick those which have been waterlogged. Store in a plastic bag, removing as much air as possible prior to securing tightly. Romaine is the most popular and most flavorful. However, there are others that are also delicious.

Peppers - Green peppers are actually unripe and should be used primarily for cooking purposes. Red and yellow peppers are mature and sweet and the ones to use in salads if they are available. When picking through green peppers, look for those with red streaks because they will usually be sweeter. Ripe peppers imported from Holland are often available; however, they are usually more expensive.

Squash - There are many varieties of squash, usually grouped as summer and winter squash. When purchasing summer squash, look for young, thin, shiny yellow crookneck or patty pans squashes or medium colored green zucchinis. Summer squash – including yellow crookneck and zucchini – are interchangeable in recipes. When purchasing winter squash, look for dark green with a touch of yellow acorn or golden butternut outer skin or Hungarian Mammoth with a pale blue-green color. Winter squash are also interchangeable.

Fruits

Most fresh fruit should be stored at room temperature (out of direct sunlight) until matured and then refrigerated. Use as quickly as possible after the fruit becomes ripe. Do not wash fruit until you are ready to use it.

Apples - Choose apples that have deep, rich coloring, especially around the stem. When picking Red or Yellow Delicious apples, the skin should be speckled with some brown lines. Apples should always be firm and not waxed. Red Delicious, Fuji, New Zealand Gala and Granny Smith apples should be extremely firm. Red Delicious apples which are elongated and slightly heart-shaped will have the best flavor. Yellow Delicious, McIntosh, Rome Beauty and Jonathan will give slightly when pressure is applied. Apples should be stored in a well-secured plastic bag in the refrigerator. Many varieties will store for months and some all winter if kept in plastic at temperatures just above freezing.

Avocados - There are many shapes, sizes and textures of avocados. The Haas avocado, my favorite, is pear-shaped, rather elongated with a dull, dark-green waxy color and a pebbly texture and are generally available all year round. Avocados should yield slightly to gentle pressure when ripe. Do not buy if they are mushy as they become rancid. Purchase ripe, or if unripe place in a closed paper bag on the counter. When ripened, refrigerate immediately unbagged. Ripened avocados have a shelf life of only about three days. When cut open, if the avocado has gray, black or brown spots, remove them, and check the yellow part for taste prior to using. The Haas has its peak season in the spring and summer while Florida varieties come in during the fall. If you use only a portion of an avocado, wrap the remainder tightly with plastic wrap and refrigerate.

Bananas - Look for bananas that are a rich yellow color from end to end and slightly speckled. Green bananas, however, will ripen if left on the counter a few days. Do not eat bananas until they are ripe. A banana is not ripe until all the green has disappeared and speckles begin to appear on the skin. Bananas that are very ripe can be purchased for peeling and freezing. Bananas that are uniformly brown or black should be avoided.

Berries - Do not buy berries that have been irradiated. (They should be labeled.) Berries should be blemish free, with dark color and no soft or bleeding spots. Do not buy strawberries with white or green tips. Overly large berries will usually lack sweetness. Smell the container. Berries should smell clean and sweet; if you can detect the odor of pesticide, do not buy them. Store in the refrigerator in a covered container.

Cherries - Should be firm and plump, not soft to the touch. The sweetest cherries will be dark red in color. There are yellow varieties as well and they, too, should be firm and plump. Wash and store in an open container in the refrigerator. Cherries do not store well and should be used within 2 or 3 days.

Figs - Ripe figs are plump and tear-drop shaped and may have a slightly wrinkled or cracked skin. Characteristics of ripe figs are softness, moistness and oozing of nectar. Hard, dry figs are not ripe and will have an undesirable flavor. Figs are very perishable and should be refrigerated uncovered.

Grapes - Peak season July through November. Never buy grapes that are not grown in the USA. Buy organic whenever possible. Many other countries use heavy chemicals on their crops. Always sniff grapes to check for pesticides. Always wash thoroughly. Grapes should be firm when touched. Green stems indicate fresh grapes while those that are old will be dark. Also old grapes will have puckering at the stem. Refrigerate exposed to some air. All green grapes are prone to be sour. Look for a yellow or golden shade.

Recipes for Life ... from God's Garden

When green grapes have reached the golden stage the sugar content is higher and the taste is sweeter. Red seedless grapes grown in the United States usually keep quite a while and are a wonderful delight when available. Black seedless grapes have a tougher skin and bolder flavor.

Grapefruit - Grapefruit should have thin, shiny skins and feel heavy. Grapefruit should be stored in the refrigerator in a sealed container.

Lemons - Should be slightly firm with a golden yellow skin. Thicker skinned lemons will have less juice. The Meyer lemon is the sweetest lemon and has an orangy flavor. Lemons can be stored at room temperature for a few days and must be refrigerated if keeping longer.

Limes - Contrary to popular opinion, limes are not interchangeable with lemons. Limes have a sweeter flavor. Look for firm bright color and refrigerate if keeping more than a few days.

Mangoes - These wonderful fruits are best when they have been allowed to ripen until they are multi-colored. Well-proportioned mangoes are usually more desirable than the long narrow ones. Mangoes should yield to pressure when ripe and are aromatic when ripe. However, they should not be mushy.

Oranges - Avoid commercial oranges that are stamped "color added." The orange rind should be shiny, smooth and thin. It should feel firm and slightly heavy and should have a sweet aroma. Oranges range in color from green-speckled yellow to deep orange, and the Good Temple Orange is more red-orange and rather dull. Oranges need to be smelled; they should not smell like chemical sprays, but rather like citrus. Look for organic whenever possible.

Peaches - When ripe, peaches yield to pressure. Peaches should be soft colored, not faded or dull. Do not buy those that are partially green. Peaches are aromatic when ripe. When ripened, refrigerate allowing air to penetrate their container. Peaches should be fragrant and have a natural rose-colored blush to their skin. Since peaches do not usually ripen well off the tree, look for peaches that feel solid, but give when gently squeezed. Other stone fruits like nectarines and apricots have these same characteristics.

Pears - Peak season is September through November. Pears ripen off the tree, and therefore they can be purchased when green and allowed to ripen at home. When ripe, summer pears such as Bartletts get soft all over while winter pears, like Bosc have a golden skin and should continue to be firm except around the stem. Oregon's large yellow skinned Comice pears are especially good in winter. Asian pears are firm but crunchy and can be eaten like apples. Refrigerate when they are ripe.

Pineapples - Peak season is March through June. Pineapples do not ripen after they have been picked – they simply rot. These flavorful fruits should be gold, orange or reddish brown from top to bottom and very aromatic. If the golden color has spread to 15 to 20 percent of the fruit, it is usually ripe. When selecting a pineapple, the top leaves should pull out easily if it is ripe. A ripe pineapple should be plump and heavy for its size. Maui, Hawaii produces the best naturally-ripened pineapples and although the cost may be a little higher, the taste treat is worth it!

Strawberries - Peak season is April through June. Strawberries are quite easy to grow and can be planted in early spring or in the fall. Medium to small berries are usually sweeter than the larger berries. Select dry berries with bright green stems attached that are firm, bright red and with no white tips. Make sure the berries you select have not been irradiated or sprayed. Be sure to remove any decaying or green berries immediately. Do not wash berries until ready to use.

Tomatoes - A good tomato is normally very red with thin skin. The stem is well-indented and the tomato will be well-proportioned. When buying tomatoes out of season, usually cherry tomatoes and Roma (pear-shaped) tomatoes are the most flavorful. Out-of-season tomatoes are almost always picked green and then gassed to turn them red. They look like a ripe tomato, but one bite and you know they are not.

Melons

Different types of melons may be mixed together at a meal, but melons should never be eaten with other foods because they do not digest well when combined with other foods. Either eat melons alone or leave them alone.   All melons should be ripened at room temperature prior to being refrigerated. To avoid heavy chemical sprays that are used on imported melons, try to buy locally.

Cantaloupes - Peak season June through August. The best way to select a cantaloupe is by smell. A ripe cantaloupe produces an enticing aroma. Usually medium to large melons are more flavorful than smaller ones. Also when ripe, the end of the cantaloupe opposite the stem should be soft and yield to gentle pressure. The skin should be golden tan and the webbing should be deep cream color (rather than green), coarse and stand out boldly. The stem end should be smooth and slightly depressed. Do not select a melon with the stem attached. An attached stem means the melon was picked green. The melon should be heavy and yield slightly to pressure. An aromatic melon indicates good flavor. Avoid melons with smooth, bald spots. Overripe melons can be detected by widespread softening and will be watery and tasteless. Cantaloupes will ripen some at room temperature; however, green melons should be avoided. When fully ripened store in the refrigerator.

Casabas - Peak season July to November, with the best flavor in September and October. Casaba melons are uniquely marked with vertical ridges rather than the webbing of cantaloupes or the smooth skin of a honeydew. The skin color of the Casaba melon depends on the variety. For example, the Golden Beauty is pointed at the stem end, with a green skin that turns golden and will have a slight give at the blossom end when fully matured. The flesh can either be white, yellow or orange. Casabas are not as sweet as a honeydew and do not have the aroma of a cantaloupe. Casabas do not fall off the vine as do other melons when mature but must be harvested by cutting the stem when the melons have neared maturity. They are then placed in storage until the blossom end becomes soft. If a Casaba melon is not ripe, the flavor will be similar to a cucumber.

Recipes for Life ... from God's Garden

Crenshaw - Peak season August and September; however, they are usually available from July through the end of October. The Crenshaw melon is a relative of the Casaba melon and prior to maturity it is a slightly wrinkled, dark green melon. Look for golden orange color with a minimum amount of green streaking. Ripe melons will feel soft to pressure all over, especially at the enlarged end. If required, ripen at room temperature prior to refrigeration. The flesh of the Crenshaw melon is vibrant orange, and is juicy with a rich, spicy flavor. Crenshaws can grow up to 9 pounds.

Honeydew - Peak season July through September. Can be either orange or green fleshed. A ripe honeydew should give to pressure all over but particularly at the stem end. Creamy white with yellow areas in the skin indicates the melon is ripe. If the veins are brown, usually the melon will have a higher sugar content. Green Honeydews should not have white skin. A golden orange cast will appear on Orange Honeydews and they will have an aroma when ripe. As with all melons, they should be heavy for their size. Ripen at room temperature prior to refrigeration. If a Honeydew melon is white or greenish, not soft to touch at the stem end, or looks shiny and smooth, it was picked too early.

Persian - Peak season for these melons is August and September. Persian melons are a member of the cantaloupe family and look like oversized cantaloupes. Selection of this melon is the same as for regular cantaloupe. The dark green rind under the netting lightens as the melon ripens. The rind should give under light pressure. The flesh of the melon is a darker orange than a regular cantaloupe.

Watermelon - Peak season May through August. Dark green or shiny watermelons are usually unripe. The ends should be rounded and full rather than pointy. The bottom of the melon should not be white or greenish but creamy off-white to yellow. The stem should look brown and shriveled, not green. A good watermelon will be well-proportioned, not gourd-shaped. A deep, hollow tuneful tone will be produced by thumping a ripe melon. A green melon, on the other hand, will squeak when it is thumped and an overripe watermelon will sound dull or flat. When opened, the flesh of the melon should be bright red with dark brown or black seeds. Store at room temperature; wrap and refrigerate after cutting.

Pantry Items

You may not be familiar with some of the following items, but they should be available at your local health food store or co-op. If the items you are looking for are not part of their regular inventory, ask if they can special order them for you.

Pasta

Pasta is made from flour and water with salt often added. Products that are called "noodles" almost always contain egg or egg whites.

Vegetable pastas are available at health food stores and are preferable to those made with white, bleached flour. Whole grain pastas include: spinach, whole wheat, buckwheat and come in a variety of shapes and sizes, such as spinach spaghetti noodles, buckwheat, corn, sorba and wheat udon noodles. These pastas add delightful color and texture to meals.

Grains

Grains, including pasta, should be used sparingly as many are acid forming in the body, and our bodies need to maintain an alkaline pH. Of the whole grains, brown rice, millet and quinoa are the best.

Brown Rice - There are several varieties of brown rice to choose from:
Basmati rice is a long grain brown rice that originated in India. This rice is very flavorful, enhancing

anything that is prepared with it. Organically grown Basmati rice is our favorite and has a delightful aroma when cooking.

Short-grain brown rice has a bold texture and a nut-like flavor, and tends to be the chewiest of the rices.

Long-grain brown rice is light and fluffy and resembles white rice the most.

Wild rice is another taste treat that has exceptional flavor and can be used alone, but is usually mixed with another variety. When mixing wild rice with other brown rice, be sure to cook them separately because it takes longer to cook wild rice than most other types of rice.

To cook brown rices, bring 2 cups of distilled water to a boil, add 1 cup of rice, lower heat and simmer, covered, for about 20 or 30 minutes. Do not stir rice while it is cooking. The rice will be done when all the water has cooked away. Remove from heat and allow to sit an additional 15 minutes without removing the lid.

Bulgur Wheat - is made from whole wheat kernels that have been steamed, dried and cracked. It has a nutty flavor and can be prepared in about 30 minutes. It is delicious in pilafs, tabouli and salads and can be used in place of rice. Bulgar is not always made from whole wheat, so be sure to check the label to make sure it is from unprocessed whole wheat. To prepare bulgar wheat, pour 2 cups of boiling water over 1 cup bulgar, cover and allow to sit for 20 minutes.

Corn Meal - corn that has been ground into flour.

Couscous - a traditional food of North Africa, is made from semolina, the refined endosperm (inside starch) of durum wheat. Couscous can be served as a side dish or in combinations with vegetables, as you would use rice. It is light and fluffy when cooked and can be prepared in about 10 minutes. Couscous is made by removing the germ and bran from durum wheat, then this semolina is ground and mixed with water and formed into long strands, which are broken into small pieces, steamed and dried. This leaves tiny yellow granules, which is couscous.

Millet - is an ancient cereal grass from Asia and Africa, now grown in the central U.S. and Canada, that can be used in place of rice, for stuffing, in pilafs, breads or burgers. It is a small yellow grain which has a slightly nutty taste. If toasted in a dry skillet prior to cooking, it will have a toasty flavor. Millet can be used in soups, stews, vegetable burgers, etc.

Oat groats – Originally, oats were a staple food grown in Scotland; however, today they are one of the main crops grown in the mid-west United States. Only about 5 percent of the oats grown commercially are for human consumption, with the greatest yield being used for animal feed. Oat hulls contain furfural, a widely used industrial solvent. The hulls must be removed before the oats can be eaten. After the hull is removed, the bran and germ remain intact. This is called the groat. Steel cut oats are hulled groats that are sliced but not rolled. They should be soaked prior to cooking.

Oat bran – is a source of soluble fiber. Oat bran received considerable publicity when it was reported several years ago that as little as $1/2$ cup of oat bran daily can lower serum cholesterol levels by as much as 20 percent. This gave oat bran the reputation as miracle food, until it was later discovered that the reason people's cholesterol levels were being reduced is that they were eating oatmeal (and other foods with oat bran) for breakfast instead of bacon and eggs, country ham, sausage, etc. The reduction in cholesterol in these studies was related more to people ***not*** eating bacon, eggs, country ham, sausage, etc. than it was to people eating oat bran. The bottom line is that although oat bran is a source of soluable fiber, raw fruits and vegetables are a better source because they are alive. And although eating oatmeal for breakfast is better than eating bacon and eggs, it is even better to eat fresh, raw fruit for your first meal of the day.

Quinoa - (pronounced keen-wah) is a delicious grain that has a subtle, pleasing flavor and fluffy texture. Quinoa originally came from the Andes Mountains of South America, and is now being grown in the Colorado Rockies. It is a food that can be prepared quickly and is alkaline, so the body can digest it easily. Quinoa should always be rinsed well in hot water to remove the saponin, a natural substance that protects it from birds and pests. Quinoa can be used in salads, pilaf, soups, casseroles, or can be ground into a flour for breads. Quinoa is small, flat and disc-shaped, ranging in color from yellow to orange, red, pink, purple and black. Quinoa is actually the fruit from an annual herb in the chenopodiaceae family. Quinoa goes well with all vegetables and beans. To cook, rinse with hot water in a strainer, then combine 1 cup quinoa with 2 cups distilled water in a saucepan. Bring to a boil, reduce heat and simmer about 15 minutes or until all water is absorbed.

Rolled oats - are hulled oats from which the bran has been removed. They have been steamed and flattened into flakes by large rollers and then baked. Rolled oats are thicker than quick-cooking oats and take longer to prepare. Quick-cooking oats often have added ingredients such as salt, caramel color, etc., and are more processed than rolled oats. We do not recommend quick-cooking oats. To cook rolled oats, boil 2 $\frac{1}{2}$ cups distilled water, add 1 cup rolled oats, stir for 2 minutes, cover and cook over low heat for about 15 minutes or until the water has been absorbed.

Rye – a cereal grass whose seeds are ground into flour.

Spelt – is a relative of wheat, but can be consumed by many people who are allergic to wheat. However, spelt is not gluton-free, and should not be consumed by anyone on a gluton-free diet. Spelt has been grown in the U.S. since the early 1900's. A grain of spelt looks very similar to a grain of hard wheat, but is not of the same biological composition. Spelt has a very high water solubility, which means the grain's nutrients can be absorbed quickly by the body. Spelt is also a good source of fiber and contains large amounts of vitamin B-17.

Whole wheat – flour made from the complete wheat kernel.

Condiments

Celtic Sea Salt- While we have earlier taken an position against the toxic effects of refined table salt, Celtic Sea Salt contains as little as 84 percent sodium chloride in the Light Grey variety and may be used in

moderation for those desiring a salt for seasoning. Celtic Salt is harvested by hand from the Celtic Sea north-west of France, is sun-dried and contains all of its natural occurring elements and contains no added chemicals. It is interesting that Dr. N. W. Walker, who is credited with developing the process of juicing vegetables and fruits, suggests in his book "Fresh Vegetable and Fruit Juices" that a specific salt that has not been subjected to high heat is a natural catalyst which the enzymes in the body can cause to be utilized constructively. The salt he refers to was only 90 to 95 percent sodium chloride and contained the natural occurring minerals. While this specific salt is no longer available, we find the Celtic Sea Salt to be a good option.

Herb Seasoning - ground herbs used to season salads, casseroles, etc. Can usually be purchased in health food stores. We especially like Frontier Herbs All-Purpose mix on steamed vegetables and rice dishes. Frontier Herbs also has an Italian and Oriental blend that make things real tasty. You can also make your own all-purpose herb seasoning. See recipes starting on page 312.

Lemon Juice - can be used in place of vinegar in most recipes.

Mayonnaise - commercial mayonnaise is made from eggs and oil, has many additives and is high in cholesterol. In your local health food store you should be able to find "mayonnaise" that is made without sugar or preservatives and is cholesterol free. However, even mayonnaise purchased in a Health Food store should be used sparingly because even these contain harmful ingredients.

Sea Vegetables

Seaweeds are extremely rich in vitamins including B-12 and minerals like iron and calcium. They are known to bond with radioactive substances, heavy metals and stagnated poisons and assist the body in eliminating them. Sea vegetables also increase the metabolic rate, purify the blood, assist the body with cleansing, help to dissolve fat and mucous and enhance the endocrine and nervous systems. When seaweed is used as a thickener in puddings and ice cream, it is usually listed in the ingredients under the name of carrageenan.

Dulse - a burgundy-colored sea lettuce. Wash and soak, and add to salads, Essene breads, vegetable dishes and seed loaves. (The Essenes, a religious group originally based in the Dead Sea region of Israel. They were a brotherhood of Jews in Palestine from the 2nd century B. C. to the 2nd century A. D. Historically, the Essenes were known for their raw vegetarian dietary philosophy, well developed wisdom, and remarkable longevity.) Can be washed and dried, then ground into a coarse powder and used as a seasoning in soups, dressings, sauces and salads.

Kelp - is the most popular of the sea vegetables and can be used as a salt substitute by simply sprinkling it on food after cooking. Sun dried kelp contains all known and even some unknown trace minerals on earth and is an excellent source of nutrients.

Kombu - is a wide-leafed deep sea vegetable that flourishes in cold northern waters. When Kombu is used for soaking and cooking with legumes, it enhances their digestibility. Kombu can also be used in soup stock to enhance the flavor. A rule of thumb is a half piece of Kombu per pound of dried beans. If the Kombu is covered with a fine white powder, it is still usable. The white powder is glutamate, which is a crystalline amino acid.

Nori - is sea algae that is pressed into sheets and has a sweet, delicate flavor. It can be crumbled and used as a garnish for many foods, or left whole and used to wrap raw veggies for a delicious live sandwich. When Nori is toasted, its color becomes bright green, as well as sweeter.

Wakame - is a pale green sea vegetable that is often found in Miso Soup to enhance the flavor. It can also be added to stews, marinaded dishes or salads. Just as Kombo softens the fiber of other foods it is added to, so does Wakame. Soak in distilled water 20 minutes to soften, rinse and chop into salads.

Recipes for Life … from God's Garden

Thickeners

Agar agar - is a gelatinous colloidal (a substance made up of small particles, too small to be seen under an optical microscope, yet too big to pass through a semipermeable membrane, that are suspended in the dispersed throughout a solid, liquid or gaseous medium) extractive of a red algae used as a gelling or stabilizing agent. Contains no calories and is a colorless, natural gelatin derived from a sea vegetable. Use to replace gelatin from animal sources – for example, to make aspics and fruit jellies. Agar agar is 75-percent carbohydrate (anything of a class of organic compounds composed of carbon, hydrogen and oxygen, including starches and sugars produced in green plants by photosynthesis) and is high in a type of fiber that passes through the body undigested, adding bulk to the diet and acts as a natural laxative. Agar agar comes in flakes, blocks or cakes. Use 1 teaspoon powder to $1/2$ cup distilled water or 2 tablespoons flakes to 2 cups of hot but not boiling liquid. When using flakes instead of powder use $1/6$ as much. If desiring to make jello-type "finger" treats, increase agar agar two to three times.

Vinegar and oxalic acid (found in cooked spinach) interfere with the gelling of agar. Fruit acids may also soften the gel, so experiment with fruit juices to see if more agar is required to achieve the amount of firmness you desire. When using citrus, tomato, or pineapple, increase the amount of agar agar by 50 percent.

Arrow Root Powder - is made from West Indian arrow root plant. Use as a thickener in place of cornstarch. Blend with a little liquid before adding to hot dishes to prevent clumps from forming. However, arrow root powder does not have to be heated to thicken. Store in a cool, dry place.

Oils

For life to be sustained, there are at least 50 essential nutrients required. These include alpha - linolenic acid, Omega 3 fatty acid, linoleic acid and Omega 6 fatty acid. Most fats consumed in America today are processed with high heat, which damages the finished product.

Hydrogenated fats are liquids that have been turned into solids and are extremely dangerous. Examples would be margarine and crisco. In our grandparents' day, butter and lard were the leading oils and fats consumed. The butter was made from raw, unpasteurized milk and rarely was salt added. Today, we have become aware that lard is very harmful to the human body, as is any other saturated fat.

Margarine and Crisco are extremely dangerous and should not be consumed. These hydrogenated fats are made by heating a liquid oil to an extremely high temperature and then pumping hydrogen gas through it until it hardens. It is then bleached, filtered and deodorized, producing an odorless, tasteless artificial fat that has the deadly effect of clogging arteries.

The process used converts the poly-unsaturated oil into a saturated fat! Saturated fats cause high cholesterol and clog arteries, which lead to heart attacks, strokes and cancer. The human body was not designed to digest these artificial, deadly poisons. Hydrogenated fat is also found in most peanut butter, and many baked and fried products.

The high heat involved in this process deranges the molecules, rendering them harmful to the body as they no longer fit properly into the cell wall. However, the body does need fat, and two of the best sources are first-pressing or extra virgin olive oil and flax seed oil.

Extra Virgin Olive Oil - first-pressing olive oil is cold-processed and the best oil to use for dressings or food preparation. The body can digest it, utilize it, and it adds a wonderful flavor. Extra virgin olive oil is a raw product made from the first pressing of the flesh of the fresh olive. If the label does not contain the words "extra virgin" before the words olive oil, it means the oil came from the seed of the olive and that a heat process was used. This form of olive oil is toxic to the body. Store in cool, dry place. If it is in a clear container, store inside a cabinet or cupboard so it is not exposed to light. Buy in small quantities unless you plan to use it often.

Flax Seed Oil - is a cold processed oil which provides the body with essential Omega 3 and Omega 6 oils. According to Udo Erasmus, in his book Fats that Heal, Fats that Kill, flax seed oil "is useful for those with cancer, inflammatory conditions, high triglycerides, cardio-vascular conditions, diabetes and other degenerative illnesses." For long-term use, Erasmus recommends a blended oil with a two to one ratio of the Omega 3 to Omega 6 fatty acids. In either case, you should purchase an organic oil or blend that has been expeller-pressed under 96 degrees so the enzymes remain intact. Find an organic oil or blend with no preservatives or additives. Don't use this oil for cooking. These oils need to be refrigerated after opening. We do not recommend fish oils, as they almost always contain chemical contaminants. Erasmus says, "for long term use," a blend of Omega 6-rich sunflower and sesame oils with flax oil will provide the best results for those who desire superior health."

Grape Seed Oil - is made from the seeds of grapes after the juice has been extracted for wine. It has a light nutty flavor that brings out the flavor of the foods, but without the heaviness of other oils, so it does not overwhelm foods or leave a greasy aftertaste. Grape seed oil will stay fresh without refrigeration because of its naturally high level of vitamin E. However, if refrigerated, it does not cloud like other oils. Using grapeseed oil provides two key nutrients in your diet: vitamin E and linoleic acid. Grapeseed oil has a high concentration (60-120 mg per 100 g of oil) of the antioxidant vitamin E. It is also a highly-concentrated source (75%) of linoleic acid, an essential fatty acid (EFA) also known as OMEGA-6. Grapeseed oil is naturally cholesterol-free. The Napa Valley Grapeseed Oil Company, based in Rutherford, California, makes their oil from California-grown grapes and uses a low-temperature direct screw press for extraction. This means that only a gentle mechanical method is used (no chemical solvents or alcohol), temperatures are kept low, and the environment is oxygen- and light-free to preserve the flavor and nutrients in the oil. It is excellent for salad dressings.

Walnut Oil - A light-colored speciality oil best used in cold sauces or dressings. It becomes bitter when heated.

Oil should not be heated. The best oils for using raw are organic flax seed oil and organic extra-virgin (or "first pressing") olive oil purchased in dark glass containers rather than pliable plastic containers, which leach the solvent toluene into the contents.

Just a reminder, there are two types of fat, saturated and unsaturated. The difference between the two are:

Saturated fats are those that harden at room temperature. They also harden in the body. Saturated fats are found in animal products, coconut and palm kernel oils. These fats cause your cardiovascular system a great deal of problems and should be avoided.

Unsaturated fats are fats that are liquid at room temperature. There are two types of unsaturated fat; monosaturated which is olive and almond oil; and polyunsaturated fats, which are found in corn, safflower, and cotton seed oils.

All saturated fats are very harmful and not recommended for human consumption. Polyunsaturated fats are also harmful.

Dried Fruits

Dried Fruits - buy organic, unsulphured, sun-dried fruits, which will usually be darker in color than those which have been treated with sulphur dioxide, but the taste is wonderful. Organic raisins have none of the harmful sprays that regular raisins do. Regular raisins are sprayed with harmful chemicals then left in the sun to dry, causing those toxic chemicals to be concentrated in the raisins. Dehydrated tomatoes and sun-dried tomatoes would also fit in this category and can be used in any recipe calling for tomatoes. (See page 298) Organic dehydrated fruits can usually be found in health food stores and by mail order. We stay away from commercially grown and processed dried fruits because they contain too many toxins. Consume dehydrated fruits in small quantities as they contain highly concentrated sugars. We must always be aware of the fact that concentrated sugars, even from a natural source, can be a problem to our bodies if consumed in too large a quantity at any one time. Dehydrated fruits are best when reconstituted with distilled water and allowed to soak until softened.

Sweeteners

The pancreas cannot differentiate between the sugar that is naturally present in fruits and vegetables, as opposed to concentrated forms of sugar, such as white sugar, honey, maple syrup and molasses. Honey, maple syrup and molasses are more natural, less processed, less potent and less harmful than white sugar, but still should be used sparingly.

Honey - raw, unfiltered, unpasteurized honey can be purchased from local bee keepers or at natural food stores. The mildest are clover and wildflower. This is another concentrated sugar and should only be used sparingly.

Maple Syrup - made from the sap of maple trees. Look for organic maple syrup as most of the commercial suppliers now use formaldehyde in their processing. Maple syrup is a delicious sweetener, but contains very concentrated amounts of sugar and thus should also be consumed in very small amounts.

Molasses - is a residual product of sugar refining and contains only minimal nutrients. Unsulphured molasses is best - use with discretion.

Apple Juice - should always be organic and freshly extracted in your own juicing machine. Commercial apple juice contains many toxins, and even bottled apple juice from an organic source has been pasteurized, thus killing the enzymes and most of the nutritional value. Apple juice as well as all fruit juices contain concentrated sugars and should be consumed only in small amounts.

Substitutions for 3/4 cup of sugar would be any of the following: 1/2 cup of honey, or 1/4 cup of molasses, or 1/2 cup fruit concentrate, or 2 cups of apple juice, or 1/2 cup maple syrup. It is important to remember when replacing sugar with a concentrated sweetener to reduce the liquid in the recipe by 1/4. If there is no liquid in the recipe, add 4 tablespoons of flour for each 3/4 cup of concentrate. When using ***concentrated sweeteners*** instead of sugar, use sparingly. For instance it takes 40 gallons of sap to make one gallon of syrup.

Seasonings

Cayenne - does not contain the harmful properties that white and black pepper do, but still should be used sparingly.

Celtic Sea Salt - Celtic Sea Salt is free of any processing, is dried only by the hot summer sun and wind, and harvested by salt farmers who gather it from the marshes. Its gray color is attributed to the pure clay of the basins, which ionizes the many minerals in the salt, making it richer in electrolytes. Use sparingly.

Nutritional Yeast - is usually golden or bright yellow in color, but it can be a dull yellow-brown. ***Do not confuse with baker's yeast which should never be consumed raw or brewer's yeast, which has a bitter taste.*** Nutritional yeast is 50 percent protein, and comes in powder or flakes. Nutritional yeast adds a rather cheesey taste to dishes in which it is used. Add toward the end of cooking time. Can be used on salads, in soups, main dishes or sauces. Nutritional yeast is a good source of several B vitamins, including B_{12}.

Tahini - made from ground sesame seeds. When made from raw sesame seeds and cold processed, tahini has most of the nutritional value of the sesame seeds remaining intact. It contains vitamins, minerals, protein and essential fatty acids that the body needs. Can be used in sauces, dressings, dips, etc.

Vegetable Seasoning - dried vegetables ground into a seasoning that can be used to season many dishes.

Honey - The color and flavor of honey depend on where bees harvest their nectar. Expect light color and mild flavor and aroma from clover, orange blossom, and sourwood honeys. Buckwheat honey boasts a full bodied flavor and deep color.

When you substitute honey for sugar in a recipe, reduce any liquid by 1/4 cup and add 1/2 teaspoon baking soda for each cup of honey used. Also reduce the oven temperature by 25 degrees to prevent over-browning.

As an ingredient, honey absorbs and retains moisture, which helps delay drying out of baked goods.

Store honey at room temperature. If it crystallizes, remove lid and place the jar in a container of warm water until the crystals dissolve.

For easy removal, coat measuring cup with vegetable cooking spray before measuring honey. Honey can be toxic for infants under one year of age.

Baking Needs

Flour - We recommend using whole grain, organically grown flour that has been stone ground. Store in the refrigerator or freezer to help preserve freshness. Remember, however, that even if you buy organic grains and grind them into a flour just before mixing of ingredients, when you place that bread dough into a 350-degree oven, most of the nutrients will be destroyed by the heat. Whole grain flour products taste good and contain fiber and fuel for the body, but leave much to be desired as far as nutritional value is concerned.

Soy Products

Braggs Liquid Aminos-Hallelujah Acres promoted the use of Bragg's Liquid Aminos until recent research revealed that it's use may be potentially harmful.

Textured Vegetable Protein (TVP) is made from soy flour which is cooked under pressure and forced into different sizes and shapes. TVP is lower in fat than tofu and can be used to replace it in many recipes. TVP will keep for a long time in a tight container. It contains no cholesterol, a minimal amount of fat and no sodium. TVP can be rehydrated easily for use in soups, stews, sauces and casseroles. To reconstitute, add an equal part of boiling liquid. I usually use tomato juice but 1 or 2 teaspoons of Celtic Sea Salt and a pinch of your favorite herb mixture in distilled water can also be used.

Tofu - is made from fermented bean curd from soybeans. It is white in appearance and has very little taste; however, it takes on the flavor of whatever it is mixed with. Tofu is a refrigerated item that comes packed in water, and must be drained before use. Tofu can be baked, braised, broiled, marinaded or steamed. For most purposes, "firm" tofu is preferred because the soft type crumbles easily.

Meat Analogs made from soybeans. They are concentrated protein but have many harmful ingredients added. We do not consider them fit for human consumption, because they cause many physical problems – similar to those experienced by consumers of animal products.

Note: Soy products are concentrated protein and should be used only occasionally.

Nuts and Seeds are also high in fat and protein, so use sparingly.

Recipes for Life ... from God's Garden

The Hallelujah Diet differs from most vegetarian diets because we emphasize the importance of raw fruits and vegetables and teach that the use of nuts, seeds, sprouts and grains should be minimized. As you will notice from the Hallelujah Acres Healthy Foods Pyramid," found on page 65, nuts and seeds are very high in fat and protein. The body has difficulty digesting these high fat and protein items and they should not be eaten in large quantities on a regular basis. Moderation should be the rule. ***High fat and high protein foods cause problems for the digestive system and for those fighting cancer. Excessive fat and protein can actually feed the cancer.***

If you do eat seeds and nuts, it is best to soak them 24 hours prior to consuming. To soak: place seeds or nuts in a container, add enough distilled water to cover. Place towel over bowl and allow to sit on the counter overnight. Drain (save soaking water for other recipes, if desired) and rinse thoroughly. This starts to break down the protein making them easier to digest. Almonds are the best of the nuts while sunflower seeds are the best of the seeds.

The Gerson Clinic in Tijuana, Mexico found that occasionally, some patients were not doing well after leaving their clinic. Upon researching to discover what was causing the problem, they discovered that some patients were consuming large amounts of alfalfa sprouts. When the patients were taken off the sprouts, their health was restored.

Legumes

Legumes fall into the similar category as nuts and seeds because they are seeds that will sprout. Legumes should be soaked 24 hours prior to being used in any recipe to begin the sprouting process. Sprouting legumes will not only shorten their cooking time but it will help to eliminate intestinal gas. Another suggestion would be to add half of a piece of Kombu to the water while cooking the beans to increase their digestibility.

Peanuts – which are a legume rather than a nut – are dangerously high in protein and fat and very difficult to digest. The protein in peanuts cannot be assimilated by the human body, and should be avoided. Peanuts and peanut butter are not healthy foods. Commercial peanut butter is a very harmful product as it not only contains ***roasted*** peanuts, but also sugar, hydrogenated oil and salt. Almond butter is a very good substitute for peanut butter.

*"Unhulled sesame seeds contain ten times more calcium than cow's milk; one and a half times more iron than beef liver; more protein than chicken, beef liver or beef steak; three times more phosphorus than eggs; and more niacin than whole wheat bread." – USDA Composition of Foods Handbook #8

Herbs

Herbs can replace salt and pepper and make your meals delightful; however, it is important to remember they are to add sparkle to your dishes, not to bury the natural flavor of the food! Following are a few of the herbs and how you might use them in your kitchen:

Basil - Sweet and full flavor - improves the flavor of pasta, salads, soups and dressings. Also good with tomatoes, eggplant, squash, mushrooms, etc. Fresh is best. Used in many Italian recipes. Basil is easy to grow with both green and purple varieties available.

Bay Leaves - Fragrant and pungent - Add depth and a sweet peppery scent - use in soups, stews, sauces and tomato dishes. Crushed bay leaves, tied in cheese cloth, may be stored with grains to help repel insects.

Cardamom - Enhances the flavor of vegetables such as sweet potatoes, pumpkin and winter squash.

138

Recipes for Life ... from God's Garden

Used in Middle Eastern and Scandinavian dishes. Member of the ginger family with a sweetly pungent aromatic flavor.

Chervil - Aromatic herb used in soups, stews and salad greens. Use like parsley. It has a similar flavor, but milder. Used in French recipes. Add at end of cooking time to preserve flavor.

Chives - Similar to the taste of scallions, only milder. Use with potatoes, tomatoes, mushrooms, steamed vegetables, grains, dips, spreads, herb butters, etc.

Cilantro - With its unique flavor, cilantro cannot be substituted for other herbs. Used in East Indian, Central and South American and Asian dishes. Much stronger dried than fresh. Cilantro is made from the leaf of the coriander plant. Note: According to recent studies, raw cilantro helps to remove mercury from brain cells.

Coriander - Made from coriander seeds and has a nutty flavor with a delightful aroma, tastes like lemon peel and sage blend. Use with cauliflower, mushrooms, rice, in stir fry, curry sauce and salads. It is dominant, so use sparingly. Use in Mexican dishes.

Cumin - Member of parsley family made from the seed and gives aromatic taste to stews, vegetables, Mexican and Indian cooking. It has a warm, robust flavor. Use sparingly. Used in curry and chilies.

Dill - Aromatic foliage and seeds. Use with potatoes, tomatoes, cucumbers, mushrooms, in sauces, dips, dressings and salads. Add at the end of cooking because flavor fades quickly when heated.

Garlic - Whole garlic in soups and sauces. It gives a unique fragrance and flavor which can easily become overpowering. The flavor of garlic when sautéed is half as strong as pressed garlic. Raw garlic is the strongest flavor. 1/8 tsp. of powder equals 1 tsp. of fresh. Garlic becomes bitter if burned.

Ginger - Pungent hot and spicy flavor, golden color. Use root in stir-fries or other middle eastern dishes. Grate or mince finely. Leaves can be used in soups. Powdered ginger is used for baking.

Marjoram - Member of the mint family. Sweet herb with mild flavor, best added toward the end of cooking time in soups, stews, salad dressings and stuffing. Also goes well with tomatoes and onions.

Mints - There are many kinds of mint: peppermint, pineapple mint, chocolate mint, orange mint, spearmint, etc. They make wonderful herb teas and enhance the flavor of beets, carrots, grains, peas, potatoes, pilafs, chutney, stir-fries, sauces, dips, dressings. Mints go well with other herbs.

Oregano - Strong, similar to marjoram. Use sparingly with basil, garlic, and extra virgin olive oil, tomatoes or potatoes, eggplant, summer squash, in marinades, herb vinegars, pizza, Greek and Italian dishes. Oregano is a member of the mint family.

Parsley - Mild flavor. Use with cauliflower, lima beans, summer squash, potatoes, pilafs, tabouli, dips, marinades, soups, stews, sauces and pasta. It blends well with most other herbs and makes a nice garnish.

Rosemary - Aromatic shrubby mint with a strong pine taste. Use with cauliflower, lemon, mushrooms, parsnips, peas, potatoes, tomatoes, in marinades, soups, stews, etc. Use sparingly as it can easily dominate.

Sage - Aromatic and spicy. Use with beans, grains, pasta, potatoes, stews, dressings, soups, sauces and marinades. Can be domineering, so use sparingly.

Savory - Aromatic, grass-like smell, with a mild peppery flavor - assertive. Use with green beans, salads, cabbage and soups.

Tarragon - Use in salads and with vegetables. Fresh tarragon has a taste similar to licorice. Great alone or mixed with parsley, chives and chervil.

Thyme - Heavy aroma and spicy taste. Use with asparagus, carrots, eggplant, leeks, mushrooms, nutmeg, onions, parsley, peas, potatoes, tomatoes, soups, stews, sauces, herb butters, marinades and bean dishes.

Turmeric - Member of ginger family native to India and SE Asia. Adds a mild, slightly musty flavor and yellow color to curries and rice dishes.

When buying spices in the market place, be sure they are non-irradiated (they should be labeled).

For soups and stews, if not using soup stock, tie the following herbs in a bag: 1 Bay Leaf, 1 tsp. each fresh thyme, parsley, marjoram, sage and rosemary or your favorite herbs. Remove before serving.

Instead of salt, use Celtic Sea Salt or try combining fresh herbs such as parsley, chives, chervil and tarragon.

Part II

Recipes for Life

The Five-Star System

As stated earlier, my goal is to set before you a simpler, healthier lifestyle. To assist you in attaining that goal, you will find the five-star system throughout the recipe section of this book. The following key will assist you in understanding this system and working toward the goal of healthier meals for your family.

☆☆☆☆☆

Recipes with five stars are all-raw and properly combined. These five-star recipes are foods that have been shown to have a profound health-producing effect on people who consume them on a regular basis. These foods should be consumed daily. It is these foods that provide the nutrients to strengthen our immune systems, which help to prevent or heal all disease. Our bodies were designed by God to be self-healing, and these five-star recipes are properly and deliciously-combined foods containing the nutrients, in their simplest, raw form – as God created them – that help this self-healing to work.

☆☆☆☆

Recipes with four stars are all raw, but not properly combined. These are still excellent recipes, but should not be consumed as often as five star recipes.

☆☆☆

Recipes with three stars are the cooked, but properly combined recipes. They can be consumed every day as part of the 15 to 25 percent cooked portion of the evening meal.

☆☆

Recipes with two stars are cooked, but not properly combined recipes. They should be consumed less frequently than the three star recipes for that 15 to 25 percent cooked food portion of the evening meal.

☆

Recipes with only one star are cooked recipes with ingredients that should be used sparingly, such as tofu, TVP, honey or maple syrup. These recipes would usually be used sparingly.

An example of a recipe that would earn no stars – and would not even be included in this book – is a recipe that includes substances that have been shown to cause disease, such as meat (including fish and chicken), dairy, eggs, sugar, salt or chemical preservatives.

Abbreviations:

tsp. = teaspoon   Tbsp. = tablespoon

Using a juicer, blender, food processor or Vita-Mix

Many of the recipes in this book call for the use of either a juicer, blender, food processor or Vita-Mix to process certain ingredients. These are all great machines to have, but the most essential and adaptable among the four is a good juicer, such as the Green Star or Champion. (Here at Hallelujah Acres we sell juicers and recommend the Green Star.)

For certain recipes, you will find there is some interchangeability among a juicer, blender, food processor and Vita-Mix. For example, if you want to puree apples to make apple sauce, any one of the four machines may be used. But if you want to juice the apples to make apple juice, only a juicer will work for this purpose.

Keep in mind that if you are pureeing food, everything you put through the machine will come out together. So you should remove the seeds and core of the apple before pureeing it to make apple sauce. On the other hand, if you are juicing an apple to make apple juice, you may put the core and seeds through the juicer because a juicer separates the pulp from the juice. The solid part of the apple core and seeds will be expelled with the pulp, while certain nutrients (such as pectin in the seeds) will be included in the juice.

To use a Champion juicer to puree food, install the solid "blank" plate instead of the screen. (The screen allows the juice to be filtered through underneath, while the pulp is expelled through the end of the juicer; whereas using the solid plate directs all the pureed food out the end of the juicer.) The Green Star juicer may be used to puree food in a similar manner, but it includes two different plates for this purpose. (See the Green Star manual that comes with the Juicer for more details.)

To make nut butters, (see Almond Butter, page 284) you may use either a Green Star or Champion juicer, but not a food processor or blender.

To coarse or fine chop vegetables, you may use a blender, Vita-Mix or food processor. (If you are using a blender or Vita-Mix, add just enough water to cover the vegetables, then turn the machine on and off until the desired consistency is reached. Place chopped vegetables through a strainer to drain the water.)

Chapter Thirteen:

Fruit Salads

A fruit lunch is ideal and can be as simple as eating an apple, banana and a few dates or a couple of oranges or a bunch of grapes; however, many prefer fruit salads, so following are some ideas to help you get started.

Blueberry, Strawberry, Banana Salad

☆ ☆ ☆ ☆

1 pint of blueberries	1 pint of strawberries
3 bananas	

Wash berries. Slice strawberries and bananas and put into bowl. Add blueberries. No dressing required for this delightful fruit combo. Serve on a bed of leaf lettuce if you like.

Fruit Delight

☆ ☆ ☆ ☆ ☆

4 bananas	1 $\frac{1}{2}$ cup green grapes
3 nectarines	2 peaches
2 pears	$\frac{3}{4}$ cup organic raisins

Soak raisins for 30 minutes in distilled water and drain. Peel and slice bananas, nectarines, peaches and pears. Cut grapes in half, combine all ingredients and mix well. Option: Top with a sauce made by blending approximately 2 cups of the fruit with the soaked raisins.

Apple / Kiwi Salad

☆ ☆ ☆ ☆

3 Red Delicious apples	3 Yellow Delicious apples
3 bananas	3 kiwis
1/2 cup organic apple juice	1 cup fresh pineapple

Peel apples, core and slice in small slices. Peel and slice kiwis, slice bananas, and cut pineapple into small pieces. Add apple juice, mix well, cover and refrigerate. Serve chilled.

Mixed Fruit Salad

☆ ☆ ☆ ☆ ☆

8 dates	3 ripe bananas
2 apples (Red or Yellow Delicious)	2 ripe pears
3/4 cup organic raisins	1/2 cup organic apple juice

Peel apples, pears, and bananas. Cut all fruit into small pieces, add raisins, pour apple juice over the fruit, cover and refrigerate. Serve chilled. Freshly grated or unsweetened coconut flakes may be added if desired.

I create the fruit of the lips;
Peace, peace to him that is far off,
and to him that is near,
saith the Lord;
and I will heal him.
– Isaiah 57:19

Avocado Fruit Salad
☆ ☆ ☆ ☆

1 banana   ½ avocado
4 dates   ¼ cup organic raisins
¼ cup organic apple juice

Soak raisins in organic apple juice 30 minutes. Peel and slice banana, peel and dice avocado and cut dates into small pieces. Combine all ingredients in a bowl and enjoy. No dressing is required.

Apple Salad
☆ ☆ ☆ ☆

3 celery ribs   2 Red Delicious apples
1 pear   1 Yellow Delicious apple
¾ cup seedless grapes *   ½ cup pecans
1 lemon   1 orange

* May substitute chopped dates for grapes

Chop celery fine and put into a bowl. Peel and chop apples and pears into small pieces, juice lemon and orange and pour over apples and pears to keep them from turning brown. Stir to coat all fruit, allow to stand for 10 minutes and then drain, saving the juice. While soaking, mince pecans.

Add chopped apples and pear to celery, grapes (or chopped dates) and half of the minced pecans. Toss to mix ingredients. Make a dressing by combining the other half of the pecans into blender along with the juice drained from the fruit and puree into a nut butter sauce. Add to salad and mix to blend all flavors. Serve on a bed of leaf lettuce.

Peach Delight
☆ ☆ ☆ ☆ ☆

2 peaches   2 apricots
2 nectarines   ½ pint of strawberries

Wash and halve berries, peel and slice peaches, nectarines, and apricots. Arrange on a bed of red tipped leaf lettuce. No dressing required.

Citrus Salad

☆ ☆ ☆ ☆ ☆

2 oranges	2 tangerines
1 tangelo	1 grapefruit
½ pineapple	1 pint strawberries

Peel and segment oranges, tangerines, tangelo and grapefruit and cut them into smaller pieces. Cut pineapple into cubes, slice strawberries and put all ingredients into a bowl. If additional liquid is needed for dressing, juice two oranges and pour over the salad before serving.

Pineapple Boats

☆ ☆ ☆ ☆

¾ cup fresh coconut or unsweetened coconut	3 bananas
1 pint of strawberries	1 pineapple

Wash strawberries. Slice pineapple lengthwise, remove the core from each half, cut out the pineapple and cut into bite-size pieces. Place in a bowl and set aside. Slice strawberries and bananas, and shred the coconut. Mix strawberries, bananas and half of the coconut and fill pineapple halves. Top with the rest of the shredded coconut to serve.

Diced Fruit Salad

☆ ☆ ☆ ☆

1 kiwi	1 mango
1 papaya	2 bananas
1 pint strawberries	

Slice kiwi and berries, dice papaya, mangos and bananas and serve on a bed of leaf lettuce. No dressing required.

Strawberry, Nectarine, Blueberry Salad

☆ ☆ ☆ ☆

2 cups fresh strawberries	2 ripe nectarines
2 cups fresh blueberries	1 1/2 Tbsp. agar agar
1/2 cup apple juice	1/4 cup shredded unsweetened coconut
2 ripe bananas	1 3/4 cup apple sauce

Mix apple juice with agar agar and heat gently until dissolved, stirring constantly. Set aside to cool. Wash, hull and slice strawberries, wash blueberries, and peel and slice nectarines. Set aside.

In a blender combine 2 ripe bananas and 1 3/4 cups of apple sauce, and blend until smooth. Combine with agar agar / apple juice mixture, add coconut, and pour over fruit. Mix gently. Pour into bundt pan or other decorative ring and chill until set.

Grape Salad

☆ ☆ ☆ ☆ ☆

1 apple
1 peach
2 bananas
1/4 cup of organic raisins
3 cups of mixed seedless grapes such as Concord, Red Flame or Thompson

Wash grapes and cut in half, peel and dice apple and peach, cut banana into quarters and slice. Combine all fruits in a bowl to serve. No dressing required.

Ambrosia Salad

☆ ☆ ☆ ☆

3 bananas	juice of 1/2 of lemon
2 oranges	3/4 cup seedless grapes
1/2 cup chopped dates	
1/2 cup freshly grated or unsweetened coconut	

Peel and slice bananas, peel and dice oranges, chop dates, halve and add grapes, sprinkle with lemon juice and chill. Grate coconut. To serve, place on a lettuce leaf and sprinkle with coconut.

Apple, Pear Molded Salad

☆ ☆ ☆ ☆

2 cups apple juice	2 Tbsp. agar agar
2 ripe pears	3 apples
1/2 cup raisins	1/2 cup pecans
1 tsp. lemon juice	

Gently heat agar agar in apple juice to dissolve, stirring constantly. Set aside to cool. Peel and chop pears and apples, chop pecans and add rest of ingredients to bowl. Pour cooled juice mixture over fruit and then pour fruit salad into bundt pan and chill until set.

Fruit Plate

☆ ☆ ☆ ☆

The difference between most fruit salads and a fruit plate is the size of the fruit and how it is served. In fruit salads the pieces are cut considerably smaller than those served on a fruit plate.

When making a fruit plate that contains avocado, brush it with lemon juice so that it will maintain its color and freshness. Normally a half avocado is considered a serving. If serving nuts or seeds – such as almonds, pecans, sunflower or pumpkin seeds – on the fruit plate, omit the avocado because these two sources of protein do not digest well together.

Celery and lettuce may be served with any fruit (except melons) and can be used with the following suggestions:

Apple, celery and grapes. Peel apple if not organically grown, and slice. Add celery sticks, bunches of washed grapes of different varieties for color. Serve on a bed of leaf lettuce.

Avocado and citrus. Peel avocado, oranges and grapefruit. (I prefer pink grapefruit.) Cut the citrus in rounds and the avocado in slices. Place on a plate that has romaine or other leaf lettuce as a bed.

Avocado and banana. Peel avocado and banana, slice and serve on a bed of leaf lettuce. For variety, try adding freshly sliced pears.

Kiwi, mango, papaya, strawberries, bananas. Slice all fruits and serve on a bed of romaine or other leaf lettuce.

Eat melons alone or leave them alone; however, a lovely melon plate comprised of slices of different melons can be served. Select any of the following melons: Watermelon, Crenshaw, Honeydew melon, Casaba melon, Cantaloupe, etc. served in slices or make a melon bowl by using a melon ball tool. Either one makes an attractive meal.

A fruit bar can make a delightful lunch. If in doubt which foods digest well together, see food combining chart on page 68-69.

Berry Salad
☆ ☆ ☆ ☆ ☆

Wash and gently mix together 1 ½ cups of each of your favorite berries. For instance, blueberries, raspberries, strawberries or blackberries. Serve plain or make a sauce by pureeing part of the berries together in a blender.

Melon Ball Salad
☆ ☆ ☆ ☆ ☆

1 medium cantaloupe	½ watermelon
1 medium honey dew melon	½ crenshaw melon
½ Casaba Melon	Any other melon available

Select the ripest melons available for this salad and plan to make it the whole meal. A melon ball tool is essential for making perfect melon balls. When all the balls have been made, place them all in the watermelon rind you have left to serve. If you don't have a melon ball tool, just cut the melons in uniform cubes to make this delightful salad.

Hint: Melon balls can be made from any melons that are available if the ones listed are not available in your area.

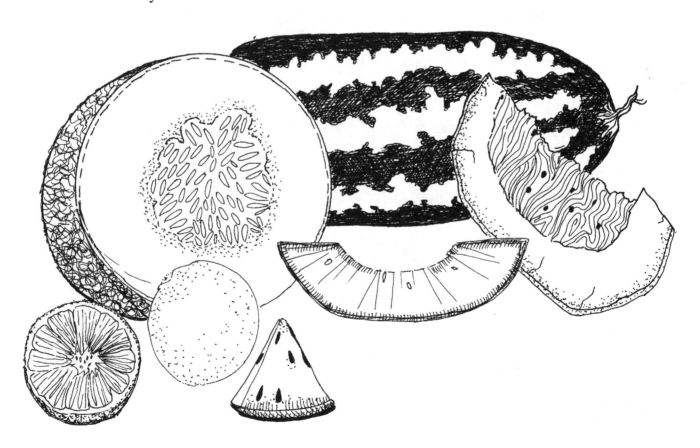

Chapter Fourteen:

Vegetable Salads

Broccoli & Cauliflower Salad
☆ ☆ ☆ ☆ ☆

try

1 bunch of broccoli   ½ head of cauliflower
2 stalks celery   ¼ cup pine nuts
¼ cup pecans   1 small onion
12 cherry tomatoes

Wash all vegetables. Chop broccoli and cauliflower into florets, dice celery, finely chop the onion, halve the tomatoes, coarsely chop the pecans and place ingredients in a large bowl and mix well. Squeeze the juice of one lemon over top and sprinkle with pine nuts. Serve on leaf lettuce.

Raw Stuffed Peppers
☆ ☆ ☆ ☆ ☆

1 red bell pepper for each person   2 celery stalks
1 large avocado   2 tomatoes
2 scallions   ½ cup grated cabbage

Wash pepper, remove top, ribs, and seeds. Set aside. Grate cabbage, finely chop celery, dice tomatoes, chop scallions, mash the avocado, combine all chopped vegetables and stuff pepper.

Hallelujah Acres Vegetable Salad

☆ ☆ ☆ ☆ ☆

Start with green leaf lettuce and/or other greens like spinach, kale or endive. ***Never use iceberg lettuce (head lettuce) because it has very little nutritional value.*** Make sure the lettuce is washed well and completely drained. This can be accomplished by using a salad spinner or by washing and loosely rolling in a dry towel and placing in the refrigerator to chill while chopping the rest of the vegetables. (Never use paper towels for drying; some are coated with formaldehyde.)

While the greens are crisping in the refrigerator, clean and prepare the rest of the vegetables. After all vegetables are prepared, you are ready to build your salad. First remove the greens from the refrigerator and tear into small, bite-sized pieces. Fill the bowl half full of greens, then add layers of the following vegetables:

Small broccoli florets   Finely chopped *sweet* onion or scallions (if desired)
Small cauliflower florets   Finely diced red or yellow peppers *
Finely diced celery   Peel and chop ½ avocado **
Top with grated California carrots

* **Hint:** green peppers are actually red peppers that have not yet ripened.
** Omit avocado for people with cancer, because excess fat and protein can be a problem.

Wonderful just plain or with a squeeze of lemon juice or top with your favorite dressing (not from the super market, as they are full of sugar and preservatives) and enjoy.

There is no end to the variety you can have in your salads. Don't be afraid to experiment. You might like to omit any of the above or add any of the following to change the flavor of your salad: Raw asparagus, raw corn off the cob, raw grated or cubed summer squash, raw grated or cubed sweet potatoes, cucumbers, cherry tomatoes, grated cabbage, Bok Choy, parsnips, radishes, turnips, beets, rutabaga, snow peas, zucchini, eggplant, chopped chives, etc. Sunflower seeds, raw grated or slivered almonds may be added for texture.

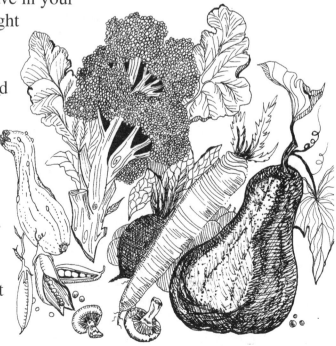

George and I share a large salad as part of our evening meal. Our salad is the main part of the meal, thus very large, usually filling a regular serving bowl.

Hallelujah Acres Blended Salad

☆ ☆ ☆ ☆ ☆

try

One of George's favorite ways to fix a salad is to blend it into a coarse or fine cold soup. He learned this method of preparing salads at the Shangri-La Health Resort in Florida. There it was used for people who had difficulty chewing or digesting raw foods. However, this is a nice variation for anyone, including children. As the name denotes, this salad does require a blender. Here is the way to prepare it:

Gather:

1 medium tomato	2 cups leaf lettuce or greens
1/4 cucumber	1 stalk of celery
1/2 ripe avocado	1/4 tsp. Celtic Sea Salt (optional)
1/4 cup broccoli florets	1/4 cup cauliflower florets
1/2 tsp. herb seasoning	

Blend tomato, cucumber, avocado, Celtic Sea Salt and seasoning to make the dressing. Then add the remainder of the ingredients to the blender except the celery. As you push the veggies down into the blades with celery stalk, quickly turn the blender on and off until all the veggies are mixed into the dressing. Then continue turning the blender on and off until desired consistency is reached. If the dressing is too dry, a *little* distilled water may be added. (If you turn your blender on and leave it on instead of pulsing it on and off rapidly, your salad will be too fine.)

The dressing part of this salad can be used on a vegetable salad as well.

Hint: People dealing with cancer should omit the avocado because of its high fat.

Asparagus Salad

☆ ☆ ☆ ☆ ☆

2 pounds of asparagus	1 bunch of Romaine lettuce
3 medium tomatoes	2 stalks of celery
1 stalk of bok choy	1 red pepper

Wash and dry vegetables, tear lettuce and place in bowl, add asparagus, which should be young tender stalks cut into bite-size pieces. Add chopped tomatoes, diced bok choy stalk, celery and red pepper. Toss to combine. A raw dressing can be made by removing 1/3 of the salad and placing it in a blender, blend until creamy. Sprinkle with grated almonds.

Broccoli Mix
☆ ☆ ☆ ☆ ☆

try

2 cups of broccoli florets	1 cup cucumber
1 medium tomato, cubed	1 sweet onion
1 red bell pepper, sliced	1 stalk of celery

Wash vegetables, cut broccoli florets, cube tomato and slice red pepper. Peel and chop cucumber, chop onion fine, dice celery then combine. Prepare a dressing by placing 1 peeled medium tomato in the blender, adding $1/3$ of a cup of sunflower seeds and blending until creamy. To serve, make a bed of fresh leaf lettuce greens, add a layer of vegetables, top with fresh dressing and add a sprinkle of sunflower seeds, if desired.

Vegetable Plate
☆ ☆ ☆ ☆ ☆

2 or 3 celery ribs cut into thirds	1 cucumber, peeled and sliced into rounds
2 broccoli heads, cut into florets	1 red bell pepper, cut into strips
1 yellow squash, sliced into rounds	1 yellow bell pepper, cut into strips
1 cauliflower head, cut into florets	1 kohlrabi, sliced into rounds
2 or 3 carrots, cut into sticks	

Arrange on leaf lettuce lined plate. Serve with one or more bowls of your favorite dressings as dips. See Chapter 16, page 175 "Delightful Dressings".

Sunshine Carrot Salad
☆ ☆ ☆ ☆

try

3 cups carrot	1 Red Delicious apple
$1/2$ cup organic raisins	1 stalk of celery

Peel and grate apple and carrots, and finely chop celery. Combine all ingredients above in a bowl and toss. Mix in the following dressing:

1 Red Delicious Apple	$1/2$ cup almonds
2 cups grated carrot	fresh apple juice or distilled water

In a blender, chop $1/2$ cup of almonds, add 1 Red Delicious apple, peeled and cored and 2 cups of grated carrot; blend until creamy. Add a small amount of distilled water or fresh apple juice to reach consistency desired.

Hallelujah Acres Cabbage Salad

☆ ☆ ☆ ☆

2 large apples
2 cups green cabbage
1/2 cup organic raisins

1 cup carrots,
2 stalks of celery

Grate apples, carrots, cabbage, chop celery and add raisins. Delicious plain or the following dressing may be added:

Combine and mix well:

1/4 cup Rhonda's No Oil Dressing (page 175)
1/2 tsp. dried onion
2 Tbsp. raw unfiltered honey

1/2 tsp. minced garlic
2 – 3 Tbsp. organic apple juice

Hint: Organic raisins have none of the harmful sprays that regular raisins do. Regular raisins are sprayed with harmful chemicals then left in the sun to dry, causing those toxic chemicals to be concentrated in the raisins.

Pea Salad

☆ ☆ ☆ ☆

Submitted by Edie Dalson

1 quart shelled peas
1/2 cup Rhonda's No-Oil Dressing (page 175)
Romaine lettuce leaves
2 cups cauliflower

1 green onion
1 cup Almond Cheese Sauce
      (See page 284)
1 cup slivered almonds

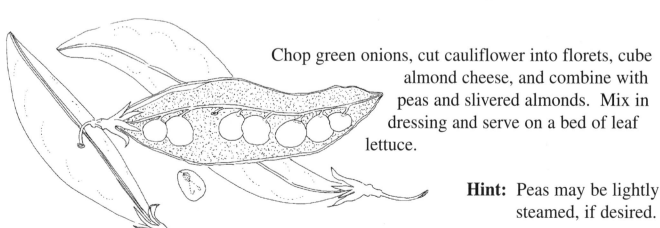

Chop green onions, cut cauliflower into florets, cube almond cheese, and combine with peas and slivered almonds. Mix in dressing and serve on a bed of leaf lettuce.

Hint: Peas may be lightly steamed, if desired.

Stacked Salad
☆ ☆ ☆ ☆ ☆

try

On a plate, place a bed of romaine lettuce or other salad greens, and add layers of the following:

large sliced tomatoes
avocado, optional
summer squash rounds
cucumber rounds
red pepper rings
yellow pepper rings
Top with grated carrot

Dressing may be added if you feel the need, but this salad is delicious without anything added.

Delightful Beet Salad
☆ ☆ ☆ ☆ ☆

try

4 large beets	1 rutabaga * /carrot
1 red onion	1 stalk of celery

Peel beets and rutabaga, cut into matchsticks, mince onion and chop celery. Mix together and top with dressing if desired.
* Carrot may be substituted for rutabaga.

Great Grated Salad
☆ ☆ ☆ ☆ ☆

try

Grate ¾ cup of each of the following vegetables and arrange them in pleasing design on a lettuce leaf and or spinach lined plate or plater:

beets	carrots
pumpkin or yellow squash	broccoli florets
cauliflower florets	red cabbage or beet
sweet potatoes	summer squash

Garnish with carrot and celery strips, chopped chives, sliced radishes or whatever other vegetable you desire. Serve with your favorite dressing.

Marinaded Broccoli, Cauliflower Salad
☆ ☆ ☆ ☆ ☆

try

2 cups of broccoli florets	1 cup cauliflower florets
2 medium carrots	½ cup onion
1 medium tomato (diced)	

Cut broccoli and cauliflower into florets, cut carrots in ¼-inch circles and thinly slice onion. Place all vegetables in a bowl. Make a marinade by placing the following in a blender:

3 Tbsp. extra virgin olive oil	1 Tbsp. fresh lemon juice
½ tsp. garlic powder	½ tsp. Celtic Sea Salt (optional)
1 Tbsp. toasted sesame seeds	1 Tbsp. Italian seasoning

Blend all but Italian seasoning and toasted sesame seeds until smooth. Pour over vegetables, add seasoning and Italian dressing. Mix well, cover and set in the refrigerator to chill overnight.

Top with toasted sesame seeds before serving.

Confetti Coleslaw
☆ ☆ ☆ ☆ ☆

try

1 cup red cabbage	2 cups green cabbage
1 large carrot	1 medium green bell pepper
2 or 3 scallions	1 stalk of celery

In a large bowl, grate cabbages and carrot, chop pepper, celery and scallions. Set aside. Make your favorite slaw dressing, combine with the above and allow to sit a few minutes for the flavors to mingle. See Chapter 16, page 175 "Delightful Dressings"

Grated Apple Combo
☆ ☆ ☆ ☆

try

1 Red or Golden Delicious apple	½ cup carrots
½ cup cabbage	1 stalk celery
¼ tsp. dehydrated onion flakes	1 tsp. of honey

Grate apple, cabbage, carrots and celery, and mix with ¼ tsp. dehydrated onion flakes and 1 tsp. of honey. Cover, refrigerate, and allow to sit to blend flavors.

Spring Garden Salad
☆ ☆ ☆ ☆ ☆

2 cups Romaine or other leaf lettuce
1/2 cup bunch curly endive
1 cup of spinach leaves
12 cherry tomatoes

6 radishes
3 green onions
1/2 red pepper
2 stalks of celery

Tear lettuce, endive and spinach into bite-size pieces, cut tomatoes in half, slice radishes thinly, chop green onions, slice pepper into thin strips, and dice celery. Toss gently and add your favorite dressing. See Chapter 16, page 175 "Delightful Dressings"

Orange Spinach Salad
Submitted by Dana Hathaway
☆ ☆ ☆ ☆

1 cup small orange slices, such as mandarin
1 handful of romaine lettuce leaves
1 handful of spinach leaves

1/2 cup green grapes
1/2 cup green onions
1 cup almonds

Tear spinach and romaine leaf lettuce into bite-size pieces and set aside. Cut grapes in half, chop onions, chop almonds and cut oranges in half. Combine with spinach and lettuce and mix well.

Serve with the following dressing. Combine ingredients and shake well before serving.

2/3 cup extra virgin olive oil
1/8 to 1/4 cup honey
1 tsp. celery seed

1/3 cup freshly extracted orange juice
3 Tbsp. of freshly-extracted lemon juice
1 tsp. dry mustard, optional

Cucumber & Tomato Salad
☆ ☆ ☆ ☆ ☆

2 large cucumbers, peeled
1 red bell pepper
1/2 small red onion

3 large tomatoes
1 stalk of celery

Peel and chop cucumbers, chop tomatoes, onion and bell pepper, and dice celery. Mix together in a bowl and top with your favorite dressing or make a dressing of 2 blended tomatoes, 1 cup of your favorite veggies, combined with your favorite herb seasoning.

Cucumber, Radish Salad
☆ ☆ ☆ ☆ ☆

2 medium cucumbers	10 radishes
3 scallions	1/3 cup parsley
2 garlic cloves	

Peel cucumbers if waxed and slice, slice radishes thin, chop scallions and mince garlic cloves and parsley. Combine ingredients. Serve with Cucumber Dressing (page 176).

Raw Sweet Corn Salad
☆ ☆ ☆ ☆ ☆

try

1 large ear of raw sweet corn
1/2 red bell pepper
1 large ripe tomato
3 Tbsp. parsley
1 celery stalk
1/4 cup sweet red onion

Husk corn, wash all vegetables, and remove kernels of corn from cob. Dice tomato and celery, chop red pepper and onion, and mince the parsley. Combine in a bowl, cover and set in refrigerator.

To Serve: Place leaf lettuce on a plate, spread with avocado dressing (see page 176) and top with raw sweet corn salad.

Hint: For those fighting cancer, avocados and all fat should be avoided. Fat feeds cancer. (See Chapter 4, page 60 for information on fats.)

Hint: Raw corn on or off the cob is delicious. Simply clean, wash and enjoy!

Red Cabbage Slaw
☆ ☆ ☆ ☆ ☆

try

2 1/2 cups red cabbage	1/2 red onion
2 cup carrots	1 cup red pepper

Grate cabbage, dice red onion and red pepper and grate carrots. Top with Cole Slaw Dressing (page 181) and enjoy.

Chef Salad
☆ ☆ ☆ ☆ ☆

try

2 cups Romaine or other leaf lettuce	1 cup spinach
2 tomatoes	4 radishes
1 green pepper	1 cucumber
1 clove garlic	

Rub salad bowl with one garlic clove. Wash, dry and tear lettuce and spinach into bite-size pieces, cut tomatoes into wedges, slice radishes thinly, slice cucumber, and cut green pepper into narrow strips. Place greens in bowl and top with the other vegetables. Serve with your favorite dressing. See Chapter 16, page 175 "Delightful Dressings"

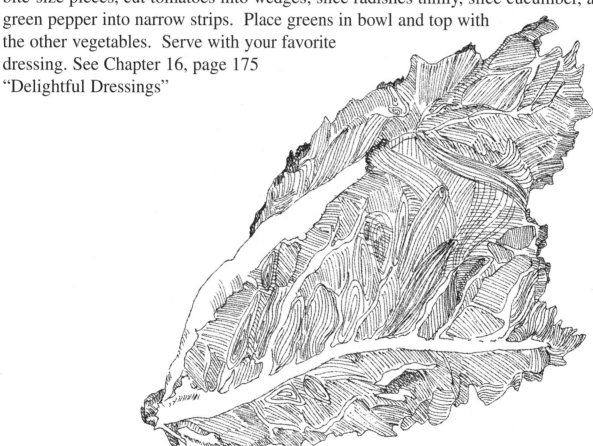

Garden Salad
☆ ☆ ☆ ☆ ☆

try

2 cups Romaine lettuce	1 cup spinach leaves
½ cup thinly sliced radishes	8 or 10 cherry tomatoes
1 or 2 green onions with tops	½ cucumber

Wash and dry veggies and tear lettuce and spinach into bite-size pieces. Slice radishes, slice onions, add cucumber and tomatoes. Top with desired dressing. See Chapter 16, page175, "Delightful Dressings."

Cauliflower Salad
☆ ☆ ☆ ☆ ☆

try

½ head of cauliflower	1 carrot
1 red bell pepper	4 Tbsp. chives
1 stalk of celery	12 cherry tomatoes

Cut cauliflower into small pieces. Quarter tomatoes, grate carrot and dice chives, celery and bell pepper. Mix together. If more color is desired add ½ cup of shredded red or green cabbage. Wonderful with Italian Dressing.

Three-Day Coleslaw
☆ ☆ ☆ ☆ ☆

try

1 medium head of cabbage	1 red bell pepper
1 medium red onion	1 yellow bell pepper

Shred Cabbage, slice red and yellow bell peppers into thin strips, slice onion into thin rings and lightly toss vegetables to mix. Pour over the following dressing:

¼ cup of honey	½ cup fresh lemon juice
½ tsp. Celtic Sea Salt (optional)	4 Tbsp. of extra virgin olive oil

Cover and allow to sit in the refrigerator up to three days. Stir well each day to mix flavors.

Green Bean Salad
☆ ☆ ☆ ☆ ☆

try

1 cup red onion	juice of one lemon, about ¼ cup
2 ½ cups green beans	10 - 12 cherry tomatoes
1 large garlic clove	½ tsp. Celtic Sea Salt (optional)
1 Tbsp. extra virgin olive oil	¼ tsp. rosemary

Cut onion into small slivers and place in lemon juice to marinate. Wash green beans and cut on an angle into 1-inch pieces, wash and cut cherry tomatoes into quarters, mince garlic or use garlic press, and place all of the above ingredients in a bowl. Crush rosemary and combine with the other seasonings, pour over the salad, cover and refrigerate several hours or overnight.

Zucchini Salad

☆ ☆ ☆ ☆ ☆

try

1 medium zucchini	3 stalks of celery
3 sprigs of parsley	1/4 red pepper
1 carrot	2 tomatoes
2 green onions with tops	2 radishes

Quarter zucchini lengthwise and slice thinly, chop parsley, grate carrot, thinly slice green onions and tops, dice celery, chop red pepper, cut tomatoes into wedges, finely chop radishes, combine all ingredients and stir gently. Serve on leaf lettuce and top with your favorite dressing. See Chapter 16, page 175 "Delightful Dressings"

Cucumber Boats

☆ ☆ ☆ ☆ ☆

try

Wash thoroughly or peel cucumbers, cut in half lengthwise and carefully remove the seeds. On a plate make a nice bed of greens and place cucumber on top.

2 medium cucumbers	2 Tbsp. tomato
1 - 2 Tbsp. celery	1 - 2 Tbsp. carrot
1 - 2 Tbsp. almond butter (page 284)	

Finely chop celery and cucumber hearts, dice tomatoes, grate carrot and process almonds in Green Star or Champion juicer. Mix enough almond butter in to hold together and fill the cucumber halves and serve.

Hint: You may change the "stuffing" by simply adding your favorite veggies or herbs such as 1 Tbsp. parsley, minced.

Spinach Salad

☆ ☆ ☆ ☆ ☆

try

3 cups spinach	8 or 10 cherry tomatoes
1/2 red onion	1/2 red pepper
1 small cucumber	

Wash and dry spinach, tear into small pieces. Thinly slice red onion and pepper. Wash and slice cucumber into small slices. Halve tomatoes. Toss in a salad bowl and serve with your favorite dressing. See Chapter 16, page 175 "Delightful Dressings"

Snow Peas with Sesame

Submitted by Georgia Cline
☆ ☆

3/4 lb. snow peas
1/2 tsp. orange rind
2 tsp. toasted sesame seeds*

1 carrot
1 tsp. sesame oil
2 Tbsp. red onion

Grate orange rind, mince onion and grate or julienne carrot. Place pea pods and carrots in a strainer. Set strainer in sink. Pour boiling water over vegetables for about one minute. Pat dry.

Place vegetables in a medium bowl, stir in orange rind, oil, onion and seeds. Serve warm or at room temperature.

*"Unhulled sesame seeds contain ten times more calcium than cow's milk; one and a half times more iron than beef liver; more protein than chicken, beef liver or beef steak; three times more phosphorus than eggs; and more niacin than whole wheat bread." – USDA Composition of Foods Handbook #8

Tomato Juice Salad

Submitted by Connie Richardson
☆ ☆ ☆ ☆ ☆

4 - 6 tomatoes

1 clove of garlic

Peel tomatoes and garlic and process in a blender or food processor . Use enough tomatoes to make 24 ounces. In a large glass or stainless steel bowl, combine the following:

4 medium tomatoes
2 cucumbers
4 Tbsp. lemon juice
Celtic Sea Salt to taste (optional)

8 green onions
1 cup celery
pinch of cayenne (optional)

Peel and chop tomatoes, chop green onions, peel and finely chop cucumbers, and celery. Combine all ingredients, mix well, cover and chill overnight. Mix before serving in small bowls.

Stuffed Cucumbers
☆ ☆ ☆ ☆ ☆

3 cucumbers	2 cups of celery
1 small zucchini	1 red bell pepper
3 scallions	1 ripe tomato
1 Tbsp. fresh basil or 1 tsp. dried	

Peel cucumbers, cut in half lengthwise, carefully remove seeds with a spoon and discard. Place remaining ingredients in a blender or food processor with basil and chop until fine. Blend in 1/2 cup of almond butter (page 284) and stuff cucumbers. Top with minced parsley.

Sweet Potato Salad
☆ ☆ ☆ ☆ ☆

2 cups carrots	1/2 cucumber
1 cup sweet potatoes	1/2 cup celery
1 tomato	

Finely grate carrots and sweet potato, shred the cucumber, chop the celery fine, and cut the tomato in wedges. Combine all but the tomato, place on leaf lettuce, arrange tomato wedges in a pleasing design and top with your favorite dressing. See Chapter 16, page 175 "Delightful Dressings"

try Great!

Cauliflower & Greens Salad
☆ ☆ ☆ ☆ ☆

1 cup shredded carrots	1 cup cauliflower pieces
1/2 cup pecans	1 1/2 cups dark salad greens

Cut cauliflower into small florets, making sure the stem pieces are sliced thin. Shred carrots and chop pecans. Tear the greens into small pieces and combine with carrots and cauliflower. When serving, top with chopped pecans. Serve with your favorite dressing. See Chapter 16, page 175 "Delightful Dressings"

try

Spinach, Orange Salad
Submitted by Dr. J. B. Silcox
☆ ☆ ☆ ☆

2 bunches of spinach leaves	1 red onion
2 small oranges (such as Mandarin)	

Wash and dry spinach leaves, place on salad plate, arrange sectioned oranges and thinly sliced onion rings on top. Serve with Strawberry Dressing on page 178.

Summer Squash Salad
☆ ☆ ☆ ☆ ☆

2 or 3 small summer squash	2 carrots
2 stalks of celery	4 scallions

Scrub squash, carrots, celery and scallions. Cut the squash and carrots into julienne strips, finely chop the celery and scallions. Squeeze the juice of a lemon or orange over the top. Sprinkle sesame seeds over the top before serving.

try

Broccoli Salad
☆ ☆ ☆ ☆

3 cups of broccoli florets	1 cup red onion
1 cup red grapes	

Combine in a bowl and mix with 1 Cup of Rhonda's No Oil Dressing (page 175). Sprinkle with sunflower seeds prior to serving.

Marinaded Tomato Salad

☆ ☆ ☆ ☆ ☆

3 tomatoes
2 cucumbers

1 or 2 medium onions
1 red or green pepper

Chop tomatoes and cucumbers, and thinly slice onion and peppers. Combine and lightly toss in a bowl. Marinate in Italian Dressing (page 181) or Three Day Coleslaw Dressing (page 161).

Summer Salad

Submitted by Elizabeth Peele

☆ ☆ ☆ ☆ ☆

¼ cup cucumber
¼ cup zucchini
⅛ tsp. kelp (optional)
½ medium-size tomato

¼ cup onion
1 cup torn leaf lettuce
Celtic Sea Salt to taste (optional)

In a food processor, chop the following: Cucumber, onions and zucchini. Place on a bed of leaf lettuce. Drizzle with avocado dressing (page 176) or your favorite dressing. Sprinkle with Celtic Sea Salt and kelp, if desired. Top with peeled and sliced tomato wedges.

Winter Salad

Submitted by Elizabeth Peele

☆ ☆ ☆ ☆ ☆

¼ cup broccoli florets
¼ cup celery
¼ cup carrots
1 cup torn Romaine lettuce
Celtic Sea Salt to taste

¼ cup cauliflower florets
1¼ cup red onion
¼ cup turnips
⅛ tsp. kelp (optional)

Chop the following: Broccoli, cauliflower, celery, red onion, carrots and turnips. Place on a bed of Romaine lettuce. Top with your favorite dressing. Cucumber dressing (page 176) is good. Add kelp and Celtic Sea Salt if desired.

Mixed Garden Salad

Submitted by Eleanor Brandow

☆ ☆ ☆ ☆

2 cups fresh green peas

3/4 cup celery

3/4 cup red onion

1 tsp. oregano or other seasoning of choice

2 cups fresh corn

3/4 cup red bell pepper

3/4 cup fresh tomatoes

1/2 tsp. Celtic Sea Salt (optional)

Shell peas and steam slightly, if desired. Remove corn from the cob, chop celery, red pepper and onion. Peel and chop tomatoes. Mix all vegetables and seasonings together, cover and refrigerate, allowing the flavors to mingle before serving.

Salad Bar Ideas
☆ ☆ ☆ ☆ ☆

Salad bars are a wonderful way to allow each person to prepare their own salad with their favorite veggies and toppings. A salad bar can be a great way to serve dinner to a crowd or your family. Select several items from the following categories:

Greens:

torn spinach   torn endive
torn leaf lettuce, any variety torn kale
chopped bok choy hearts

Chopped or sliced vegetables:

cucumbers   yellow bell peppers
cauliflower florets red bell peppers
tomatoes   green onions
kohlrabi   mushrooms
avocado   red onion
asparagus   radishes
broccoli florets   celery

Whole vegetables:

cherry tomatoes   raw okra
raw sweet corn   raw snow peas

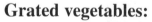

Grated vegetables:

sweet potato   crookneck or other summer squash
green cabbage   red cabbage
raw beets   zucchini
turnips   carrot

Minced vegetables:

chives   parsley
garlic chives scallions

Serve with two or three of your family's favorite dressings.

Chapter Fifteen:

Salad & Grain Combinations

Tabouli
★ ★ ★ ☆

This dish is best when flavors have had a chance to mingle. It can be made the night before. Soak 1 cup of bulgar wheat in 2 cups of distilled water for 30 to 60 minutes. While soaking, chop the scallions, tomatoes and cucumber. Drain bulgar and pat dry. Add vegetables, parsley, mint, Celtic Sea Salt, lemon juice and oil. Mix well. Cover and refrigerate at least one hour before serving.

1/2 cup fresh parsley or 1/4 cup dried	2 large tomatoes
1/2 cup cucumber	1/2 cup scallions
1/2 tsp. Celtic Sea Salt (optional)	1 to 2 Tbsp. extra virgin olive oil
1/4 cup fresh lemon juice	2 Tbsp. minced fresh mint or 1 tsp. dried

Hint: You can change the flavor of Tabouli by adding or omitting different vegetables or seasonings. For example, 1 garlic clove, minced may be added. You can also vary the taste by using quinoa, couscous or prepared brown rice rather than the soaked bulgar wheat. Tabouli may be served on a bed of lettuce or stuffed into a fresh tomato.

Basmati Rice Salad

☆ ☆ ☆

1 cup basmati rice   2 cups distilled water

Bring distilled water to a boil and stir in the rice. Cover and turn to lowest heat, cook for 25 minutes without lifting lid. Turn heat off and allow to sit for 15 additional minutes, covered.

While rice is cooking prepare the following:

1 cup yellow squash	1 cup broccoli florets
1 cup sliced radishes	½ cup green onions with tops
1 cup shredded carrots	1 cup zucchini
1 cup bell pepper	

Cut yellow squash and zucchini into thin strips, slice radishes, shred carrots, chop bell pepper, chop broccoli florets into small pieces, chop green onions combine and set aside.

Make the following dressing:

¼ cup lemon juice	2 Tbsp. extra virgin olive oil
1 large garlic clove	1 tsp. honey (optional)
2 Tbsp. fresh dill	1 Tbsp. fresh parsley

Press garlic and combine with other ingredients in a container. Shake well to mix. Pour over rice mixture and mix to combine flavors. Cover and refrigerate several hours.

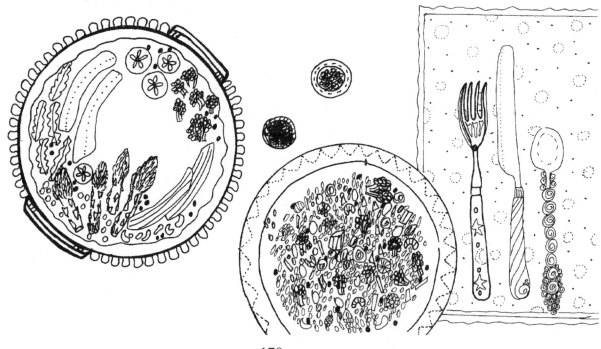

Wild Rice Salad
☆ ☆ ☆

2 cups cooked wild rice	$\frac{1}{2}$ cup red bell pepper
$\frac{1}{2}$ cup tomato	$\frac{1}{2}$ cup green beans
$\frac{1}{2}$ cup corn	$\frac{1}{2}$ cup green peas
$\frac{1}{2}$ cup celery	$\frac{1}{2}$ cup carrot

Cook rice by stirring slowly into 4 cups of boiling distilled water, cover and turn to lowest heat for 30 minutes. Turn off heat and allow to sit an additional 15 minutes with the lid on. Place in bowl, cover with a clean towel and place in the refrigerator and allow to cool.

While the rice is cooling, chop the tomato and green beans, dice bell pepper, celery and grate carrot. Lightly steam peas, corn and green beans, if desired.

Make a dressing of the following:

4 Tbsp. apple juice	2 Tbsp. lemon juice
1 Tbsp. fresh parsley	1 Tbsp. fresh basil
1 Tbsp. fresh tarragon	1 Tbsp. lime juice
Celtic Sea Salt to taste (optional)	

Pour dressing over salad and allow to sit until flavors have mixed and most of the liquid is absorbed.

Potato Salad
☆ ☆ ☆

8 medium potatoes	2 cups celery
$\frac{1}{4}$ cup each red and green pepper	$\frac{1}{2}$ cup diced onion
$\frac{1}{4}$ cup parsley flakes	fresh dill weed (optional)

Peel and boil potatoes. When tender, remove from stove, drain hot water and run cold water over them until cool enough to handle, then dice. Chop peppers, celery and onion. Fold in with diced potatoes and add dill weed to taste.

Combine with Rhonda's No-Oil Salad Dressing (see page 175).

Hint: For a change of pace and whole new taste sensation, try substituting a couple of sweet potatoes or yams for a couple of regular potatoes.

Rainbow Pasta Salad

☆ ☆ ☆

try

Bring 6 cups of water to a boil, add 3 cups of whole grain spiral pasta. Cook al dente (firm but tender). Drain, run cold water over to cool.

While pasta is cooking, chop the following vegetables to be added raw to the salad.

1 cup green pepper	1 cup red pepper
3/4 cup red onion	3/4 cup celery
1 small cucumber	1 medium zucchini
1 medium tomato	1 cup grated carrot

Chop green and red pepper, celery, cucumber, zucchini and tomato, dice onion, and grate carrot. Combine in a bowl with pasta and add Cucumber and Herb Dressing found on page 177 or Rhonda's No-Oil Dressing on page 175.

Three Bean Salad

☆ ☆ ☆

2 cups cooked kidney beans	2 cups cooked green beans
2 cups cooked yellow wax beans	1 cup red onion
1 green pepper	1 red pepper

Cook beans and drain well and place in bowl. Add peppers and onions cut into small rings or slices. Pour over the following marinade and allow to sit overnight in covered bowl in the refrigerator.

1/3 cup lemon juice	1/3 cup unfiltered honey
1/2 tsp. Celtic Sea Salt (optional)	1/2 cup extra virgin olive oil

Option: Garnish with sunflower seeds just prior to serving.

Taco Lentil Salad

☆ ☆ ☆

Submitted by Kimberly & Randy Patterson

1 bunch of Romaine lettuce	1 cup of lentils
1 Tbsp. Mexican Seasoning (no salt added)	¼ cup onion
¼ cup Almond Slicing Cheese (page 285)	1 tomato
¼ to ½ cup distilled water	3 cloves of garlic

Soak lentils, drain, cover with fresh water and bring to a boil, turn down heat, cover and cook until tender. Remove from heat and drain. Meanwhile chop onion and tomato, mince garlic and tear leaf lettuce. Steam sauté onions and garlic, add lentils, continue to sauté for 3 minutes. Add Mexican seasoning, and ¼ to ½ cup of water, and allow lentils to simmer on low heat for 5 minutes. Line plate with a large mound romaine lettuce, spoon lentil mixture over lettuce, add chopped tomato, salsa and crumbled blue corn chips. Top with almond cheese, if desired.

French Potato Salad

☆ ☆ ☆

3 cups potatoes (4 or 5 medium)	2-3 Tbsp. chopped green onions, including tops
2 Tbsp. lemon juice	1 tsp. Herb Seasoning
2 Tbsp. extra virgin olive oil	¼ cup vegetable soup stock (page 207)
⅛ tsp. Celtic Sea Salt (optional)	⅛ tsp. dry mustard
pinch of cayenne pepper	

Boil potatoes until tender, peel and slice into thin circles. (Do not dice). Combine all remaining ingredients except 1 Tbsp. of chopped green onions. Mix well and pour over potatoes. Mix very gently to prevent potatoes from breaking. Garnish with green onions. Place in a bowl, cover and serve at room temperature.

Hint: If keeping overnight, store in refrigerator and allow to reach room temperature again before serving.

Vegetable Aspic

☆ ☆ ☆

2 medium carrots	2 stalks of celery
2 ears of corn	3 cups fresh tomato juice
6 scallions	2 Tbsp. minced parsley
1 bay leaf	1 tsp. lemon juice
1/4 cup grated onion	5 Tbsp. agar agar
1 tsp. Celtic Sea Salt (optional)	1 tsp. paprika

Prepare cleaned vegetables by grating carrots, chopping celery fine, decobbing corn, chopping scallions, mincing parsley and grating onion.

Dissolve agar agar in tomato juice and add bay leaf. Heat gently and when warm, take pan off stove, remove bay leaf, allow to cool. Add Celtic Sea Salt, lemon juice, paprika and onion, and mix well to combine, add chopped vegetables. Pour into bundt pan or individual molds and refrigerate until set.

Chapter Sixteen:

Delightful Dressings

Rhonda's No-Oil Salad Dressing
☆ ☆ ☆ ☆

1 cup raw almonds   1 cup distilled water

Pour water over almonds, cover and leave on counter to soak for 24 hours. At the end of 24 hours, drain almonds and discard water.

Place almonds in Vita Mix or blender with the 1 cup of distilled water and blend about 2 minutes until creamy. Stop the blender and add the following ingredients:

2 tsp. nutritional yeast flakes	2 tsp. garlic powder
1 tsp. kelp	2 Tbsp. dried onion flakes
2 Tbsp. lemon juice	1 tsp. dill weed
1/4 tsp. Celtic Sea Salt (optional)	pinch of cayenne pepper
1 tsp. herb seasoning (optional)	1 Tbsp. raw unfiltered honey *
1 Tbsp. minced parsley	

* or 1 1/2 Tbsp. chopped dates

Blend to mix then add the following thickener:

In a blender combine 2 cups room temperature distilled water or vegetable broth with 2 Tbsp. Arrow root powder. Blend until smooth. Pour into a sauce pan, heat until clear and beginning to thicken. Add this mixture to the blender with the other ingredients and blend well. Pour into glass jar and allow to cool. The mixture will thicken as it cools. Store in refrigerator. This dressing can be used in any recipe which calls for salad dressing.

An even whiter dressing can be made by pouring boiling water over the almonds after soaking. Allow them to soak 15 minutes, then drain and remove hulls. However, the boiling water will destroy the enzymes and much of the nutritional benefit of a raw dressing.

Cucumber Dressing
☆ ☆ ☆ ☆ ☆

1 large cucumber
1 Tbsp. fresh lemon juice
1/8 tsp. Celtic Sea Salt (optional)

1 green onion including top
2 Tbsp. dehydrated onion flakes
1/2 cup toasted sunflower seeds

If the cucumber is not organic, peel it. If it is organic, *some* of the skin may be left on. Blend all until smooth and creamy. If a thinner dressing is desired, add distilled water.

Hint: To toast sunflower seeds, place in a dry skillet on medium heat, shake the skillet until the seeds are brown and be careful not to burn.

Herb Lemon Dressing
☆ ☆ ☆ ☆ ☆

1/3 cup lemon juice
1/3 cup honey
1 garlic clove
1/2 tsp. basil

1/3 cup distilled water
1/2 tsp. Celtic Sea Salt
1 Tbsp. minced onion
1 tsp. oregano

Mince garlic clove and onion and combine with liquids. Add herbs and allow to sit several hours for the flavors to combine.

Avocado Dressing
☆ ☆ ☆ ☆ ☆

1 ripe avocado   1 lemon, juiced

Mash the avocado until smooth, and add the lemon juice until a creamy consistency is obtained. Add herbs of choice to vary the flavor.

Avocado & Tomato Dressing
☆ ☆ ☆ ☆ ☆

2 ripe tomatoes   1 stalk of celery
1 ripe avocado

Blend all ingredients in blender until smooth, add herbs of your choice.

Lemon & Oil Dressing
☆ ☆ ☆ ☆ ☆

try - ok

Combine the following:
> juice of two lemons
> 1 - 2 cloves of garlic, crushed
> 1 Tbsp. extra virgin olive oil

Mix dressing ingredients together and allow to stand several hours before serving. Garlic should be removed prior to serving. Any of your favorite herbs can be added to vary the flavor.

Cucumber & Herb Dressing
☆ ☆ ☆ ☆ ☆

1 large cucumber	1 small garlic clove
2 Tbsp. lemon juice	2 Tbsp. organic maple syrup
3 Tbsp. dried dill	1 tsp. flax seed oil

Peel and seed cucumber, put all ingredients into blender, and blend until smooth. If not thick enough, chop celery to add to the mixture, and blend until pureed.

You may substitute 1 tsp. cilantro or $\frac{1}{2}$ tsp. cumin, for dill if desired.

Orange Dill Dressing
☆ ☆ ☆ ☆

$\frac{1}{2}$ cup lemon juice	3 cloves garlic, peeled
1 cup orange juice	1 Tbsp. honey
2 Tbsp. red onion, chopped	$\frac{1}{4}$ red bell pepper
$\frac{1}{2}$ tsp. dried dill	$\frac{1}{2}$ cup distilled water

Blend all ingredients in blender or VitaMix. Makes one pint. This dressing has a sweet and zesty taste. The longer it sits, the more flavorful it becomes. You can substitute sage or thyme for dill.

Strawberry Dressing

Submitted by Dr. J. B. Silcox
☆ ☆ ☆ ☆ ☆

1 Tbsp. honey	1 Tbsp. lemon juice
1/4 cup fresh orange juice	1/2 cup fresh strawberries

Combine all ingredients in a blender. Use more strawberries if additional thickener is required. This is a nice dressing for fruit salads.

Green Dressing
☆ ☆ ☆

Use 1 Cup Rhonda's No Oil Dressing (page 175) and add the following:

1/2 cup fresh parsley*	4 scallions, green part only
1 tsp. tarragon	dash of cayenne
1 tsp. maple syrup (optional)	1/2 tsp. dill weed

* More or less to taste.

Garlic Dressing
☆ ☆ ☆

Use 1 cup of Rhonda's No-Oil Dressing (page 175) and fold in the following ingredients:

1 garlic clove, minced
1/8 tsp. cayenne pepper
1/2 tsp. ground celery seed
2 Tbsp. unsalted tomato paste

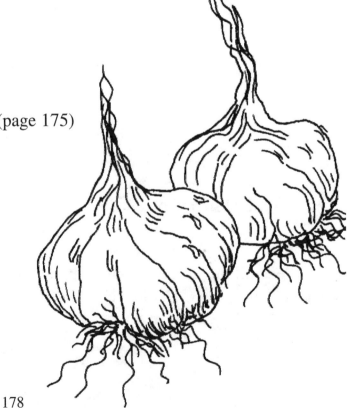

No-Oil Poppy Seed Dressing
☆ ☆ ☆

1 cup distilled water or vegetable soup stock (page 207)
1 Tbsp. arrow root powder

Mix well and pour into a small saucepan, heat until clear and thickened, allow to cool slightly, pour into blender and add the following:

⅓ cup lemon juice	⅓ cup honey
2 Tbsp. poppy seeds	¼ tsp. Celtic Sea Salt (optional)
1 tsp. dry mustard (optional)	1 tsp. paprika

Blend well, pour into jar and refrigerate until ready to serve.

Poppy Seed Dressing
☆ ☆ ☆

1 cup distilled water or vegetable soup stock (page 207)
1 Tbsp. arrow root powder

Mix well and pour into a small saucepan, heat until clear and thickened, allow to cool slightly, pour into blender and add the following:

⅓ cup **unsweetened** pineapple juice	¼ cup date pieces
2 Tbsp. poppy seeds	¼ tsp. Celtic Sea Salt
1 tsp. paprika	3 Tbsp. lemon juice
1 tsp. grated onion (optional)	1 tsp. ground celery seed

Blend well, pour into jar and refrigerate until ready to serve.

All-Natural Thousand Island Dressing
☆ ☆ ☆

Use 1 Cup Rhonda's No Oil Dressing and add the following:

2 Tbsp. ketchup (page 290)	1 Tbsp. finely chopped cucumber
1 Tbsp. finely chopped onion	2 tsp. chopped parsley
1 Tbsp. finely chopped celery	

No-Oil French Dressing
☆ ☆ ☆

1 cup distilled water or vegetable soup stock (page 207)
1 Tbsp. arrow root powder

Mix well and pour into a small saucepan, heat until clear and thickened, allow to cool slightly, pour into blender and add the following:

1/3 cup lemon juice	1/3 cup honey
1 Tbsp. paprika	1 Tbsp. onion powder
1/2 tsp. garlic powder	1/2 tsp. Celtic Sea Salt (optional)
3/4 cup fresh tomato puree	

Blend well, pour into jar and store in refrigerator.

Celery Seed Dressing
☆ ☆ ☆

1/2 cup distilled water or vegetable soup stock (page 207)
1 1/2 tsp. arrow root powder

Mix well and pour into a small saucepan, heat until clear and thickened, allow to cool slightly, pour into blender and add the following:

1/3 cup pineapple juice
1/4 cup date pieces
1/2 tsp. celery seeds

Blend until creamy. This dressing is good on fruit salads.

Carrot Dressing
☆ ☆ ☆

½ cup distilled water or vegetable soup stock (page 207)
1 ½ Tbsp. arrow root powder

Mix well and pour into a small saucepan, heat until clear and thickened, allow to cool slightly, pour into blender and add the following:

1 medium carrot, chopped	½ onion
3 Tbsp. sesame seeds	1 tsp. Celtic Sea Salt (optional)
2 Tbsp. lemon Juice	

Blend until creamy.

Italian Dressing
☆ ☆ ☆ ☆ ☆

2 red bell peppers	2 stalks of celery
2 small cucumbers	2 cloves of garlic
½ cup lemon juice	3 Tbsp. extra virgin olive oil
1 tsp. basil	Celtic Sea Salt to taste (optional)
1 tsp. oregano	½ tsp. honey
½ cup of parsley	

Seed peppers and cucumber, chop celery into chunks, and put all ingredients except parsley into blender. Blend until desired consistency is reached, adding soup stock (page 207) or distilled water to thin.

Mince ½ cup of parsley and add after blending.

To make this a Creamy Italian Dressing add one cup of Rhonda's No Oil Dressing (page 175) instead of distilled water.

Cole Slaw Dressing
☆ ☆ ☆

Combine 1 Cup of Rhonda's No Oil Dressing (page 175) with the following ingredients and mix well:

2 Tbsp. honey	3 cloves of garlic, minced
¼ tsp. Celtic Sea Salt (optional)	1 tsp. poppy seeds

Creamy Dill Dressing
☆ ☆ ☆

Combine 1 Cup of Rhonda's No Oil Dressing (page 175) with the following:

1 tsp. dill weed	1 Tbsp. garlic powder
1 tsp. basil	1 tsp. onion flakes

Mix well and allow to sit in the refrigerator 30 minutes for flavors to mingle.

Tomato Basil Dressing
☆ ☆ ☆ ☆ ☆

2 cups tomatoes	2 garlic cloves
2 Tbsp. lemon juice	1/4 cup fresh basil or 2 tsp dried
dash of Herb Seasoning	1 green onion

Chop basil and pack loosely, chop tomatoes and onion, press garlic and place with the balance of ingredients in a blender and blend for 45 seconds. For added flavor, place 2 or 3 pieces of dehydrated or sun-dried tomato in a blender or food processor and grind to a powder, and add to the above dressing.

Pecan, Tomato Dressing
☆ ☆ ☆ ☆ ☆

1/4 cup pecans	3 fresh tomatoes
2 green onions	1/2 cup fresh celery juice
1 tsp. ground chervil	

Cut celery in small pieces and run through juicer. Chop pecans, tomatoes and onion and place in blender along with chervil. Blend until smooth.

Cilantro Dressing

Submitted by Marion Foster

☆ ☆ ☆

¼ cup raw unfiltered apple cider vinegar

1 cup extra virgin olive oil

1 cup of fresh cilantro stems and/or leaves

4 cloves of organic raw garlic

2 Tbsp. raw unfiltered honey

Put into blender and process until desired consistency of dressing is reached.

Hint: According to recent studies, raw cilantro helps to remove mercury from brain cells.

Beet Salad Dressing

☆ ☆ ☆ ☆ ☆

4 cups raw beets

juice of 2 lemons

2 - 3 cups hulled sunflower seeds

1 avocado

Celtic Sea Salt to taste (optional)

distilled water

Place beets, juice, sunflower seeds, avocado and Celtic Sea Salt into a blender adding enough distilled water to reach the consistency desired.

Hint: This recipe was sent to me, but the name was not on it, and the envelope was separated from it.

Tomato & Herb Dressing

☆ ☆ ☆ ☆ ☆

Blend 2 ripe tomatoes and 1 stalk of chopped celery with 1 tsp flax seed oil or extra virgin olive oil, add one of the following fresh herbs: anise, basil, oregano or rosemary.

Chapter Seventeen

Fresh Vegetable Juices ... The Healers

When juicing carrots, the rule of thumb is one pound of carrots will produce approximately 8 fluid ounces of juice. The body can only assimilate the nutrients from 8 ounces of juice at any one time, so drink 8 ounces and then wait another hour before drinking another 8 ounces. Or if you are drinking juice before a meal, wait at least 30 minutes after the juice to eat. This allows the juice to be assimlated by the body before you put something in your stomach that requires digestion.

For this same reason, always drink juice on an empty stomach. If you put juice and solid food into your stomach at the same time, this nullifies one of the best features of fresh juice by requiring it to sit around in your stomach during the process of digestion. Because the fiber (or pulp) has been removed, no major digestive effort is required, so nutrients from freshly-extracted juice are assimilated and get into the bloodstream and on the way to feed your cells in a matter of minutes.

There is no better way of getting health-producing nutrition into your body than by daily consumption of freshly-extracted vegetable juice, because:

• The nutrients are straight from the raw, living vegetables God designed for human nutrition, without being cooked, processed or altered in any way;

• Removal of fiber allows us to consume the nutrients from an entire pound of carrots in one sitting, which is much more than anyone would ever be able to eat;

• And because no digestion is necessary, these nutrients are able to get to the cellular level within minutes to provide the nutritional building blocks required to create healthy new living cells.

Vegetables have a much higher nutritional content than most fruits, so this is the reason the Hallelujah Diet emphasizes daily consumption of fresh vegetable juice. Although fresh fruit juices are cleansing (see Chapter 18, page 191) it is nice occasionally, but it does not have the same cell-building and healing capabilities as fresh vegetable juice. ***Always strain carrot juice before drinking.*** For more information on juicing, see page 76.

Carrot Juice
☆ ☆ ☆ ☆ ☆

If the carrots are organic, scrub the outer skin and remove the top and bottom tip. If the carrots are not organic, remove the skin, tops and bottoms and trim to fit the feeding tube of your juicer. Run 1 pound of carrots through the juicing machine. Serving size is 8 ounces.

Carrot juice is the number one juice in our diet. It contains natural vitamins B, C, D, E, K and beta carotene, a precursor of vitamin A, as well as calcium, phosphorous, potassium, sodium, and many other minerals and trace minerals. Carrot juice contains calcium and magnesium, which help to maintain the intestinal walls and helps to strengthen bones and teeth. Carrot juice acts as a cleanser for the liver, explaining why we sometimes get a little orange tint in the palms of our hands when first starting to consume carrot juice. The body is simply releasing toxins from the liver to be removed from the body. Contrary to popular opinion, turning orange is not a sign of too much vitamin A. The pro-vitamin A (beta carotene) in carrot juice is converted to vitamin A within the body. If you feel your skin is turning too orange, simply cut back a little on your consumption or dilute the carrot juice slightly with other vegetable juices or an apple. Another advantage of consuming carrot juice on a regular basis is the liver is able to release stale bile and excess fat which contribute to high cholesterol levels.

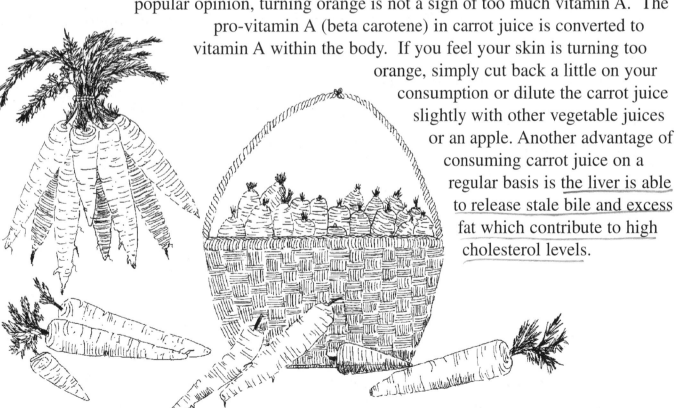

185

Carrot, Beet Juice
☆ ☆ ☆ ☆ ☆

Carrot and beet juice is not only delicious, but beautiful. Prepare the carrots for juicing. Clean the beet, peel if necessary. Cut into smaller pieces that will easily fit into the juicing machine. Use ³/₄ of a pound carrots and ¹/₂ of beet. Juice and enjoy. **Hint:** if the juice does not total 8 ounces, add more carrots. Serving size is 8 ounces.

Hint: Beets and beet greens are very cleansing to the body and help to build strong blood cells as well as cleanse the kidneys. Dr. N.W. Walker advocated that beet juice is very beneficial during the menstrual cycle. Beets are such powerful cleansers that it is best to use only a couple of ounces at one time and always in combination with another juice.

Carrot, Apple Juice
☆ ☆ ☆ ☆ ☆

Process ³/₄ of a pound of cleaned carrots with the ends removed, add ¹/₂ Gala, Delicious or Granny Smith apple, including the skin and seeds, which has been washed. If not organic, the apple should be peeled. Process through the juicing machine. Serving size is 8 ounces.

Hint: Apples are the only fruits that should be mixed with carrot juice. Vegetable and fruit juices otherwise do not combine well and should not be mixed.

Carrot, Apple, Celery Juice
☆ ☆ ☆ ☆ ☆

Wash ³/₄ of a pound of carrots, one apple (peel if not organic) and 1 stalk of celery. Process through your juicing machine. Serving size is 8 ounces.

Carrot, Celery Juice
☆ ☆ ☆ ☆ ☆

Make ready ³/₄ pound of carrots. Wash and remove debris from 2 - 4 ribs of celery, and feed through juicing machine. Serving size is 8 ounces.

Hint: When juicing celery in a Champion Juicer, cut stalks in half-inch pieces to prevent the strings from winding around the blade, which causes the motor to overheat.

Carrot, Beet & Cucumber Juice
☆ ☆ ☆ ☆ ☆

Prepare ¾ pound of carrots, ½ beet with stem and ½ cucumber. If vegetables are organic, scrubbing is required. If not organic, peel the vegetables. Run through juicing machine adding more carrots if needed to make 8 ounces. Serving size is 8 ounces.

Hint: Dr. N.W. Walker states that cucumber juice is a natural diuretic, is beneficial for those with rheumatic ailments, is high in potassium, promotes hair and fingernail growth and helps to eliminate skin eruptions.

Carrot, Beet & Greens Juice
☆ ☆ ☆ ☆ ☆

Scrub and make ready ¾ pound carrots, ½ beet including greens, 1 or 2 leaves of leaf lettuce, spinach or you may wish to add other greens from your garden. Juice and enjoy. If you are in a hurry and don't have time for lunch, this drink is a wonderful substitute. Serving size is 8 ounces.

Carrot, Bell Pepper Juice
☆ ☆ ☆ ☆ ☆

Prepare ¾ pound of carrots, trim if necessary to fit feeding tube of juicer, wash and seed ½ of a small bell pepper or ¼ of a medium to large one. Try adding an apple or handful of spinach to this juice for variety. Process through the juicing machine and enjoy. Serving size is 8 ounces.

Hint: Bell peppers have a very hearty flavor which can be dominant in juice. Peppers are rich in vitamin C and also beta carotene.

Carrot, Spinach Juice
☆ ☆ ☆ ☆ ☆

Prepare ¾ pound of carrots, trim if necessary to fit feeding tube of juicer, wash a handful of spinach leaves and process through the juicer. An apple may be added to change the flavor. Serving size is 8 ounces.

Hint: Raw spinach is a rich source of vitamins A and E as well as a wonderful source of iron. Spinach is also higher in useable protein than many of its other counterparts. However, spinach should never be juiced alone.

Carrot, Apple, Broccoli Juice
☆ ☆ ☆ ☆ ☆

Clean and prepare 3/4 pound of carrots, 1 apple and 3 to 4 broccoli florets. Process and enjoy. Serving size is 8 ounces.

Hint: Broccoli contains a copious amount of beta carotene as well as many other valuable nutrients that make it a powerful cancer-fighting food.

Carrot, Cabbage, Celery Juice
☆ ☆ ☆ ☆ ☆

Prepare 3/4 pound of carrots, 2 ribs of celery, and a 3-inch wedge of cabbage (red or green). Process through juicer. (If using a Champion juicer, cut the celery into half-inch pieces.) Serving size is 8 ounces.

Hint: If your system is acidic this juice may cause you to feel "gassy."

Carrot, Cucumber, Bell Pepper Juice
☆ ☆ ☆ ☆ ☆

Prepare 3/4 pound of carrots, scrub (or peel, if not organic) 1 small cucumber or 1/2 of a large cucumber, and 1/4 of bell pepper. Juice in your machine. Other green leaves from your garden may be added to enhance the flavor. Serving size is 8 ounces.

Carrot, Celery, Parsley, Lettuce & Spinach Juice
☆ ☆ ☆ ☆ ☆

Prepare 3/4 pound of carrots, 1 stalk of celery cut into 2 inch pieces, wash 2 or 3 sprigs of parsley, a handful of leaf lettuce and a handful of spinach. Run through the juicing machine and enjoy. Serving size is 8 ounces.

Carrot, Cucumber Juice
☆ ☆ ☆ ☆ ☆

Prepare 3/4 pound carrots, scrub or peel, if not organic, 1 small cucumber or 1/2 of a large cucumber. Cut the cucumber into quarters lengthwise and process with the carrots in your juicer. Serving size is 8 ounces.

Carrot, Celery & Parsley Juice
☆ ☆ ☆ ☆ ☆

Clean and prepare 3/4 pound carrots, clean 2 stalks of celery and cut into half-inch pieces, wash 1/2 to 3/4 cup of parsley. Run through your juicing machine. Serving size is 8 ounces.

This particular juice makes a pleasing combination and can be very relaxing at the end of a hectic day. Celery juice contains alkaline minerals which have a very calming effect on the body's nervous system. It also helps to curb the desire for sweets for those who desire to lose weight.

Celery juice also contains organic sodium combined with many minerals the body requires.

Parsley juice is also nutritionally dense and is very concentrated, which is why it is mixed in combination with other vegetables.

Carrot, Celery & Spinach Juice
☆ ☆ ☆ ☆ ☆

Prepare 3/4 pound of carrots, 2 stalks of celery cut into half-inch pieces, and 5 or 6 spinach leaves. Process through juicing machine. Serving size is 8 ounces.

Carrot, Cucumber, Beet Juice
☆ ☆ ☆ ☆ ☆

Scrub or peel, if not organic, 3/4 pound of carrots, peel 1/2 large cucumber or 1 small cucumber, scrub beet and add 1/4 to 1/2 beet including greens. Run through your juicing machine. Serving size is 8 ounces.

Tomato, Cucumber, Celery Juice
☆ ☆ ☆ ☆ ☆

Wash 1 vine-ripened tomato, cut in small pieces, prepare 1 small cucumber and cut 1 or 2 stalks of celery into 1 inch pieces. Process in juicer. A small piece of lime may be added, if desired. Process all in juicer and enjoy.

Hint: Although tomatoes are a fruit, most people think of them as a vegetable so this juice is listed here. Fresh, raw tomato juice will taste and look quite different from those found in bottles and cans. Never use hot house tomatoes since they are picked green and gassed to make them turn color.

Tomato Juice Cocktail
☆ ☆ ☆ ☆ ☆

Prepare 1 large, vine-ripened tomato, cut into pieces, clean ½ medium cucumber, 1 stalk of celery*, 3 carrots, 1 handful of greens like spinach, kale or leaf lettuce, 1 scallion, 1 small beet and ½ red bell pepper. Juice and enjoy. Serving size is 8 ounces.

Hint: If you are using a Champion juicer, cut celery into half-inch pieces to prevent the strings from wrapping around the blade.

Carrot, Vegetable Juice
☆ ☆ ☆ ☆ ☆

Clean and prepare ¾ pound of carrots, ½ beet with tops, 1 stalk of celery cut into half-inch pieces, along with a handful of your favorite greens like spinach, kale, lettuce, or cabbage. Process in your juicer and enjoy. Serving size is 8 ounces.

Chapter Eighteen:

Fruit Juices ... The Cleansers

As stated earlier on page 185, fruit juices are too high in sugar to be consumed on a regular basis, and no more than one fruit juice per day is recommended. A person who has been advised to limit sugar intake should confine fruit juices to no more than 16 ounces spread out during the week, and you may consider diluting the fruit juice with distilled water.

As mentioned at the beginning of the previous chapter, there are many advantages to consuming vegetables in the form of fresh juice rather than eating them in their whole form. The same is not necessarily true for fruits. First of all, the fiber in fruit is more easily digested than the fiber in vegetables. Most fruits, if eaten in proper combination, can be fully digested in about 30 minutes. (Never eat fruit with other foods, because fruit digests much faster than vegetables and grain. If you eat fruit with other foods, this will require the fruit to sit around in your stomach much longer than necessary, leading to fermentation.) Because fruit is able to go through your system so quickly, it is an excellent cleanser. Eating fruit is a great way of adding fiber to your diet, and this fiber helps the body to deal with the sugar content of the fruit. And fruits are not as high in nutritional content as vegetables. For all these reasons, a good rule of thumb for maximum nutrition is to "Juice your vegetables and eat your fruits."

Citrus fruits should be used in moderation since they can leach calcium from the body, leading to soft bones and teeth unless a vigorous exercise program is followed. (Vigorous exercise speeds up the metabolism to enable to the body to burn up the excess acid.) Citrus should be peeled before juicing, except lemons and limes. Pineapples should be peeled and cut into strips.

Fruit and vegetable juices do not mix well, except apples which can be juiced with fruits or vegetables.

Apple Juice
☆ ☆ ☆ ☆ ☆

Select one pound of apples for each 8-ounce serving of apple juice. Prepare the apples for juicing and run them through your juicer. Serving size is 8 ounces.

Fresh apple juice is delicious and can be made from a variety of apples such as Granny Smith, Gala, Delicious, Golden Delicious, McIntosh, Ida Red, Cortland and many others. Firmer apples are best for juicing – the softer varieties tend to get "soupy" when juiced. Do not buy apples that have been sprayed with Alar, which is a known carcinogen. If apples are waxed, they should be peeled before juicing, while organic apples can be washed and juiced peel and all.

If using organic apples, be sure and check for worms! Although the worms will not harm you, it is doubtful that you will want to drink them!

Hint: You may not be aware that the U.S. Government allows commercial canners to use some wormy apples in every batch the canneries produce. Canneries are also allowed to use old fruit which can be disfigured and rotten. Apple juice sold in the grocery stores which is clear has been pasteurized, or cooked, then filtered, thus destroying the nutrients.

Apple, Strawberry Juice
☆ ☆ ☆ ☆ ☆

Wash 1 or 2 medium apples, or peel if not organic, wash and hull 1 cup of strawberries and run through juicer. Add 1 squeeze of fresh lemon juice. Serving size is 8 ounces.

Apple, Pear Juice
☆ ☆ ☆ ☆ ☆

Wash and peel if not organic 2 or 3 apples and one pear. Juice and enjoy. Serving size is 8 ounces.

Grapefruit Juice
☆ ☆ ☆ ☆ ☆

Peel grapefruit, preferably organic, leaving the white, mealy inner layer in place. Separate into sections and run through juicing machine. This juice will be quite thick. Serving size is 8 ounces.

Hint: Drink citrus juice in moderation, because excess acidity can leach calcium from the body, leading to softened bones and teeth. Vigorous daily exercise speeds up the metabolism, which helps to burn up excess acidity.

Grapefruit, Orange Juice
☆ ☆ ☆ ☆ ☆

Peel 1 grapefruit and 1 orange, leaving the white mealy layer, separate into sections and process through the juicing machine. Serving size is 8 ounces.

Hint: Try adding some fresh strawberries for a whole different taste sensation.

Orange Juice
☆ ☆ ☆ ☆ ☆

Peel the orange, preferably organic, leaving the white mealy inner layer intact. Separate into sections, and process through the juicing machine. Serving size is 8 ounces.

Peach Juice
☆ ☆ ☆ ☆ ☆

Wash and pit 2 peaches and run through the juicing machine. For an added taste treat, add one pear and/or an apple. Serving size is 8 ounces.

Grape Juice
☆ ☆ ☆ ☆ ☆

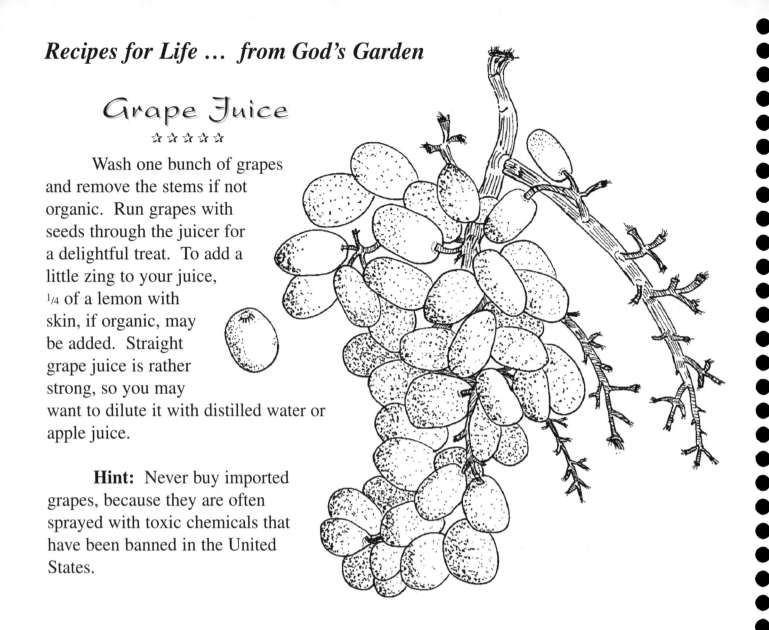

Wash one bunch of grapes and remove the stems if not organic. Run grapes with seeds through the juicer for a delightful treat. To add a little zing to your juice, 1/4 of a lemon with skin, if organic, may be added. Straight grape juice is rather strong, so you may want to dilute it with distilled water or apple juice.

Hint: Never buy imported grapes, because they are often sprayed with toxic chemicals that have been banned in the United States.

Pineapple Juice
☆ ☆ ☆ ☆ ☆

Scrub pineapple, if organic or peel if not organic. Cut into pieces about 1 to 1 1/2-inch thick and run through the juicing machine. Serving size is 8 ounces.

Hint: 6 or 8 strawberries or 1/2 of an orange can be used to vary the flavor.

Pineapple, Grape Juice
☆ ☆ ☆ ☆ ☆

Peel pineapple, slice pieces about 1 to 1 1/2 inches thick, clean 1 small bunch of red or green grapes (remove stems if not organic), run through juicing machine. Serving size is 8 ounces.

Pineapple, Orange Juice
☆ ☆ ☆ ☆ ☆

Peel pineapple, slice a piece about 2 inches thick, add one medium orange which has been peeled. A squeeze of lemon may be added for variety. Serving size is 8 ounces.

Mixed Fruit Juice
☆ ☆ ☆ ☆ ☆

Wash 6 strawberries, 1 apple (peel if not organic), wash pineapple and peel, add ¼ of it to juice, and 1 bunch of washed grapes. Run through juicing machine. Serving size is 8 ounces.

Melon Juices

Melons are in a class by themselves because they do not digest well with other foods. However, melons are very high in nutrients. Any of the melons may be mixed together for a variety of flavors, but not with other foods.

When shopping for melons, check to see if they have a sweet aroma and a soft spot opposite the stem end. Choose the heavier melons since they contain more water.

There are several kinds of melons all of which can be used for juicing. For a review of the types of melons available see Chapter 12, page 129.

It takes approximately one pound of melon to make eight ounces of juice.

Cantaloupe, Honeydew & Watermelon Juice
☆ ☆ ☆ ☆ ☆

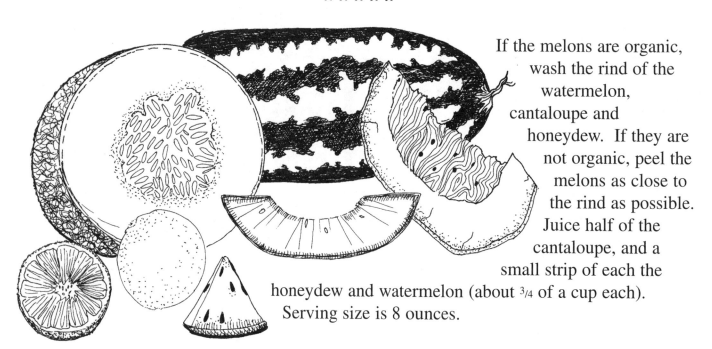

If the melons are organic, wash the rind of the watermelon, cantaloupe and honeydew. If they are not organic, peel the melons as close to the rind as possible. Juice half of the cantaloupe, and a small strip of each the honeydew and watermelon (about ¾ of a cup each). Serving size is 8 ounces.

Cantaloupe Juice
☆ ☆ ☆ ☆ ☆

If the melon is organic, scrub cantaloupe, cut open, remove seeds, cut into slices and run through your juicing machine. If the melon is inorganic, remove the outer skin. Each 8 ounce glass takes approximately ¼ of a melon. Serving size is 8 ounces.

Honeydew Juice
☆ ☆ ☆ ☆ ☆

Cut open a honeydew melon and remove the seeds, remove the outermost rind and run about ¼ of the melon through the juicer.   Serving size is 8 ounces.

Hint: For an added zest, a squeeze of lime juice can be added

Watermelon Juice
☆ ☆ ☆ ☆ ☆

If the melon is organic, scrub the outside of the melon. If the melon is inorganic, peel off the outermost rind. Cut about 1 pound of a watermelon into strips. Run the rind, pulp and seeds through the juicing machine. This makes a wonderful juice cooler in the summer time. Serving size is 8 ounces.

Delicious Soups & Stews

Chapter Nineteen:

Raw Soups

For soups and stews, if not using soup stock, tie the following herbs in a bag: 1 Bay Leaf, 1 tsp. each fresh thyme, parsley, marjoram, sage and rosemary or your favorite herbs. Remove before serving.

Asparagus Soup
☆ ☆ ☆ ☆ ☆

try

2 cups blended tomatoes *
2 stalks of celery
1/8 tsp. thyme
Celtic Sea Salt to taste (optional)

1 bunch of asparagus (1 lb.)
1/8 tsp. oregano
1/8 tsp. basil
1/2 cup almonds

Soak almonds overnight and drain. Remove tough ends and half spear heads from asparagus, discard the tough ends, set the spear heads aside, and chop the remainder into 1-inch pieces. Peel and quarter tomatoes, cut celery into 1-inch pieces, and grind the almonds into a fine meal. Combine ingredients in the blender or food processor and add the seasonings. Process to desired consistency. Use reserved tips for garnish.
*May substitute vegetable soup stock (page 207) for tomatoes

Golden Barley Soup
☆ ☆ ☆ ☆ ☆

1/2 cup carrots
3/4 cup barley
2 cups carrot juice
1/2 cup parsley

1 cup crookneck squash
1 cup distilled water
1/2 cup celery
1/2 cup scallions

Place barley in a bowl, cover with distilled water, and soak overnight. The next day, grate carrot and squash, chop celery and scallions and mince parsley. Drain and rinse barley in hot water, drain well. Combine all ingredients and heat slightly. Serve in heated bowls.

Avocado Soup
☆ ☆ ☆ ☆ ☆

1 ripe avocado	1 tsp. chives
2 cloves of garlic	1 stalk of celery
1 carrot	2 tomatoes
1 cup vegetarian soup stock (page 207)	Celtic Sea Salt to taste (optional)

Peel and mash avocado, peel and mince garlic, grate carrot, dice celery, peel and chop tomatoes into small pieces. Combine all ingredients and mix well or place in a blender and chop to desired consistency.

try

Broccoli Zucchini Soup
☆ ☆ ☆ ☆ ☆

1 ½ cups broccoli	½ cup vegetarian soup stock
1 ½ cups zucchini	½ cup celery
½ cup red onion	1 tsp. basil
Celtic Sea Salt to taste (optional)	

Blend zucchini, half of the broccoli, basil and Celtic Sea Salt with soup stock, finely chop onion, celery and remaining broccoli, and pour blended zucchini-broccoli mixture over other vegetables in a bowl. Add seasonings, stir to blend.

Carrot Soup
☆ ☆ ☆ ☆ ☆

try

2 cups of carrots	¼ cup red onion
¼ cup red pepper	¼ cup broccoli florets
½ cup celery	1 cup fresh carrot juice
¼ tsp. paprika	½ tsp. thyme
Celtic Sea Salt to taste (optional)	

Clean and grate carrots, and finely chop onion, red pepper, broccoli and celery. Mix together. Add carrot juice, Celtic Sea Salt and seasonings. Stir to blend.

try

Celery Chowder
☆ ☆ ☆ ☆ ☆

4 stalks of celery
4 green onions
1 clove of garlic
1 cup carrot juice
1 Tbsp. minced parsley

1 small zucchini
1/2 bell pepper
1/2 cup celery juice
Celtic Sea Salt to taste (optional)

Dice all vegetables, mince garlic. Blend half of the vegetables with the juices, add the remaining vegetables, minced parsley and Celtic Sea Salt to taste.

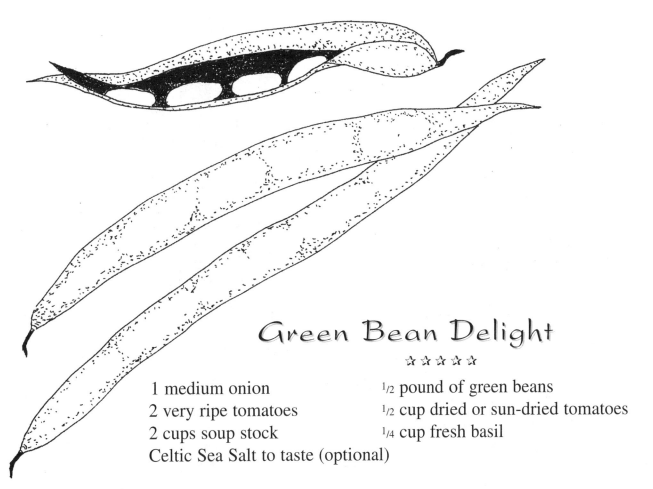

Green Bean Delight
☆ ☆ ☆ ☆ ☆

1 medium onion
2 very ripe tomatoes
2 cups soup stock
Celtic Sea Salt to taste (optional)

1/2 pound of green beans
1/2 cup dried or sun-dried tomatoes
1/4 cup fresh basil

Wash and remove ends from beans, chop onion and tomatoes. Place the beans and onion and 1 tomato, dried tomato, basil and soup stock in blender. Blend until smooth. Add Celtic Sea Salt to taste. Finely chop the other tomato, place a small amount in the bottom of each bowl, and top with soup.

Cucumber Soup

☆ ☆ ☆ ☆ ☆

3 large cucumbers
1 small red onion
1 zucchini

½ cup of celery
Celtic Sea Salt to taste (optional)

Peel and remove seeds from cucumbers, and finely chop two of the cucumbers and celery, mince onion, and grate zucchini. Place these ingredients in a bowl. Run the third cucumber through a food processor to mince. Combine with rest of the ingredients.

To vary the taste of this soup, add your favorie herb, for example 1 Tbsp. of dill or top with scallions.

Corn Chowder (Raw)

☆ ☆ ☆ ☆ ☆

4 cups fresh corn kernels
1 cup zucchini
2 medium tomatoes
4 green onions
½ bell pepper
1 stalk of celery
1 cup fresh carrot juice
¼ tsp. thyme
½ tbsp. Celtic Sea Salt
(optional)
½ tsp. basil

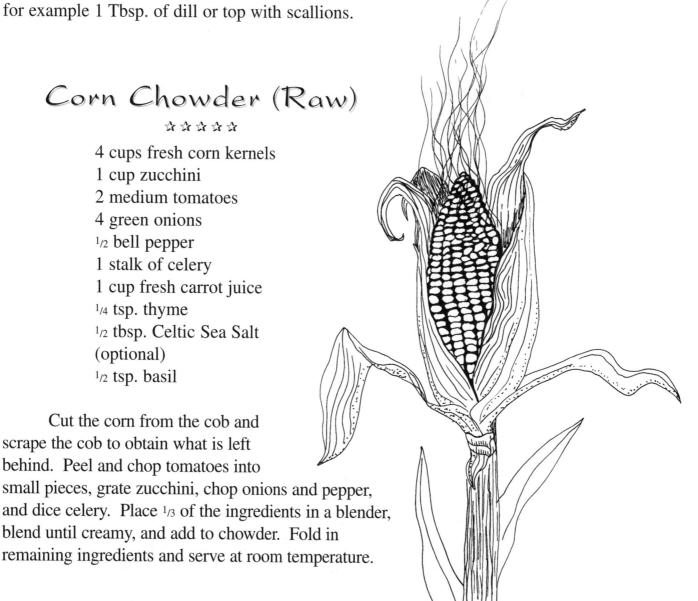

Cut the corn from the cob and scrape the cob to obtain what is left behind. Peel and chop tomatoes into small pieces, grate zucchini, chop onions and pepper, and dice celery. Place ⅓ of the ingredients in a blender, blend until creamy, and add to chowder. Fold in remaining ingredients and serve at room temperature.

Borscht
☆ ☆ ☆ ☆ ☆

1 cup shredded beets
1 small onion or 2 green onions
3/4 cup fresh carrot juice
1 medium tomato

1 stalk of celery
1/4 cup fresh beet juice
1/2 tsp. dill weed
1/4 head medium cabbage

Shred beets and cabbage and set aside. Peel and chop tomato, chop celery and onion, place in blender with juices, blend until smooth consistency. Mix in dill and pour over shredded beets and cabbage and serve at room temperature.

Tomato Soup
☆ ☆ ☆ ☆ ☆

3 cups fresh tomatoes
1 small onion
1 ripe avocado
1 tsp. oregano
1 tsp. basil

1 Tbsp. lemon juice
1 stalk of celery
Celtic Sea Salt to taste (optional)
1/2 cup fresh carrot juice

Peel tomatoes and avocado, place in blender and puree. Chop the onion and celery, and add to the blended seasoning and Celtic Sea Salt. Puree to desired consistency, stir in carrot juice just before serving.

Kohlrabi Soup
☆ ☆ ☆ ☆ ☆

6 scallions
2 ripe tomatoes
1/2 tsp. cumin
2 cups fresh tomato juice

1 lb. of kohlrabi
1 tsp. thyme
1 cup vegetable soup stock
Celtic Sea Salt to taste (optional)

Juice enough tomatoes to make 2 cups of juice. Chop scallions, peel and chop tomatoes, peel and remove ends from kohlrabi, grate kohlrabi using the coarse side of the grater. In a food processor or blender, place half the kohlrabi, half the chopped scallions, the soup stock, seasonings and tomato juice, and blend until smooth. Place the other half of the vegetables in a bowl, top with soup and garnish with the remaining scallions.

Green Pea Soup

☆ ☆ ☆ ☆ ☆

1 very ripe avocado	2 cups of fresh peas
1 medium zucchini	1 cup of soup stock
1 cup carrot	½ cup carrot juice
2 sprigs of parsley	1 tsp. dill weed
Celtic Sea Salt to taste (optional)	

Peel and pit the avocado, shell the peas, peel and chop the zucchini, peel and grate the carrot, and mince the parsley. Place the soup stock, carrot juice, the avocado, the zucchini, half of the carrot, half of the peas and half of the parsley in a blender. Blend until smooth, add the dill weed and Celtic Sea Salt. Place remaining peas and carrots in bowls, top with soup mixture, and garnish with the rest of the parsley.

Raw Vegetable Soup

☆ ☆ ☆ ☆ ☆

1 large tomato	½ cucumber
1 tsp. Italian seasoning (page 313)	1 green onion
2 - 3 cabbage leaves	1 stalk of celery
½ cup vegetable soup stock	1 clove of garlic
Celtic Sea Salt to taste (optional)	½ c shelled peas

Peel tomato, mince garlic and place in blender, along with soup stock and Celtic Sea Salt and blend until smooth. Add herbs.

Finely chop cabbage, celery, and cucumber and mince green onion. Place vegetables in heated bowls and pour soup over top.

Gazpacho Soup
☆ ☆ ☆ ☆ ☆

3 cups ripe tomatoes
2 cups cucumbers, peeled & diced
2 stalks celery, diced
1/2 green bell pepper, seeded & diced
1 red bell pepper, seeded & diced
3 green onions, sliced or 2 Tbsp. dry onion flakes

2 Tbsp. extra virgin olive oil
1 1/2 – 2 Tbsp. lemon juice
1/2 tsp Celtic Sea Salt (optional)
All-Purpose Seasoning to taste
    (see page 313)
1/4 cup soup stock, optional

Place 1 1/2 tomatoes, 1/4 cup soup stock in a food processor and pureé. Place in a glass container, add remaining vegetables, stir in olive oil, lemon juice, Celtic Sea Salt and All Purpose Seasoning to taste. Cover and chill. Do not heat. This soup is served cold. Garnish each bowl with a few parsley flakes.

Hint: See recipe Chapter 25, page 313 or Frontier Herbs currently makes an All Purpose Seasoning It should be available at your local health food store.

Zucchini Chowder
☆ ☆ ☆ ☆ ☆

1 small red onion
1 cup red bell pepper
1 medium tomato
1 cup fresh carrot juice
1/2 tsp. oregano
Celtic Sea Salt to taste (optional)

2 cups zucchini
1 medium carrot
1 cup vegetable soup stock
1 garlic clove
1 tsp. basil

Chop the onion, bell pepper and tomato, grate the zucchini and carrot, and mince the garlic. Combine half of the grated and chopped ingredients with the soup stock and process until smooth. Stir in the fresh juice and remaining ingredients. Grated carrot may be added as a garnish.

Raw Carrot Soup
☆ ☆ ☆ ☆ ☆

2 cups hot Vegetable Soup Stock (page 207) or distilled water
1/2 cup almonds
1 cup fresh parsley or 1 Tbsp. dried
1/2 tsp. Celtic Sea Salt (optional)
1 cup shredded carrot
1/4 cup finely chopped scallions, green onions or chives

Blend first four ingredients, then add carrots. Pulse blender to chop carrots to desired consistency. Pour into bowls, and garnish with green onions before serving. A garden salad and soup make a wonderful meal.

Sweet Potato Soup
☆ ☆ ☆ ☆ ☆

1 cup Vegetable Soup Stock (page 207)   1 cup fresh carrot juice
3 cups sweet potato   1 cup parsnip
1/4 cup fresh parsley   1/4 cup onion
Celtic Sea Salt to taste (optional)   1/2 tsp. dill weed

Grate sweet potato and parsnip, chop onion and mince parsley. Place half of the sweet potato, parsnip and parsley, and all of the onion in a blender or food processor with soup stock and blend until smooth. Stir in the carrot juice and seasonings. Place the remainder of the vegetables in bowls, top with soup.

Chapter Twenty:

Delicious Cooked Soups & Stews

For soups and stews, if not using soup stock, tie the following herbs in a bag: 1 Bay Leaf, 1 tsp. each fresh thyme, parsley, marjoram, sage and rosemary or your favorite herbs. Remove before serving.

Vegetable Soup Stock
☆ ☆ ☆

Every cook knows the secret to any good soup is the soup stock from which it is made. Here is a recipe that will give your soups lots of extra flavor and body:

8-10 cups distilled water
2 onions, cubed, leave skins on if clean
2 to 3 cloves of garlic
3 carrots
3 to 4 stalks of celery
2 potatoes with skin

1/2 to 1 cup parsley
1 bay leaf
1 tsp. thyme
1 tsp. basil
2 cups broccoli pieces (stems are fine)
2 cups cauliflower pieces

Chop all vegetables into 1-inch pieces. Place in stock pot or large stainless steel kettle, and add seasonings. Steam sauté until slightly tender. Cover with distilled water, bring to a boil, and reduce heat and simmer over low heat for 45 minutes to one hour. Cool and strain twice to remove all debris, and discard vegetables. Stock may be frozen or will keep in refrigerator up to one week. Use for soups or stews.

If you would like a more delicate bouquet, omit the cauliflower and broccoli, and spices may be changed to just 1-2 tsp. dill, omitting other herbs. Celtic Sea Salt may be added to taste.

Minestrone Soup

☆ ☆ ☆

For that cold winter evening, a thick, full-bodied soup with homemade, whole-grain bread (Chapter 23 page 274 or 279) can be a welcome treat following your large salad. This was the most popular soup at our restaurant.

8 cups of vegetable soup stock (page 207)	1 cup cabbage
1 ¹/₂ cups of garbanzo beans	¹/₄ tsp. oregano
2 cups of red kidney beans	³/₄ tsp. basil
¹/₂ cup of carrots	¹/₄ tsp. thyme
3 medium tomatoes*	¹/₂ cup celery
¹/₂ cup fresh parsley (or 1 Tbsp. dried)	¹/₂ cup onion
Celtic Sea Salt (optional) (add slowly to taste)	1 clove garlic

1 package spinach noodles - prepare according to directions and set aside.

*or one 14-oz. can of unsweetened and unsalted Italian tomatoes with juice
Soak garbanzo and kidney beans overnight, drain and rinse.

Peel and dice tomatoes. Cook and drain kidney and garbanzo beans. Mince garlic and parsley. Chop carrots, onion, celery, cabbage and garlic and sauté in water or soup stock over medium heat until the onion is translucent - about 5 minutes. Stir in cooked and drained kidney beans, garbanzo beans, diced tomatoes and minced herbs. Bring to a simmer, then turn heat down and simmer about 10 minutes. Stir in cabbage and parsley and simmer with lid partially on for about 15 minutes or until cabbage is tender (be careful not to burn). As the soup cooks, it will thicken. Add more tomatoes or soup stock as needed. Serve over spinach noodles.

Split Pea Soup

☆ ☆ ☆

Great!
even better when put thru blender

2 carrots	2 cups split peas
1 med. onion	3 stalks celery
1 tsp. garlic powder	1 medium potato
1 tsp. ground cumin	¹/₂ tsp. cayenne
¹/₂ cup parsley flakes	2 qts. soup stock *or distilled water*
Celtic Sea Salt to taste (optional)	

Soak peas overnight. Drain and rinse, set aside. Shred carrots, chop or dice onion and celery, and cube potato. Sauté onion and spices in distilled water for 1 minute. Add Celtic Sea Salt, peas and vegetable soup stock (page 207). Bring to boil, simmer for one hour. Add potatoes, carrots and celery. Cook additional hour on low until peas have reached a creamy consistency. Stir often to prevent soup from sticking.

Acorn Squash Soup
☆ ☆

3 cups Vegetable Soup Stock (page 207) | 2 medium acorn squashes
1 yellow or red bell pepper | 1 Tbsp. Vegetarian Worcestershire Sauce
3 apples (not green variety) | 1 tsp. curry powder
2 Tbsp. Better Than Milk | 1 large onion
Celtic Sea Salt to taste (optional)

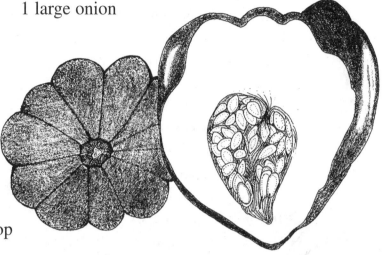

Scrub, halve and seed squash. In a large pan, bring 4 cups of distilled water to a boil. Add squash, cover and boil 15 to 20 minutes or until tender. While squash is cooking, peel, core and dice apples, and dice pepper and onion. Remove squash and allow to cool. Save liquid. When cool enough to handle, scoop out squash and set aside.

In a large sauce pan, steam onion and bell pepper until onion is transparent. Add squash, reserved liquid, apples, curry, Worcestershire, Vegetable Soup Stock and Celtic Sea Salt. Bring to a boil, and then reduce heat to simmer. Partially cover and cook for about 15 minutes, stirring occasionally.

Remove about half of the squash mixture, and allow to cool. When cool, place into a blender or food processor, add 2 Tbsp. of Better Than Milk and curry and puree. Return to soup pot, adjust seasonings, if needed, continue to heat until heated through, do not boil.

White Bean Soup
Submitted by Terri Stralow
☆ ☆ ☆

Try Good

1½ 2 cups white beans | 1 cup yellow or red pepper
2 cups onions | 1 cup cabbage
1 cup broccoli | 2 cups vegetable soup stock (page 207) *or water*
Celtic Sea Salt to taste (optional)
herbs of your choice such as sage, savory, basil, thyme

Soak beans overnight and drain. Place in pot with soup stock, cook for 1 ½ hours, adding more soup stock or distilled water if needed. While beans are cooking, chop onions, broccoli, pepper and cabbage.   Add these veggies, seasonings and Celtic Sea Salt to the beans after 1 ½ hours and cook an additional hour.

Cauliflower Chowder
☆ ☆ ☆

1 small onion	2 garlic cloves
1 tsp. caraway seed	1/2 tsp. Celtic Sea Salt (optional)
1 medium head of cauliflower	1 large carrot
1 or 2 steamed potatoes	6 cups vegetable soup stock (page 207)

Finely chop onion and mince garlic. Grind caraway seeds in a blender or food mill. Place onion, garlic, ground caraway and Celtic Sea Salt in a small pan and sauté in soup stock until tender.

Remove florets from the cauliflower and chop until bite-sized, and chop carrots into small pieces. Place potato in blender or food processor and puree. If necessary, add a small amount of soup stock. Add vegetables to soup stock and cook until just tender. Add Celtic Sea Salt to taste. Garnish with chopped scallions.

To make this a raw soup: Place florets, carrots and potatoes in a food processor and chop until very fine, place in pot with onion, garlic, and ground caraway seeds, add vegetable soup stock and heat just until warm. Do not boil. Garnish with scallions.

Corn Chowder (Cooked)
☆ ☆ ☆

6 cups vegetable soup stock (page 207)	4 cups potatoes
2 large onions	1 cup celery with leaves
1/2 cup fresh parsley	4 cups of fresh corn
1 Tbsp. Better Than Milk	Celtic Sea Salt to taste (optional)
1 Tbsp. garlic powder	1 Tbsp. dried onion flakes

Peel and dice potatoes, dice onions, mince parsley. Combine in a pan with the vegetable stock and cook until tender. Add celery and corn and continue to cook until just done. Take soup off heat and add seasonings. Remove about 1/3 of the soup and allow it to cool. In blender or food processor, place one cup of vegetable soup broth, add 1 Tbsp. of Better Than Milk and 1 Tbsp. whole wheat flour, the cooled soup and blend until smooth. Add to soup pot and heat to serving temperature, stirring constantly.

Barley Vegetable Soup
☆ ☆ ☆

8 cups vegetable soup stock (page 207)	1 cup onions
2 stalks of celery	2 parsnips or turnips *potatoe*
1 cup green beans	1 cup whole peas
1 cup barley, uncooked	1 cup carrots
2 Tbsp. parsley	1 tsp. Celtic Sea Salt
1/2 tsp. marjoram	1/2 tsp. thyme

Chop onions, dice carrots, celery, parsnips or turnips and slice green beans. Place in pot with small amount of water or soup stock and steam for about 10 minutes. Add the remainder of the soup stock and bring to a boil, add barley and allow to come back to a boil. Cover and turn down to low for about 45 minutes. Add peas and all seasonings except parsley and continue cooking another 40 minutes. Mix in parsley just prior to serving.

Black Bean Soup
☆ ☆ ☆

8 cups vegetable soup stock (page 207)	1 pound of black turtle beans
1 1/2 cup onion	1 yellow or red pepper (optional)
1 cup celery	1 cup carrots
1 potato	2 Tbsp. cilantro
2 garlic cloves	1 tsp. oregano
1 tsp. honey	1 tsp. apple cider vinegar
2 bay leaves	1 Tbsp. parsley
Celtic Sea Salt to taste (optional)	2 Tbsp. marjoram
chopped scallions for garnish	1 whole medium onion with 2 cloves in it

Sort turtle beans, removing broken beans or other foreign objects, rinse, cover with distilled water and soak overnight, drain. Place in pot with vegetable soup stock, onion with cloves and bay leaves, bring to a boil and cook about 2 1/2 hours or until beans are tender. Remove onion with cloves and bay leaves.

Meanwhile chop onion, pepper and celery (including leaves), and grate carrots and potato on a large grater. Mince garlic and sauté in a small amount of distilled water until al dente (firm but tender).

During the last hour of cooking, combine vegetables and seasonings with beans. Bring to a boil, lower heat to simmer and cook until the vegetables and beans are tender.

To serve, place in bowl and top with chopped scallions.

Carrot & Barley Soup

☆ ☆ ☆

8 cups vegetable soup stock (page 207)	2 cups onion
1/2 cup barley	Celtic Sea Salt to taste (optional)
2 cups carrots	3 garlic cloves
3 cups celery	1 Tbsp. garlic powder
1 tsp. basil	1 tsp. oregano
1/4 cup fresh parsley	1/2 tsp. cumin
2 cups tomatoes	1 tsp. Italian seasoning

Slice carrots and celery into thin slices, chop onions and tomatoes, mince parsley and garlic cloves and set aside. In a large pot combine soup stock (or distilled water if soup stock is not available) and barley, cover and cook over medium heat for 40 minutes. Add reserved vegetables and remaining ingredients. Reduce heat to low and cook an additional 45 minutes. If needed, add Celtic Sea Salt to taste.

If soup gets too thick, add more soup stock or tomato juice.

Curried Vegetable Stew

☆ ☆ ☆

2 cups onion	2 Tbsp. garlic
6 carrots	4 russett potatoes
1 medium cauliflower	2 cups green beans
2 cups fresh tomatoes	4 cups brown rice
1 1/2 Tbsp. curry powder	2 Tbsp. honey
1/2 cup golden raisins	1 cinnamon stick
1/2 cup fresh parsley	Celtic Sea Salt to taste (optional)
8 cups vegetable soup stock (page 207)	

Chop onions, peel and dice potatoes, peel carrots, cut in half and then into 1-inch pieces. Cut green beans into 1-inch pieces, cut tomatoes into small chunks (removing seeds), cut cauliflower into small pieces and mince garlic.

In a soup pan, dry roast rice for 2 minutes on medium heat, add onion and garlic to a small amount of soup stock, and cook until vegetables are tender. Sprinkle curry powder over onions, garlic and rice. Mix to mingle flavors.

Add the rest of the vegetable soup stock, the balance of the seasonings, bring to a boil, cover and reduce heat to its lowest setting and cook 20 minutes.

After 20 minutes, add the raisins, the rest of the vegetables except tomatoes and parsley, cover and continue to cook an additional 25 minutes, stirring occasionally.

The tomatoes and parsley should be added just prior to serving.

OK-) but not real great (handwritten)

Cream of Broccoli Soup
☆ ☆ (use ⅓ recipe) = 6 servings (handwritten)

1½ 4 - 6 cups broccoli	*⅔* 2 cups celery
1t 1 Tbsp. garlic powder	*dash* ⅛ tsp. cayenne *(use less !!!)*
4C 12 cups vegetable soup stock (page 207)	*⅔* 2 cups onions
Celtic Sea Salt to taste (optional)	*dash* ½ tsp. basil
2t 2 Tbsp. Better Than Milk	*⅔* 2 cups carrot
⅔ 2 cups basmati rice	*¼* ¾ cup red pepper

Prior to making the soup, prepare the thickener by using the following steps: for 2 minutes, dry roast 2 cups basmati rice in a dry skillet on low heat, add 2 minced garlic cloves and ¾ cup of each of the following: celery, onion and red pepper. Add 4 cups soup stock, cover and cook on lowest possible heat for 30 minutes, remove from heat and allow to sit 15 more minutes without removing the cover. Set aside to cool.

Peel and chop tender broccoli stalks and heads into small pieces, grate carrots or cut into small pieces and dice onions and celery. In a large soup kettle, steam carrots, celery and onions in a small amount of water for about 3 minutes. Add seasonings and remove from heat, and leave covered.

In a blender or Vita Mix, combine ⅓ of the rice with enough soup stock to cover and blend at high speed one minute or until creamy. Continue to blend the rest of the rice mixture, ⅓ at time. To the last ⅓ of rice, add 2 or 3 cups of the chopped broccoli and blend until mixed well. When all rice is blended, add to soup pot, along with the remainder of the soup stock, stirring to blend.

Place over medium heat, add the rest of the broccoli, steamed vegetables, two Tbsp. of "Better Than Milk" powder, which has been mixed in a blender with distilled water or cold soup stock, and Celtic Sea Salt. Cook until broccoli is al dente (firm but tender). To serve, top with a few broccoli florets.

Creamy Carrot Soup
☆ ☆

6 cups vegetable soup stock (page 207)	2 large onions
4 cups carrot	1 tsp. dill weed
2 Tbsp. honey	2 Tbsp. Better Than Milk
1/3 cup basmati rice	Celtic Sea Salt to taste (optional)

Grate carrots and dice onions, then sauté in a small amount of water for 3 to 5 minutes, add honey and mix well. Stir in rice, soup stock and dill weed. Heat to boiling, stir, cover and reduce heat to low. Cook until rice is done, about 45 minutes. Ladle about half of the soup into a food processor, and allow to cool, add Better Than Milk, then puree. Return to pot, heat, but do not boil. Add Celtic Sea Salt to taste. Serve with seasoned croutons and chopped scallions or green onion tops.

Country Stew
☆ ☆ ☆

1/4 cup barley	6 cups vegetable soup stock (page 207)
1 cup celery	1 cup onion
1 cup cabbage	1 garlic clove
3 cups raw potatoes	1/2 cup fresh minced parsley
	1 cup carrot
	1 cup peas
	Celtic Sea Salt to taste (optional)

Dice celery and onion, chop cabbage, cube potatoes, cut carrots into 2-inch sticks and mince garlic and parsley. Cook barley in soup stock. Lightly steam onion, celery and garlic in small amount of soup stock, add to barley. Add remaining ingredients except peas. When other vegetables are almost tender, add peas.

To thicken, remove 1/3 of the barley/ vegetable mixture, and allow to cool. When cool, blend in blender or food processor, adding 1 Tbsp. of whole wheat flour. Slowly add back into stew, stirring constantly until desired consistency and temperature is reached. Add Celtic Sea Salt to taste.

Potato, Squash Soup
☆ ☆

8 to 10 cups of vegetable soup stock (page 207)	2 carrots
1 butternut squash or 2 acorn squash	2 medium onions
6 medium potatoes	4 garlic cloves
1 ½ cup of celery	2 cups broccoli
½ cup fresh parsley	1 tsp. basil
Celtic Sea Salt to taste (optional)	1 tsp. sage
2 Tbsp. Better Than Milk	

Peel and cube squash, potatoes, and dice onion and celery. Shred carrots, chop broccoli into small pieces and mince parsley and garlic cloves. In a soup kettle, place vegetables and seasonings, along with vegetable soup stock, and cook 45 to 60 minutes until all vegetables are tender. Remove 4 to 6 cups of the mixture and allow to cool. When cool, place in blender or food processor, add Better Than Milk and blend, return to soup and heat but do not boil.

Lentil, Barley Stew
☆ ☆ ☆

14 oz. dried lentils	4 cups vegetable soup stock (page 207)
1 medium onion	2 cloves of garlic
2 stalks of celery with leaves	4 medium carrots
3 cups fresh tomatoes	1 tsp. dried rosemary
½ cup barley	½ tsp. oregano
½ tsp. cumin	Celtic Sea Salt to taste (optional)
1 potato	

Peel and dice tomatoes, chop carrots and mince garlic. Dice celery and onion. In a soup stock pan, bring lentils, barley, onion, garlic, celery, carrots and vegetable stock to a boil, reduce heat to lowest temperature, cover, and simmer for 35 minutes. Add the tomatoes and seasonings, cover and simmer 20 to 25 minutes longer or until the lentils are tender.

Curried Millet Spinach Soup

Submitted by Jean Jacobson

☆ ☆ ☆

1 ½ cups onions	²/₃ cup millet
7 cups vegetable soup stock (page 207)	2 cloves of garlic
2 medium potatoes	1 large carrot
2 cups fresh tomatoes	1 tsp. ginger root
2 tsp. curry powder	1 cup spinach

Peel and dice tomatoes and potatoes, chop onion and carrot, mince garlic, grate ginger, and cut spinach into pieces. Dry roast millet until one shade darker, add vegetables, **except spinach**, and sauté lightly in a small amount of vegetable broth. Add rest of vegetable broth and curry powder, and bring to a boil. Simmer, covered over a low heat until millet is tender. Add the juice of ½ of a lemon. For additional flavor add 2 heaping tsp. of your favorite herb mixture. After cooking, add spinach for a garnish when serving.

Soupe au Pistou (Vegetable Soup with Basil)

Submitted by Joann Hicks, Past President of American Nutrition Society

☆ ☆ ☆

Pesto Sauce:

1 Tbsp. sweet basil	4 cloves of garlic
1/4 cup olive oil	

Mince cloves and mix with basil and olive oil. Refrigerate while soup is cooking:

Vegetable Soup:

3 cups Italian tomatoes	2 cups fresh green beans
3 medium potatoes	1 onion
Celtic Sea Salt to taste (optional)	4 cups distilled water

Peel tomatoes, cut green beans into 1-inch lengths, peel and cube potatoes, grate or finely chop onion. Add enough distilled water so that the vegetables are just covered. Place in crock pot, turn on low and cook overnight. Just prior to serving, remove from slow cooker, and mix in pesto sauce. Mix well to combine.

Hearty Vegetable Stew
☆ ☆ ☆

try

1 quart vegetable soup stock (page 207)	6 medium red potatoes
1 medium onion	1 garlic clove
4 cups tomatoes	4 carrots
1 cup green beans	2 cups fresh peas
4 stalks of celery with tops	6 sprigs of parsley or 3 tsp. dried
1/2 tsp. thyme	1/4 tsp. basil
1 bay leaf	Celtic Sea Salt to taste (optional)

Dice celery and onion, peel and cube tomatoes and potatoes, slice carrots and green beans, mince garlic, remove stems from parsley, if using fresh, and mince. Steam sauté vegetables in a small amount of soup stock until al dente. Add the rest of the soup stock and the seasonings, bring to boil, cover and reduce heat to low. Cook an additional 30 minutes, add peas, cover and continue cooking 15 minutes.

Serve in deep bowls with toasted whole grain bread.

Sea Shell Stew

☆ ☆ ☆

8 cups vegetable soup stock (page 207)	2 cups celery
4 garlic cloves	3 cups red or yellow pepper
4 cups onions	Celtic Sea Salt to taste (optional)
2 tsp. oregano	2 tsp. basil
4 cups zucchini	4 cups carrot
3 cups garbanzo beans	6 cups whole-grain shells
1 cup fresh parsley or 1/2 cup dried	2 cups fresh tomatoes

Wash and soak garbanzo beans overnight, drain, cover with fresh water and cook until tender. Drain and set aside.

Mince garlic, parsley (if fresh), and chop onions, peppers, carrots and celery. Cut zucchini into quarters and then into 1/2-inch pieces. Peel and chop tomatoes into bite-sized pieces. Sauté garlic, pepper, celery and onion in a small amount of water until tender. Add tomatoes, soup stock and seasonings and simmer 30 minutes. Add zucchini, carrots and parsley and simmer an additional 15 to 20 minutes. Add cooked garbanzos.

In a separate pan cook whole-grain pasta shells. Place 1/2 cup in each bowl when serving.

Two-Potato Soup

☆ ☆

3 large sweet potatoes	3 large baking potatoes
2 cups of celery	2 medium onions
2 cloves of garlic	1/2 cup parsley
1 cup carrots	1 tsp. dill weed
2 Tbsp. Better Than Milk	Celtic Sea Salt to taste (optional)
Pinch of cayenne	1 Tbsp. All Purpose Seasoning

Cube all potatoes, finely chop celery and onions, crush the garlic, and shred the carrots. Sauté onion and celery in small amount of distilled water for 3 minutes. Add the rest of the ingredients except Better Than Milk and enough distilled water to cover. Bring to a boil, then turn down to medium heat. Cook about 45 minutes until the vegetables are tender.

Remove 3 to 4 cups of vegetables, cool partially, place the veggies in a food processor with the Better Than Milk and puree. Add back to the soup, heat to serving temperature and serve.

Veggie Stew

submitted by Michael Dye

☆ ☆ ☆

distilled water

tomato sauce

1 cup split peas

3/4 cup lentils

1/3 cup millet or couscous

1/3 cup barley

1/3 cup buckwheat

1/4 cup brown rice

1 tsp. curry powder

2 potatoes

1 - 2 onions

2 large carrots

2 stalks celery

2 small yellow squash or zucchini

1 1/2 cups broccoli florets

1/4 tsp. garlic

1/4 tsp. cayenne powder (optional)

herbs of your choice (such as oregano, cumin, parsley, thyme)

Begin by bringing a large kettle of distilled water and 1 tsp. olive oil to a boil and adding each of the grains and curry powder from the left column. Let the grains begin cooking before you start preparing the vegetables from the right column. The grains will need to simmer for about 90 minutes, while being stirred occasionally, to result in a thick, full-bodied texture. These grains will expand while cooking, so add more distilled water when necessary. But don't add so much water that the stew becomes too thin or watery.

While the grains are cooking, begin washing and chopping the vegetables. I wash, chop and add to the stew each of the vegetables from the right column in the order listed, because some vegetables need to cook longer than others. As you are adding the vegetables and stirring the stew, you will notice it getting thicker and thicker as the grains expand, which requires you to add more distilled water. Toward the end of preparing the vegetables, instead of adding more water, begin to add tomato sauce.

If, in the last 30 minutes of cooking, you add just enough water and tomato sauce to keep it from sticking, this will be a very thick and hearty stew.

Chapter Twenty-one:

Live Food Delicacies

Marinaded Tomatoes
☆ ☆ ☆ ☆ ☆

3 tomatoes	1 or 2 medium onions
2 cucumbers	1 red pepper

   Chop tomatoes and cucumbers, and thinly slice onion and pepper. Combine and lightly toss in a bowl. Marinate in Italian dressing or Three-Day Coleslaw Dressing (see page 161).

Marinaded Broccoli Salad
try
☆ ☆ ☆ ☆ ☆

2 bunches of broccoli florets	1 red bell pepper
1/2 red onion	1 green bell pepper
1 tsp. Celtic Sea Salt (optional)	1/4 cup extra virgin olive oil

   Into a medium bowl, cut broccoli into small florets, chop peppers fine and dice onion. Add Celtic Sea Salt and olive oil, mix well. Cover and allow to sit at least 1/2 hour for flavors to blend.

Cucumber Pickles
☆ ☆ ☆ ☆ ☆

4 - 6 cucumbers	1 medium red onion
1/3 cup lemon juice	2 Tbsp. fresh parsley
1/2 tsp. turmeric	1/8 tsp. cayenne
1 garlic clove	1/2 cup Celtic Sea Salt
2 Tbsp. honey	1 tsp. dill weed
1 tsp. All Purpose Seasoning	1 cup distilled water

Scrub cucumbers and peel if not organic. Slice cucumbers into rounds, slice red onion thin, mince parsley and combine in a bowl.

In a separate bowl, combine the lemon juice, crushed garlic and seasonings. Add Celtic Sea Salt and distilled water, and pour over cucumbers. Cover, refrigerate and allow to sit at least half an hour for flavors to mingle. The flavor improves the longer the ingredients are allowed to marinate.

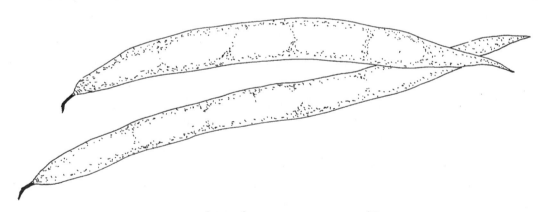

Marinaded Green Beans
☆ ☆ ☆ ☆ ☆

1 pound of green beans	2 Tbsp. red onion
1 garlic clove	2 stalks of celery
1/2 tsp. dried rosemary	1 cup tomato
1/4 cup fresh basil	juice of 1/2 lemon
1 Tbsp. extra virgin olive oil	Celtic Sea Salt to taste (optional)

Wash and remove ends from green beans, slice lengthwise and then diagonally into 1-inch pieces, seed and chop tomato, dice celery, mince garlic and basil. Combine with other ingredients and allow to marinate one hour before serving.

Sauerkraut
☆ ☆ ☆ ☆ ☆

Red or green cabbage, or a combination of the two, may be used to make sauerkraut. Remove outer leaves and set aside about 8 leaves. Finely chop about 4 heads of cabbage and set aside. In a food processor using an "S" blade, feed another 4 heads of cabbage through the feeding tube to create a very fine mush. This also can be accomplished by processing through the Green Star or Champion juicer using the blank instead of the screen.

Combine all cabbage. Place about 4 inches of the cabbage mixture in a crock, and sprinkle with a tablespoon of kelp powder and a layer of wakame. Continue to layer until all of the cabbage is used. Cover with the cabbage leaves, which have been set aside. Wipe down the sides of the crock or glass container so they are clean (this helps to prevent spoilage).

Place a plate over the leaves and weight it down with jars filled with water or use a plastic bag about 3/4 full of water and tied tightly. Cover with a clean dish towel, move to a cool, dark place and allow it to work for approximately five to seven days, depending on temperature (the warmer the temperature, the faster the cabbage will work).

When the sauerkraut has fermented, remove jars and plate or plastic bag. Discard the cabbage leaves from the top and remove any residue which may be on the sides of the container or on the top layer of kraut. Place the sauerkraut in jars or other glass containers to be stored in the refrigerator until needed. Sauerkraut will usually keep about a month if stored properly.

For variation, add any of the following to your "kraut" when preparing it: Grated carrots, dill weed, chopped scallions, chopped red onion, garlic cloves, grated beets, celery slices or apple pieces, or your favorite vegetables.

Marinaded Vegetable Combo
☆ ☆ ☆ ☆ ☆

1/8 cup Celtic Sea Salt	1 cup distilled water
1/3 cup lemon juice	2 medium zucchini
1/2 head of cauliflower florets	1/2 head broccoli florets
4 garlic cloves	1 carrot
1/2 red onion	1 handful of cherry tomatoes
1/4 cup extra virgin olive oil	

Mix Celtic Sea Salt, distilled water, olive oil and lemon juice, and set aside.

Prepare cauliflower and broccoli florets, dice zucchini, and thinly slice carrots and onion. Cut tomatoes in half, and peel whole garlic cloves. Combine all ingredients and marinate. Allow to sit 2 hours, mixing occasionally. Drain before serving.

For added flavor, add 1 tsp. of your favorite herbs to the marinade.

try

Sunflower Loaf
☆ ☆ ☆ ☆ ☆

1 cup hulled sunflower seeds
1 cup almonds
1 cup pumpkins seeds
$1/2$ red pepper
$1/4$ cup parsley
$1/2$ red onion
1 garlic clove
1 carrot

Soak seeds and almonds overnight and drain. In food processor with an "S" blade, a Green Star using the blank and with the least amount of tension, or a Champion Juicer with the blank in place, put the seeds, carrot, garlic and almonds through. To this mixture, add the minced parsley, finely chopped red pepper and onion.

Make a sauce of the following in a blender or food processor.

2 medium tomatoes   1 Tbsp. basil
1 tsp. Celtic Sea Salt (optional)   1 Tbsp. oregano

Mix half of the sauce into the loaf mixture, form into loaf, cover and set aside unrefrigerated for 4 to 6 hours*. To serve, place the loaf on a bed of lettuce and pour the remaining tomato mixture over the top.

***Hint:** The longer this loaf is allowed to marinate, the stronger the flavors become.

Almost Turkey
☆ ☆ ☆ ☆ ☆

2 cups almonds	2 cups celery
2 medium tomatoes	2 cups carrots
1 cup zucchini	1 cup yellow squash
1/4 tsp. sage	1 Tbsp. fresh parsley
1/2 tsp. kelp	2 Tbsp. flaxseed meal
lecithin	leaf lettuce

In a blender or food processor, grind 1 cup of almonds into meal and grind one cup of almonds into almond butter in your Champion or Green Star juicer (see page 284). Peel and dice tomatoes into small pieces. Shred carrots, squash and zucchini. Cut 1/2 of the celery into 1-inch pieces and juice, dice the other 1/2 of the celery fine. Combine all ingredients, making a stiff dough-like consistency. Add more ground almonds or flaxseed if the dough is too thin. Press mixture into a lecithin-lined pan or turkey mold and chill. Serve on a bed of lettuce, garnished with cherry tomatoes and carrot slices. Serve with cranberry sauce (page 293).

Asparagus with Cream Sauce
☆ ☆ ☆ ☆ ☆

    1 lb. of young asparagus
    1 cup red bell pepper
    1/2 cup celery
    Celtic Sea Salt to taste (optional)
    1 Tbsp. parsley
    leaf lettuce

Cut asparagus into 1-inch pieces, mince parsley, dice celery and red pepper into small pieces. Combine asparagus, celery and half of the pepper in a bowl. Toss to mix. Pour over one recipe of Almond-Sunflower Seed Sauce (page 285). Garnish with the rest of the red pepper and minced parsley. Serve on a bed of leaf lettuce.

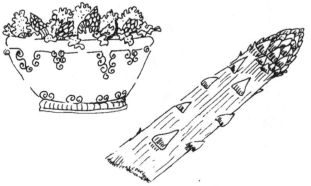

Preparing Raw Whole Grains

Whole grains that are soaked can be used for babies, toddlers, the elderly or anyone else who may have trouble chewing. Because the grain has been soaked, the enzymes have become active, which aids the digestive system and makes a nice texture for cereals.

Measure the amount of grain to be used. Place in a strainer and rinse thoroughly with cold water. Coarsely chop the grain to break the protective outer layer, using a grain mill, food mill or coffee grinder. Place in a container with an equal amount of distilled water (for example, one cup of grain to one cup of distilled water). As the grain absorbs the water, *it will double in volume.* One cup dry equals two cups soaked.

Place a cover over the container and allow to *soak at room temperature* from 18 to 24 hours. (Placing grains in the refrigerator will slow the absorption process.) Grains soaked 18 hours will be more chewy, while those allowed to soak 24 hours will be a much softer texture. During the soaking process, the grain will absorb most of the moisture and may begin to sprout.

Soaking more than 24 hours may start the fermenting process and the grain will be unpalatable. Therefore, after soaking, drain the grain to remove any excess liquid and keep it in the refrigerator in a covered container. Soaked grain will keep for several days.

Fruit and vegetable juices do not penetrate whole grains well, even when soaked at room temperature. Therefore always soak grains in distilled water. If a recipe calls for juice, add it after the grain has been soaked and drained. In recipes that do not specify "soaked grain," soaking is not required.

Almond Paté
☆ ☆ ☆ ☆ ☆

2 cups almonds	1 cup chopped cucumber
1/4 cup red onion	1 stalk celery
1/2 cup carrot	1/4 cup fresh dill
dash of cayenne	1 Tbsp. fresh basil
1/4 tsp. cumin	2 Tbsp. tahini
1 Tbsp. sesame seeds	Celtic Sea Salt to taste (optional)

Process nuts, seeds and vegetables through a Green Star or Champion juicer using the blank instead of the screen, or in a food processor or Vita Mix until creamy. Add seasonings and mix well. Form into a loaf. Chill before serving. Delicious with Vegetable Crisps on page 305.

Italian Vegetables & Bulgar
☆ ☆ ☆ ☆ ☆

1½ cups bulgar wheat	½ cup carrot
½ cup rye flakes	¼ cup celery
1 cup oat flakes	3 cups tomatoes
1 cup red onion	½ tsp. Italian seasoning
3 tsp. ground sesame	1 cup zucchini
1 cup bell pepper	

Cover grains with distilled water and soak overnight, drain. Grate carrot, mince onion, chop tomatoes, zucchini, celery, and bell pepper. Combine with grain mixture, add seasonings and ground sesame seeds. Spoon into bowls, top with Italian dressing (page 181), if desired.

Vegetable Nut Loaf
☆ ☆ ☆ ☆ ☆

1 cup hulled sunflower seeds	1½ cup almonds
½ cup sesame seeds	¾ cup celery
¾ cup parsley	1 garlic clove
1 cup ground carrots	¼ cup red onion or chives
1 tsp. Celtic Sea Salt (optional)	½ tsp. caraway seeds
1 cup red bell pepper	¾ cup tomatoes

Soak sesame seeds and almonds overnight in separate bowls. After 12-24 hours, drain, rinse, and process through Champion juicer using the blank instead of the screen, or through the Green Star Juicer using the closed blank with the least amount of tension, or process in a food processor using the "S" blade. Process enough carrots to equal 1 cup. Combine all ingredients.

Finely chop celery, onion, tomatoes, and bell pepper. Mince garlic and parsley. Combine all ingredients and mix to blend flavors. Form into a loaf, cover and allow to sit unrefrigerated on the counter for 4 or 5 hours* to allow flavors to blend.

Serve on a bed of lettuce, parsley, or spinach.

***Hint:** The longer this loaf is allowed to sit, the stronger the flavors become.

Almost Crab

☆ ☆ ☆ ☆ ☆

6 cups parsnips
3 Tbsp. green onion
1 small clove garlic
1/4 tsp. dry mustard (optional)

1/2 cup celery
1/2 cup carrot
1 1/2 cups Rhonda's Dressing (page 175)
1/8 tsp. cayenne pepper

Coarsely grind parsnips, chop celery and green onions, mince garlic and finely grate carrot. Combine and serve on a bed of mixed salad greens. Garnish with paprika.

Cabbage Rolls

☆ ☆ ☆ ☆ ☆

1/2 cup yellow squash
1/2 cup zucchini
1 cup celery
1 cup kohlrabi
1 cup red cabbage
1/2 cup carrot

Dice celery fine, shred squashes, cabbage, carrot and kohlrabi, combine in a bowl and add avocado dressing (pg 176) or almond butter (pg 284) to reach a creamy consistency.

Wash and prepare 6 or 8 outer cabbage leaves or napa cabbage leaves. Divide the filling equally and roll each leaf and secure with a toothpick.

Stuffed Tomatoes
☆ ☆ ☆ ☆

Stuffed tomatoes can be absolutely scrumptious! Just take a large, ripe, tomato and core out the stem end. Cut the tomato (stem-end up) into 8 wedges – but stop about a half inch from the bottom. If the bottom is rounded and will not sit flat, flatten it by cutting a little off. Place on plate on top of a large piece of leaf lettuce (not head lettuce). Stuff with your favorite stuffing and serve with celery and carrot sticks, red and/or green pepper rings, etc.

For *Taboule* stuffing, place in small mixing bowl: 1 cup bulgar wheat soaked in 2 cups of distilled water a half hour before adding the following ingredients:

> 2 Tbsp. fresh parsley (or 1 tsp. dry)
> 2 Tbsp. each of chopped onion, celery and pepper
> 1 tomato chopped
> 2 Tbsp. cucumber, chopped fine
> ½ tsp. Celtic Sea Salt (optional)
> 1 to 2 Tbsp. extra virgin olive oil
> ¼ cup fresh lemon juice
> 2 Tbsp. fresh mint (or 1 tsp. dried)

Toss lightly. Refrigerate at least one hour before stuffing the tomato. You can change the flavor of Taboule by adding or omitting different vegetables or seasonings. Taboule can also be served on a bed of lettuce without being stuffed into a tomato.

You can also use quinoa, couscous or brown rice cooked according to directions in place of the wheat in the above recipe.

Another stuffing for the tomato would be to chop your favorite veggies into small pieces - as great a variety as desired. Sauté till desired tenderness in vegetable broth, distilled water or small amount of extra virgin olive oil. (Add some herbs while sautéing if desired.) Place into prepared stuffing tomato as explained above. Top with a sauce made from two blended tomatoes, three garlic cloves, Celtic Sea Salt and your favorite herbs (basil, oregano or mixed herbs).

Still another excellent stuffing for tomatoes is the guacamole recipe on page 288.

Better than Tuna
☆ ☆ ☆ ☆ ☆

try

2 cups carrots	2 stalks of celery
1 medium ripe bell pepper	1/2 medium red onion
1 tomato (optional)	1/2 cup parsley
1/2 tsp. Celtic Sea Salt (optional)	1/2 tsp. kelp
4 Tbsp. Rhonda's No-Oil Dressing	

Finely chop the pepper, celery, onion and tomato, and place in a bowl. Finely grate carrots, resembling carrot pulp, and add the carrot to the vegetable mixture.

Combine 4 Tbsp. of Rhonda's dressing, Celtic Sea Salt, parsley and kelp and add to the above chopped vegetables. Mix well and allow to marinate for flavors to blend. May be served on a bed of lettuce, on a sandwich, or to stuff a pita or tomato.

Broccoli & Cauliflower with "Cheese"
☆ ☆ ☆ ☆ ☆

try

2 bunches of broccoli	1/2 head of cauliflower
1/3 cup tahini	2 small garlic cloves
1/4 cup lemon juice	1/3 cup distilled water
3/4 cup sunflower seeds	Celtic Sea Salt to taste (optional)
1/4 cup red onion	

Cut broccoli florets from the stalks and cauliflower into small florets and place in a large bowl. Mince onion. In a blender or food processor combine the tahini, garlic, lemon juice, water and Celtic Sea Salt and process until creamy. Pour over broccoli and cauliflower, and stir to combine. Garnish with sunflower seeds and onion.

Lemon & Herb Marinade
☆ ☆ ☆ ☆ ☆

1/4 cup lemon juice	1/2 cup extra virgin olive oil
1/4 cup flax seed oil or olive oil	2 Tbsp. chives
1 tsp. chevril	1/4 cup parsley
2 garlic cloves	1/8 tsp. cayenne pepper (optional)

Mince chives, parsley and garlic clove. Combine with other ingredients and mix well.

Bulgar Wheat Surprise
☆ ☆ ☆ ☆

$2/3$ cup bulgar wheat (cracked)	$2/3$ cup distilled water*
$1/2$ tsp. garlic powder	1 tsp. Celtic Sea Salt (optional)
1 Tbsp. extra virgin olive oil	$1/2$ cup bell pepper
$1/4$ cup red onion	$1/2$ cup carrot
$1/2$ cup tomato	$1/2$ cup cucumber

Place bulgar wheat in a bowl, add spices, olive oil and Celtic Sea Salt, and mix well. Add distilled water and stir well. The water should cover all of the bulgar wheat. Cover and let sit for approximately 30 minutes.**

Dice bell pepper, onion, tomato and cucumber, and shred carrot. Add the vegetables and mix well. Taste and adjust seasonings if necessary. Experiment with other seasonings, such as a pinch of curry, cayenne or ginger.

* Vegetable soup stock on page 207 may be substituted for water.
** Bulgar wheat has already been cracked, not requiring a longer soaking time.

Garden Delight Aspic
☆ ☆ ☆

1 cup red pepper	1 cup fresh corn
$1/2$ cup red onion	1 $1/2$ cups celery
1 cup cucumber	1 cup carrot
$1/2$ cup lemon juice	$3/4$ cup Rhonda's No Oil Dressing
1 tsp. Celtic Sea Salt (optional)	3 Tbsp. agar agar
1 cup Vegetable Soup Stock (page 207)	leaf lettuce
chives	

Peel, seed and finely chop cucumber. Peel and shred carrot. Chop red pepper, onion and celery fine, place all vegetables in a bowl. Dissolve agar agar in Vegetable Soup stock, and heat slowly, stirring with a whisk to blend. Pour over vegetables, add lemon juice, Celtic Sea Salt, and No Oil Dressing. Mix well, pour into mold, and refrigerate until firm. Serve on a bed of leaf lettuce and garnish with chopped chives.

Tacos
☆ ☆ ☆ ☆ ☆

try

lettuce or Napa cabbage leaves	chopped tomatoes
diced celery	shredded zucchini squash
shredded yellow squash	finely chopped red or yellow bell pepper
finely chopped cucumber	finely chopped red onion
finely chopped chives	

Prepare all ingredients and place in separate bowls. On a lettuce or cabbage leaf, place a row of desired vegetables down the center, top with raw salsa (page 288) or guacamole (page 288), fold up bottom and fold one side over the other.

Chili
☆ ☆ ☆ ☆ ☆

try

1 tsp. garlic	
2 tsp. cumin	
1 tsp. oregano	2 tsp. basil
5 Tbsp. lemon juice	1 tsp. Celtic Sea Salt (optional)
6 cups tomato	1 cup celery
1 cup red onion	1/2 cup corn kernels (optional)
1 small garlic clove	1 cup red, yellow or orange bell pepper
1/2 cup honey	1 cup cracked Bulgar Wheat (optional)

Juice tomatoes to equal 3 cups of juice. Squeeze lemon. Mince garlic, finely chop onion, bell peppers and celery, chop 3 cups of tomatoes, husk corn and remove kernels. Place these ingredients in a bowl with the tomato juice and seasonings. Cover and refrigerate overnight to allow flavors to mingle. If chili is too thick, add more juiced tomatoes.

For more texture, cracked bulgar wheat may be added. Soak bulger wheat in 1 cup of distilled water or Vegetable Soup Stock for 25 to 30 minutes before adding to chili.

Hint: If desired, chili may be warmed slightly. Do not boil; remember enzymes start to die at 107 degrees.

Summer Squash, Italian Style
☆ ☆ ☆ ☆ ☆

4 cups summer squash
2 red peppers
1 avocado
1 cup shredded carrot

1 cup celery
2 large tomatoes
12 - 14 cherry tomatoes
1 tsp. Italian seasoning

Shred summer squash, finely chop celery and peppers, and quarter cherry tomatoes. Blend avocado and large tomatoes until creamy. Mix in the celery, quartered cherry tomatoes, half the squash, Italian seasoning and peppers. Place the remainder of the summer squash on a bed of mixed greens, add a layer of the avocado and tomato mixture, and top with shredded carrot.

Stuffed Peppers
Submitted by Max Majireck
☆ ☆ ☆ ☆ ☆

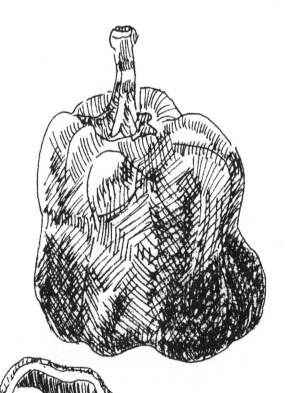

Cut yellow or red bell pepper in half lengthwise, remove seeds and ribs and stuff raw pepper with raw vegetables of your choice, such as minced broccoli, onions, cauliflower, shredded cabbage, carrot, beet, parsnip, squash, turnip and chopped tomato. Drizzle with 1 Tbsp. flax seed oil or extra virgin olive oil and season with your favorite herb mixture.

Hint: It takes a little practice eating these without spilling the liquid contents!

Options: Omit oil and use mashed avocado or almond butter.

Garlic & Herb Seed Cheese
☆ ☆ ☆ ☆ ☆

1 cup Basic Seed Sauce (page 277)	3 garlic cloves
1 tsp. dill weed*	2 tsp. onion & garlic
1 tsp. basil*	1 tsp fresh lemon juice
2 tsp. parsley*	1/4 tsp. Celtic Sea Salt (optional)

Mince onion, parsley and garlic. Combine all ingredients in a small bowl. Cover and allow to sit 4 to 8 hours for flavors to mingle.

* If herbs are fresh, use 1/2 Tbsp.

Butternut Squash & Veggies
☆ ☆ ☆ ☆ ☆

2 pounds tender asparagus	10 radishes
1 avocado	1 cup red pepper
1 cup red onion	1 head leaf lettuce
3 Tbsp. fresh parsley	1 butternut squash

Snap tough ends off asparagus. Cut off tips and slice stalks on the diagonal into 1/2-inch pieces. Julienne cut (into fine shreds) radishes and red pepper. Dice onion and mince parsley, tear leaf lettuce into bite-sized pieces. Shred butternut squash.

On a plate, make a bed of leaf lettuce, top with squash and arrange veggies in a colorful display. Just prior to serving, add finely diced avocado and top with Italian Dressing on page 181.

Cucumber Medley
☆ ☆ ☆ ☆ ☆

3 cucumbers	1 cup of celery
1 small zucchini	1/2 red bell pepper
3 scallions	1 ripe tomato
1 cup carrot	1/2 yellow bell pepper

Peel cucumbers, cut in half lengthwise, carefully remove seeds with a spoon. Grate carrot, finely chop zucchini, scallions, peppers, celery and tomato. Add 1 Tbsp. fresh basil or 1 tsp. dried basil and mix well. Add Celtic Sea Salt to taste, if desired. Blend in 1/2 cup of almond butter (page 284) and stuff cucumbers. Top with minced parsley.

Chinese Vegetables
☆ ☆ ☆ ☆ ☆

1 large garlic clove	2 cups celery
1 large red onion	1 medium red bell pepper
1/2 tsp. Celtic Sea Salt (optional)	2 cups Chinese cabbage
1/3 cup almonds	

Sliver almonds into small slices. Mince garlic, cut celery into thin U-shaped pieces, cut pepper and onion into thin strips and shred Chinese cabbage.

On a warmed plate, make a bed of shredded cabbage, top with vegetables and slivered almonds.

Make the following sauce and stir until well blended. Place in a saucepan and heat until thickened, cool slightly, and pour over vegetables:

2 Tbsp. arrow root powder	1 tsp. Celtic Sea Salt (optional)
3/4 cup distilled water.	

Lettuce Leaf Rolls
☆ ☆ ☆ ☆ ☆

6 large leaves of leaf lettuce
4 cups carrots
2 cups bell peppers
1 cup celery
1 tomato
1/2 cup green onions
1/2 cup almond butter
1 Tbsp. red onion

1/2 tsp. fresh basil
1 garlic clove

In a Green Power or Champion Juicer, process enough almonds to make 1/2 cup of almond butter (page 284). Set aside. Shred carrots, chop bell pepper, tomato, green onion and celery and red onion fine, sliver almonds, press garlic and mince basil.

Spread each lettuce leaf with a layer of almond butter. Sprinkle with peppers, carrots, tomatoes, green onions, almonds and seasonings.

Roll up the leaves using toothpicks to hold them together.

Marinaded Mixed Vegetables

☆ ☆ ☆ ☆ ☆

1 head of cauliflower	2 cups broccoli florets
3 large carrots	1 red bell pepper
1 yellow bell pepper	1 small red onion
1 Tbsp. Italian Seasoning (page 313)	$1/4$ cup Distilled water
$1/3$ cup extra virgin olive oil	1 tsp. Celtic Sea Salt

Cut cauliflower and broccoli into small florets, cut carrots into $1/4$-inch rounds, cut peppers into $1/4$ inch strips, and cut onion into thin rings. Combine all vegetables in a bowl and toss to mix. Combine Celtic Sea Salt, olive oil and Italian seasoning in a covered jar and shake. Pour over vegetables, cover and refrigerate for at least one hour to allow flavors to mingle.

Marinaded Vegetables & Rye

☆ ☆ ☆ ☆ ☆

1 cup cauliflower florets	1 cup broccoli florets
1 $1/2$ cups zucchini	$1/2$ cup beets
1 cup green onions	$1/2$ cup celery
$1/2$ cup carrots	2 $1/2$ cups soaked rye

Soak rye as directed on page 225, remembering 1 cup dry is equal to 2 cups soaked.

Cut the cauliflower and broccoli into florets and place in a bowl. Combine with the Lemon & Herb Marinade (page 229) overnight. The next day, slice the zucchini into rounds, grate the carrots and beets, dice the celery and finely chop the green onions.

Combine marinaded broccoli and cauliflower with the other vegetables. Serve on a plate lined with leaf lettuce, place a mound of soaked rye topped with marinaded vegetables.

Cauliflower, Broccoli & Bok Choy

☆ ☆ ☆ ☆ ☆

2 cups broccoli florets	$1/3$ cup almonds, pecans, or walnuts
1 cup bok choy stems and leaves	1 cup cauliflower florets
2 medium tomatoes	

Cut cauliflower and broccoli into florets, cut bok choy stems and leaves lengthwise and then diagonally. Chop tomatoes and nuts. Combine all ingredients and top with Avocado Tomato Dressing (page 176).

Seed Cheese Pie
☆ ☆ ☆ ☆ ☆

2 cups vegetable seed cheese (page 295) $1/2$ cup broccoli
4 cups greens (lettuce, spinach, kale) $1/2$ cup cauliflower
$1/2$ cup carrot   1 cup almonds
$1/2$ cup scallions

Mince broccoli and cauliflower minute florets, shred carrots very fine, sliver almonds, mince scallions and shred greens.

In a 10-inch pie plate, layer $1/4$ of the greens, and with a knife, spread a layer of seed cheese, add a layer of broccoli, a layer of cheese, a layer of greens, a layer of cauliflower, a layer of cheese, a layer of carrots, a layer of greens, a layer of cheese, a layer of scallions, and top with the balance of the greens. Cover and chill. To serve, place a plate over the pie plate and invert. Garnish with slivered almonds.

Millet Burgers
☆ ☆ ☆ ☆ ☆

1 cup millet $3/4$ cup celery
$1/4$ cup soft wheat berries $1/4$ cup carrot
$1/4$ cup chives $1/3$ cup tahini
$1/4$ cup red onion   2 garlic cloves
1 tsp. Celtic Sea Salt (optional) $1/3$ cup distilled water
2 tsp. oregano   2 tsp. cumin

Place millet and wheat berries in separate bowls in enough distilled water to cover and soak overnight. Drain and rinse. Place wheat berries, garlic, tahini, seasonings and distilled water in a food processor and blend well. Set aside.

Place millet in the food processor and pulse chop, add to sauce mixture. Fold in finely grated carrot, finely minced chives, onion and celery. Add Celtic Sea Salt.

Form into burgers and dehydrate at 105 degrees until they reach a consistency you desire. It will take about 24 hours.

Raw Vegetarian Pizza
☆ ☆ ☆ ☆ ☆

Crust:

1/2 medium tomato	1/2 cup dehydrated tomatoes
3/4 cup almonds	1/8 tsp. Celtic Sea Salt (optional)
3/4 cup sunflower seeds	

In food processor, blender or Vita Mix machine grind almonds and sunflower seeds to a fine powder. Add fresh and dehydrated tomatoes and Celtic Sea Salt and mix until a dough-like consistency is reached. Press dough onto a dehydrator sheet and dehydrate at 105 degrees for about 8 hours.* Remove and top with the following sauce:

Sauce:

30 dehydrated tomatoes	1 tsp. Celtic Sea Salt (optional)
1 tsp. Italian seasoning	1/4 cup plus 1 Tbsp. extra virgin olive oil
1 tsp. oregano	1/2 tsp. basil
1/2 tsp. garlic powder	

Place tomatoes in a bowl, add enough distilled water to cover them. Add 1/4 cup olive oil and 1 tsp. Celtic Sea Salt. Stir well, cover and allow to sit overnight. Pour off liquid and discard. Place tomatoes in a food processor, blender or Vita Mix and puree. Add seasonings plus 1 Tbsp. olive oil and mix well. Pour into bowl and stir in your favorite vegetables.

Vegetable Samples:

shredded zucchini	shredded yellow squash	diced tomatoes
minced red onion	diced bell peppers	

OR

After turning over crust, cover with sauce, seasonings and vegetables and return to the dehydrator to dry for an additional eight to ten hours or until dry.

* If dehydration is not an option, place dough in a lecithin-lined pan, preheat oven to 200 degrees, ***turn the oven off,*** place crust in oven leaving door open. When baked, top with the sauce.

These are great for school lunches, picnics or traveling.

Raw Spaghetti
☆ ☆ ☆ ☆ ☆

3 cups zucchini
3 cups summer squash
3/4 cup red bell pepper
3/4 cup yellow bell pepper
1/2 cup celery
1/2 cup chives
1 small clove garlic
3 Tbsp. fresh parsley
3 Tbsp. fresh sweet basil
3/4 pound fresh tomatoes
2 Tbsp. extra virgin olive oil

Peel squash, cut in half lengthwise, and remove seeds. Grate in a food processor. Refrigerate in a covered bowl. Finely chop bell peppers, celery and chives. Mince garlic. Quarter tomatoes and put in food processor or blender with garlic and almond, extra virgin olive, or flax oil to make spaghetti sauce. Fold in vegetables and herbs.

Place a bed of squash on a plate, and top with spaghetti sauce.

Stuffed Avocados
☆ ☆ ☆ ☆ ☆

2 ripe avocados
1/4 cup carrot
1/4 cup green onion
1/4 cup celery
2 tsp. fresh lemon juice
1/4 cup beet
2 Tbsp. olive oil

Mince green onion, shred carrot and beet and finely dice celery. Peel avocados, cut in half and remove pit. For each serving, place 2 halves of avocado on a bed of mixed greens and stuff with vegetables. Combine lemon juice and oil and drizzle over stuffed vegetables.

Hint: To vary the flavor, change the vegetable combination.

Tomato Aspic
☆ ☆ ☆

3 cups fresh tomato juice	2 Tbsp. lemon juice
1/4 cup green onion	2 Tbsp. parsley
1 Tbsp. onion	1 cup vegetable soup stock (page 207)
1/2 cup agar agar	1/2 cup celery
1/2 cup carrot	1/2 tsp. Celtic Sea Salt

Juice tomatoes, squeeze lemon, and set aside. Into a medium sized bowl, place chopped green onion, minced onion and parsley, grated carrot and diced celery, and set aside.

In a small bowl, dissolve agar flakes in vegetable soup stock, using a whisk to combine. Place in a saucepan and bring to a boil, stirring constantly until thickened. Quickly add agar mixture to blender with Celtic Sea Salt, tomato and lemon juice and pulse to blend. Pour over vegetables and stir to blend. Pour into a ring mold and refrigerate until firm.

To serve, unmold onto a plate lined with lettuce leaves, and garnish with avocado slices.

Tomato Bowls
☆ ☆ ☆ ☆ ☆

6 large ripe tomatoes	1 ripe avocado
1/4 cup parsley	1/2 cup celery
1/2 cup carrot	1 bell pepper
4 tsp. caraway seeds	1/4 cup sunflower seeds
1 cup mixed greens	1/4 cup corn kernels (optional)

Wash tomatoes, cut off the tops, and scoop out the insides. Chop the removed tomato pulp and place in a bowl. Turn tomato bowls upside down on a towel to drain. Mince the parsley, dice celery and pepper, finely shred the carrot, chop the greens and tomato tops and mix into the bowl of tomato pulp.

Mash the avocado and add caraway seeds, sunflower seeds and corn kernels. Mix well and combine with the other vegetables. Stuff tomatoes and serve on a bed of greens.

You may top with a dressing, if desired.

Tostada
☆ ☆ ☆ ☆ ☆

To make tortillas:

³/₄ cup cornmeal	¹/₄ cup flaxseed meal
¹/₄ cup vegetable soup stock	1 tsp. cumin

Mix ingredients together and knead. Form into 6 patties and place between 2 sheets of wax paper. Roll into thin circles. Remove top layer of wax paper and allow to air dry for 6 or 8 hours or dehydrate on flexible sheets at 105 degrees for 4 to 6 hours. Turn once during drying time, removing flexible sheet from dehydrator.

To make topping:

1 cup red bell pepper	¹/₂ cup carrot
¹/₂ cup green onions	1 cup of celery
1 cup green cabbage	1 cup purple cabbage
1 cup spinach leaves	

Finely chop green onion and celery, finely shred carrot and cabbages, cut pepper into small match sticks and chop spinach.

To make tostada:

Put the tortilla on a plate, top with layers of vegetables, and garnish with raw salsa (page 288) and guacamole (page 288).

What's For Dinner Loaf
☆ ☆ ☆ ☆ ☆

1 ¹/₂ cups flaxseeds	¹/₂ cup pumpkin seeds
¹/₂ cup almonds	1 cup carrots
¹/₂ cup red onion	1 cup celery
4 cloves of garlic	1 Tbsp. rosemary
1 tsp. Celtic Sea Salt (optional)	1 Tbsp. sage

Process almonds and seeds in a Vita Mix or food processor until a meal consistencey is reached. Mince onion, press garlic cloves and finely shred carrots. Juice celery and discard the pulp. Combine all ingredients and set aside for three to four hours for flavors to blend. The longer it sits, the stronger the flavor becomes.

Tomato Bowls with Grain
☆ ☆ ☆

6 large ripe tomatoes	2 cups grain*
¼ cup parsley	¼ cup celery
¼ cup chives	¼ cup carrots
2 Tbsp. basil	¼ cup Rhonda's No Oil Dressing

Soak grain (see page 225). Slice tops off tomatoes and set aside. Using a spoon, carefully scoop out the pulp, creating "tomato bowls," and set aside. Turn tomato bowls upside down on a paper towel to drain.

Chop tomato tops and pulp, mince parsley, finely chop celery and chives and grate carrot. Combine with soaked grain and dressing. Stuff tomatoes and serve on a bed of leaf lettuce and spinach leaves.

*Some grains that can be used are: buckwheat groats, rye, oat groats, quinoa, millet, basmati rice, wheat or cracked bulgar wheat.

Cucumber Delight
☆ ☆ ☆ ☆ ☆

6 cucumbers	4 green onions
4 cups carrots	4 cups celery
1 cup fresh peas	¼ cup fresh dill weed
1 tsp. Celtic Sea Salt (optional)	2 Tbsp. extra virgin olive oil
leaf lettuce or endive	

Peel cucumbers if they have been waxed or sprayed (organic are best). Cut them in half lengthwise and hollow out the centers. Chop the cucumber hearts, thinly slice the onions, finely shred the carrots (reserve one cup), mince the dill weed, and dice the celery into small pieces, and place in a bowl with the peas. Mix in the olive oil and Celtic sea salt and combine with the vegetables, and stir to coat the vegetables. Stuff the cucumbers and place on a bed of leaf lettuce or endive, sprinkle with reserved carrots.

Vegetable Pot Pie
☆ ☆ ☆ ☆ ☆

To make the crust:

3 cups soaked buckwheat	½ cup celery
2 cups soaked pine nuts	2 Tbsp. chives
herb seasoning to taste	Celtic Sea Salt to taste (optional)

Soak pine nuts and buckwheat overnight in separate bowls with enough water to cover. Drain well, cover and allow to sit for 6 to 8 hours. Place buckwheat in a food processor and process until blended. Remove and process the pine nuts. When both are processed, combine and set aside. Mince celery and chives and combine with nut and buckwheat mixture. Add herb seasoning and Celtic Sea Salt to taste. Press into 9-inch pie plate and dehydrate at 105 degrees for about 4 hours.

To make the filling:

In Green Power or Champion juicer insert the blank rather than the screen to process:

2 sweet potatoes	1 carrot

Place juiced carrots and sweet potatoes in a bowl and combine with your choice of grated or finely chopped vegetables such as green beans, celery, onion, fresh whole peas and corn. Add Celtic Sea Salt or additional Herb Seasoning, if desired. Layer pie with this mixture and your choice of greens and/or seed cheese. Top with favorite dressing if desired.

Raw Veggie Stew
☆ ☆ ☆ ☆ ☆

1 large broccoli stalk	1 head cauliflower
6 cups cabbage	3 cups carrots
6 large tomatoes	3 cups zucchini
2 cups red onions	20 spinach leaves
1 tsp. garlic powder	1 tsp. curry powder
¼ tsp. oregano	¼ cup olive or flaxseed oil
1 Tbsp. organic honey	Celtic Sea Salt to taste (optional)
2 cups fresh carrot juice	

Peel tomatoes and place half in a blender or food processor until smooth. Cut the balance of the vegetables into bite-sized pieces and place in a large bowl. Add the seasonings and oil, and mix well. Cover and marinate in the refrigerator. Just prior to serving, add 2 cups of fresh carrot juice.

Yam Burger

☆ ☆ ☆ ☆ ☆

2 cups yams or sweet potatoes	1 cup carrots
1/4 cup red onion	1/4 cup celery
1/2 tsp. Celtic Sea Salt (optional)	2 Tbsp. tahini
1 1/2 tsp. basil	1/2 tsp. oregano
4 Tbsp. nutritional yeast flakes	1/2 Tbsp. rice syrup
1/2 cup soft wheat berries	

Cover wheat berries with distilled water and soak overnight; drain and set aside. Grate yams and carrots in a food processor using a fine blade, and set aside. Place the onion, celery, Celtic Sea Salt and tahini in a food processor with an "S" blade. When pureed, add the rest of the ingredients and process until well-blended. Form into patties and serve.

Option: May be dehydrated at 105 degrees for about 8 hours or until desired texture is reached. Remember the bottom shelves dry faster.

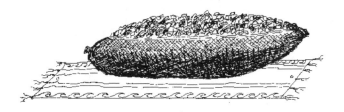

Zucchini Boats

☆ ☆ ☆ ☆

2 pounds zucchini	1/4 cup lemon juice
1/2 cup extra virgin olive oil	2 cloves garlic
2 cups soaked grain of choice	1/2 cup radishes
1/2 cup red pepper	1/4 cup green onions
1/2 cup carrot	

Cut zucchini in half lengthwise, and carefully remove the pulp, creating "zucchini boats." Set aside.

In a bowl, slice green onion and radishes, dice pepper and zucchini pulp and grate carrot. Add minced garlic. Mix in the soaked grain.

Place the lemon juice and olive oil in a blender and whiz to combine. Mince garlic and add to mixture. Pour over vegetables and mix well. Stuff into zucchini boats and serve on a bed of leaf lettuce. Garnish with radish roses and curled carrot slivers.

Winter Squash

☆ ☆ ☆ ☆ ☆

2 cups shredded squash
1 or 2 Tbsp. maple syrup
1/2 tsp. cinnamon (optional)

2 Tbsp. distilled water
1/4 tsp. Celtic Sea Salt (optional)
pinch of nutmeg (optional)

Peel squash and shred, and combine with other ingredients.

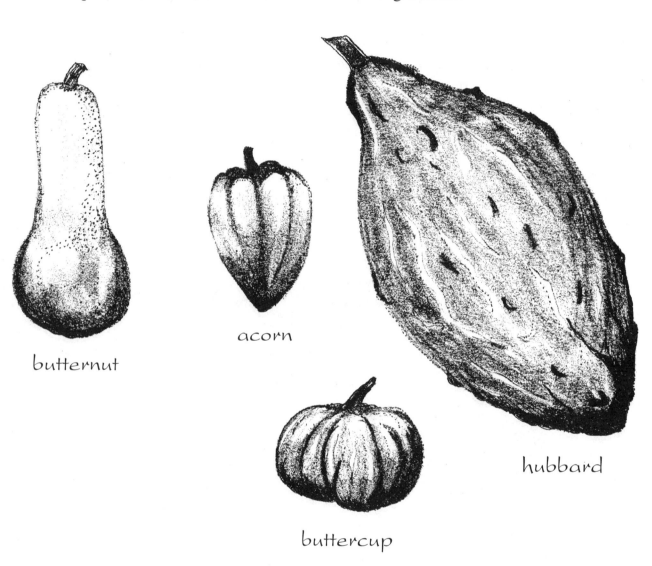

butternut

acorn

buttercup

hubbard

Chapter Twenty-two

Tempting Cooked Foods

Here at Hallelujah Acres we teach that all nutrients needed by the body are found in live foods and freshly extracted juices. We also realize that it is extremely difficult to stay all raw, and we have found that by eating a diet of about 75 to 85 percent raw and 15 to 25 percent cooked the body can function at an optimal level. These cooked recipes are included for the 15 to 25 percent of the diet which is cooked, and for those in transition from the Standard American Diet.

Baked Beans

☆ ☆ ☆

2 cups Great Northern beans	7 cups distilled water
1 medium onion	1/4 cup molasses
1/2 cup pure maple syrup	1/2 tsp. Celtic Sea Salt (optional)
1 tsp. dry mustard (optional)	1/2 tsp. ground cinnamon
1 tsp. ground ginger	1/4 cup honey

Cover beans with water and allow to soak overnight in a covered bowl.

Preheat oven to 350 degrees. Drain and rinse beans. In a 2-quart saucepan, pour the 5 cups of distilled water and add the soaked beans. Bring to a boil over high heat. Cover, reduce heat to simmer and cook for 2 hours. Drain.

In a 2-quart baking dish lined with lecithin, combine the beans, onion, 2 cups distilled water, and the remaining ingredients, and mix well. Cover and bake for 2 hours, stirring occasionally, adding more distilled water if necessary. Uncover and bake 35 to 45 minutes more or until the top is brown and crusted.

Baked Spaghetti Squash
☆ ☆ ☆

1 large spaghetti squash

Preheat oven to 350 degrees. Cut squash in half and remove seeds. Place on a baking sheet, cut side down, and bake until tender, about 30 to 40 minutes. Carefully remove squash with a fork, separating the spaghetti-like strands.

Serve with your favorite sauce.

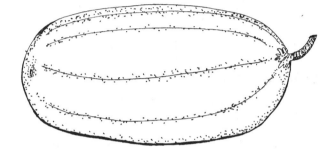

Black Bean Burrito
☆ ☆

1 ⅓ cup dried black beans	2 cups onion
1 large bell pepper	3 cups fresh tomato
3 garlic cloves	2 tsp. ground cumin
2 tsp. ground corriander	juice of 2 oranges
Celtic Sea Salt to taste (optional)	

Sort beans, removing any that are discolored or shriveled, and place in a pot. Add enough distilled water to cover beans (5 cups of water to 1 cup of black beans) and soak overnight or at least 12 hours. Drain, add fresh water and cook until tender, about 2 hours. Drain when finished cooking. Steam sauté onion, bell pepper, garlic, add cumin and corriander until onions are soft and translucent.

Place beans in a food processor and process until most of the beans are mashed (if you do not have a food processor, this can be accomplished with a potato masher). Add the beans to the pan with the onion and garlic mixture. Add tomatoes and orange juice, cover and simmer over low heat for 5 or 10 minutes, stirring frequently to prevent sticking. Add Celtic Sea Salt to taste.

To make burrito, use soft tortillas shells. Place the black bean mixture down the center, top with shredded leaf lettuce, diced tomatoes, grated almond cheese (page 285), salsa (page 288) and guacamole (page 288). Roll burrito, fold up the bottom, then fold over each side.

Broccoli with Onion Sauce
☆ ☆ ☆

Steam 1 bunch of broccoli heads until al dente (firm but tender). Meanwhile, make the following sauce:

1 cup diced onion
1 cup distilled water
1 tsp. arrow root powder

$1/4$ tsp. ground thyme
4 tsp. dehydrated vegetables

In a blender, grind dehydrated vegetables to a powder, add arrow root, thyme and distilled water and blend well.

Steam sauté onions until tender. Pour sauce in with onions and heat until thickened, stirring frequently to prevent sauce from burning. Pour over broccoli and serve or serve separately.

try

Carrot Burgers *make ½*
☆ ☆ ☆

8 carrots
1 cup celery
3 cups onion
$1/2$ cup wheat germ
Celtic Sea Salt to taste (optional)
$1/2$ tsp. garlic powder
1 tsp. paprika
1 tsp. parsley

1 cup cauliflower
2 garlic cloves
1 cup bell pepper (optional)
$1/2$ cup tahini
5 Tbsp. almond butter (page 284)
1 tsp. basil
1 tsp. oregano

Peel carrots and cut into chunks. Cut cauliflower into chunks. Place carrots and cauliflower in a medium saucepan with enough water to cover and steam until soft. Drain and mash with a potato masher or food processor.

Dice onion, celery and bell pepper, mince garlic and steam sauté until tender.

In a large bowl, combine mashed carrots, steamed vegetables and other ingredients. Mix well and form into patties. Place on lecithin-lined baking sheet.

Preheat oven to 350 degrees. Bake for 10 to 12 minutes, until golden. Turn and bake until other side is golden.

Chow Mein
☆ ☆ ☆

2 large onions	2 carrots
4 stalks of celery	1 red pepper
1 cup of mushrooms (optional)	1 cup of water chestnuts
1 cup bean sprouts	Celtic Sea Salt to taste (optional)
1 Tbsp. vegetarian Worcestershire Sauce	1 tsp. Oriental seasoning*

Thinly slice onions, thinly cut carrots and celery diagonally, and cut pepper into thin strips. In a wok, steam sauté onions, carrots, celery and pepper for 5 minutes. Add other vegetables, simmer over low heat, stirring occasionally until the vegetables are al dente (firm but tender). Add Celtic Sea Salt, Worchestershire sauce and seasoning.

Serve with seasoned Basmati Rice or chow mein noodles.

*Frontier Herbs makes a good one.

Cornbread Dressing
☆ ☆ ☆

Prepare George's famous Hallelujah Acres Corn Bread on page 275. Set aside to cool.

To make the dressing:

2 cups celery
1 cup 7-Grain Bread (or other whole grain bread) cut into small cubes
1 ¹/₂ tsp. marjoram
¹/₂ tsp. thyme
¹/₂ tsp. sage
Celtic Sea Salt to taste (optional)
1 ¹/₂ cup onion

Dice onion and celery into small pieces and place in a saucepan. Steam sauté onion and celery in distilled water or vegetable stock until tender. Cut bread into small cubes and toast in a dry skillet.

In a large bowl, combine crumbled corn bread, toasted bread cubes and vegetables. Add seasonings and mix well. Add vegetable stock until the mixture is very moist. Put into a baking pan that has been lined with liquid lecithin. Bake 350 degrees for 45 to 60 minutes.

Couscous & Raw Veggies
☆ ☆ ☆

The veggies:

1 cup carrots	1 cup green onion
1 cup broccoli florets	1 cup cauliflower florets
1/2 cup zucchini	1/2 cup yellow squash
1/2 cup red pepper	

Cut carrots and red pepper into match-stick size pieces, cut broccoli and cauliflower into florets, chop green onion and grate zucchini and yellow squash. Set aside raw veggies.

The couscous:

4 cups distilled water	2 cups couscous
1/2 tsp. nutmeg	1/4 tsp. cinnamon
1 1/2 tsp. cumin	1/4 tsp. tumeric
Celtic Sea Salt to taste (optional)	

Bring water to a boil, add couscous and boil for one minute, stirring constantly. Remove from heat, add fresh vegetables, nutmeg, cinnamon, cumin, tumeric and Celtic Sea Salt. Cover and allow to sit 10 to 15 minutes.

Eggplant & Rice Casserole
☆ ☆ ☆

3 1/2 cups eggplant	3 to 4 medium tomatoes
1 bell pepper	1 tsp. Celtic Sea Salt (optional)
2 garlic cloves	1 medium onion
2 Tbsp. salsa (page 288)	1 tsp. All Purpose seasoning

Wash and chop eggplant, leaving the skin on. Dice onion, pepper and tomatoes, and mince garlic.

Steam eggplant for 5 minutes. Add pepper and onion and minced garlic, and steam an additional 2 minutes. Mix in tomatoes and salsa, simmer until juicy, about 5 minutes. Add seasonings and mix well.

Serve over seasoned basmati rice (page 271).

Lentil Loaf
☆ ☆

2 stalks of celery	1 cup scallions
2 cups lentils	$\frac{1}{2}$ cup wheat germ
$\frac{1}{2}$ cup whole grain bread crumbs	$\frac{1}{2}$ cup sunflower seeds
$\frac{1}{2}$ tsp. dried sage	2 Tbsp. nutritional yeast
$\frac{1}{2}$ cup almonds	
6 cups distilled water or vegetable soup stock	

Soak lentils in distilled water for 24 hours. Drain. Add fresh distilled water or soup stock and bring to boil. Cook for 10 minutes or until most of the moisture is absorbed. Drain any excess moisture. Chop scallions, dice celery, and steam sauté until tender. Grind almonds into a fine meal. Combine all ingredients and mix well, place in a non-stick or liquid lecithin-lined loaf pan and bake at 350 degrees for about 40 minutes, or until firm.

Grain Burgers
☆

1 cup cooked Basamati rice	1 cup cooked barley
1 cup bulgur wheat	1 cup texturized vegetable protein (TVP)
$\frac{1}{2}$ cup uncooked rolled oats	1 medium onion
$\frac{1}{2}$ cup dehydrated onion flakes	$\frac{3}{4}$ cup red bell pepper
1 clove garlic	$\frac{1}{2}$ cup mushrooms, opt.
1 tsp. Celtic Sea Salt (optional)	$\frac{1}{2}$ cup celery
$\frac{1}{2}$ tsp. basil	$\frac{1}{2}$ tsp. oregano
$\frac{1}{2}$ tsp. ground celery seed	

Prepare grains according to package directions, and set aside to cool. Finely chop all vegetables by hand or with a food processor and set aside. When grains have cooled, place them in food processor, blender or Vita Mix and process until a creamy texture is reached. Fold in minced vegetables and seasonings, and mix thoroughly. Form into patties and freeze, separating with wax paper or plastic wrap. To serve, heat in the oven until golden on a non-stick pan.

Hallelujah Burgers

☆ ☆ ☆

try

We sold hundreds of these veggie burgers at our restaurant!

6 cups distilled water	3 cups millet
4 garlic cloves	6 onions
2 cups celery	1 cup chopped carrots
1 cup green pepper	1 cup red pepper
Celtic Sea Salt to taste (optional)	1 cup almond butter
1 cup sunflower seeds	4 cups finely grated carrot
4 cups whole grain bread crumbs	½ cup dehyrated onion flakes
½ cup dried parsley	½ tsp. cumin
2 Tbsp. Italian seasoning	1 tsp. each basil, garlic powder and paprika

Bring 6 cups of distilled water to a boil. Add millet and turn down to low heat, cooking for 20 to 25 minutes or until soft and water is absorbed. Set aside to cool.

Dice celery, peppers and onions, mince garlic, and grate carrots Steam sauté vegetables until tender. Remove from heat and fold in almond butter.

Combine vegetable mixture, millet, bread crumbs, sunflower seeds, carrots, Celtic Sea Salt, onion flakes and seasonings. Mix well, cover, and allow to sit several hours or overnight in the refrigerator for flavors to blend.

Preheat oven to 350 degrees, and put liquid lecithin on cookie sheet. Form mixture into patties and place them on a cookie sheet. Bake 10 minutes, remove from oven and allow to sit 10 minutes. Turn and bake an additional 10 minutes. Remove from oven and serve immediately or allow to cool, wrap in plastic wrap and freeze for later use. To reheat, place frozen patty on a non-stick, oven-proof or lecithin-lined pan in a 350-degree oven and heat about five minutes or until defrosted.

This recipe makes about 60 burgers.

Baked Sweet Potatoes

☆ ☆ ☆

try

Bake one potato per person at 350 degrees for 45 minutes or until tender when pricked with a fork (larger potatoes take longer). Remove from the oven, cool slightly, peel and mash.

Add a small amount of pure maple syrup and herb seasoning like Frontier Herb's All Purpose (this seasoning can be found at your health food store).

Fettuccine Alfredo
☆

4 cups distilled water	1/2 cup almonds
1/2 cup tofu parmesan	1/2 tsp. Celtic Sea Salt (optional)
3 Tbsp. arrow root powder	3 cloves of garlic
1 onion	1 cup chives
1 tsp. dill weed	2 tsp. cilantro

Pour 1 cup boiling water over almonds, and allow to sit for 15 minutes. Drain almonds and discard water, remove and discard skins. Place almonds, 3 cups distilled water and arrow root powder in a blender or Vita Mix and blend until a creamy consistency is reached.

Chop onion and mince garlic, steam sauté until soft, and add to blended mixture. Pour into saucepan and heat until thickened, stirring with a whisk. Remove from heat. Just prior to serving, add chives, tofu parmesan and Celtic Sea Salt and seasoning and stir with whisk to mix well.

Cook whole grain fettucini of your choice until al dente (firm but tender), rinse and drain. Pour sauce over top or serve on the side.

Orzo Pasta with Garden Veggies
☆ ☆ ☆

12-ounce orzo pasta	10 - 12 spears of asparagus
1 medium red bell pepper	2 - 4 garlic cloves
1 medium yellow squash	1 medium zucchini
1 cup sugar snap peas	1 small red onion
1/4 cup fresh chives	1/3 cup fresh herbs *
1/4 cup vegetable soup stock	Celtic Sea Salt to taste (optional)

Diagonally slice asparagus in 1/2-inch to 1-inch pieces. Slice red pepper into thin strips, mince garlic, cut squashes into quarters and thinly slice, cut sugar snap peas into 1-inch diagonal slices. Chop onion and mince herbs and chives.

Prepare pasta according to directions, drain and set aside. Steam sauté vegetables in soup stock until al dente (tender but firm). Combine with pasta, herbs and Celtic Sea Salt.

* Herbs may include dill, tarragon, basil, thyme or other of your favorites. If fresh herbs are not available, dried herbs may be substituted. If using dried herbs, decrease by one half.

Manicotti (stuffed shells)
☆

1 box whole grain manicotti shells	1 pound of firm tofu
1 cup green onion or scallions	2 garlic cloves
1 tsp. oregano	1 tsp. basil
1/8 tsp. marjoram	1/2 tsp. Celtic Sea Salt (optional)
1 Tbsp. parsley	4 cups tomato sauce (page 286)
2 cups tofu mozzarella	1/2 cup onion

Cook manicotti noodles according to directions on the box. Drain, rinse and set aside. Mince garlic and onion. Drain and rinse tofu, place in a blender or food processor with 1/2 cup tomato sauce, 1 cup tofu mozzarella, onion and garlic, and process until smooth. Fold in the green onions. Stuff the shells with the tofu mixture.

Combine remaining tomato sauce, oregano, marjoram, basil, Celtic Sea Salt and parsley, and mix well. Cook for approximately 15 minutes for flavors to blend. Pour some of the sauce over the bottom of the pan. Arrange stuffed shells in the dish. Pour the remaining sauce over the top of the shells, and cover with the remaining shredded tofu mozzarella. Bake 350 degrees for 20 minutes.

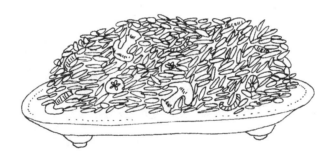

Herbed Rice
☆ ☆ ☆

1 medium red onion	2 1/2 cups vegetable soup stock
1 cup basmati rice	1/2 tsp. dried thyme
1/4 cup wild rice	1/2 tsp. dried basil
1/2 tsp. marjoram	1/2 cup fresh parsley

Bring vegetable soup stock to a boil, and add rices, herbs, and chopped onion. Allow to come to a boil and reduce heat to simmer. Cover and cook 30 minutes. Turn off burner and allow to steep 15 to 20 minutes. Fluff before serving.

Hint: Vary the herbs for a completely different flavor.

Scalloped Potatoes
☆ ☆

8 to 10 large Russet potatoes	1 cup red onion
1 cup chives	8 Tbsp. unbleached flour

Peel and slice potatoes thinly, dice onions and chop chives. In a 9 x 13-inch baking pan, place a layer of potatoes, onions and chives, then sprinkle with a layer of about 1 Tbsp. of unbleached white flour. Continue layering, finishing with potatoes as the top layer.

In a blender, make the following sauce and pour over the potaotes:

4 cups distilled water	¼ cup nutritional yeast flakes
8 cups Better Than Milk	¼ cup veggie parmesan cheese
½ tsp. Celtic Sea Salt (optional)	

Sprinkle potatoes generously with parsley, cover and bake in a 350 degree oven about one hour. Remove, cover and continue to bake until potatoes are tender.

Hint: For variation and color, add your favorite herbs, bell peppers or other steamed vegetables.

Potato Medley
☆ ☆ ☆

5 large russet potatoes	2 cups broccoli
2 cloves garlic	1 cup celery
1 green pepper	1 red pepper
2 green onions	1 tsp. oregano
1 tsp. basil	2 Tbsp. parsley
Celtic Sea Salt to taste (optional)	

Peel and cube potatoes, and boil for 10 minutes. Add broccoli and steam for an additional 5 minutes or until potatoes are tender. Drain.

Meanwhile in a large skillet, dry roast over medium heat garlic, pepper, onions and celery. When they are slightly browned, add the potatoes, broccoli and seasonings. Add about ¼ cup of Distilled water or Vegetable Soup stock (page 207) and continue to steam for about seven more minutes.

Layered Casserole
☆ ☆ ☆

try

8 potatoes	1 large onion
3 medium carrots	1 bell pepper
1/2 zucchini	1/2 cup yellow squash
1 cup corn	1 cup peas
1 cup green beans	1/2 cup mushrooms (optional)

Slice potatoes, onion, carrots, bell pepper, green beans and squash. Layer all vegetables into a liquid lecithin lined casserole dish. Top with the Tomato Basil Sauce on page 293. Bake in a 350-degree oven for about 1 1/2 hours or until vegetables are tender.

Nutted Rice & Orzo Pilaf
☆ ☆

1 cup onion	1/2 cup dried orzo (pasta shaped like rice)
1 cup Basmati rice	1 tsp. Celtic Sea Salt (optional)
1 tsp. cinnamon	1/4 cup slivered almonds
1/4 cup pine nuts	1/4 cup pistachios
1 tsp. marjoram	2 3/4 cup distilled water
1/4 tsp. nutmeg	

In a pan, dry roast rice and orzo 2 or 3 minutes or until golden, set aside. In a separate pan steam sauté onion until translucent, mix in spices. Combine all onion mixture, rice and orzo, nuts and pistachios, seasonings and distilled water, stirring to mix thoroughly. Bring to a boil, cover and turn the heat to its lowest setting and simmer for 30 minutes. Turn burner off, do not lift lid, allow to sit an additional 15 minutes until all of the moisture is absorbed.

Pasta Primavera Alfredo
☆

Prepare one recipe of Alfredo Sauce (see page 252). Steam sauté any or all of the following vegetables until al dente (firm but tender).

carrot match sticks	cauliflower florets
broccoli florets	red bell pepper match sticks
zucchini match sticks	diced red onion

Combine steamed vegetable with Alfredo Sauce and serve over whole grain fettucini, which has been prepared according to the package directions.

try it but takes a lot of time to prepare *OK*

Shepherd's Pie

☆ ☆ ☆

8 medium potatoes	1 cup green beans
3 cups carrots	1 cup celery
1 cup onion	1 cup peas
1/2 tsp. thyme	1 tsp. Celtic Sea Salt (optional)
3 Tbsp. fresh basil	1/2 tsp. marjoram
3 cups corn kernels (optional)	

Dice potatoes and onion, and place *half of each* in a pan with just enough water to cover. Cook until just tender. Drain, saving the water, and set aside.

In a separate pan, place the carrots, green beans, celery, peas and the other half of the potatoes and onion, with just enough water to cover, and cook until just tender. Drain and set aside.

In a dry sauce pan, dry roast 1/3 cup whole grain or unbleached flour until browned. Remove from heat and place in blender with 2 1/2 cups distilled water or vegetable soup stock, 1/2 cup nutritional yeast flakes, Celtic Sea Salt and 1/4 tsp. nutmeg. Blend until mixed well. Return to saucepan and heat to boiling, reduce heat and cook for about 4 minutes, until thickened.

Combine steamed vegetables, Celtic Sea Salt, and seasonings with as much of the sauce as desired. (Refrigerate leftover sauce for up to one week). Pour into shallow baking dish.

Mash the balance of the potatoes and onion until creamy, using some of the reserved potato water, if needed. Spread over the casserole, and sprinkle with All Purpose seasoning (see page 313) and paprika. Bake in 400-degree oven for 15 to 20 minutes or until the crust is golden.

Two-Potato Casserole

☆ ☆ ☆

3 large sweet potatoes	3 large red potatoes
1 cup fresh carrot juice	1/2 cup fresh celery juice
1/2 cup celery	1/4 cup onion
1 Tbsp. dry mustard	1 Tbsp. dried sage

Dice potatoes and sweet potatoes, and mince celery and onion. Combine vegetables with carrot juice, celery juice and seasonings. Pour into a covered casserole dish and bake at 350 degrees for about one hour or until the vegetables are tender.

Pecan Loaf

? try   Very Good
½ = 6 pieces ☆☆

2 cups pecans
¼ tsp. garlic powder
½ cup celery
2 cups whole grain bread crumbs
2 cups basmati rice

¼ tsp. sage
1 medium onion
2 cups tomatoes
½ tsp. Celtic Sea Salt (optional)

Prepare 2 cups basmati rice by stirring rice into 4 cups boiling water, turn down heat, replace lid and cook for 30 minutes. Turn off and allow to sit 15 minutes with lid on. While rice is cooking, place pecans in a food processor or blender, grind to a fine meal and pour into a bowl. Chop tomatoes fine and add to the bowl. Dice and steam sauté onions and celery in a small amount of distilled water.   Combine rice, onions, celery, tomatoes, seasonings and bread crumbs with pecan mixture and mix well. Spread into a lecithin-coated loaf pan and bake at 350 degrees for 45 minutes. Remove from oven, spread homemade tomato ketchup (page 290) over the top and continue to bake an additional 15 minutes.

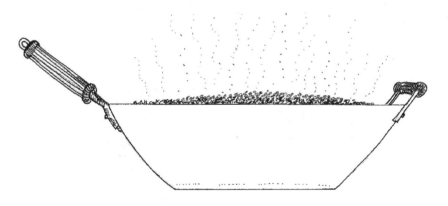

Stir-Fry Vegetables
☆ ☆ ☆

1 red onion
3 stalks of celery
½ cup broccoli
1 bell pepper
1 tsp. Celtic Sea Salt (optional)

3 carrots, peeled & sliced
½ cup cauliflower
1 cup zucchini
1 cup yellow squash
1 Tbsp. Oriental seasoning

Cut onion into thin rings, peel and slice carrots on a diagonal, thinly slice celery, zucchini and yellow squash, chop broccoli and cauliflower, and cut pepper into match sticks.
Stir-fry in small amount of water until al dente (firm but tender). Add Celtic Sea Salt and 1 Tbsp. Oriental seasoning. Serve alone, over rice or with Udon noodles.

Stuffed Acorn Squash
☆ ☆

Use 1 small to medium acorn squash for two people. This recipe serves 8.

To make the stuffing:

¹/₂ cup organic raisins	1 - 1 ¹/₂ cups vegetable soup stock
2 onions	4 garlic cloves
2 apples or about 1 1/2 cup	1 tsp. grated lemon peel
1 tsp. Celtic Sea Salt (optional)	¹/₄ cup celery

1 ¹/₂ cup cubed whole-grain bread, toasted slightly in ungreased fry pan
1 – 2 tsp. each of parsley, basil, sage or your favorite herbs.

Cut squash in half. If the squash will not sit up, slice ¹/₄-inch from the bottom to make it stable. Remove the seeds. Bake cut side down (not the side the ¹/₄-inch was cut from) on a baking pan coated with liquid lecithin until soft (about 50 minutes). Remove from oven.

While squash is baking, heat vegetable stock. Remove vegetable stock from heat, add raisins and soak for 10 minutes. Peel, core and chop apples and onions. Dice celery and mince garlic. Steam sauté the onion, celery and garlic over medium heat until soft (3 to 4 minutes). Add apple and steam another 3 minutes or until apple is tender.

Transfer to a large mixing bowl and mix in the bread crumbs, herbs, grated lemon, raisins, vegetable stock and Celtic Sea Salt. The mixture should be moist. Taste and adjust seasonings if needed. Spoon into squash. Return to the oven and bake an additional 15 minutes.

The Wild Rice Dressing on page 265 can also be used to stuff the squash if you prefer.

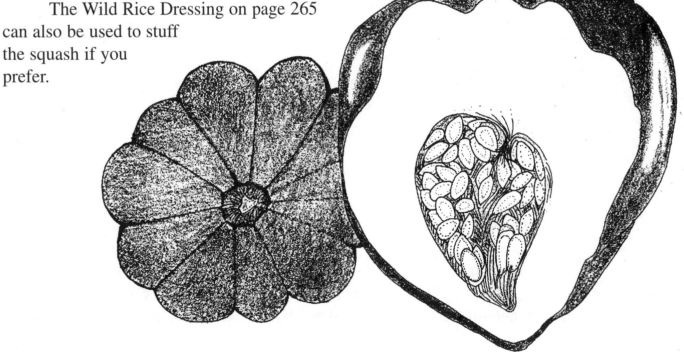

Stuffed Baked Potatoes
☆ ☆ ☆

2 large baking potatoes	1 cup onion
3/4 cup carrots	3/4 cup bell pepper
1/2 cup broccoli florets	1/2 cup cauliflower florets
1 tsp. ground corriander	1/2 tsp. tumeric
1/8 tsp cardamom	1/8 tsp. cloves
Celtic Sea Salt to taste (optional)	1/2 cup almond "cheese" sauce (optional, page 284)

Scrub and bake potatoes at 400 degrees for one hour or until done. Meanwhile, prepare filling. Steam sauté onion, carrots, broccoli and cauliflower until tender, or about 8 minutes. Add bell pepper and spices and continue to sauté for a couple minutes longer. Add more distilled water or vegetable soup stock; cover and steam until bell pepper is just tender. Stir in almond cheese and Celtic Sea Salt to taste. Set aside.

When potatoes are cool enough to handle, make a lengthwise cut in the top of each one and remove at least half of the potato pulp, leaving a 1/2-inch rim of potato attached to the skin. Mash the scooped-out potato, and add to it the vegetable and cheese mixture. Lower oven temperature to 350 degrees, stuff the potato shells, place on a no-stick baking dish, cover with parchment paper and bake for 15 to 20 minutes.

try

Spanish Rice
☆ ☆ ☆

1 cup basmati rice	1 cup vegetable soup stock
1 cup fresh tomato juice	1 tsp. oregano
1/3 cup green pepper	1/3 cup carrot
1/3 cup celery	1/3 cup onion
1 medium tomato	2 small garlic cloves
2 tsp. chives	1 tsp. Celtic Sea Salt (optional)
1 tsp. basil	

Combine tomato juice and vegetable soup stock and place in a pan and bring to a boil, then add rice and reduce heat to simmer. Cover and cook for 25 minutes. Remove from heat and add the following: diced tomato, celery and onion, minced garlic, chopped chives, grated carrots, seasonings, and Celtic Sea Salt. Replace cover and allow to sit another 15 to 20 minutes.

Stuffed Eggplant
☆ ☆ ☆

2 eggplants	1 cup onion
1/2 cup green pepper	1/2 cup celery
2 cloves garlic	1 cup tomato
2 Tbsp. fresh basil	2 Tbsp. fresh Italian parsley
2 cups basmati rice	1/2 tsp. cinnamon

Cook basmati rice according to directions. While rice is cooking, cut eggplants in half length-wise and place on non-stick baking sheet, cut side down. Bake at 400 degrees for 20 minutes or until tender. Remove from oven and set aside to cool.

Chop onion, celery, green pepper and tomato and mince garlic. Steam sauté until tender and set aside.

Spoon out the cooked eggplant, leaving a 1/4-inch rim aroung the outside edge. Place the pulp in a food processor and process until a creamy consistency is reached. Remove and place in a bowl. Stir in rice and onion mixture.

Mince the parsley and basil and add to the eggplant, rice and onion mixture, along with the cinnamon, and mix well. Add Celtic Sea Salt to taste (optional). Fill the eggplant shells with the mixture, top with 1/2 cup whole-grain bread crumbs and bake at 350 degrees for 30 minutes.

Stuffed Red Bell Peppers
☆ ☆ ☆

4 medium red bell peppers	1/4 cup chives
1/4 cup onion	1/4 cup carrots
1 cup celery	1 cup basmati rice
1 cup corn kernels	1 clove garlic
1/2 tsp. rosemary	1 tsp. parsley flakes
2 cups vegetable soup stock (page 207)	Celtic Sea Salt to taste (optional)

Bring soup stock to a boil, add basmati rice, reduce heat, cover and cook for 25 minutes. Turn off heat and allow to sit an additional 15 to 20 minutes.

Slice tops off peppers, remove seeds and stems, and dice the remaining red part of the top of pepper. Dice the onion, celery, chives and carrots and combine with diced red pepper and corn. Mince garlic and steam sauté this vegetable mixture until tender – about 5 minutes.

Preheat oven to 350 degrees. Combine rice, vegetables and seasonings. Fill peppers and bake about 30 minutes.

Stuffed Cabbage Rolls
☆ ☆

Outer leaves from 1 large head of cabbage

Gently remove outer leaves of the cabbage by cutting off the bottom of the cabbage. Steam the outer leaves over boiling water for 5 minutes.
Make the following filling:

2 Tbsp. onion	1 cup raw basmati rice
1 ¹/₂ cup vegetable soup stock	2 Tbsp. organic raisins
¹/₄ cup almonds	¹/₄ cup carrot
¹/₄ cup celery	¹/₂ tsp. cinnamon
¹/₂ tsp. Celtic Sea Salt (optional)	

Mince the onion, grate the carrot, chop the celery and steam sauté these veggies in a small amount of distilled water until tender. Sliver almonds. Combine almonds and rice in a pan and dry roast for 2 to 3 minutes over medium heat. Add soup stock, vegetables, raisins and seasonings. Bring to a boil, cover and lower heat to its lowest setting and cook for 45 minutes.
While rice is cooking, prepare the following sauce:

1 red onion	1 Tbsp. whole grain flour
¹/₂ tsp. Celtic Sea Salt	¹/₄ tsp. ground cloves
2 cups tomatoes or tomato sauce (page 286)	

Combine all ingredients in a blender and process until thoroughly combined. Place in a small sauce pan and simmer until thickened, stirring constantly.
In the bottom of the baking dish, place a generous amount of sauce to prevent cabbage rolls from sticking. Place 2 Tbsp. of filling on each leaf. Fold in the sides and roll it up. Place the prepared leaves in the sauce-covered pan with the seam-side down. Pour the remaining sauce over the stuffed cabbage, cover and bake approximately 45 minutes.

Sweet Potato Casserole

Submitted by Myra Idol

☆ ☆

For the sweet potatoes:

3 cups mashed sweet potatoes	1 Tbsp. pure vanilla extract
maple syrup or honey to taste	2 Tbsp. soy powder
½ cup non-dairy milk or more to reach desired consistency	

Bake 3 or 4 sweet potatoes, enough to yield 3 cups of sweet potato. Mix together and put in a casserole coated with liquid lecithin to prevent sticking.

For the topping:

Combine the following ingredients and spread over sweet potatoes. Bake 20 minutes at 300 degrees.

1 cup maple syrup
⅓ cup whole wheat pastry flour
1 cup chopped pecans

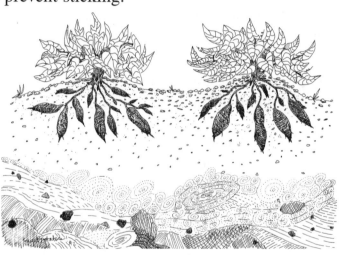

Vegetables & Rice Casserole

☆ ☆ ☆

3 cups seasoned basmati rice (page 271)	1 cup peas
2 cups carrots	1 cup celery
2 cups green beans	1 cup corn kernels
1 cup onion	1 cup bell pepper
2 cups vegetable soup stock (page 207)	1 tsp. dried oregano
Celtic Sea Salt to taste (optional)	1 tsp. dried basil

Cook rice according to the directions. While cooking rice, dice carrots, bell pepper and celery, mince onion and slice green beans into small pieces. Remove rice from heat and combine with vegetables and seasonings. Stir to mix thoroughly. Place in a covered casserole dish, pour vegetable stock over the mixture, cover and bake at 350 degrees until the vegetables are tender.

Vegetable Lo Mein
☆ ☆ ☆

½ pound brown rice udon noodles	½ cup green onion
1 clove garlic	1 cup zucchini
1 cup yellow squash	¾ cup carrots
2 cups broccoli florets	½ cup cauliflower florets
¾ cup cabbage	¾ cup bell pepper (red, yellow or orange)
1 tsp. Celtic Sea Salt (optional)	2 Tbsp. arrow root powder
½ cup mushrooms (optional)	1 small red onion
½ tsp. freshly-grated ginger	vegetarian soup stock (page 207)
2 tsp. Oriental seasoning	

Thinly slice green and red onions, cut zucchini, yellow squash, carrots and peppers into thin matchsticks, grate ginger, mince garlic, cut broccoli and cauliflower into florets, and chop cabbage fine. If using dehydrated mushrooms, soak for 20 minutes in distilled water. Place all prepared vegetables near wok as they will need to be added quickly.

Prepare noodles according to package directions, set aside but keep warm.

In a blender, combine arrow root powder, mushroom soaking water and enough vegetarian soup stock to equal ¾ cup. Blend until mixed well and set aside.

If using mushrooms, drain soaking water through strainer and set aside.

Heat wok, adding a small amount of vegetable stock, along with broccoli, cauliflower and carrots. Steam sauté these vegetables for 4 minutes and set aside.

Steam sauté green onion, garlic, zucchini, squash, and cabbage until vegetables are al dente (firm but tender) and bright in color. Remove from pan.

Place mushrooms and onion in the wok and cook approximately 3 minutes. Add the rest of the vegetables back to the wok to reheat for about 3 minutes.

Pour the Soup Stock/mushroom soaking water mixture over the vegetables, stirring constantly, and bring to a boil for about 1 minute.

Reduce heat and add noodles and Oriental seasoning and Celtic Sea Salt, heating about 1 minute, mixing gently until vegetables and noodles are thoroughly heated.

Vegetarian Spaghetti
☆ ☆ ☆

try

Another recipe from our restaurant, loved by hundreds and missed by all, is this vegetarian spaghetti! I have been asked for this recipe hundreds of times. The secret is in the sauce!

Make one batch of spaghetti sauce found on page 291. Add to the sauce the following chopped and steam sautéed vegetables:

2 cups chopped onions	1 cup chopped bell pepper
2 cups chopped celery	1 cup grated carrot (optional)

Serve over spaghetti squash, spinach, artichoke or any other whole grain spaghetti.

Vegetarian Taco Salad
☆

try

Rinse and soak the following beans (organic if possible) overnight in distilled water:

1 ½ cups black turtle beans	1 ½ cups red kidney beans

The following morning, drain the soaking water, rinse and cover beans with fresh water. Cook until tender, drain and set aside.

To prepare taco sauce:

1 cup carrots, chopped	½ tsp. garlic powder
1 tsp. oregano	1 cup green pepper, chopped
½ tsp. cumin	1 cup onions
2 or 3 large tomatoes	Celtic Sea Salt to taste (optional)
1 cup texterized vegetable protein, opt.	

Chop carrots, green pepper, onion and tomato. Sauté vegetables in small amount of distilled water. Stir in prepared beans, add seasoning and texturized vegetable protein (TVP). If additional liquid is required, add unsalted tomato juice.

To prepare toppings:

black olives (optional)	3 to 4 bunches of scallions, chopped
3- 4 large tomatoes, chopped	non-dairy cheddar cheese, shredded
Romaine lettuce, shredded	no salt or low salt corn chips, crumbled

To build the salad:

On a large dinner plate crumble a layer of blue corn chips and top with shredded lettuce. Add 1 ladle of taco mix and top with scallions, tomatoes, shredded cheese, and black olives. Serve with Salsa if desired, recipe on page 288.

Bok Choy with Ginger

☆ ☆ ☆

Submitted by Lorna Spring

1 head of bok choy
1 clove garlic
Celtic Sea Salt to taste (optional)

2 Tbsp. fresh ginger
2 tomatoes

Cut bok choy on the bias, including the greens, grate ginger, press garlic and cut tomatoes into wedges. Steam sauté in a small amount of Distilled water or Vegetable soup stock, add bok choy, ginger, pressed garlic and tomatoes. Cover and heat through over couscous with additional Celtic Sea Salt, if desired.

Veggie / Rice Medley

☆ ☆ ☆

2 cups seasoned basmati rice (page 271)
1 green pepper, diced
7 garlic cloves, pressed
5 large onions, sliced thin
2 celery stalks, sliced diagonally
1 cup carrot, sliced diagonally $1/8$-inch thick

$1/2$ tsp. sweet basil
$1/4$ tsp. ginger
Celtic Sea Salt to taste (optional)
1 cup bean sprouts
1 cup water chesnuts

Cook rice according to directions. Add garlic, onions, celery, pepper, carrots and steam sauté for 5 minutes. Add other vegetables. Simmer on low heat, stirring occasionally until vegetables are al dente (tender but firm). Add Celtic Sea Salt and other seasoning. Serve over seasoned rice.

Wild Rice Dressing

☆ ☆ ☆

4 cups vegetable broth
$1/4$ tsp. Celtic Sea Salt (optional)
$3/4$ cup basmati rice
$3/4$ cup wild rice
$1/8$ tsp. marjoram
1 small onion, chopped

1 lb. fresh mushrooms, cleaned & sliced (optional)
$1/2$ cup fresh chopped parsley
1 cup diced celery
$1/4$ tsp. sage
$1/8$ tsp. dried thyme
1 cup pecan halves, broken length-wise

Bring soup stock to a boil; add rice; reduce heat to lowest temperature, cover and cook until tender (about 30-40 minutes). Pre-heat oven to 350 degrees. In a large skillet, steam sauté onion and mushrooms (optional) until onion is transparent. Mix parsley, celery and cooked rice, seasonings and pecans. Add Celtic Sea Salt to taste; stir to mix. Cover and bake 15 minutes.

Vegetarian Lasagna
☆

try

This recipe is one that was served at our Hallelujah Acres Restaurant and was a favorite of our customers. It is a little labor-intensive, but worth the effort.

The noodles:

3 quarts distilled water   12 whole wheat lasagna noodles

Put 3 quarts of distilled water in a pot and bring to a boil. Stir frequently to prevent noodles from sticking. Add noodles and cook 7 or 8 minutes. Remove from heat, drain and cover with cold water until needed.

Tofu ricotta:

1 pound of tofu	$\frac{1}{2}$ tsp. nutmeg
$\frac{1}{2}$ tsp. Celtic Sea Salt (optional)	1 tsp. basil
$\frac{1}{8}$ tsp. tumeric	$\frac{1}{3}$ cup lemon juice
$\frac{1}{4}$ cup parsley	$\frac{1}{3}$ cup tahini
$\frac{1}{3}$ cup nutritional yeast flakes	1 cup chopped scallions or spinach

Combine above-listed ingredients in a blender or food processor to prepare one batch of tofu ricotta. When tofu ricotta is made, fold in 1 cup chopped scallions or spinach and $\frac{2}{3}$ cup tofu parmesan cheese.

The sauce:

1 Tbsp. basil	1 Tbsp. oregano
2 tsp. Italian seasoning	2 tsp. parsley
2 cups carrots	1 cups zucchini
1 cup onions or scallions	1 cup yellow squash
1 batch of tomato sauce (page 286)	2 cups broccoli stalks (optional)
1 batch of tomato paste (page 287)	Celtic Sea Salt (optional)

Grate carrots, yellow squash and zucchini, chop onion, and peel and chop broccoli stalks if using. Steam sauté vegetables for about 3 minutes. Add oregano, basil, Italian seasoning, parsley, and continue to sauté for an additional 3 minutes, adding more distilled water if required. Add tomato sauce and paste, and stir to mix well. Cover and simmer for 30 minutes, stirring frequently.

To assemble lasagna, spoon a thin coating of the vegetable sauce into the bottom of a
(continued – please see next page)

9 x 13-inch glass baking dish. Top with a layer of 4 noodles, spoon $^1/_3$ of the tofu ricotta over the noodles, smooth it out with the back of the spoon, and top with tomato sauce. Repeat the layers of sauce, noodles (place the opposite way of the first layer), ricotta, ending with tomato sauce to cover the top layer of noodles. Sprinkle with tofu parmesan.

Cover with parchment paper, and bake 20 minutes at 350 degrees. Remove paper and bake an additional 20 minutes. Remove from oven and allow to sit 15 minutes prior to serving. The lasagna firms as it cools.

Pizza Dough
☆ ☆ ☆

try

1 Tbsp. active dry yeast	1 $^1/_2$ cup whole wheat pastry flour
2 Tbsp. honey	1 $^1/_2$ cup unbleached white flour
1 $^1/_4$ cup very warm distilled water	corn meal

Mix honey into distilled water, heat until honey is dissolved and the water is warm to the touch but not boiling. Add dry yeast and mix until dissolved. Let rest 5-10 minutes. Bubbles should form on the surface. Gradually add flour and knead about 10 minutes. Dough may be sticky – if so, use a small amount of flour on hands. After kneading, cover and put in a warm place to rise for approximately 1 to 1 $^1/_2$ half hours. Roll out until $^1/_4$ inch thick, place on pizza pan, sprinkle with corn meal. Allow dough to rise for about $^1/_2$ hour. Add toppings and bake at 350 degrees for twenty minutes.

Vegetarian Pizza
☆ ☆ ☆

try

1 prepared crust from above
2 cups pizza sauce (page 291)
1 $^1/_2$ cups tomato paste (page 287)
1 cup grated almond cheese (page 285) *need veg Parmeson Cheese*
1 tsp. Italian Seasoning (page 313)
3 cups vegetables such as: diced bell pepper, grated onion, grated zucchini
or yellow squash, mushrooms, etc.

Preheat oven to 375 degrees. Combine pizza sauce, tomato paste and Italian seasoning and simmer on low for about 20 minutes to blend flavors. Spread onto the crust recipe from above. Lay down a thick layer of vegetables and top with grated almond cheese. Bake 20 minutes.

Red Bell Pepper with Bulgur

Submitted by Kathy Kojundic
☆ ☆

1/2 cup bulgur	4 medium sweet peppers
3/4 cup distilled water	4 large plum tomatoes
4 cloves of garlic	4 green onions with tops
1/2 cup carrot	4 Tbsp. organic raisins
4 Tbsp. walnuts or pecans	pinch of cayenne pepper (optional)
1 cup vegetable soup stock (page 207)	

Place bulgur in a heavy heat-proof bowl. Bring distilled water to a boil and pour over bulgur, allow to sit for 30 minutes or until all of the liquid has been absorbed.

Preheat oven to 375 degrees. Remove the tops from the peppers, saving the flesh and discarding the stem. Scrape out the seeds and ribs, leaving the peppers whole. Drop whole peppers into a large kettle of distilled boiling water for about five minutes. Remove promptly, drain and set aside.

Chop pepper tops, tomatoes, onions, grate carrot, mince garlic and chop the nuts. Combine bulgur with the prepared vegetables, raisins, and cayenne and 1/3 of the vegetable soup stock, and stir well to combine. Fill each pepper with 1/4 of the mixture and place in an ungreased casserole that has a lid. Pour the remaining soup stock in the bottom of the casserole. Cover and bake about 20 minutes or until tender.

Hawaiian Rice

Submitted by Diane Brandow
☆ ☆

1 3/4 cup vegetable soup stock (page 207)	3/4 cup basmati rice
1/3 cup green pepper	1/4 cup celery
1/4 cup fresh pineapple	1 Tbsp. honey
1 Tbsp. apple cider vinegar, optional	1/2 cup green onion

Chop green pepper, celery and green onions. In a medium saucepan, bring 13/4 cups of soup stock to a boil over high heat. Add rice, cover and reduce heat to a low setting. Cook 30 minutes, turn heat off and allow to sit covered for an additional 15 minutes until the moisture is absorbed.

After the rice has been turned off, steam sauté green pepper, pineapple and celery in 1 - 2 Tbsp. of vegetable soup stock until softened.

When rice is finished cooking, add green pepper, pineapple, celery, vinegar and honey, and mix well. Garnish with green onion when serving.

Wild Rice Pilaf

Submitted by Jean Jacobson
☆ ☆ ☆

2 stalks celery
1 cup Basmati rice
1/2 cup Wild rice
2 Tbsp. parsley
1 onion
1 cup fresh or frozen peas

3 1/2 cups vegetable soup stock (page 207)
1/3 cup raw almonds
1/2 tsp. Celtic Sea Salt (optional)
1/2 cup whole wheat or rye berries
1 clove garlic

Soak wheat or rye berries overnight in distilled water. Drain. Chop celery and onion, mince garlic and parsley, sliver almonds, and set aside. Place almonds in a dry skillet and roast lightly. Bring vegetable stock to a boil, add all ingredients except almonds and peas, reduce heat to simmer, cover and cook about 25 minutes. After 25 minutes, turn off heat, add peas and almonds, cover and allow to sit another 15 to 20 minutes.

Sweet Potato Delight

☆ ☆

Wonderful for the holidays or any time you want a special treat.

4 sweet potatoes, peeled and cut in 1-inch chunks
1 large green apple, peeled and diced
1/4 cup raw cranberries (optional)

2 Tbsp. raw, unfiltered honey
1/2 cup of raisins
1/2 cup fresh orange juice

Preheat oven to 350 degrees. Place sweet potato chunks in a large baking dish. Top with a diced apple, cranberries and raisins. Drizzle with honey and pour orange juice over everything. Cover and bake approximately one hour, or until sweet potatoes are tender.

Kathleen's Tabouli

Submitted by Kathleen Newsome
☆ ☆ ☆

2 cups distilled water
3 garlic cloves
4 scallions
1/2 tsp. Celtic Sea Salt (optional)
juice of 1 large lemon or 2 small lemons

1 cup millet
1/2 cup fresh parsley
1 Tbsp. olive oil
4 large tomatoes
1/2 tsp. kelp (optional)

Bring distilled water to a boil, add millet, reduce heat, cover and simmer until all moisture has been absorbed. Remove from heat and cool. Mince garlic and parsley, chop scallions and tomatoes, place in a large bowl and add olive oil, Celtic Sea Salt, lemon juice and kelp. **Options:** diced celery, chopped broccoli, cauliflower, etc.

Quick Mexican Supper

Submitted by Jean Stoltzfus
☆ ☆ ☆

2 Hallelujah Burgers (page 251) or other veggie patty
1 cup dark red kidney beans
1/2 tsp. mild chili powder (optional)
diced tomatoes

salsa (page 288)
1/2 tsp. cumin
shredded leaf lettuce
avocado slices

Place veggie patties in a pan and put into oven preheated to about 300 degrees until the patties are warmed through.

Use kidney beans that have been prepared ahead of time; rinse well, and heat with 1/4 cup of distilled water until hot. Mash with a potato masher, and add seasonings. When the veggie patties are heated, crumble and add to bean mixture.

Serve on warmed tortillas or pita pockets and top with prepared lettuce, avocado, tomatoes and salsa.

Pasta Primavera

☆ ☆ ☆

1 cup chopped broccoli
1 cup chopped cauliflower
1 cup carrots, sliced in thin diagonals
1/2 cup onion, diced
2 Tbsp. minced parsley (fresh is best)
2 cups snipped fresh chives or basil, if available
1/4 cup diced red pepper
1/2 pound angel hair pasta
5 - 6 cherry tomatoes or 1 roma tomato

Bring large pot of distilled water to boil. Blanch broccoli, cauliflower, carrots and onions for 3 to 5 minutes or until tender. Remove veggies with slotted spoon, rinse in cold water and pat dry. Return vegetable water to a boil. Add pasta and cook until al denté (tender but firm), about 3 - 5 minutes.

While pasta is cooking, steam sauté vegetables, red pepper, seasoning and tomatoes for 3-5 minutes. Drain pasta and transfer to large bowl. Add 1 Tbsp. olive oil. Toss with vegetables. Season with herb seasoning.

Seasoned Basmati Rice

☆ ☆ ☆

try

This is one of our favorites on a cold winter evening after we have had our Barleygreen and salad. The aroma of this rice cooking will tantalize your taste buds.

1 cup brown basmati rice, rinsed and set aside
1/2 cup of celery, chopped
1/4 cup onion chopped

1/4 cup red and/or green pepper
3 cups distilled water

Steam sauté the celery, onion and peppers in water or vegetable soup stock, until onion is translucent. Add rice and sauté a few minutes (do not let it burn). Then add 3 cups of distilled water and bring quickly to a boil. Cover, reduce heat and simmer for 30 minutes. Turn burner off and allow it to sit covered for an additional 15 to 30 minutes. Do not lift lid. Stir, season with Celtic Sea Salt and herbs to taste. Serve alone or use as a base on which to place stir-fried or steamed vegetables.

Vegetarian Chili

☆

try

A Hallelujah Acres Restaurant sell-out every week! We served it with the corn bread recipe on page 275.

3/4 cup bell pepper
1/2 cup carrot
2 cups organic black beans
1 tsp. basil
1 tsp. cumin
1/2 tsp. garlic powder
1 Tbsp. onion flakes
3/4 cup TVP

1 cup onions
1/2 cup celery
2 cups organic kidney beans
1 tsp. Celtic Sea Salt (optional)
1/4 tsp. paprika
1/2 tsp. oregano
2 quarts tomato sauce (page 286)

Sort, rinse and soak beans overnight in enough water to cover. Drain and add enough water to cover and cook until tender. This can be done a day ahead.

Chop pepper and celery, dice onions, shred carrot, and sauté in a small amount of water until almost tender. Add cooked beans, TVP, herbs, seasonings and tomato sauce. Cook over low heat for about an hour, allowing the flavors to mingle.

Hint: If too thin, add more TVP. If too thick, add more tomato sauce.

Black Beans & Rice

Submitted by Georgeanna Seal

☆ ☆ ☆

1 medium yellow onion	1 small sweet red pepper
2 cloves of garlic	2 cups black beans
3/4 cup Basmati rice	1 1/2 cup vegetable soup stock (page 207)
1/4 tsp. red pepper flakes (optional)	1/4 tsp. dried thyme
1 bay leaf	

Sort, rinse and soak beans overnight. Drain soaking water, cover with fresh water and bring to a boil. Turn down heat, cover and cook until tender.

Core, seed and finely chop red pepper and onion, mince garlic and crumble thyme. In a large, heavy saucepan, steam onion and red pepper until the onion becomes translucent.

Add the remaining ingredients and bring to a boil. Adjust heat so that the mixture bubbles gently. Cover and cook 30 minutes. Remove from heat and allow to sit covered for an additional 15 minutes.

Remove bay leaf, spoon the rice and beans onto heated plates, and sprinkle with almond cheese, if desired.

Rice-Stuffed Tomatoes

Submitted by Cindy King

☆ ☆ ☆

6 large tomatoes	2 cups cooked basmati rice
1/2 cup organic raisins	2 Tbsp. fresh mint
2 Tbsp. chopped green pepper	2 Tbsp. parsley
2 Tbsp. green onions	

Remove the stem and cut a thin slice from the top of each tomato. Chop the edible portion of the tomato top and set aside. Scoop the pulp and seeds from the tomato, and invert the tomato shells to drain.

In a bowl, combine chopped tomato, rice, raisins, green pepper, onion, parsley and mint. Prepare lemon and oil dressing; stir into rice until well blended. Season to taste.

Fill tomato shells with equal portions of rice mixture, cover and chill. Serve with Rhonda's No-Oil Dressing on the side or

Dressing: In a small bowl, combine the following:

1/4 cup extra virgin olive oil	2 Tbsp. lemon juice
1 Tbsp. ketchup (page 290)	1/2 tsp. dry mustard, optional
1 tsp. mild chili powder (optional)	1 tsp. curry powder

Basmati Rice
☆ ☆ ☆

2 cups distilled water   1 cup rice

To cook brown rices, bring 2 cups of distilled water to a boil, add 1 cup of rice, lower heat and simmer, covered, for about 20 or 30 minutes. Do not stir rice while it is cooking. The rice will be done when all the water has cooked away. Remove from heat and allow to sit an additional 15 minutes without removing the lid.

Bulgur Wheat
☆ ☆ ☆

2 cups water   1 cup bulgur

To prepare bulgar wheat, pour 2 cups of boiling water over 1 cup bulgar, cover and allow to sit for 20 minutes.

Quinoa
☆ ☆ ☆

1 cup quinoa   2 cups distilled water

To cook, rinse with hot water in a strainer, then combine 1 cup quinoa with 2 cups distilled water in a saucepan. Bring to a boil, reduce heat and simmer about 15 minutes or until all water is absorbed.

Rolled Oats
☆ ☆ ☆

1 cup rolled oats   2 $\frac{1}{2}$ cups distilled water

To prepare, bring distilled water to a boil, add rolled oats and stir for 2 minutes. Reduce heat to low, cover and cook for 15 minutes or until water has been absorbed.

Chapter Twenty-three:

Tasty Breads, Snacks & Sandwiches

Poor Man's Bread

Submitted by Mrs. Thomas Bradbury
☆ ☆ ☆

8 cups distilled water   1 tsp. yeast
5 pounds freshly ground whole wheat flour

Warm water, mix in the yeast and half of the flour. Cover and allow to sit to make a sponge (takes about 4 to 6 hours, depending on temperature). Punch down and knead, mixing in additional flour. Let rise in an oiled, covered pan overnight in a cool place.

Shape into rounds or loaves. Cover and let rise until it doubles in size (about 1 hour). Bake at 350 degrees for approximately 50 minutes.

Hallelujah Acres Cornbread
☆

try

In first bowl, combine:

¹/₂ cup corn meal	
¹/₂ cup unbleached white flour	
¹/₂ cup rye flour	1 Tbsp. onion flakes
1 tsp. Italian Seasoning (page 313)	2 tsp. Rumford *Aluminum-Free* baking powder

In second bowl, combine the following:

1 cup water	1 Tbsp. raw, unfiltered apple cider vinegar
1 ¹/₂ Tbsp. honey	¹/₂ tsp. Celtic Sea Salt (optional)

Line muffin tin with liquid lecithin. Mix wet ingredients well until honey is dissolved. Add dry ingredients. Mix quickly and pour into a 6-muffin pan, filling each half full. Bake 20 min. in 350-degree oven. Let cool 5 to 10 minutes, remove from muffin pan and cool on wire racks. Store covered in refrigerator.

Broccoli / Red Pepper Pita Pocket
☆ ☆ ☆

try

¹/₂ red bell pepper	¹/₄ cup broccoli florets
¹/₂ ripe tomato	¹/₄ cup cauliflower florets
¹/₂ avocado	juice from ¹/₂ lemon
1 tsp. herb seasoning	

Finely chop broccoli, cauliflower and red pepper, dice tomato and drain off excess juice. Mash avocado and mix with lemon juice and seasonings, and spread onto pita. Add chopped vegetables.

Hint: Whole grain bread may be substituted for pita pocket.

Cucumber Sandwich
☆ ☆ ☆

2 slices whole grain bread or pita pocket   ¹/₂ avocado
2 leaves leaf lettuce   ¹/₂ cucumber
1 or 2 tomato slices

Slice tomato, cucumber and avocado in very thin slices. Spread the bread with Rhonda's No-Oil Dressing. Top with other ingredients, and sprinkle with herb seasoning, if desired.

Hint: If packing in a lunch, place vegetables in separate containers.

Hummus in a Pita
☆ ☆ ☆

Use the Hummus recipe on page 289 to spread on one half of the pita pocket. Add chopped lettuce, grated carrot, cucumber or your favorite minced vegetables. Top with a small amount of your favorite dressing.

Hint: If packing in a lunch, put dressing in a separate container.

Pizza Lover's Sandwich
☆ ☆

¹/₄ green pepper rings   ¹/₄ red onion rings
¹/₄ cup tomato sauce (page 286)   1 Tbsp. tomato paste (page 287)
1 slice almond cheese (page 285)   ¹/₄ tsp. Italian season (page 313)

Slice green pepper and onions into thin rings. Toast whole grain bread, pita or bagel, top with remaining ingredients and serve.

Power House Sandwich
☆ ☆

2 slices of whole grain bread   2 leaves of leaf lettuce
2 slices of tomato   2 slices of almond cheese (page 285)

Spread bread with Rhonda's No-Oil Dressing (page 175), sprinkle with herb seasoning, then add lettuce, tomato and cheese.

Almond Butter Sandwiches
☆ ☆ ☆

Make fresh almond butter (see page 284), mix with a small amount of raw, unfiltered honey and spread on whole-grain bread or pita pockets.

Almond Cheese Delight
☆ ☆ ☆

Slice "almond cheese" (pg 285) and place on whole-grain bread, bagel or in a pita spread with dressing of choice. Top with leaf lettuce, thinly sliced onion or other vegetables of choice.

Sloppy Joe Mix
☆ ☆ ☆

1 onion	1 cup dry bean flakes
1 cup raw Basmati rice	1 cup tomato sauce (page 286)
1 tsp. dry mustard	1/2 tsp. Celtic Sea Salt (optional)
3 cups distilled water or vegetable broth	

Dry roast onion and rice until onion is translucent. In a blender or food processor, mix bean flakes and distilled water until smooth. Combine with other ingredients in a sauce pan. Cover, bring to a boil, reduce heat to simmer and cook approximately 30 minutes, turn off heat and allow to sit an additional 15 minutes until rice is done.

Veggie Combo Sandwich
☆ ☆ ☆

2 slices whole grain bread or pita pocket	leaf lettuce or spinach
sliced tomatoes*	thinly sliced onions
sliced avocado or sliced almond cheese	grated carrots
sliced cucumbers	chopped red peppers

Any other fresh veggies of your choice may be added. Add Rhonda's No Oil Dressing (page 175) and enjoy. Or mash the avocado and omit the dressing.

*If sending in a lunch, put tomatoes and dressing in separate containers to prevent the sandwich from getting soggy.

Tomato & Avocado Pita Pocket
☆ ☆ ☆

1 whole grain pita pocket
1/2 tomato
2 Tbsp. shredded carrot

1/4 avocado*
juice from 1/4 lemon
1 leaf of lettuce

Cut pocket in half, mash avocado and spread half on each pita. Dice tomato fine and drain excess juice, put in pita, place on top of avocado, shred lettuce and place on top of tomato, top with a small amount of shredded carrot.

*If using for a bagged lunch, wrap all veggies separately and replace avocado with Rhonda's Dressing because avocados do not keep well after being cut.

Tomato on a Burger Bun
☆ ☆ ☆

whole grain burger bun
1/2 cup guacamole (page 288)

3/4-inch slice of large tomato
1 slice red onion

On a toasted bun, spread with guacamole and Rhonda's Dressing (optional), place tomato and thinly sliced onion.

If taking for lunch, place guacamole, tomato and onion in separate containers.

Tofu Eggless Salad in a Pita Pocket
☆

Spread Tofu Eggless Salad (page 295) in each half of a pita pocket, add torn lettuce and other thinly-sliced vegetables, if desired. If more dressing is desired, spread with Rhonda's No-Oil Dressing (page 175) or one of your choice.

Hallelujah Acres Colonial Bread

☆ ☆ ☆

At Hallelujah Acres Restaurant, this bread was extremely popular. We could never make enough!

1 package yeast
2 ½ cups unbleached white flour
½ tsp. Celtic Sea Salt (optional)
1 ½ cups very warm distilled water

1 cup rye flour
1 cup yellow corn meal
½ cup raw unfiltered honey

Heat water to between 110 and 115 degrees. Combine honey, yeast, Celtic Sea Salt and water, and stir to dissolve. Allow to work for 10 to 20 minutes. Add corn meal, mixing thoroughly, then add rye flour while continuing to mix. Work in unbleached flour ½ cup at a time until dough is smooth and elastic – about 5 to 10 minutes. Dough should be stiff.

Place the dough on a well-floured cutting board, and sprinkle with enough flour to cover lightly. Flour your hands. Knead* dough to form an even, elastic consistency. This step is extremely important as it develops the gluten. The gluten acts as a net to hold in air bubbles formed by the yeast. The result is a bread that is more airy and light.

Place the dough in a bowl lined with liquid lecithin. Cover with a clean dish towel. Place in a warm location and allow to rise until doubled. This usually takes about 1 ½ hours.

Remove the dough from the bowl, punch it down and knead for a few seconds. Divide dough in two, and shape each half into a loaf. Place into lecithin-lined loaf pans (8" x 4" x 2"), cover and allow to rise until doubled. About 45 minutes.

Bake in a preheated oven at 350 degrees for 40 to 45 minutes. The crust should be golden brown. Remove from oven and place pans on a wire rack to cool.

*Kneading consists of folding the dough in half, pushing it down and away from you. Turn the dough a one-quarter turn and repeat until all the dough is kneaded. The harder the dough is worked, the better the texture will be and the more the bread will rise. If the dough is sticky, add a small amount of flour. After kneading 5 or 10 minutes, press slightly to see if the dough returns to its original shape. If so, it is ready to rise.

279

Honey Nut Oatmeal Bread

☆ ☆ ☆

Submitted by Kay Frost

1 ¹/₃ cups distilled water	2 Tbsp. unsweetened applesauce
¹/₄ cup honey	1 cup rolled oats
1 cup whole wheat flour	2 cups bread flour
2 ¹/₂ tsp. yeast	²/₃ cup walnuts

Place all ingredients in a bread machine except walnuts. Turn machine on to the Sweet Bread setting. Chop walnuts. At the beep, add the walnuts and continue baking until the machine shuts off.

This recipe can also be made by hand following the directions for Hallelujah Acres Colonial Bread.

Open Face Sandwiches

Submitted by Jolene Trickle

☆ ☆ ☆

3 whole grain rolls	2 leaves of romaine lettuce
2 green onions	¹/₂ cucumber
6 tomato slices	6 sweet red pepper

Cut rolls in half lengthwise and spread each half with Rhonda's No-Oil Dressing. Chop green onions, and thinly slice tomatoes, pepper and cucumber. Layer each bun half with onions, almond cheese (page 285), and leaf lettuce. Spread with a small amount of Rhonda's No-Oil Cucumber Dressing, then add tomato, sweet pepper and cucumber. Sprinkle with Herb Seasoning and serve.

Hero Sandwich

Submitted by Julie Zumach
☆ ☆ ☆

2 medium carrots
1 medium zucchini
1 cup tomato sauce (page 286)
1/2 tsp. dried sweet basil
1 loaf (8 ounces) French or Italian whole-grain bread

1/2 red bell pepper
1 large red onion
1/2 tsp. dried oregano
sliced almond cheese (page 285)

Slice onion, zucchini and peppers into thin rings, grate the carrots, and place in pan with a small amount of Celtic Sea Salt or distilled water and steam until tender. Add tomato sauce and seasonings and simmer uncovered for 3 minutes.

Preheat broiler. Slice bread in half lengthwise and remove and discard soft center from the bottom half and part of the top half. Place the halves, cut side up, on a baking sheet and broil 4 inches from the heating unit for one minute until lightly toasted. Remove and set aside.

Spoon the vegetable mixture into the bread, top with almond cheese (page 285) and return to pan. Place under broiler and broil 1 minute or until the cheese has melted. Remove to cutting board, and top with toasted upper half. Cut to serve immediately.

Laurie's Granola

Submitted by Laurie Ousley
☆ ☆ ☆ ☆

10 cups rolled oats
2 cups pine nuts (optional)
1 pound of organic raisins
1 pound of organic figs
2 cups unsweetened coconut
1 - 2 cups sesame seeds (optional)

2 cups pepitas (pumpkin seeds)
2 cups raw sunflower seeds
1 pound bag of organic dates
2 cups slivered almonds
1 cup wheatgerm (optional)

Combine all ingredients in a large bowl. Store in a tightly sealed container.

Essene Bread

☆ ☆ ☆

1/4 cup almonds (soaked overnight and drained)
1/4 cup walnuts (soaked overnight and drained)
3 pitted dates (soaked in a separate bowl until soft, about one hour and drained)

1/2 apple, peeled and shredded
1 clove garlic, minced (optional)
1 teaspoon fresh parsley, minced
2 tablespoons extra virgin olive oil
2 cups sprouted wheat berries, kamut or spelt*

Place drained sprouts and dates into food processor along with remaining ingredients and process until a dough consistency is reached. Or remove the screen and replace it with the blank on the Champion or Green Star and run through into a catch container. Place dough on a solid dehydrating sheet and shape a loaf about 3 1/2 inches wide, about 6 inches long and1 1/2 inches thick. Dehydrate at 100 degrees for 13 to 17 hours. The bread will be crispy on the outside and moist on the inside.

*To sprout grains place them in a large bowl and cover with distilled water. Allow them to soak 2 to 3 days. Place colander over a large bowl and pour soaked grains into colander draining all of the soaking water. Cover colander and allow it to sit overnight. The following morning, rinse by placing them in a bowl of fresh water and swirling lightly with your hand. Return to colander until next the next morning and repeat the process. Repeat this process until a small "tail" about 1/4" forms. When the "tail" has formed, place the sprouts in a container in the refrigerator, this helps slow down the growing process. Sprouts should keep two to three days in the refrigerator.

Chapter Twenty-four:

Healthy Condiments, Sauces, Dips & Spreads

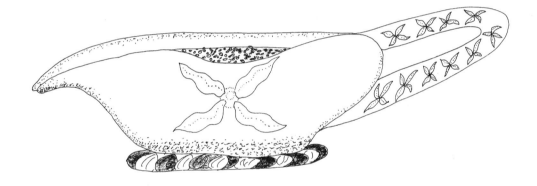

Basic Seed Sauce

☆ ☆ ☆ ☆ ☆

1 cup sunflower seeds   1 cup almonds
3 cups distilled water

In a food processor, blender, Green Star or Champion Juicer, grind seeds to a fine meal. Pour into blender, add distilled water and puree. Pour into a glass bowl or jar and cover with a cloth. Allow to sit at room temperature for approximately 4 to 8 hours until the "cheese" separates from the liquid (the "cheese" will be at the top).

Herbs may be added while blending the seeds and nuts to vary the flavor.

Hint: Seed sauces are slightly fermented which creates live enzymes and friendly bacteria for the body. However, if the sauce has fermented too much and is tart, add a bit of minced onion.

Almond Butter
☆ ☆ ☆ ☆ ☆

Almond butter is a much healthier alternative to peanut butter. It can be made in your Green Star or Champion Juicer. Cover almonds with distilled water, cover and soak overnight. Drain and discard soak water. If using a Champion, replace the screen with the solid plate and slowly feed the almonds through. In a Green Star, place the open blank or homogenizing blank (the thinner side towards the front of the machine) over the gears. Replace discharge casing and tighten the knobs. Loosen the outlet adjusting knob. When the almonds are processed, they will be a paste-like consistency. If a thinner consistency is desired, add distilled water a little bit at a time after putting almonds through the machine until desired consistency is reached.

Almond butter can be used to stuff celery or to replace peanut butter in any recipe. To add variety, add 1 Tbsp. honey or 3 dates. Use immediately, does not store well.

Almond & Garlic Dip
☆ ☆ ☆ ☆ ☆

1/2 cup almond butter	1/4 cup fresh basil, parsley or cilantro
2 Tbsp. minced garlic	1/8 tsp. Celtic Sea Salt (optional)
1/4 Cup Rhonda's No Oil Dressing (page 175)	

Combine all ingredients and mix thoroughly. If too thick add a little distilled water to reach desired consistency. Can be used on raw crackers, with raw veggies or on bread.

Almond "Cheese" Sauce
☆ ☆ ☆ ☆ ☆

1 cup almonds	2/3 cup distilled water
1/4 tsp. Celtic Sea Salt (optional)	1 Tbsp. fresh lemon juice
1/2 tsp. garlic powder	1/2 cup red bell pepper
1 1/2 tsp. onion powder	1/4 cup nutritonal yeast flakes

Place all ingredients in a blender or Vita Mix and blend until smooth. Place in a glass container and store in the refrigerator. This cheese will thicken in the refrigerator.

Almond Slicing "Cheese"
☆ ☆ ☆

1 cup distilled water
1/2 cup red bell pepper
1/4 cup nutritional yeast flakes
1/2 tsp. garlic powder
1/2 tsp. Celtic Sea Salt (optional)
2 tsp. onion flakes

4 Tbsp. agar agar flakes or arrow root powder
1 cup almonds
1 Tbsp. tahini or 2 Tbsp. sesame seeds
2 Tbsp. lemon juice
1 tsp. paprika
1 Tbsp. Vegetarian Parmesan Cheese

Place water and almonds into blender and process until a creamy milk consistency is reached. Pour into saucepan. Mix in agar agar (or arrow root powder) and bring to a boil. Immediately, reduce heat and simmer for 5 minutes or until agar agar (or arrow root powder) is completely dissolved. Place mixture in blender, Vita Mix or food processor and add remaining ingredients and blend until smooth. Scrape sides until all ingredients are mixed well. Pour into container and refrigerate until set. This cheese can be sliced in the size you prefer.

Almond, Sunflower Seed Sauce
☆ ☆ ☆ ☆ ☆

1/2 cup almonds
1/2 cup sunflower seeds
1 cup distilled water
1/2 cup dates
1/2 lemon
Celtic Sea Salt to taste (optional)

Soak almonds, sunflower seeds and dates overnight in distilled water using separate containers. The following morning, drain, saving soaking water. Juice lemon, pit dates, add to blender with almonds and sunflower seeds and mix to desired consistency using soaking water to thin, if needed. Serve sauce with fruits or vegetables.

Honey Mustard
☆ ☆ ☆

Mix in a saucepan the following:

> $\frac{1}{4}$ cup distilled water or vegetable broth
> $\frac{1}{2}$ cup lemon juice
> 3 tsp. arrow root powder

Cook over high heat, stirring until thickened. The amount of arrow root used will determine the thickness of the mustard. Remove from heat and cool. After it has cooled, combine this mixture with the following ingredients in a blender and blend until creamy.

2 Tbsp. honey	2 tsp. tumeric or paprika
$\frac{1}{4}$ tsp. Celtic Sea Salt (optional)	1 tsp. garlic powder (optional)
2 Tbsp. Rhonda's No-Oil Dressing	

Hint: Honey may be omitted if a less sweet mustard is desired.

Tomato Sauce
☆ ☆ ☆

7 pounds of ripe tomatoes	5 large garlic cloves
3 celery stalks with leaves	6 cups onions
3 cups green pepper	2 cups carrot
2 bay leaves	1 Tbsp. garlic powder
1 Tbsp. basil	2 Tbsp. oregano
$\frac{1}{4}$ cup parsley	$\frac{1}{2}$ tsp. marjoram
$\frac{1}{2}$ tsp. rosemary	1 Tbsp. thyme
Celtic Sea Salt to taste (optional)	

Peel and cube tomatoes, mince garlic cloves, dice onions, celery and green pepper and grate carrot.

For fresh sauce: Place in a large glass bowl and add seasonings, cover and allow to sit for flavors to mingle. Remove bay leaves. Serve at room temperature or heat slightly but do not boil.

For a cooked sauce: Place in a large stainless steel kettle, cover and bring to a boil. Turn the heat down to simmer and cook without a cover until the amount has decreased to one third to one half. Remove bay leaves. Transfer about one third of the mixture, cool and blend in a blender or food processor until smooth. Return to kettle and mix with the rest of the sauce.

Hint: This Tomato Sauce Recipe makes about 5 $\frac{1}{2}$ quarts. It can be served immediately with the balance being dehydrated, canned or frozen.

Tomato Paste
☆ ☆ ☆

1 cup fresh tomatoes	1 cup carrot
1/4 cup onion	2 dates
1/8 tsp. oregano	1/8 tsp. basil
Celtic Sea Salt to taste (optional)	1 tsp. arrow root powder

Blend tomatoes, onion, carrots and dates until well blended. Add seasonings and arrow root powder, and simmer until desired consistency is reached. You may add more arrow root to thicken faster.

Baba Gannouj
☆ ☆ ☆ ☆ ☆

2 medium eggplants
1/2 cup tahini
juice of 2 lemons
Celtic Sea Salt to taste (optional)
3 cloves of garlic
1/4 tsp. basil
1/4 cup fresh parsley
1/2 cup red onion

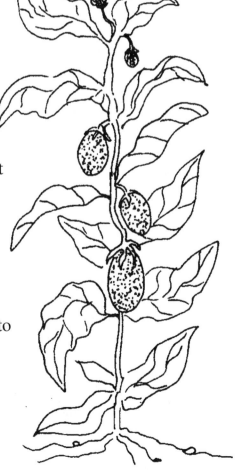

Remove stem and peel eggplant, chop into small pieces, sprinkle with Celtic Sea Salt and allow to soak for at least one hour. Drain and rinse. In a blender combine eggplant, tahini, lemon juice, garlic and onion. Blend until creamy. Mix in fresh parsley and basil just prior to serving. Additional Celtic Sea Salt and a pinch of cayenne pepper may be added, if desired.

Hint: This is a raw recipe; however, some may prefer to bake eggplant prior to mixing with other ingredients. If so, preheat oven to 400 degrees, and bake eggplant one hour until soft.

Salsa

☆☆☆☆☆

1 cup tomatoes	2 Tbsp. onion
¹/₂ cup red bell pepper	¹/₂ cup green bell pepper
¹/₂ cup fresh corn, optional	¹/₂ cup cucumber
¹/₂ cup celery	2 Tbsp. extra virgin olive oil
1 tsp. each, basil, oregano and cilantro	1 clove fresh garlic
Celtic Sea Salt to taste (optional)	2 Tbsp. honey, optional

Peel and chop tomatoes, mince onion, garlic, peppers, celery and cucumber. Place half of the vegetables in blender or food processor and blend until smooth. Combine with the remaining vegetables, add seasonings and oil and mix well. Cover and place in refrigerator to chill until served.

Guacamole

☆☆☆☆☆

2 very ripe avocados	2 Tbsp. onion
1 clove of garlic	¹/₂ red pepper
1 cup tomato, optional	1 stalk of celery
1 Tbsp. lime or lemon juice	

Press garlic, mince onion, chop tomato, red pepper and celery and place in bowl. Halve avocados, remove pits and scoop flesh into a bowl and mash well, add to other ingredients, add lemon or lime juice, and mix well. Cover and chill. Use as a dip, in pitas or sandwiches.

Option: Add a small amount of Rhonda's No Oil Dressing (page 175) for a unique flavor and creamier consistency.

288

Hummus

Submitted by Judy Moore
☆ ☆ ☆ ☆ ☆

2 cups dried garbanzo beans (chick peas)	1/4 cup dried parsley
1/4 cup fresh lemon juice	1/2 tsp. Celtic Sea Salt (optional)
2 cloves of garlic	1/3 cup tahini (page 292)
1/2 tsp. cumin	pinch of cayenne

Soak garbanzo beans at least 24 hours. If soaked less, they will be too hard to use. Do not cook.

Stir the tahini to mix well and mince the garlic. Use the "S" blade in a food processor and process the soaked garbanzo beans about one minute. Add tahini and minced garlic while the processor is still running, process one minute. With the machine still running, add the Celtic Sea Salt, seasonings, and lemon juice and process until a creamy consistency is reached, perhaps up to 10 minutes. Stir the parsley in by hand.

Hint: If the garlic is not minced prior to adding to the bean mixture, it may be too chunky.

Pesto

☆ ☆ ☆ ☆ ☆

1/3 cup fresh basil leaves	1/3 cup fresh cilantro leaves
1/4 cup almonds	1/4 cup pine nuts
2 garlic cloves	1 Tbsp. lemon juice
1/4 tsp. Celtic Sea Salt	1 cup tomato (optional)
1/4 cup extra virgin olive oil	

Grind almonds and pine nuts to a fine texture. To measure fresh basil and cilantro, pack herb tightly into measuring cup. Place in a blender or food processor with the remaining ingredients. Pulse to chop, scraping sides until well blended. If using tomatoes, add and pulse just to blend, do not puree.

Hint: This blend can be stuffed into celery, served with crackers, served with rice, pasta, steamed vegetables or used as a dip with fresh vegetables. Can use 2/3 cup basil if desired. Basil and cilanro have strong flavors. If a lighter (milder) flavor is desired, use less.

Ketchup

☆ ☆

2 cups freshly extracted tomato juice	3 stalks of celery with tops
2 cloves of garlic	1 bay leaf
1 cup onion	$1/2$ cup of parsley
1 6-ounce can low-salt tomato paste	6 ounces of distilled water

Juice tomatoes, mince garlic and parsley, chop onion and celery. Place ingredients in a pan and bring to a boil, reduce heat and cook for about 20 minutes. Remove bay leaf and press the rest of the ingredients through a sieve into a clean pan.

Add the following:

1 cup lemon juice	$1/2$ tsp. cinnamon
$1/8$ tsp. cayenne	1 tsp. dry mustard
$1/2$ tsp. mace	1 tsp. allspice
$1/2$ tsp. celery seed	$1/4$ cup raw unfiltered honey or maple syrup
$1/2$ tsp. Celtic Sea Salt (optional)	

Simmer over low heat without a cover for about one and one half hours, stirring on occasion to prevent sticking. Cool, place in jar and store in the refrigerator.

To serve raw: Omit the cooking time of 20 minutes, allow to sit with bay leaf for one hour at room temperature. Remove bay leaf and put through a sieve, add the rest of the ingredients, cover and store in the refrigerator.

For a little different flavor replace the above spices with:

$1/4$ tsp. thyme
1 tsp. sweet basil
1 tsp. marjoram
1 tsp. garlic powder
2 tsp. dehydrated onion flakes

Hint: 1 Tbsp. of commercial ketchup contains 170 mg. of sodium, along with sugar and preservatives.

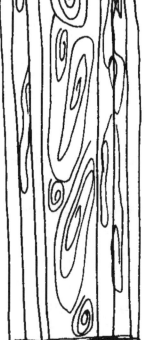
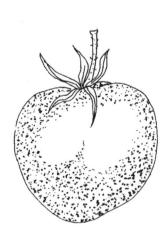

Pizza Sauce
☆ ☆ ☆

try

2 garlic cloves	1 onion
1 cup tomato paste	2 cups tomato sauce
1 Tbsp. lemon juice	2 tsp. raw, unfiltered honey
1/2 tsp. oregano	1/2 tsp. basil

Mince garlic, chop onions fine. To use for a raw pizza, add the remaining ingredients and allow to sit until flavors are blended.

To use for cooked pizza, place onions and garlic in a pan with a small amount of water to steam until tender. Add the remainder of the ingredients and cook until it has reached the desired consistency. Spread on pizza crust and top with your favorite veggies.

Spaghetti Sauce
☆ ☆ ☆

try

1 quart of tomato sauce	1 large garlic clove
1 celery stalk with leaves	1 cup onion
1/2 cup green pepper	1 small carrot
1 bay leaf	1 tsp. garlic powder
2 tsp. basil	1 tsp. oregano
1/2 tsp. Italian seasoning	1 tsp. marjoram
1/4 cup parsley	2 Tbsp. vegetarian Worchestershire sauce
2 Tbsp. raw unfiltered honey	1 cup tomato paste
Celtic Sea Salt to taste (optional)	3 large tomatoes

Peel and cube tomatoes, mince garlic cloves, dice onions, celery and green pepper and grate carrot.

For fresh, raw Spaghetti Sauce: Place in a large glass bowl and add the rest of the ingredients, cover and allow to sit for flavors to mingle. Remove bay leaves. Serve at room temperature or heat slightly but do not boil.

For a cooked Spaghetti Sauce: Place in a large stainless steel kettle, cover and bring to a boil. Turn the heat down to simmer and cook without a cover until the amount has decreased to one third to one half. Remove bay leaves. Transfer about one third of the mixture, cool and blend in a blender or food processor until smooth. Return to kettle and mix with the rest of the sauce.

Hint: The secret to the wonderful taste of this Spaghetti Sauce is the abundant amount of veggies.

Tofu Ricotta
☆

1 pound firm tofu	2 Tbsp. extra virgin olive oil (optional)
1/2 tsp. nutmeg	1 tsp. basil
1/8 tsp. turmeric	1/2 tsp. Celtic Sea Salt (optional)
1/4 cup dried parsley	1/3 cup lemon juice
1/3 cup nutritional yeast flakes	1/3 cup tahini

Place all ingredients in blender or food processor. Blend until a creamy consistency is reached.

Tahini
☆ ☆ ☆ ☆ ☆

1 cup distilled water	1 cup sesame seeds
1/4 cup lemon juice	2 cloves of garlic
1/4 tsp. Celtic Sea Salt (optional)	

In a Champion or Green Star Juicer, process 1 cup of sesame seeds and 2 garlic cloves to create nut butter. Combine the nut butter with the remaining ingredients, mix well. Adjust water and lemon to reach desired consistency.

Hint: Use as a spread or dip or use in recipes calling for tahini. Thin to use as a dressing.

Tomato Chutney
☆ ☆ ☆ ☆

4 cups ripe tomatoes	1 apple
1 cup onion	1 pear
1/4 cup fresh lemon juice	1/4 cup organic raisins
1 tsp. pickling spices	Celtic Sea Salt to taste (optional)

Peel tomatoes, remove seeds. Place in food processor with "S" blade, chop to chunky consistency, set aside. Quarter onion, mince in food processor with "S" blade, set aside. Peel and core apple and pear, place in food processor with "S" blade, chop to a chunky consistency. Combine with remaining ingredients and allow to sit for several hours before serving.

Tomato Basil Sauce

☆ ☆ ☆ ☆ ☆

3 cups tomatoes
3/4 cup fresh basil leaves
Celtic Sea Salt to taste (optional)
1/4 tsp. oregano

2 garlic cloves
juice of 1/2 lemon
1 tsp. ground thyme

Peel tomatoes, cut in quarters and remove seeds. Mince the garlic. Wash the basil and place in a blender or food processor along with the minced garlic and lemon juice. Pulse chop a few times. Add the tomato pieces and pulse to chop only (do not puree). Add Celtic Sea Salt to taste.

Serve over vegetables, spaghetti squash, veggie pizzas or vegetable burgers.

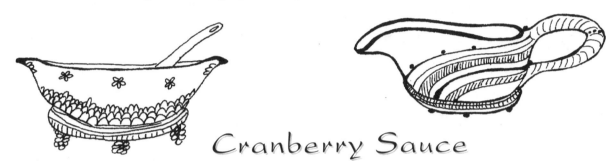

Cranberry Sauce

☆ ☆ ☆

2 cups fresh or frozen cranberries
1 medium Delicious apple
1 orange
1/4 cup apple juice or orange juice
1/2 cup dates
1/8 tsp. cloves

2 ripe pears
1/2 cup raisins
1/2 cup honey
1/4 grated organic orange rind
1/4 tsp. cinnamon, ginger & allspice

In food processor, grind cranberries, pour into bowl, chop peeled orange and add to cranberries, chop the apple and pears and combine with the cranberry/orange mixture. Add raisins, honey, orange rind and apple juice and allow to sit overnight in the refrigerator for the flavors to blend. If more sweetener is required add more raisins, pears or honey.

If a gelatin salad is desired, simply increase the apple juice to 1/2 cup and dissolve 4 tablespoons of agar agar for a few minutes, put in a saucepan and boil for 5 minutes before adding to the salad.

If a cooked sauce is desired, place whole cranberries with remaining ingredients in a saucepan, bring to a boil, reduce heat and cook gently for about 20 to 30 minutes uncovered.

Hint: Cranberries are a seasonal food that can usually be found October through December.

Raw Raisin Chutney

submitted by Michael Dye
☆ ☆ ☆ ☆ ☆

This is a unique chutney recipe because it is all raw (and therefore more nutritious than most chutneys, which usually include a main ingredient cooked for a lengthy time in spices). The amounts of cayenne and ginger can be increased to make this recipe quite spicy, if you desire. The sweetness of the raisins balance out this spiciness, but you may want to adjust the amount of cayenne and ginger to suit your personal taste.

This recipe can be made using a blender, a Champion juicer (using the solid blank plate instead of the screen) or a Green Star juicer (using the solid blank). I always multiply this recipe several times, because it keeps at least two weeks refrigerated in an air-tight container. Keep in mind that when you multiply the main ingredient(s) of a recipe, you can't always multiply the spices by that same amount without it being too spicy. I have included the original recipe, along with my proportions for an extra large batch in parenthesis.

2 cups organic raisins (or 10 cups)
1 ¹/₂ Tbsp. chopped fresh ginger (or 5 Tbsp.)
¹/₂ tsp. cayenne (or 1 ¹/₂ tsp.)
juice from 1 lemon (or 5 lemons)

First, let the raisins soak in a bowl of distilled water for about 30 minutes, so they become plump, then drain the raisins of excess water. Cut the ginger into thin slices (or if you are using a blender, you will need to chop the ginger much finer). Begin by putting a handful of raisins and all the cayenne and ginger through the juicer; then put this blended mix of raisins, ginger and cayenne back into the bowl of raisins and mix well to evenly distribute the spices. Now put these raisins, ginger and cayenne through the juicer. Finish by pouring the lemon juice through the juicer, which will help clean the other ingredients from the inside of the juicer. Mix well by hand to evenly distribute the lemon juice with the other ingredients. This raisin chutney is great on toast as a spicy jam or can be served with brown rice or Indian foods.

Vegetable Seed Cheese
☆ ☆ ☆ ☆ ☆

1/2 cup basic seed cheese (page 283) 1/2 cup vegetable pulp*
1/2 tsp. Celtic Sea Salt (optional) 1 tsp. garlic
1 tsp. onion

Mince onion and garlic, and mix into seed cheese. Add vegetable pulp and Celtic Sea Salt. Use as a sandwich filling, on dehydrated crackers or for a veggie dip.
*Carrot, celery, pepper, squash, etc.

Creamy Onion Dip
☆

1 8-oz. package low fat tofu, drained 2 Tbsp. lemon juice
1/2 tsp. Celtic Sea Salt (optional) 2 tsp. nutriontional yeast
1/2 cup dehydrated onion flakes 1/2 tsp. garlic powder
2 tsp. raw, unfiltered honey or maple syrup

Combine all ingredients in a blender and blend until smooth.

Hint: For added flavor or a change of pace, try adding some different dehydrated vegetables before blending.

Tofu Eggless Salad
☆

1 8-oz. package low fat tofu, drained 1 tsp. Celtic Sea Salt (optional)
5 Tbsp. Rhonda's No Oil Dressing (page 175) 1/4 tsp. ground coriander
2 tsp. ground mustard (optional) 1/2 tsp. curry powder
1 tsp. tumeric 1/4 tsp. ground cumin
1/4 cup each diced celery, onion, bell pepper pinch of cayenne

Crumble tofu into a medium bowl, mash large chunks with a fork until a uniform texture is reached. Add diced vegetables, seasonings and dressing. Mix well.
Can be served in a pita or on a bed of lettuce with tomato slices.

Chapter Twenty-five:

Dehydrated Foods

The most efficient, healthy, palatable and simple way to preserve foods in their natural state is through dehydration. When food is dehydrated at approximately 105 degrees, the food's enzymes, proteins, vitamins, minerals, etc. stay intact. The moisture is simply removed from the food by the flow of heat and air. When the moisture is removed, microorganisms such as yeast, bacteria and mold cannot grow. No other method of food preservation is as nutritionally sound. It is important, however, not to over-dry foods.

Dehydration as a method of food preservation has been around for centuries. Ancient civilizations relied on the sun as a method to dry food, and later fire was used. When ancient pyramids were opened, dried foods were often found intact.

Dehydrating vegetables can also be a rewarding experience. It is important to remember that the quality of the fresh vegetable will determine the texture and taste of the dehydrated produce. Wash the vegetables well, dry, remove any blemishes, cut uniformly and fill the dehydrator trays. Once the dehydrator has been filled and started, it is best not to add additional fruits or vegetables as the added moisture will delay the processing time. It is important to dehydrate vegetables immediately after picking or place them in the refrigerator. Do not allow them to sit at room temperature. Dried vegetables do not contain natural sugars that cushion the enzymatic activity in dried fruits; therefore, the longer the vegetables are stored, the more they begin to lose their flavor, color, texture and nutrients. Dehydrated vegetables should be stored in the refrigerator or freezer if they will not be consumed within one year. Always date and then rotate the stored items, placing the oldest to be consumed first.

The peels of some foods, like cucumbers, have a bitter taste compared to the sweetness of the fruit when dehydrated. The higher the concentration of sugar in the fruit, the more the rind will taste bitter. When fruits dry, their sugar concentrates and they sweeten; however, the peels do not. This leaves a contrasting taste between the pulp and the peel which can be quite distinct.

Rehydrating takes longer for vegetables than it does for fruit because more of the moisture has been removed. To prevent a tough texture when adding to hot foods, rehydrate in cool water for no longer than two hours, unless refrigerated. If large pieces need to be rehydrated, it may be best to soak overnight in the refrigerator. Use only the amount of liquid required for rehydrating because valuable nutrients will be lost when excess liquid is drained off. A good rule of thumb is to soak 1 cup of dehydrated food in 1 cup of liquid. If necessary, gradually add more liquid until the desired texture is obtained and the food will not absorb any more. The liquid drained from dehydrated fruits and vegetables can be saved and later used in soups, stews, pies, sauces or leathers.

Vegetables that do not dehydrate well are brussels sprouts, lettuces, potatoes, artichokes and hard squashes.

When using dehydrated vegetables and fruits in quick breads, pies, dough or batters, use 2 parts liquid to 3 parts dried ingredients. For vegetable dishes, fruit toppings, and compotes, 1 to 1 1/2 parts liquid to 1 part dehydrated food is usually sufficient. Additional liquid may be added during cooking, if required.

When drying fruits, wash them well, discard any bruised or rotten pieces. If the skin is not removed, it must be perforated so that the moisture can escape. Slicing, halving, pitting or removing the skin will all allow the moisture to be removed. Fill the dehydrator trays with fruits that are cut in similar sizes and shapes so that they will dry evenly. When the dehydrator is filled, it may be started. It is important not to add more fresh fruit later as the added moisture will delay the process time of the first batch. When dehydrating a fruit leather it is important to use the solid plastic trays or parchment paper which can usually be purchased from kitchen specialty shops or from some bakeries. *Never use aluminum foil, wax paper or plastic wrap.* Once the food is dried, remove and place in storage containers immediately. (Allowing dehydrated foods to sit out of a container will allow it to absorb moisture from the room air.) Store in airtight glass or plastic containers in a cool, dark, dry place. Vacuum sealing provides the maximum protection, especially if stored in a temperature of under 60 degrees. The average shelf life of dried fruits is 6 to 12 months. Plan to use rehydrated fruits immediately because they tend to spoil a little more quickly than fresh fruits.

Fruits that do not dry well are avocados, acid fruits, melons and berries with seeds. However, the peels of citrus fruits can be dried and then pulverized into a powder and added for flavor to many recipes.

Fruits that have been commercially dried have chemicals such as lye applied to perforate the skins, or they are coated with toxins like sulfur dioxide, sodium bisulfate or refined sugar. Although spoilage is retarded, the health hazards are not worth the risk. Read labels before purchasing commercial dried fruit.

Herbs are great to dehydrate and their aroma will make your home smell wonderful. For the best flavor, harvest herbs on a bright, sunny morning just after the dew has evaporated and before the sun has dispersed the oils. Most herbs should be gathered while green and tender prior to flowering; however, plants in the mint family have the best flavor while in full bloom. Use a scissors to collect the leaves and stems that are required. Lightly rinse with cold water, shake off excess water, remove and discard discolored leaves or stems. Dehydrate herbs by themselves, not with fruits or vegetables. Most herbs take only a few hours to dehydrate and it is important not to over-dry so that they maintain their essential oils. Store in dark glass jars away from heat, light and air (brown glass is best). Do not use paper or cloth bags, lightweight plastic bags, bread wrappers or any container without a tight fitting lid. When using dried herbs or spices in recipes rather than fresh herbs, cut the amount down about two-thirds.

Equipment Needed:

A dehydrator with a thermostat which can be adjusted to 107 degrees or lower is a must for proper dehydrating. Dehydrators with a set thermostat are too hot and will kill enzymes along with many nutrients.

Sharp paring knife with stainless steel blade - a carbon steel blade discolors some fruits and vegetables.

A vegetable peeler.

Cutting board.

Blender for making flakes, powders and leathers.

Dehydrating Vegetables

Asparagus

Moisture content of fresh food: 92%

Selecting vegetable: Select fresh, young, well-formed aspapagus with closed, compact tips. Asparagus comes in two varieties, white and green. When harvesting fresh asparagus, choose stalks which are 6 to 8 inches in height, cut off at ground level. If not dehydrating immediately, store in the refrigerator at a temperature between 35 and 40 degrees.

Preparation for dehydrating: Remove any blemishes and any part of the stalk that is woody. Wash only when ready to place on dehydrator trays, do not soak. Dry whole or diagonal slice into half-inch lengths.

Optional pretreatment: Steam 3 to 5 minutes or boil 2 to 4 minutes

Testing for dryness: Brittle

Uses: Small spears rehydrate well, and can be added to soups, stews, casseroles or served as a side dish. Larger pieces should be used for dressings or salad sprinkles as they do not rehydrate well.

Beans, Green and Yellow

Moisture content of fresh food: 90%

Selecting vegetable: Beans for dehydration should be bright in color, young, tender and that snap easily. Look for beans with thick walls and small seeds. Pods that are discolored, rusted, limp or bulging with beans should not be used. Beans should be dried as quickly as possible after harvesting.

Preparation for dehydrating: Wash, remove ends and strings. For best results, french cut or cut on the diagonal as this method exposes more of the surface, resulting in faster dehydration.

Optional pretreatment: Blanch in water 5 to 6 minutes or steam 6 to 8 minutes

Testing for dryness: Brittle

Uses: Add to soups, stews, casseroles, sauces, salads or serve as a vegetable.

Beets

Moisture content of fresh food: 87%

Selecting vegetable: Look for beets that are approximately 3 inches in diameter, fresh, deep in color, firm to the touch, with fresh green tops. If not processing immediately, store in refrigerator at a temperature between 35 and 40 degrees.

Preparation for dehydrating: Wash, trim beet greens but do not remove, in order to prevent bleeding, do not remove root. Steam 12 to 15 minutes, cool, trim off greens and root, remove skin. Cut into $1/8$ to $1/2$-inch slices, cubes or strips.

Optional pretreatment: Not required.

Testing for Dryness: Crisp

Uses: In blender, grind into powder for seasonings, dressings or salads. Beet pieces can be added to soups and stews. Season beets with dill, cloves, nutmeg, basil or mint. To rehydrate, soak in a small amount of distilled water overnight in the refrigerator. Beet powder can be used as a sweetener due to high sugar content.

Carrots

Moisture content of fresh food: 88%

Selecting vegetable: Select dark orange, crisp, well-formed carrots. Do not use carrots with green patches or yellow tops or that are woody.

Preparation for dehydrating: Scrub or peel, remove tops and ends if needed. Grate, cut crosswise, lengthwise, diagonally or cube. Store at a temperature of 35 to 40 degrees if not dehydrating immediately.

Optional pretreatment: Steam blanch 4 to 5 minutes

Testing for dryness: Hard

Uses: Soups, stews, breads or process in blender and use for baby foods or as seasonings.

Celery

Moisture content of fresh food: 94%

Selecting vegetable: Look for tender, young stalks with leaves that snap when bent. Stalks should be smooth inside. Store at 35 to 40 degress in the refrigerator if not dehydrating right away.

Preparation for dehydrating: Trim and wash stalks and leaves, remove any dark spots. Slice crosswise 1/4 to 1/2-inch slices.

Optional pretreatment: Blanch 30 seconds

Testing for dryness: Brittle

Uses: Soups, stews and with other vegetables. Process in blender to make celery flakes for seasoning.

Corn

Moisture content of fresh food: 73%

Selecting vegetable: Select tender, young ears that have no space between rows and that have green husks and dark brown silks.

Preparation for dehydrating: Remove husks and silks, cut away any damaged areas.

Optional pretreatment: Steam blanch 4 to 6 minutes. Immediately place in cold water, when cool remove kernels.

Testing for dryness: Crunchy

Uses: Chowders, soups, stews, casseroles, process in blender or food processor to make corn flour.

Cucumber

Moisture content of fresh food: 95%

Selecting vegetable: Select small, fresh cucumbers with dark green skins. Seeds should be small and the flesh white in color.

Preparation for dehydrating: Wash and peel (the skins get tough and bitter when dehydrated). Slice 1/4 to 1/2-inch thick.

Optional pretreatment: May season with Celtic Sea Salt before drying.

Testing for Dryness: Crisp

Uses: After dehydration, keep in the freezer. Chop in a food processor or blender and use dry on salads. May be used as a chip with dip. Tend to be tough if rehydrated.

Eggplant

Moisture content of fresh food: 93%

Selecting vegetable: Select firm, young eggplant that is heavy for its size. Look for a smooth skin with a uniform color, dark purple, almost black.

Preparation for dehydrating: Wash, cut off ends, peel eggplant and cut in $1/4$ to $1/2$-inch slices or cube.

Optional pretreatment: Steam blanch 3 to 5 minutes

Testing for dryness: Brittle

Uses: Use in tomato dishes.

Onions

Moisture content of fresh food: 88%

Selecting vegetable: Any onion can be dried; however, the white varieties have the most flavor when dehydrated. Select onions that are heavy for their size.

Preparation for dehydrating: Trim the top and bottom ends of the onion. Remove outer layer, cut into $1/4$-inch rings or dice.

Optional pretreatment: Not required

Testing for dryness: Brittle, light weight

Uses: Soups, stews, salads, dressings, onion flakes

Parsley

Moisture content of fresh food: 84%

Selecting vegetable: Cut fresh, curly leaved bright green in color. Store in refrigerator in plastic bag if not dehydrating immediately.

Preparation for dehydrating: Wash, remove and discard stems.

Optional pretreatment: Not required

Testing for dryness: Brittle, light weight

Uses: In food processor make into flakes, use in salads or as called for in recipes.

Parsnips

Moisture content of fresh food: 79%

Selecting vegetable: Parsnips are a root vegetable which are similar to carrots in appearance. They are usually harvested in the spring and fall.

Preparation for dehydrating: Wash, remove top and bottom ends, peel. Cut into $1/4$ to $1/2$-inch slices, cubes or strips

Optional pretreatment: Blanch or steam 3 to 5 minutes

Testing for dryness: Brittle

Uses: Soups, sauces, or rehydrated with other vegetables or mashed

Peas

Moisture content of fresh food: 78%

Selecting vegetable: Select peas that are bright green, full but not old and snap easily.

Preparation for dehydrating: Shell

Optional pretreatment: Blanch 3 to 4 minutes

Testing for dryness: Shriveled and hard

Uses: Soups, stews, casseroles or mixed with other vegetables

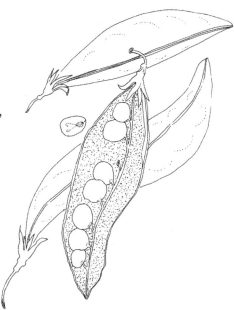

Peppers – Red, Green & Orange

Moisture content of fresh food: 93%

Selecting vegetable: Select well-shaped, fresh, bright colored, firm peppers with thick walls.

Preparation for dehydrating: Wash, remove stem and seeds, chop into $1/2$-inch pieces or slice into strips or rings.

Optional pretreatment: Not required.

Testing for dryness: Hard and crisp

Uses: Add to soups, stews or casseroles or rehydrate and use in salads, on pizzas or anywhere fresh peppers are used.

Pumpkin

Moisture content of fresh food: 91%

Selecting vegetable: Choose pumpkins that are heavy for their size, bright orange in color and that have a shiny, unblemished skin.

Preparation for dehydrating: Wash and cut into large pieces, remove seeds.

Optional pretreatment: Place pumpkin with the rind side down in $1/2$-inch of water in a large baking pan and cover. Bake at 350 degrees for 45 minutes or until tender, cool, remove pulp and puree in blender. Flavor with cinnamon, ginger, nutmeg, allspice, pumpkin pie spice, maple syrup, honey, chopped dates, raisins or finely shredded coconut. Use approximately 1 cup per sheet. Or cut into $1/4$-inch strips and dry until brittle.

Testing for Dryness: Ready to be removed when the strips can be rolled.

Uses: Pies, breads, cakes, soups.

Tomatoes

Moisture content of fresh food: 94%

Selecting vegetable: Select firm, red tomatoes that are not overly ripe. Tomatoes that are too ripe discolor when dehydrated.

Preparation for dehydrating: Wash and core. Peel, if desired. To peel, dip in boiling water 20 - 30 seconds, immediately place in cold water and peel. Slice into uniform slices.

Optional pretreatment: Not required.

Testing for dryness: Crisp or brittle

Uses: Chop in blender to use in salads, add to sandwiches, sauces, soups, mix with other vegetables, completely pulverize to make tomato paste or sauce.

Hint: I have only listed some vegetables that can be successfully dehydrated. There are many books on the market, if you would like additional information on dehydrating foods for your family.

Delightful Dehydrates

When using dehydrated vegetables rather than fresh vegetables in recipes, $^1/_2$ to $^2/_3$ cup equals one cup fresh vegetables. In most cases, dehydrated vegetables should be rehydrated prior to using. If vegetables are not rehydrated prior to using, addition liquid should be added to the recipe.

Vegetable Grain Crisps
☆ ☆ ☆ ☆ ☆

Raw crackers can be made by using any grain, such as rye, oats, rice, millet, wheat or barley. Soak the grain overnight (about 12 hours) in distilled water. Drain the water, reserving for use later (do not refrigerate). Place grain in a bowl, cover with a cloth and allow to sit out of the refrigerator.

Put the soaked grain in a blender, add equal amount of liquid reserved from soaking grain (1 cup of grain to 1 cup of liquid - add distilled water if there is not sufficient liquid). Blend until a creamy consistency is reached. Add spices and blend long enough to mix well.

Pour a thin layer onto solid plastic dehydrator trays. Do not use trays lined with plastic wrap, wax paper or aluminum foil. Dehydrate 10 - 12 hours at 105 degrees.

Hint: The longer they dry, the crispier they become. When dry, break and put into a tightly covered container.

$^1/_4$ - $^1/_2$ cup	soaked rye
1 $^1/_2$ - 1 $^3/_4$ cup	soaked wheat berries
2 cups	distilled water used to soak berries
1 Tbsp.	dehydrated onion flakes
$^1/_2$ - 1 Tbsp.	dill weed
1 tsp.	caraway seeds
$^3/_4$ tsp.	Celtic Sea Salt (optional)

To vary the flavor, replace the above seasonings with your own favorites or add finely chopped vegetables.

Sweet Potato Chips
☆ ☆ ☆ ☆ ☆

4 sweet potatoes   8 Tbsp. Distilled Water
Pinch of cayenne (optional)   3 tsp. Celtic Sea Salt

Wash and slice sweet potatoes or yams into thin (1/8 inch) slices. Blend all other ingredients. Dip slices into spice mixture. Place on plastic sheets or parchment paper and place in dehydrator and process at 105 degrees until dry. Serve as other chips would be served.

Fruit Crisps
☆ ☆ ☆ ☆ ☆

Prepare grains as for veggie crisps, omit the onion, dill and caraway and add 2 bananas, 1 Tbsp. cinnamon, 1 tsp. nutmeg or your favorite spices. If desired, soaked raisins or dates may be added for extra sweetness.

Vegetable Chips
☆ ☆ ☆ ☆ ☆

Vegetable chips can be made by slicing vegetables to be dried very thin, similar to potato chips. Vegetable chips are wonderful served with dips. Some vegetables that can be selected for vegetable chips are: tomato, cucumber, eggplant, zucchini or parsnips. Peel, if not organic, slice very thin, about 1/8-inch thick, dip in distilled water and sprinkle with herbs. Dry until brittle.

Vegetable Flakes & Powders
☆ ☆ ☆ ☆ ☆

Vegetable flakes can be made by simply crushing dehydrated pieces of vegetables in a blender, food processor, with hands or a rolling pin. Coarsely chopped flakes may be added to soups, stews, dressings, salads or sauces. After crushing, label and store in airtight containers out of bright sunlight.

Vegetable powders can be made by dehydrating vegetables in a blender or food processor and grinding pieces to a fine powder or by dehydrating pureed vegetables until brittle and then pulverizing. The most widely used vegetables for powders are onion, tomato, garlic and celery; however, any vegetable can be used. These can be used in place of salt, as a seasoning, for instant soup mix, on salads, baby foods or in juices.

Vegetable Soup Broth
☆ ☆ ☆ ☆ ☆

One example of a vegetable powder combination would be 1 tsp. each of the following vegetable powders: carrot, onion, tomato, garlic, chives, bell pepper, celery, parsley and rice flour or corn meal. When rehydrating, add Celtic Sea Salt, if desired. This mixture can be used for a seasoning or made into instant broth for soup by mixing 1 rounded Tbsp. of the mix with 2 cups of distilled water.

Vegetable Leathers
☆ ☆ ☆ ☆ ☆

Vegetables can be made into leathers which make convenient foods for traveling, hiking or just snacking. The vegetable leather will be more consistent if foods are first blanched. Any of your favorite vegetable combinations can be blanched, blended into a puree, seasoned to taste, poured onto flat dehydrator trays and dried at a low temperature.

Tomatoes, for instance, make wonderful leather, and onions may be added. Season to taste. Dehydrate until pliable, remove, roll into cylinders, store in plastic bags in the refrigerator or freezer. Can be rehydrated and used in sauce, paste or juice.

Fruit Roll-Up Leathers
☆ ☆ ☆ ☆ ☆

Fruit leather is a delightful chewy treat made in the dehydrator without added sugar or chemicals. Fresh fruit is pureed and poured onto a flat dehydrator sheet (do not use wax paper, plastic wrap or aluminum foil) and dried at a low temperature. Perfect for lunch boxes, traveling or snacking. The flavor can be varied by adding spices, garnishes or fillings, however, when adding sweeteners it is important to remember that dehydrating concentrates the natural sugars. Following are some examples to experiment with:

Apple Leather
☆ ☆ ☆ ☆ ☆

Wash and core apples (peel if not organic). Puree in a blender in a small amount of distilled water or apple juice. Dates, peaches, apricots, berries or your favorite fruit may be added. Continue to blend until a creamy consistency is reached. Any of the following spices may be added: allspice, cinnamon, cloves, coriander, lemon, mint, nutmeg, honey or maple syrup.

Apricot Leather
☆ ☆ ☆ ☆ ☆

Wash and pit apricots (peel if not organic). If apricots are ripe, they may be pureed in a blender without additional liquid. Start with a few, blend well, then add additional apricots until the desired capacity is reached. Apples, pineapple or plum may be pureed and added for extra flavor. The same spices may be added as with the apple.

Apricot puree can be used as a binder in confections.

Banana Leather
☆ ☆ ☆ ☆

Peel and puree very ripe bananas (the dark speckled ones) in a blender with no added liquid. If desired, apple, any berry, pineapple, pecans or walnuts may be added. Continue to puree until desired consistency is reached. Spices which enhance the flavor are: cinnamon, cloves, coriander, nutmeg, lemon, orange, honey or maple syrup.

Berry Leather
☆ ☆ ☆ ☆ ☆

Wash and puree, put through sieve to remove most of the seeds. Combine with pureed apple, which adds texture, and/or bananas. Spices which can be added to enhance the flavor are cinnamon, lemon, maple syrup or honey.

Blueberry Leather
☆ ☆ ☆ ☆ ☆

Wash and puree in a blender. Combine with pureed apples or peaches. Add cinnamon, lemon, maple syrup or honey.

Cherry Leather
☆ ☆ ☆ ☆ ☆

Wash, remove stems and pits. Puree in a blender. Apple, pineapple, banana or raspberry may be pureed and combined with cherries. Cinnamon, cloves, lemon, orange or honey may be added.

Cranberry Leather
☆ ☆ ☆ ☆ ☆

In a bowl place 1 cup of dates, which have been pitted and chopped, cover with water to soak. Sort one cup of cranberries and discard berries which are soft or discolored. Blend dates with soaking water until smooth, add cranberries.

Grape Leather
☆ ☆ ☆ ☆

Wash, puree in a blender, sieve to remove the seeds. Mix with pureed apple or raspberry, lemon or maple syrup. Heat to thicken, but do not boil, and pour onto plastic sheet which has been placed in the dehydrator.

Peach or Nectarine Leather
☆ ☆ ☆ ☆ ☆

Peel, remove stones, puree in a blender. Delicious alone or add pureed apple, blueberry, pineapple, plum or raspberries. Cinnamon, coriander, cloves, ginger, almond, nutmeg or honey may be added. **Hint:** Peaches and nectarines may darken but the flavor is wonderful.

Pineapple Leather
☆ ☆ ☆ ☆ ☆

Peel outer skin, eyes and core and puree in the blender. Any of the following may be pureed and added: apricots, cherries, strawberries, lemon, orange or a small amount of honey.

Plum Leather
☆ ☆ ☆ ☆ ☆

Wash (peel if not organic), remove pits, puree in a blender. If desired also blend apple, apricot, peach or pear. Spices that enhance flavor are cinnamon, coriander, lemon or maple syrup.

try

Granola
☆ ☆ ☆ ☆ ☆

Granola makes a wonderful snack for children or when traveling. Granolas can be varied depending upon the dehydrated foods you have available. Following is one example:

In a large bowl combine:

> 4 or 5 cups old fashioned rolled oats (not instant)
> $^3/_4$ cup of wheat germ
> $^1/_2$ cup bran or bran flakes (optional)
> $^1/_2$ cup sesame seeds
> $^3/_4$ cup fresh or dried coconut
> $^3/_4$ cup raw sunflower seeds
> $^1/_2$ cup almonds, slivered
> $^1/_2$ cup walnuts, chopped (optional)
> $^3/_4$ cup flax seeds

In a separate bowl mix the following:

> $^1/_3$ cup raw, unfiltered honey
> 2 tsp. vanilla
> $^1/_3$ cup fresh apple juice

Pour over dry ingredients a little at a time, stirring to distribute evenly. Pour onto plastic sheets, dehydrate. To dry more quickly, spread thin. Drying time is about 2 days.*

When dried, add 2 cups dried fruit cut into small pieces. (Can use dates, organic raisins, figs, apples, pears, cherries, etc.). Cool to room temperature and store in airtight container. Makes about 10 cups. Use within 4 weeks.

*To dry in the oven, preheat to 300 degrees. Pour mixture into a lecithin lined 9 x 13-inch pan. Bake for one hour, stirring every 15 minutes. After removing from the oven, add dried fruit, cool to room temperature and store in airtight container.

Strawberry Leather
☆ ☆ ☆ ☆ ☆

Wash, hull, puree and put through small strainer to remove seeds. Put in blender and puree with apple, peach or pineapple. Lemon, orange, maple syrup or honey may be added.

Pear Leather
☆ ☆ ☆ ☆ ☆

Peel and core, puree in a blender. Pears dehydrate best when mixed with other pureed fruits such as apple or pineapple. Spices that enhance the flavor are cinnamon, cloves, coriander, lemon, maple syrup, honey or a dash of mace. **Hint:** Pears may discolor but the flavor is delightful.

Raspberry Leather
☆ ☆ ☆ ☆ ☆

Wash, puree in blender and put through sieve to remove seeds. May combine with pureed apple. Flavor with lemon, mint, orange or maple syrup.

Fruit Leather Fillings

Once the fruit leather is prepared, if you would like to add a filling, any of the following can be added. Spread the filling on the fruit leather, roll it up and enjoy.

Almond butter
Fruit fillings
Natural fruit preserves without additives or sugar

Baby Foods

Dehydrated foods are easy to rehydrate and prepare for babies. All that is required is to soak and then puree in a blender or food processor. When preparing pureed food, it is important to add liquid just prior to serving. Add it gradually until the desired consistency is reached. Reconstituted foods should be stored in the refrigerator after being rehydrated. Discard leftovers that have been at room temperature for an hour or more.

As the baby grows, the foods can be ground to a coarser texture. When introducing new foods to babies, it is recommended to introduce them one new food at a time. By doing so, it will be easy to determine if a child has food sensitivities.

For more information on baby foods, see Chapter 10.

Herbs

Dehydrated herbs are much more cost-effective than those purchased in any store. They are all natural, have better flavor and have not been irradiated. Even if you don't grow your own herbs but buy them in a farmers' market to dehydrate at home, you will save money and have peace of mind about what you are serving your family.

Prepare herbs for drying by washing the leaves in cool water and pat dry with towels (if not dried prior to dehydrating they may darken more). A salad spinner can also help remove excess moisture.

The best storage containers for dried herbs are dark glass jars with tight fitting lids. The darker glass reduces exposure to light and helps to retard the fading of the dried product. It is best to store herbs in the form they were dried, crushing them when ready for use to retain more of their natural bouquet. Dried herbs can be pulverized in the blender when needed.

parsley, sage, rosemary & thyme

My Version of Fines Herbs

☆ ☆ ☆ ☆ ☆

1 Tbsp. dried chives	1 Tbsp. dried chervil
1 Tbsp. dried tarragon or rosemary	1 Tbsp. dried parsley
1 tsp. garlic powder	1 tsp. dried celery

Combine and store in a tightly sealed dark glass jar. Use to flavor salads, casseroles, steam vegetables, baked potatoes, rice or squash.

Hint: Although celery and garlic are not herbs, they add a nice flavor.

Bouquet Garni

☆ ☆ ☆ ☆ ☆

2 dried bay leaves	1 tsp. dried thyme
2 Tbsp. dried parsley	1 tsp. dried celery leaves
1 tsp. dried rosemary	1 tsp. tarragon

Tie herbs into a 3 or 4-inch square of cheesecloth or muslin bag, tie with a string and add to soups or stews. Remove before serving.

Italian Seasoning

☆ ☆ ☆ ☆ ☆

1 Tbsp. dried marjoram or sage	1 Tbsp. dried basil
1 Tbsp. dried thyme	1 Tbsp. dried rosemary
1 Tbsp. dried oregano	1 Tbsp. dried savory

Do not grind herbs. Put in bowl to mix, store in tightly covered, dark glass jar.

All Purpose Seasoning

☆ ☆ ☆ ☆ ☆

1 Tbsp. dried oregano	1 Tbsp. dried parsley
1 Tbsp. dried marjoram	1 Tbsp. dried onion flakes
1 Tbsp. dried basil	1 tsp. dried thyme
1 tsp. dried summer savory	
1 tsp. dried rosemary	

Do not grind herbs, put in a bowl and mix well. Pour into a tightly covered dark glass jar and store until needed. Herbs can be added or deleted to adjust flavor.

Herb Teas

Herb teas can be easily made with dried herbs. A rounded teaspoon per cup is a good rule of thumb. A small, porous stainless steel (don't use aluminum) container can be obtained to place herbs into, or place herbs in strainer over cup and pour boiling water through or place in cup, add boiling water and strain before drinking. Allow herbs to steep 5 to 15 minutes depending on the strength and temperature desired.

Chapter Twenty-six:

Special Occasion Treats

Hallelujah Acres Date Nut Bread
☆ ☆ ☆ ☆

1 cup organic pitted, whole dates, chopped into pieces
1 cup organic raisins
1 1/2 cup boiling distilled water
1 cup whole wheat flour
1 cup unbleached flour
1 tsp. baking soda
1 tsp. aluminum-free baking powder
1/2 cup flax seed mixture (as egg replacement, see page 123)
1 tsp. vanilla
1/2 cup chopped pecans

Place raisins and chopped dates in small bowl and pour boiling water over them. Set aside to cool while preparing remainder of recipe.

In a large bowl, stir together flour, baking soda and powder. Stir in pecans. Add vanilla to egg whites (or egg replacer) and blend. Add date and raisin mixture and egg white mixture; stir until well blended. Mixture will be thick. Spread evenly into a lightly-oiled 9 x 5 x 3-inch loaf pan.

Bake at 350 degrees for 35 to 40 minutes or until it tests done. Cool in pan 10 minutes. Remove from pan and cool thoroughly on wire rack. Best wrapped and stored overnight before serving.

Fresh Strawberry Pie
☆ ☆ ☆ ☆

Pie Shell:

     1 cup raw almonds, soaked overnight
     1 cup soft, pitted dates
     1/2 tsp. vanilla (optional)

Soak the almonds in distilled water for about 12 hours. Grind the nuts in a food processor until finely chopped. Add the dates and vanilla, and **blend well.** Press thinly into a pie plate (from center to the outside rim) to form the shell.

Binder:

     7 or 8 *large* ripe strawberries   2 bananas, fairly ripe
     5 soft dates, pitted   1 Tbsp. fresh lemon juice

Blend all binder ingredients in food processor or blender until well mixed.

Fruit Filling

Cut 2 pints of fresh strawberries into quarters, and fold into binder and fill shell. Decorate with approximately 1/2 pint of quartered strawberries. Cover with plastic wrap and store in refrigerator. Chill before serving.

Almond Pie Crust
☆ ☆ ☆ ☆ ☆

     1 1/2 cup almonds   2 cups distilled water
     1/3 cup dates   1 1/2 cup sunflower seeds
     4 Tbsp. almond butter   1/2 cup fresh coconut

Cover almonds with distilled water and soak overnight. Drain. Grate coconut. Place almonds and sunflower seeds in blender or Vita Mix and process until evenly ground. Add coconut, dates and almond butter and mix well. With machine running, add distilled water by the tablespoon until desired consistency is reached. Press into pie plate. Refrigerate four hours to set.

Pecan Pie
☆

This recipe is included for those special occasions like Thanksgiving and Christmas, which just don't seem the same without pecan pie! It is rich and should only be served on a rare occasion.

3 cups pecans
¹/₂ cup rice syrup
¹/₄ cup organic apple juice
2 Tbsp. arrow root powder
1 tsp. cinnamon
1 Tbsp. agar agar

¹/₂ cup maple syrup
¹/₄ cup unsulphured molasses
1 tsp. pure vanilla
¹/₄ tsp. Celtic Sea Salt (optional)
¹/₂ tsp. nutmeg

Make whole-grain pie crust (page 323) and place in a 10-inch pie pan lined with liquid lecithin. Set aside. Blend one cup of pecans with the rest of the ingredients to a creamy consistency. Put the remaining pecans in the pie pan, and pour over the blended mixture. Bake at 350 degrees for 35 minutes. Remove from oven and cool before serving. Pie will harden as it cools.

Almond Cookies
☆ ☆ ☆ ☆ ☆

2 cups almonds
zest from whole lemon
coconut

¹/₂ cup raw unfiltered honey
¹/₂ whole vanilla bean or 1 tsp liquid

Grind almonds into a fine meal. Mix ground almonds, vanilla and lemon zest together. Work in enough honey to make a sticky dough. Roll into balls or log shape and roll in coconut. Chill then slice.

Banana Cream Pie
☆ ☆ ☆ ☆ ☆

Crust:

2 cups unsulfered banana chips   2 cup dates
1 ripe banana

Pulverize banana chips in food processor using "S" blade. Add dates and ripe banana. Continue to process until a dough consistency is reached. Press into a 9-inch pie plate.

Filling:

2 cups almonds   2 cups organic dates
3 ripe bananas   ½ cup organic grated coconut
2 cups unsulfured banana chips   ½ cup dried unsulphured pineapple
1 tsp. ground cinnamon or nutmeg   2 tsp. pure vanilla extract

Soak dates in enough distilled water to cover for one hour. Place banana chips, pineapple and almonds in a food processor, and process to a fine meal. Add bananas and soaked dates and process, adding a small amount of apple juice if needed until a pudding consistency is reached. Add vanilla, coconut, and cinnamon, and mix well. Pour into the prepared crust and refrigerate until set.

Creamy Fruit Pie
☆ ☆ ☆ ☆ ☆

2 ripe bananas   2 frozen bananas
3 kiwis   2 pints organic strawberries
¼ organic pineapple

Peel 2 ripe bananas, place in a plastic bag and freeze 24 hours.

Make a pie shell of choice. In this pie shell, layer 2 sliced bananas, sliced kiwis and 1 pint of sliced strawberries and pineapple, cut into small slices.

In a Green Star or Champion Juicer, combine the remaining strawberries with the frozen banana to make banana-strawberry "ice cream." Pour over fruit and serve immediately or place in freezer until ready to use. If freezing, thaw slightly before serving.

Hint: Strawberries and pineapple are often heavily sprayed, so organic is always recommended.

Carob Sauce

Submitted by Mrs. Harold Cherney
☆ ☆ ☆ ☆

This sauce can be used to replace chocolate sauce in any recipe.

1 cup dates	1 cup distilled water
1/3 cup carob powder	1 - 2 tsp. vanilla

Heat water, but do not boil. Soak dates until soft. Drain dates, reserving liquid, pit dates and place in blender with soaking water, carob and vanilla. Blend until creamy.

Date-Pecan Squares
☆ ☆ ☆ ☆ ☆

1 cup organic dates	1 cup organic raisins
1/2 cup pecans	2 cups dried, unsweetened coconut
1 tsp. pure vanilla extract	

In a food processor, using a "S" blade, grind pecans to a fine meal, add pitted dates and raisins. Process until a dough-like consistency is reached. By hand, work in 1/2 cup of the coconut. Sprinkle 3/4 cup coconut in a pan, place date-pecan mixture on top and spread to cover bottom layer. Top with remaining coconut. Cover and place in refrigerator. When chilled, cut into squares.

Hint: This mixture can also be used as a pie crust, if desired.

Fresh Fruit Aspic
☆ ☆ ☆

2 cups fresh blueberries	2 fresh peaches or nectarines
1/4 cup shredded coconut	1 1/2 Tbsp. agar agar
2 1/4 cup organic apple juice	2 very ripe bananas

Slice peaches or nectarines and place in a bowl with blueberries and coconut. In a blender, combine bananas and 1 1/2 cups of apple juice. Combine remaining apple juice with the agar agar and mix well. Bring to a boil, stirring constantly. Remove from heat, cool slightly and pour over fresh fruit. Add banana mixture and mix well.

Pour into a decorative mold, cover and place in the refrigerator overnight or freeze for a couple of hours prior to serving.

Couscous Delight

Submitted by Connie Head
☆ ☆

1 cup couscous	1/2 cup organic raisins
2 cups organic apple juice	1 Tbsp. arrow root powder
1 cake soft tofu	1 jar All Fruit Spread
1 cup organic fruit	$^1/_2$ cup almonds

Pour raw couscous in a 2 $^1/_2$-inch deep, 10 x 10-inch pan, and sprinkle with raisins. Boil 1 cup of apple juice and pour over the coucous, allow to cool.

Combine arrow root powder, and the second cup of apple juice in a blender and blend until there are no lumps. Add fruit and blend to desired consistency. Pour into a pan and bring to a boil, stirring constantly. Remove from heat and allow to cool. Pour over couscous and raisins.

Place the tofu and all-fruit spread in a blender, and blend until creamy. Pour over the fruit layer, sliver almonds and sprinkle on top. Cover and refrigerate until ready to serve.

Banana & Date Pie Crust

☆ ☆ ☆ ☆ ☆

1 $^1/_2$ cup organic banana chips	1 cup organic dehydrated pineapple
1 $^1/_2$ cup organic dates	$^1/_2$ cup organic coconut

In a food processor, process banana chips until they reach a flour-like consistency. Add pineapple, dates and coconut. Process for 2 or 3 minutes until all ingredients begin to form a ball. Place dough into a 9-inch pan and press out until the plate is covered. Flute the edges as with a regular pie crust.

Hint: All dried fruits should be organic, unsweetened and unsulfered.

Date-Coconut Logs
☆ ☆ ☆ ☆ ☆

2 cups organic dates   1 cup unsweetened, shredded coconut

In a food processor using "S" blade, or a Green Star or Champion Juicer with blank in place, grind dates until a dough-like consistency is reached. (Be sure to first remove pits and the caps that are sometimes left.)   Wet your hands, shape into logs, and roll in coconut to cover.

Fresh Fruit Tart
☆ ☆ ☆ ☆

8 nectarines or peaches   2 cups raspberries
1/4 cup blueberries   1 kiwi
2 cups organic apple juice   2 Tbsp. agar agar

Peel and slice nectarines or peaches and kiwi, wash and stem berries, and place in a bowl. Gently mix to combine. Pour into 9-inch crust of your choice.

Dissolve agar agar in fruit juice and bring to a boil for one minute. Reduce heat and cook several minutes, stirring constantly. Set aside to cool slightly. Pour over fruit and refrigerate to set.

Hint: Fruit may be varied to change flavor.

Fruit Bars
☆ ☆ ☆

1 cup oat flour   1 ripe banana, mashed
3 cups rolled oats   1 cup apple juice
1 cup unsweetened coconut   2 cups chopped dates
1/2 cup chopped almonds
20 oz. can unsweetended crushed pineapple

Use the "S" blade of your food processor or blender to make oat flour out of a cup of rolled oats. Mix with all remaining ingredients except dates and pineapple. Use more apple juice to hold the mixture together, if needed. Press half of the mixture into a 9 x 12-inch glass baking pan. Chop pineapple and dates in a food processor until the pieces are small. Place in a saucepan and cook until thickened. Spread over the bottom crust. Top with remaining whole grain mixture and bake at 350 degrees for 30-40 minutes.

Raw Pumpkin Pie
☆ ☆ ☆ ☆ ☆

1 ¹/₂ - 2 cups raw pumpkin
2 - 4 Tbsp. fresh lemon or orange juice
2 Tbsp. raw, unfiltered honey
1 tsp. cinnamon
¹/₂ cup coconut, unsweetened

¹/₂ cup organic raisins, soaked
1 cup almonds
¹/₂ tsp. ginger
¹/₄ tsp. nutmeg

In a blender, food processor or Vita Mix, combine the pumpkin, almonds, juice and honey. Add coconut, raisins and spices. If too thin, add more almonds.

Pour pie into pie crust found on page 315, under the strawberry pie recipe. Cover and chill overnight.

Hint: The pie will firm up some when chilled; however, the consistency should be that of pancake batter.

Baked Pumpkin Pie *Very Good*
☆ ☆ ☆

¹/₂ cup almonds - *(soak first)*
2 cups pumpkin
✶ ¹/₂ tsp. ginger
1 ¹/₂ tsp. pure vanilla
¹/₄ cup maple syrup

³/₄ cup distilled water
¹/₄ cup raw unfiltered honey
✶ 1 tsp. cinnamon
2 Tbsp. arrow root powder
✶ ¹/₄ tsp. nutmeg

In a saucepan, place pumpkin in a small amount of water and steam until tender. Meanwhile, place the almonds and distilled water in a blender, food processor or Vita Mix and blend until a creamy texture is obtained. When the pumpkin is tender, cool it slightly, then add to the blender with the remaining ingredients, and blend well.

Pour into a whole-grain crust and bake at 350 degrees for about one hour or until a knife comes out clean when inserted in the middle.

✶ *substitute with 2 t pumpkin pie spice*

Frozen Raw Birthday Cake

Submitted by Gracie Gordon
☆ ☆ ☆ ☆ ☆

1 bundt cake pan which can be used in the freezer
1 16 oz. bag of dried organic figs, soaked overnight in distilled water*
1 16 oz. bag of dried organic dates, seeds removed, soaked overnight in distilled water*
1 12 oz. bag of organic almonds
2 big bunches fully ripe bananas (organic if possible)

* The water level for soaking is about half full. Do not cover the dried fruits completely.

Remove stems from soaked figs, puree figs and set aside. Puree dates and put in a separate bowl, chop almonds in food processor or blender and set aside in its own container. Peel and puree the bananas in a blender or food processor.

To Build the Cake

Place in the bottom of the mold, almonds, a second layer pureed figs, a third layer of almonds, a fourth layer of pureed bananas, and continue to layer almonds, figs, bananas, dates or whatever order you desire. However, almonds should be the first layer and end with dates or figs as the last layer. Cover and freeze overnight.

To Serve

Remove from the freezer, place upside down on a plate and allow to sit a few minutes until thawed enough to release from the pan. You also may carefully set the frozen bundt pan in warm water just long enough to release the cake, being very careful not to get water in the cake.

This cake has so many possibilities. For example, you could use strawberries and blue berries for a beautiful, healthy 4th of July cake. Any of your favorite fruits can be used to make a new family tradition!

Fruit Cake
☆ ☆ ☆ ☆ ☆

1 cup organic dates	1 cup organic raisins
1 cup mixed dehydrated fruits	1 cup pecans
1 cup fresh orange juice	2 Tbsp. organic lemon rind
2 Tbsp. organic orange rind	2 Tbsp. ground corriander
1 Tbsp. ground cardamom	½ cup raw unfiltered honey

Grate outer layer of lemon and orange rind, put in a small container. Cover with honey and allow to sit for seven days. Remove pits from dates and cut into small pieces. Soak dates and raisins in warm distilled water overnight. Drain. Chop mixed fruit and pecans. Combine dates and raisins with the rest of the ingredients and mix well. Pack firmly into a wax paper or saran wrap-lined loaf pan or rectangular pan. Cover and refrigerate at least 48 hours. Slice and serve.

Whole Grain Pie Crust
☆ ☆ ☆

1 cup almonds	1 cup whole wheat pastry flour
½ cup cold organic apple juice	1 cup rolled oats

Put the "S" blade in food processor and grind almonds fine, add rolled oats and process until fine, add pastry flour and process until fine. While machine is running, add apple juice 1 Tbsp. at a time, until ball forms. Stop machine immediately. Remove dough and wrap in plastic, refrigerate at least 1 hour. Roll out between plastic wrap.

Mixed Berry Pie
☆ ☆ ☆ ☆

1 cup organic strawberries	1 cup organic raspberries
1 cup organic blueberries	1 cup organic blackberries
1 cup organic apple juice	1 Tbsp. agar agar
½ cup grated fresh coconut	

Make almond, granola or banana crust, and set aside. Wash and stem berries, place in strainer and allow to dry. Place in granola or almond pie crust.

In a blender, mix the apple juice and agar agar, pour into a saucepan and bring to a boil for one minute. Turn down and simmer for another minute, remove from heat and allow to cool slightly. Pour over fruit. Chill to set.

Peach Pie
☆ ☆ ☆ ☆ ☆

6 cups organic peaches	2 ripe bananas
1/2 cup organic blueberries	1 organic lemon
1/2 cup pineapple	

Squeeze lemon and set juice aside. Slice peaches and bananas and pineapple, place pineapple, bananas and 4 cups of the sliced peaches in food processor and blend until creamy. Slice remaining peaches and fold into blended mixture. Pour into prepared pie shell. Top with blueberries. Lemon juice should be misted over the top to prevent discoloration. Cover with plastic wrap and refrigerate to set.

Pritikin Apple Pie
☆

The crust:

Moisten:　1 cup Grape Nuts cereal with
3 Tbsp. frozen apple concentrate, thawed.
Pat into bottom of pie plate.

The filling:

Peel 5 to 6 large Red and Yellow Delicious apples. Cut, core and slice half of the apple slices into pie, and sprinkle generously with cinnamon. Add remaining apple slices and sprinkle again with cinnamon. Do not skimp. Cover with foil and bake approximately 50 minutes at 350 degrees.

Remove from oven and make glaze.

In saucepan, heat and stir the following mix until clear & thickened:

1/2 cup (or a little more) frozen apple juice
1/2 cup water, distilled
2　heaping Tbsp. cornstarch

Pour over top of apples, covering **all** of them. Cool, cover with clean plastic wrap and refrigerate. Serves 8.

Granola Pie Crust
☆ ☆ ☆

Prepare Crust:

2 ¹/₂ cups granola see page 310	1 ¹/₂ tsp. coriander
¹/₂ tsp. coconut flakes	¹/₄ cup maple syrup *

Place granola in a blender, food processor or Vita Mix and make into fine crumbs. Pour crumbs into a bowl and add the rest of the ingredients. Mix well and press into a pie pan, which has been lined with lecithin. Place crumbs on the bottom and up the sides.

Bake 5 minutes at 350 degrees before adding filling.

* or frozen organic apple juice concentrate

Tofu Cheese Cake
☆

Prepare granola pie crust.

Preheat oven to 325 degrees. In a blender, food processor or Vita Mix, place the following and blend until very smooth and creamy.

1 lb. of tofu	¹/₄ cup fresh lemon juice
¹/₂ cup raw unfiltered honey	1 tsp. grated lemon zest
¹/₂ tsp. Celtic Sea Salt (optional)	2 Tbsp. almond meal
¹/₂ tsp. pure almond extract	1 tsp. pure vanilla extract
3 Tbsp. flour or 2 Tbsp. arrow root powder	

When blended, pour into prepared crust and bake for 50 minutes or until set. Cool on a wire rack. When cool, refrigerate. May be served plain or with the following topping.

Topping:

2 cups fresh or frozen fruit	¹/₄ cup raw unfiltered honey or maple syrup
2 Tbsp. distilled water	1 Tbsp. arrow root powder

In a blender, food processor or Vita Mix, combine 1 cup of fruit, arrow root powder and distilled water, and blend until smooth. Pour into a saucepan and add remaining fruit. Heat, stirring constantly until the mixture has thickened. Taste for sweetness, and adjust if needed. Spoon over cheese cake and return to the refrigerator to cool before serving.

Almond Butter Balls

submitted by Jeanne Serafin
☆ ☆ ☆ ☆ ☆

$1/2$ cup almond butter	$1/2$ cup honey
1 cup wheat germ	$1/4$ cup crushed nuts or unsweetened coconut

Mix almond butter, wheat germ and honey and roll into small balls. Then roll the balls in crushed nuts or unsweetened coconut. Serve fresh, refrigerate or they may also be frozen.

Frozen Banana Berry Pie

submitted by Michael Dye
☆ ☆ ☆ ☆ ☆

This pie, which can be made with a Green Star juicer, is so delicious that it will be hard to believe that the ingredients are all natural and all raw. Begin by freezing the bananas (make sure you peel them before you freeze them); and soaking the almonds in distilled water for 12 hours.

For the crust:

1 cup chopped dates *	1 $1/2$ cups soaked almonds *
$1/2$ cup raisins	

* For variation, you may also add some pineapple or other dried fruit, or you may add some soaked sunflower seeds in with the almonds. Whatever combination of dried fruits and soaked nuts (and seeds) you use, make this a mix of about equal parts soaked nuts and dried fruit for the crust. (Or you can make all-raw "candy" instead of crust by using a mix of about two parts dried fruit to one part soaked nuts, then rolling this in unsweetened ground coconut.)

Rinse the soaked nuts and put the nuts and dried fruit through your Green Star juicer, using the solid blank. Pat the blended dried fruit and nuts into the bottom of a pie pan or a bowl if individual servings are being made. If you make extra crust, it will keep several days refrigerated.

For the filling:

2 - 3 frozen bananas per person	1/2 cup frozen berries per person

Put the frozen bananas and frozen berries (your choice of berries) through the juicer and let them come out directly into the pie pan or bowl containing the patted-out crust.

For the topping:

Top with fresh strawberries or other fruit of your choice and consume immediately.

Fruit Smoothies

Fruit smoothies are a wonderful taste treat that can be substituted as a meal at lunch time or when life's activities make it seem impossible to have a meal. Even though they are made of fruit and fruit juice, their creamy consistency reminds one of a shake made from dairy. Fruit smoothies, however, contain none of the dairy, additives, cholesterol, fat or artificial ingredients found in those milk-shakes made commercially.

For the weight conscious, it is interesting to note that when fruit smoothies are consumed on an empty stomach, no weight will be gained … only energy and valuable nutrients.

Use bananas that are very ripe and speckled. (If your bananas are green, allow them to set a few days at room temperature to ripen before they are used for this recipe or any other consumption. Until a banana is speckled and no longer green, it is not ready to eat.) Before freezing, peel and place bananas in an airtight container or double bag them in plastic bags. Freeze only as many bananas as can be used in seven to ten days as they begin to discolor if kept longer.

To make a smoothie, place the following in a blender or Vita Mix:

1 cup fresh or organic apple juice	1 cup fresh or frozen fruit
1 1/2 to 2 frozen bananas	1 or 2 organic dates (optional)

Blend until a creamy consistency is reached, which takes about 45 seconds. Smoothies are best when consumed immediately, before the bananas have a chance to oxidize and turn brown.

Hint: Smoothies can be made with fresh ripe bananas, cold fresh fruit and cold juice; however, they will not be as cold or thick as when using frozen bananas and fruit.

Fruit Smoothie Combinations

The possibilities for great-tasting fruit smoothies are endless, and following are a few examples to help you get started. Use the food combining chart on pages 68-69 to help you to know what fruits to mix together.

Apple Banana Royal
☆ ☆ ☆ ☆ ☆

2 large Delicious or other sweet apples
dash of cinnamon and nutmeg (optional)

2 or 3 pitted organic dates
1 ripe banana, fresh or frozen

Run one sliced apple through a juicer (peel this apple if it is not organic). Peel, seed and core the second apple and cut it into small pieces. Combine the juice from the first apple with the sliced second apple, dates (be sure to remove pits and end caps), banana, cinnamon and nutmeg and puree in a blender, Vita-Mix, Green Star or Champion juicer. If you are using a Green Star or Champion juicer, use the "blank plate" to puree.

Heavenly Mango
☆ ☆ ☆ ☆ ☆

1 apple
1 Tbsp. shredded coconut

2 cups fresh mango
1 -1 ½ banana, fresh or frozen

Slice the apple (peel if it is not organic), and run through a juicer. Combine this juice with remaining ingredients and puree in a blender, Vita-Mix, Green Star or Champion juicer. If you are using a Green Star or Champion juicer, use the "blank plate" to puree.

Apple, Pineapple & Strawberry Surprise
☆ ☆ ☆ ☆ ☆

1 sweet apple   2 cups fresh pineapple
7 or 8 fresh strawberries

Slice the apple (peel if it is not organic), and peel and slice the pineapple. Run the apple and one cup of pineapple through a juicer. Combine this juice with the other cup of pineapple and strawberries, and puree in a blender, Vita-Mix, Green Star or Champion juicer. If you are using a Green Star or Champion juicer, use the "blank plate" to puree.

Hint: Try to use organic pineapples because most commerical crops are heavily sprayed.

Blueberry Delight
☆ ☆ ☆ ☆ ☆

1 cup fresh or frozen organic blueberries   1 large apple
1 or 2 pitted organic dates   1 ½ - 2 bananas, fresh or frozen

Slice the apple (peel if it is not organic) and run it through a juicer. Combine this juice with the blueberries, pitted dates and bananas and puree in a blender, Vita-Mix, Green Star or Champion juicer. If you are using a Green Star or Champion juicer, use the "blank plate" to puree.

Cranberry Blush
☆ ☆ ☆ ☆ ☆

1 cup fresh cranberry juice   2 sweet apples
1 orange

Peel the orange and slice one apple (peel if it is not organic). Run the orange sections, one apple and cranberries through a juicer. Peel, core, seed and slice the second apple. Combine the apple / orange / cranberry juice with the apple slices and puree in a blender, Vita-Mix, Green Star or Champion juicer. If you are using a Green Star or Champion juicer, use the "blank plate" to puree.

Melons Alive
☆ ☆ ☆ ☆ ☆

1 cup fresh melon   1 cup frozen melon

Use the flesh from any of the melon family alone or mixed together in any combination, and run through a juicer. (Remember to not combine melons with other foods at the same meal.)

Peaches & Cream
☆ ☆ ☆ ☆ ☆

1 apple   1 ½ - 2 bananas, fresh or frozen
2 ripe peaches, peeled and pitted

Slice the apple and peach (peel if they are not organic), and remove the peach pit, and run through a juicer. Peel, slice and remove pit from the second peach. Combine the apple / peach juice with the sliced peach and bananas and puree in a blender, Vita-Mix, Green Star or Champion juicer. If you are using a Green Star or Champion juicer, use the "blank plate" to puree.

Strawberry & Grape Combo
☆ ☆ ☆ ☆ ☆

1 cup frozen strawberries   1 cup green grapes
1 cup red grapes   1 or 2 organic dates, pitted

Run the red and green grapes through a juicer. (If the grapes have seeds, you do not have to remove them because they will be expelled with the pulp.) Combine this juice with the strawberries and dates and puree in a blender, Vita-Mix, Green Star or Champion juicer. If you are using a Green Star or Champion juicer, use the "blank plate" to puree.

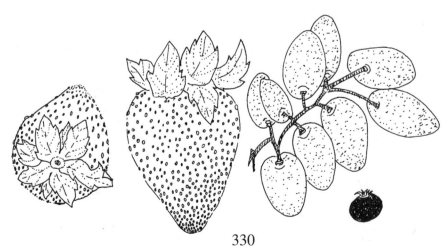

Fourteen Days of Menu Suggestions

The Hallelujah Diet can be as simple as raw fruits for lunch and raw vegetables for supper, cleaned or peeled and eaten whole, without extensive preparation, with BarleyMax and sometimes carrot juice before each meal. We also include a regular exercise workout in the morning, followed by a serving of carrot juice and/or BarleyMax. (After a workout is a good time for fresh vegetable juice or BarleyMax, because our cells have just been depleted of some nutrients, and fresh vegetable juice and BarleyMax replenishes these nutrients without requiring our digestive system to do any extra work.) The following daily menus are offered as an example of the variety of meals that may be served on The Hallelujah Diet. Certainly, there are many, many ideas and combinations that can be created. These are provided to help you get started. Feel free to substitute your favorite fruit or vegetable, soup, salad or entrée for any day. Where you go from here is up to you and your creativity.

Day 1

Breakfast	BarleyMax (1 tsp. dry powder or mixed into 4-8 oz of distilled water)
	See pages 66 for more on BarleyMax
Mid morning	8 oz. Carrot Juice (freshly extracted, never bottled, canned, frozen or powdered) page 185

$1/2$ hour before lunch, one serving of BarleyMax

Lunch	Apples (eat until satisfied)
Mid afternoon	8 oz. Carrot, Celery Juice (page 186)

$1/2$ hour before evening meal, one serving of BarleyMax

Dinner	Hallelujah Acres vegetable salad (page 152)
	Vegetable Grain Crisps (page 305)
	Gazpacho Soup (page 205)

Day 2

Breakfast	BarleyMax
Mid morning	8 oz. Carrot, Apple Juice (page 186)

$1/2$ hour before lunch, one serving of BarleyMax

Lunch	Pears (eat until satisfied)
Mid afternoon	8 oz. Carrot, Cucumber Juice (page 188)

$1/2$ hour before evening meal, one serving of BarleyMax

Supper	Zucchini salad (page 162)
	Baked sweet potatoes (page 251)

Day 3

Breakfast	BarleyMax
Mid morning	8 oz. Carrot, Beet, Cucumber Juice (page 187)

$^{1}/_{2}$ hour before lunch, one serving of BarleyMax

Lunch	Bananas (eat until satisfied)
Mid afternoon	8 oz. Carrot Juice

$^{1}/_{2}$ hour before evening meal, one serving of BarleyMax

Supper	Hallelujah Acres Cabbage Salad (page 155) Carrot Soup (page 200) Vegetable Nut Loaf (page 226)

Day 4

Breakfast	BarleyMax
Mid morning	8 oz. Carrot, Apple, Broccoli Juice (page 188)

$^{1}/_{2}$ hour before lunch, one serving of BarleyMax

Lunch	Nectarines (eat until satisfied)
Mid afternoon	8 oz. Carrot, Cabbage, Celery (page 188)

$^{1}/_{2}$ hour before evening meal, one serving of BarleyMax

Supper	Broccoli Mix (page 154) Lentil, Barley Stew (page 215) Whole Grain Rolls

Day 5

Breakfast	BarleyMax
Mid morning	8 oz. Carrot, Celery, Spinach Juice (page 189)

$^{1}/_{2}$ hour before lunch, one serving of BarleyMax

Lunch	Plums (eat until satisfied)
Mid afternoon	8 oz. Carrot, Cucumber, Bell Pepper Juice (page 188)

$^{1}/_{2}$ hour before evening meal, one serving of BarleyMax

Supper	Confetti Coleslaw (page 157) Lentil Loaf (page 250) Steamed Vegetables

Day 6

Breakfast	BarleyMax
Mid morning	8 oz. Tomato, Cucumber, Celery Juice (page 190)

$^1/_2$ hour before lunch, one serving of BarleyMax

Lunch	Peaches (eat until satisfied)
Mid afternoon	8 oz. Carrot, Celery, Spinach Juice (page 189)

$^1/_2$ hour before evening meal, one serving of BarleyMax

Supper	Sunshine Carrot Salad (page 154) Green Pea Soup (page 204) Sunflower Loaf (page 223)

Day 7

Breakfast	BarleyMax
Mid morning	8 oz. Carrot, Beet, Greens Juice (page 187)

$^1/_2$ hour before lunch, one serving of BarleyMax

Lunch	Raw Apple Sauce (page 113) – Eat until satisfied
Mid afternoon	8 oz. Carrot Juice (page 185) with BarleyMax added

$^1/_2$ hour before evening meal, one serving of BarleyMax

Supper	Garden Salad (page 160) Minestrone Soup (page 208) Vegetable Grain Crisps (page 305)

Day 8

Breakfast	BarleyMax
Mid morning	8 oz. Carrot, Apple, Celery Juice (page 186)

$^1/_2$ hour before lunch, one serving of BarleyMax

Lunch	Melon or melon combination, when in season (eat until satisfied)
Mid afternoon	8 oz. Carrot, Beet Juice (page 186)

$^1/_2$ hour before evening meal, one serving of BarleyMax

Supper	Spinach Salad (page 162) Baked Potato with Raw or Steamed Veggies

Day 9

Breakfast   BarleyMax

Mid morning   8 oz. Carrot, Vegetable Juice (page 190)

     1/2 hour before lunch, one serving of BarleyMax

Lunch   Grapes (eat until satisfied)

Mid afternoon   8 oz. Carrot, Celery, Parsley Juice (page 189)

     1/2 hour before evening meal, one serving of BarleyMax

Supper   Mixed Garden Salad (page 167)
                 Tomato Soup (page 203)
                 Vegetable Grain Crisps (page 305)

Day 10

Breakfast   BarleyMax

Mid morning   8 oz. Carrot Juice (page 185)

     1/2 hour before lunch, one serving of BarleyMax

Lunch   Mixed Fruit Salad (page 145) – Eat until satisfied

Mid afternoon   8 oz. Carrot, Cucumber Juice (page 188)

     1/2 hour before evening meal, one serving of BarleyMax

Supper   Stacked Salad (page 156)
                 Hearty Vegetable Stew (page 217)
                 Whole Grain Bread

Day 11

Breakfast   BarleyMax

Mid morning   8 oz. Carrot, Cabbage, Celery Juice (page 188)

     1/2 hour before lunch, one serving of BarleyMax

Lunch   Pineapple Boats (page 147)

Mid afternoon   8 oz. Tomato Juice Cocktail (page 190)

     1/2 hour before evening meal, one serving of BarleyMax

Supper   Hallelujah Acres Vegetable Salad (page 152)
                 Vegetarian Spaghetti (page 264)
                 Whole Grain Bread

Day 12

Breakfast BarleyMax

Mid morning 8 oz. Carrot, Celery Juice (page 186)

$^1/2$ hour before lunch, one serving of BarleyMax

Lunch Strawberries (eat until satisfied)

Mid afternoon 8 oz. Mixed Fruit Juice (page 195)

$^1/2$ hour before evening meal, one serving of BarleyMax

Supper Cucumber & Tomato Salad (page 158)
Almost Turkey (page 224)
Asparagus with Cream Sauce (page 224)

Day 13

Breakfast BarleyMax

Mid morning 8 oz. Carrot, Parsley, Lettuce, Spinach Juice (page 188)

$^1/2$ hour before lunch, one serving of BarleyMax

Lunch Banana, Apple and 3 or 4 Dates

Mid afternoon 8 oz. Carrot Juice (page 185)

$^1/2$ hour before evening meal, one serving of BarleyMax

Supper Hallelujah Acres Vegetable Salad (page 152)
Steamed Vegetables
Seasoned Basmati Rice (page 271)

Day 14

Breakfast BarleyMax

Mid morning 8 oz. Carrot Juice (page 185)

$^1/2$ hour before lunch, one serving of BarleyMax

Lunch Carrot, Celery, Cucumber Sticks, with Cherry Tomatoes

Mid afternoon 8 oz. Carrot Juice (page 185) with BarleyMax added

$^1/2$ hour before evening meal, one serving of BarleyMax

Supper Asparagus Salad (page 153)
Better Than Tuna (page 229) served on a bed of lettuce
Vegetable Grain Crisps (page 305)

Conclusion

Writing this book has been a life-long dream, and it's rather sad to bring it to a close. Although the months have quickly gone by, I feel there is much left undone. I could have spent many more months writing, testing and preparing recipes. However, it must go to press, as its contents are desperately needed.

My prayer is that through the pages of this book, you will find the encouragement to change your diet and lifestyle toward one of vibrant health and well being; and that by taking charge of your health you can restore your body/temple to the abundant life God has promised.

I am reminded of Daniel 1:11- 20: *"Then said Daniel to Melzar, whom the prince of the eunuchs had set over Daniel, Hananiah, Mishael and Azariah, prove thy servants, I beseech thee, ten days; and let them give us pulse (vegetables) to eat, and water to drink.*

Then let our countenances be looked upon before thee, and the countenance of the children that eat of the portion of the king's meat: and as thou seest, deal with thy servants.

So he consented to them in this matter, and proved them ten days. And at the end of ten days their countenances appeared fairer and fatter in flesh than all the children which did eat the portion of the king's meat.

Thus Melzar took away the portion of their meat, and the wine that they should drink; and gave them pulse (vegetables).

As for these four children, God gave them knowledge and skill in all learning and wisdom: and Daniel had understanding in all visions and dreams.

Now at the end of the days that the king had said he should bring them in, then the prince of the eunuchs brought them in before Nebuchadnezzar.

And the king communed with them; and amoung them found none like Daniel, Hananiah, Mishael and Azariah: therefore they stood before the king.

And in all matters of wisdom and understanding, that the king inquired of them, he found them ten times better than all the magicians and astrologers that were in all his realm."

If you doubt the wisdom set before you in this book, I challenge you to try it for 90 days and see what a blessing restored health can be! If you are like me, after you have experienced in your own body the health benefits of the Genesis 1:29 diet, you will never want to "look back" or return to those agonizing days of pain and suffering! Life is too precious to waste in poor health, when most ills can be overcome by simply changing diet and lifestyle. Money that is spent needlessly on drugs, hospital and doctor bills could be used for the Lord's work.

The Most Important Decision of Life

Finally, let me share with you the most important decision you will ever make. Even though you may regain your health and may live 120 years or more, there is one question for which we are all accountable. It is simply this: ***"What have you done with Jesus?"*** My friend, if you have not asked Jesus to be the Lord and Master of your life, trusted Him as your personal Savior, won't you do so today? Our Lord Jesus Christ was born, lived, shed his sinless blood as full payment for your sins, died, was buried and rose again for your justification. By placing your faith and trust in Him and His shed blood alone, you can be saved and become a new creature in Christ. If you need more information regarding this most important decision you will ever make, ***please*** contact us at Hallelujah Acres.

Recipes for Life ... from God's Garden

Bibliography

Dr. Allen Baniki, *The Choice is Clear,* Acres USA, Metairie, LA, 1971.

Neal Barnard, M.D., *Food for Life,* New York, New York, Crown Publishers, 1993.

F. Batmanghelidj, M.D., *Your Body's Many Cries for Water,* Falls Church, VA, 1994.

Mary Bell, *Complete Dehydrator Cookbook,* New York, New York, William Morrow and Company, Inc., 1994.

Victoria Bidwell, *The Health Seekers' Yearbook,* Mt. Vernon, Washington, Get Well Stay Well America, 1990.

Stephen Blauer, *The Juicing Book,* Garden City Park, New York, 1989.

Paul C. Bragg, N.D., Ph.D, Patricia Bragg, N.D., Ph.D., *Healthful Eating without Confusion,* Santa Barbara, California, Health Science.

-------------------------------, *Toxicless Diet, Body Purification and Healing System* , Santa Barbara, California, Health Science.

Albert E. Carter, *The New Miracles of Rebound Exercise,* A.L.M. Publishers, Scottsdale, AZ, 1988.

Deanna DeLong, *How to Dry Foods,* Los Angeles, California, H P Books, 1979.

Marilyn Diamond, *American Vegetarian Cookbook from the Fit for Life Kitchen,* New York, NY, 1990.

Ford Foundation Project, *The Nutriture of the American People,* James Beasley, M.D., Project Leader, 1986.

Recipes for Life ... from God's Garden

Yoshihide Hagiwara, M.D., *Green Barley Essence,* New Canaan, Connecticut, Keats Publishing, 1985.

Dr. Edward Howell, *Enzyme Nutrition, the Food Enzyme Concept,* Wayne, New Jersey, Avery Publishing Group, Inc., 1985.

Beatrice Hunter, *Consumer Beware* , Simon & Schuster, NY 1971.

Michael F. Jacobson, Ph.D. and Bruce Maxwell, *What are we Feeding our Kids?,* New York, New York Workmen Publishing Inc., 1994.

H. E. Kirschner, M.D., *Live Food Juices,* Monrovia, California, H. E. Kirschner Publications, 1991.

Michael Klaper, M.D., *Pregnancy, Children and the Vegan Diet,* Umatilla, FL, Gentle World, Inc., 1987.

Jay Kordich, *The Juiceman's Power of Juicing,* New York, New York, 1992.

Dr. George Malkmus, *Why Christians Get Sick,* Shippensburg, Pennsylvania, Destiny Image, Inc., 1995.

------------------------, *God's Way to Ulimate Health,* Eidson, Tennessee, Hallelujah Acres, Inc., 1995.

Earl Mindell, *Unsafe at Any Meal,* Warner Books, NY, 1987.

Dean Ornish, M.D., *Eat More Weigh Less*, New York, New York, 1991.

Frank A. Oski, M.D., *Don't Drink Your Milk!,* Brushton, New York: Teach Services, 1993.

John Robbins, *Diet for a New America,* Warpole, New Hampshire, Stillpoint Publishing Company, Inc., 1987.

----------------*Diet for a New World,* New York, New York, William Marrow and Company Inc., 1992.

Rita Romano, *Dining in the Raw, Cooking in the Buff,* Prato, Italy, Prato Publications, 1993.

Humbart Santillo, B.S., M.H., *Food Enzymes, the Missing Link to Radiant Health,* Prescott, Arizona, Hohm Press, 1991.

Teresa Schumacher and Toni Lund, *Cleansing the Body and the Colon for a Healthier, Happier You,* Health is Wealth, St. George, Utah 1987.

Dr. Mary Ruth Swope, *Green Leaves of Barley,* Phoenix, Arizona, Swope Enterprises, 1987.

Agatha Thrash, M.D., *Home Remedies*, Yucchi Pines Institute, Seale, AL 1981.

Dr. Norman W. Walker, *Fresh Vegetable and Fruit Juices*, Prescott, Arizona, Norwalk Press, 1936.

---------------------------, *The Vegetarian Guide to Diet and Salad,* Prescott, Arizona, Norwalk Press, 1940.

----------------------------, *The Natural Way to Vibrant Health,* Prescott, Arizona, Norwalk Press, 1972.

---------------------------, *Water Can Undermine Your Health,* Prescott, Arizona, Norwalk Press, 1974.

Anna Belle Lee Warren, Ph.D. and Jo Williard, *Blueprint for Health,* New Win Publishing, Inc. 1995.

Dr. Ann Wigmore, *Recipes for Longer Life*, Wayne, New Jersey, Avery Publishing Group, Inc., 1978.

Sharon Yntema, *Vegetarian Baby,* Ithaca, New York, McBooks Press, 1951.

-------------------, *Vegetarian Children,* Ithaca, New York, McBooks Press, 1951.

Index of Recipes – by Chapter

Chapter 10 – Breakfast Recipes for Children 109
  Strawberries, Kiwis, & More 109
  Blueberries, Peaches & Cream 109
  Apple Blueberry Cereal .110
  Melon Balls 110
  Mixed Fruit Combo 110
  Creamy Banana Milk 111
  Sweet Almond Milk 111
  Peaches & Cream Cereal 111
  Raw Whole-Grain Cereal 112
  Fruit Plate 112
  Granola 113
  Apple Sauce 113
Chapter 13 – Fruit Salads 144
  Blueberry, Strawberry, Banana Salad 144
  Fruit Delight 144
  Apple / Kiwi Salad 145
  Mixed Fruit Salad 145
  Avocado Fruit Salad 146
  Apple Salad 146
  Peach Delight 146
  Citrus Salad 147
  Pineapple Boats 147
  Diced Fruit Salad 147
  Strawberry, Nectarine, Blueberry Salad 148
  Grape Salad 148
  Ambrosia Salad 148
  Apple, Pear Molded Salad 149
  Fruit Plate 149
  Berry Salad 150
  Melon Ball Salad 150
Chapter 14 – Vegetable Salads 151
  Broccoli and Cauliflower Salad 151
  Raw Stuffed Peppers 151
  Hallelujah Acres Vegetable Salad 152
  Hallelujah Acres Blended Salad 153
  Asparagus Salad 153
  Broccoli Mix 154
  Vegetable Plate 154
  Sunshine Carrot Salad 154
  Hallelujah Acres Cabbage Salad 155
  Pea Salad 155
  Stacked Salad 156
  Delightful Beet Salad 156
  Great Grated Salad 156
  Marinaded Broccoli, Cauliflower Salad 157
  Confetti Coleslaw 157
  Grated Apple Combo 157
  Spring Garden Salad 158
  Orange Spinach Salad 158
  Cucumber & Tomato Salad 158
  Cucumber, Radish Salad 159
  Raw Sweet Corn Salad .159
  Red Cabbage Slaw 159

Chef Salad 160
Garden Salad 160
Cauliflower Salad 161
Three-Day Coleslaw 161
Green Bean Salad 161
Zucchini Salad 162
Cucumber Boats 162
Spinach Salad 162
Snow Peas with Sesame .163
Tomato Juice Salad 163
Stuffed Cucumbers 164
Sweet Potato Salad 164
Cauliflower & Greens Salad 165
Spinach, Orange Salad 165
Summer Squash Salad 165
Broccoli Salad 165
Marinaded Tomato Salad 166
Summer Salad 166
Winter Salad 166
Mixed Garden Salad 167
Salad Bar Ideas 168
Chapter 15 – Salad & Grain Combinations 169
  Tabouli 169
  Basmati Rice Salad 170
  Wild Rice Salad 171
  Potato Salad 171
  Rainbow Pasta Salad 172
  Three Bean Salad 172
  Taco Lentil Salad 173
  French Potato Salad 173
  Vegetable Aspic 174
Chapter 16 – Delightful Dressings 175
  Rhonda's No-Oil Salad Dressing 175
  Cucumber Dressing 176
  Herb Lemon Dressing 176
  Avocado Dressing 176
  Avocado & Tomato Dressing 176
  Lemon & Oil Dressing 177
  Cucumber & Herb Dressing 177
  Orange Dill Dressing 177
  Strawberry Dressing 178
  Green Dressing 178
  Garlic Dressing 178
  No-Oil Poppy Seed Dressing 179
  Poppy Seed Dressing 179
  All-Natural Thousand Island Dressing 179
  No-Oil French Dressing .180
  Celery Seed Dressing 180
  Carrot Dressing 181
  Italian Dressing 181
  Cole Slaw Dressing 181
  Creamy Dill Dressing 182
  Tomato Basil Dressing 182
  Pecan, Tomato Dressing 182

Cilantro Dressing 183
Beet Salad Dressing 183
Chapter 17 – Fresh Vegetable Juices - The Healers 184
Carrot Juice 185
Carrot, Beet Juice 186
Carrot, Apple Juice 186
Carrot, Apple, Celery Juice .186
Carrot, Celery Juice 186
Carrot, Beet & Cucumber Juice 187
Carrot, Beet & Greens Juice 187
Carrot, Bell Pepper Juice 187
Carrot, Spinach Juice 187
Carrot, Apple, Broccoli Juice 188
Carrot, Cabbage, Celery Juice 188
Carrot, Cucumber, Bell Pepper Juice 188
Carrot, Celery, Parsley, Lettuce & Spinach Juice 188
Carrot, Cucumber Juice 188
Carrot, Celery & Parsley Juice 189
Carrot, Celery & Spinach Juice 189
Carrot, Cucumber, Beet Juice 189
Tomato, Cucumber, Celery Juice 190
Tomato Juice Cocktail 190
Carrot, Vegetable Juice 190
Chapter 18 – Fruit Juices - The Cleansers 191
Apple Juice 192
Apple, Strawberry Juice 192
Apple, Pear Juice 193
Grapefruit Juice 193
Grapefruit, Orange Juice 193
Orange Juice 193
Peach Juice 193
Grape Juice 194
Pineapple Juice 194
Pineapple, Grape Juice 194
Pineapple, Orange Juice 195
Mixed Fruit Juice 195
Cantaloupe, Honeydew & Watermelon Juice 196
Cantaloupe Juice 196
Honeydew Juice 197
Watermelon Juice 197
Chapter 19 – Raw Soups 199
Asparagus Soup 199
Golden Barley Soup 199
Avocado Soup 200
Broccoli Zucchini Soup 200
Carrot Soup 200
Celery Chowder 201
Green Bean Delight 201
Cucumber Soup 202
Corn Chowder (Raw) 202
Borscht 203
Tomato Soup 203
Kohlrabi Soup 203
Green Pea Soup 204
Raw Vegetable Soup 204

Gazpacho Soup 205
Zucchini Chowder 205
Raw Carrot Soup 206
Sweet Potato Soup 206
Chapter 20 – Delicious Cooked Soups & Stews 207
Vegetable Soup Stock 207
Minestrone Soup 208
Split Pea Soup 208
Acorn Squash Soup 209
White Bean Soup 209
Cauliflower Chowder 210
Corn Chowder (Cooked) 210
Barley Vegetable Soup 211
Black Bean Soup 211
Carrot & Barley Soup 212
Curried Vegetable Stew 212
Cream of Broccoli Soup 213
Creamy Carrot Soup 214
Country Stew 214
Potato, Squash Soup 215
Lentil, Barley Stew 215
Curried Millet Spinach Soup 216
Soupe au Pistou (Vegetable Soup with Basil) 216
Hearty Vegetable Stew 217
Sea Shell Stew 218
Two-Potato Soup 218
Veggie Stew 219
Chapter 21 – Live Food Delicacies 220
Marinaded Tomatoes 220
Marinaded Broccoli Salad 220
Cucumber Pickles 221
Marinaded Green Beans 221
Sauerkraut 222
Marinaded Vegetable Combo 222
Sunflower Loaf 223
Almost Turkey 224
Asparagus with Cream Sauce 224
Preparing Raw Whole Grains 225
Almond Paté 225
Italian Vegetables & Bulgar .226
Vegetable Nut Loaf 226
Almost Crab 227
Cabbage Rolls 227
Stuffed Tomatoes 228
Better than Tuna 229
Broccoli & Cauliflower with "Cheese" 229
Lemon & Herb Marinade 229
Bulgar Wheat Surprise 230
Garden Delight Aspic 230
Tacos 231
Chili 231
Summer Squash, Italian Style 232
Stuffed Peppers 232
Garlic & Herb Seed Cheese .233
Butternut Squash & Veggies 233

Index of Recipes – by Chapter

Cucumber Medley 233
Chinese Vegetables 234
Lettuce Leaf Rolls 234
Marinaded Mixed Vegetables 235
Marinaded Vegetables & Rye 235
Cauliflower, Broccoli & Bok Choy 235
Seed Cheese Pie 236
Millet Burgers 236
Raw Vegetarian Pizza .237
Raw Spaghetti 238
Stuffed Avocados 238
Tomato Aspic 239
Tomato Bowls 239
Tostado 240
What's for Dinner Loaf 240
Tomato Bowls with Grain 241
Cucumber Delight 241
Vegetable Pot Pie 242
Raw Veggie Stew 242
Yam Burger 243
Zucchini Boats 243
Winter Squash 244

Chapter 22 – Tempting Cooked Foods 245
Baked Beans 245
Baked Spaghetti Squash 246
Black Bean Burrito 246
Broccoli with Onion Sauce 247
Carrot Burgers 247
Chow Mein 248
Cornbread Dresssing 248
Couscous & Raw Veggies 249
Eggplant & Rice Casserole 249
Lentil Loaf 250
Grain Burgers 250
Hallelujah Burgers 251
Baked Sweet Potatoes 251
Fettuccine Alfredo 252
Orzo Pasta with Garden Veggies 252
Manicotti (stuffed shells) 253
Herbed Rice 253
Scalloped Potatoes 254
Potato Medley 254
Layered Casserole 255
Nutted Rice & Orzo Pilaf 255
Pasta Primavera Alfredo 255
Shepard's Pie 256
Two-Potato Casserole .256
Pecan Loaf 257
Stir-Fry Vegetables 257
Stuffed Acorn Squash .258
Stuffed Baked Potatoes 259
Spanish Rice 259
Stuffed Eggplant 260
Stuffed Red Bell Peppers 260
Stuffed Cabbage Rolls 261

Sweet Potato Casserole 262
Vegetables & Rice Casserole 262
Vegetable Lo Mein 263
Vegetarian Spaghetti 264
Vegetarian Taco Salad 264
Bok Choy with Ginger 265
Veggie / Rice Medley .265
Wild Rice Dressing 265
Vegetarian Lasagna 266
Pizza Dough 267
Vegetarian Pizza 267
Red Bell Pepper with Bulgar 268
Hawaiian Rice 268
Wild Rice Pilaf 269
Sweet Potato Delight .269
Kathleen's Tabouli 269
Quick Mexican Supper 270
Pasta Primavera 270
Seasoned Basmati Rice 271
Vegetarian Chili 271
Black Beans & Rice 272
Rice-Stuffed Tomatoes 272
Basmati Rice 273
Bulgar Wheat 273
Quinoa 273
Rolled Oats 273

Chapter 23 – Tasty Breads, Snacks & Sandwiches 274
Poor Man's Bread 274
Hallelujah Acres Cornbread 275
Broccoli / Red Pepper Pita Pocket 275
Cucumber Sandwich 276
Hummus in a Pita 276
Pizza Lover's Sandwich 276
Power House Sandwich 276
Almond Butter Sandwiches 277
Almond Cheese Delight 277
Sloppy Joe Mix 277
Veggie Combo Sandwich 277
Tomato & Avocado Pita Pocket 278
Tomato on a Burger Bun 278
Tofu Eggless Salad in a Pita Pocket 278
Hallelujah Acres Colonial Bread 279
Honey Nut Oatmeal Bread 280
Open Face Sandwiches 280
Hero Sandwich 281
Laurie's Granola 281
Essene Bread 282

Chapter 24 – Condiments, Sauces, Dips & Spreads 283
Basic Seed Sauce 283
Almond Butter 284
Almond & Garlic Dip .284
Almond "Cheese" Sauce 284
Almond Slicing "Cheese" 285
Almond, Sunflower Seed Sauce 285
Honey Mustard 286

Tomato Sauce 286
Tomato Paste 287
Baba Gannouj 287
Salsa 288
Guacamole 288
Hummus 289
Pesto 289
Ketchup 290
Pizza Sauce 291
Spaghetti Sauce 291
Tofu Ricotta 292
Tahini 292
Tomato Chutney 292
Tomato Basil Sauce 293
Cranberry Sauce 293
Raw Raisin Chutney 294
Vegetable Seed Cheese 295
Creamy Onion Dip 295
Tofu Eggless Salad 295
Chapter 25 – Dehydrated Foods 296
Asparagus 299
Beans, Green and Yellow 299
Beets 300
Carrots 300
Celery 301
Corn 301
Cucumber 301
Eggplant 302
Onions 302
Parsley 302
Parsnips 303
Peas 303
Peppers – Red, Green & Orange 303
Pumpkin 304
Tomatoes 304
Vegetable Crisps 305
Sweet Potato Chips 306
Fruit Crisps 306
Vegetable Chips 306
Vegetable Flakes & Powders 306
Vegetable Soup Broth 307
Vegetable Leathers 307
Fruit Roll-Up Leathers 307
Apple Leather 307
Apricot Leather 308
Banana Leather 308
Berry Leather 308
Blueberry Leather 308
Cherry Leather 309
Cranberry Leather 309
Grape Leather 309
Peach or Nectarine Leather 309
Pineapple Leather 309
Plum Leather 309
Granola 310

Strawberry Leather 310
Pear Leather 311
Raspberry Leather 311
Fruit Leather Fillings 311
Baby Foods 311
Herbs 312
My Version of Fines Herbs .312
Bouquet Garni 313
Italian Seasoning 313
All Purpose Seasoning 313
Herb Teas 313
Chapter 26 – Special Occasion Treats 314
Hallelujah Acres Date Nut Bread 314
Fresh Strawberry Pie 315
Almond Pie Crust 315
Pecan Pie 316
Almond Cookies 316
Banana Cream Pie 317
Creamy Fruit Pie 317
Carob Sauce 318
Date-Pecan Squares 318
Fresh Fruit Aspic 318
Couscous Delight 319
Banana & Date Pie Crust 319
Date-Coconut Logs 320
Fresh Fruit Tart 320
Fruit Bars 320
Raw Pumpkin Pie 321
Baked Pumpkin Pie 321
Frozen Raw Birthday Cake .322
Fruit Cake 323
Whole Grain Pie Crust 323
Mixed Berry Pie 323
Peach Pie 324
Pritikin Apple Pie 324
Granola Pie Crust 325
Tofu Cheese Cake 325
Almond Butter Balls 326
Frozen Banana Berry Pie 326
Fruit Smoothies 327
Fruit Smoothie Combinations 328
Apple Banana Royal 328
Heavenly Mango 328
Apple, Pineapple & Strawberry Surprise 329
Blueberry Delight 329
Cranberry Blush 329
Melons Alive 330
Peaches & Cream 330
Strawberry & Grape Combo 330

Index of Recipes – by Alphabet

Acorn Squash Soup 209
All Purpose Seasoning 313
All-Natural Thousand Island Dressing 179
Almond "Cheese" Sauce 284
Almond & Garlic Dip 284
Almond Butter 284
Almond Butter Balls 326
Almond Butter Sandwiches 277
Almond Cheese Delight 277
Almond Cookies 316
Almond Paté 225
Almond Pie Crust 315
Almond Slicing "Cheese" .285
Almond, Sunflower Seed Sauce 285
Almost Crab 227
Almost Turkey 224
Ambrosia Salad 148
Apple / Kiwi Salad 145
Apple Banana Royal 328
Apple Blueberry Cereal 110
Apple Juice 192
Apple Leather 307
Apple Salad 146
Apple Sauce 113
Apple, Pear Juice 193
Apple, Pear Molded Salad 149
Apple, Pineapple & Strawberry Surprise 329
Apple, Strawberry Juice 192
Apricot Leather 308
Asparagus 299
Asparagus Salad 153
Asparagus Soup 199
Asparagus with Cream Sauce 224
Avocado & Tomato Dressing 176
Avocado Dressing 176
Avocado Fruit Salad 146
Avocado Soup 200
Baba Gannouj 287
Baby Foods 311
Baked Beans 245
Baked Pumpkin Pie 321
Baked Spaghetti Squash 246
Baked Sweet Potatoes 251
Banana & Date Pie Crust .319
Banana Cream Pie 317
Banana Leather 308
Barley Vegetable Soup 211
Basic Seed Sauce 283
Basmati Rice 273
Basmati Rice Salad 170
Beans, Green and Yellow .299
Beet Salad Dressing 183
Beet 300
Berry Salad 150

Berry Leather 308
Better than Tuna 229
Black Bean Burrito 246
Black Bean Soup 211
Black Beans & Rice 272
Blueberry Delight 329
Blueberry Leather 308
Blueberries, Peaches & Cream 109
Blueberry, Strawberry, Banana Salad 144
Bok Choy with Ginger 265
Borscht 203
Bouquet Garni 313
Broccoli & Cauliflower with "Cheese" 229
Broccoli / Red Pepper Pita Pocket 275
Broccoli and Cauliflower Salad 151
Broccoli Mix 154
Broccoli Salad 165
Broccoli with Onion Sauce 247
Broccoli Zucchini Soup 200
Buglar Wheat 273
Bulgar Wheat Surprise 230
Butternut Squash & Veggies 233
Cabbage Rolls 227
Cantaloupe Juice 196
Cantaloupe, Honeydew & Watermelon Juice 196
Carob Sauce 318
Carrot & Barley Soup 212
Carrot Burgers 247
Carrot Dressing 181
Carrot Juice 185
Carrot Soup 200
Carrot, Apple Juice 186
Carrot, Apple, Broccoli Juice 188
Carrot, Apple, Celery Juice 186
Carrot, Beet & Cucumber Juice 187
Carrot, Beet & Greens Juice 187
Carrot, Beet Juice 186
Carrot, Bell Pepper Juice .187
Carrot, Cabbage, Celery Juice 188
Carrot, Celery & Parsley Juice 189
Carrot, Celery & Spinach Juice 189
Carrot, Celery Juice 186
Carrot, Celery, Parsley, Lettuce & Spinach Juice . . .188
Carrot, Cucumber Juice 188
Carrot, Cucumber, Beet Juice 189
Carrot, Cucumber, Bell Pepper Juice 188
Carrot, Spinach Juice 187
Carrot, Vegetable Juice 190
Carrots 300
Cauliflower, Broccoli & Bok Choy 235
Cauliflower & Greens Salad 165
Cauliflower Chowder 210
Cauliflower Salad 161
Celery 301

Celery Chowder 201
Celery Seed Dressing 180
Chef Salad 160
Cherry Leather 309
Chili 231
Chinese Vegetables 234
Chow Mein 248
Cilantro Dressing 183
Citrus Salad 147
Cole Slaw Dressing 181
Confetti Coleslaw 157
Corn 301
Corn Chowder (Raw) 202
Corn Chowder (Cooked) 210
Cornbread Dresssing 248
Country Stew 214
Couscous & Raw Veggies 249
Couscous Delight 319
Cranberry Blush 329
Cranberry Leather 309
Cranberry Sauce 293
Cream of Broccoli Soup 213
Creamy Banana Milk 111
Creamy Carrot Soup 214
Creamy Dill Dressing 182
Creamy Fruit Pie 317
Creamy Onion Dip 295
Cucumber 301
Cucumber & Herb Dressing 177
Cucumber & Tomato Salad 158
Cucumber Boats 162
Cucumber Delight 241
Cucumber Dressing 176
Cucumber Medley 233
Cucumber Pickles 221
Cucumber Sandwich 276
Cucumber Soup 202
Cucumber, Radish Salad 159
Curried Millet Spinach Soup 216
Curried Vegetable Stew 212
Date-Coconut Logs 320
Date-Pecan Squares 318
Delightful Beet Salad 156
Diced Fruit Salad 147
Eggplant 302
Eggplant & Rice Casserole 249
Essene Bread 282
Fettuccine Alfredo 252
French Potato Salad 173
Fresh Fruit Aspic 318
Fresh Fruit Tart 320
Fresh Strawberry Pie 315
Frozen Banana Berry Pie 326
Frozen Raw Birthday Cake 322
Fruit Bars 320

Fruit Cake 323
Fruit Crisps 306
Fruit Delight 144
Fruit Leather Fillings 311
Fruit Plate 149
Fruit Plate (for children for breakfast) 112
Fruit Roll-Up Leathers 307
Fruit Smoothie Combinations 328
Fruit Smoothies 327
Garden Delight Aspic 230
Garden Salad 160
Garlic & Herb Seed Cheese 233
Garlic Dressing 178
Gazpacho Soup 205
Golden Barley Soup 199
Grain Burgers 250
Granola 310
Granola (for children for breakfast) 113
Granola Pie Crust 325
Grape Juice 194
Grape Leather 309
Grape Salad 148
Grapefruit Juice 193
Grapefruit, Orange Juice 193
Grated Apple Combo 157
Great Grated Salad 156
Green Bean Salad 161
Green Bean Delight 201
Green Dressing 178
Green Pea Soup 204
Guacamole 288
Hallelujah Acres Blended Salad 153
Hallelujah Acres Cabbage Salad 155
Hallelujah Acres Colonial Bread 279
Hallelujah Acres Cornbread 275
Hallelujah Acres Date Nut Bread 314
Hallelujah Acres Vegetable Salad 152
Hallelujah Burgers 251
Hawaiian Rice 268
Hearty Vegetable Stew 217
Heavenly Mango 328
Herb Lemon Dressing 176
Herb Teas 313
Herbed Rice 253
Herbs 312
Hero Sandwich 281
Honey Mustard 286
Honey Nut Oatmeal Bread 280
Honeydew Juice 197
Hummus 289
Hummus in a Pita 276
Italian Dressing 181
Italian Seasoning 313
Italian Vegetables & Bulgar 226
Kathleen's Tabouli 269

Ketchup	290
Kohlrabi Soup	203
Laurie's Granola	281
Layered Casserole	255
Lemon & Herb Marinade	229
Lemon & Oil Dressing	177
Lentil Loaf	250
Lentil, Barley Stew	215
Lettuce Leaf Rolls	234
Manicotti (stuffed shells)	253
Marinaded Broccoli Salad	220
Marinaded Broccoli, Cauliflower Salad	157
Marinaded Green Beans	221
Marinaded Mixed Vegetables	235
Marinaded Tomato Salad	166
Marinaded Tomatoes	220
Marinaded Vegetable Combo	222
Marinaded Vegetables & Rye	235
Melon Balls (for children for breakfast)	110
Melon Ball Salad	150
Melons Alive	330
Millet Burgers	236
Minestrone Soup	208
Mixed Berry Pie	323
Mixed Fruit Combo (for children for breakfast)	110
Mixed Fruit Juice	195
Mixed Fruit Salad	145
Mixed Garden Salad	167
My Version of Fines Herbs	312
No-Oil French Dressing	180
No-Oil Poppy Seed Dressing	179
Nutted Rice & Orzo Pilaf	255
Onions	302
Open Face Sandwiches	280
Orange Juice	193
Orange Dill Dressing	177
Orange Spinach Salad	158
Orzo Pasta with Garden Veggies	252
Parsley	302
Parsnips	303
Pasta Primavera	270
Pasta Primavera Alfredo	255
Pea Salad	155
Peach Delight	146
Peach Juice	193
Peach or Nectarine Leather	309
Peach Pie	324
Peaches & Cream	330
Peaches & Cream Cereal	111
Pear Leather	311
Peas	303
Pecan Loaf	257
Pecan Pie	316
Pecan, Tomato Dressing	182
Peppers – Red, Green & Orange	303
Pesto	289
Pineapple Boats	147
Pineapple Juice	194
Pineapple Leather	309
Pineapple, Grape Juice	194
Pineapple, Orange Juice	195
Pizza Dough	267
Pizza Lover's Sandwich	276
Pizza Sauce	291
Plum Leather	309
Poor Man's Bread	274
Poppy Seed Dressing	179
Potato Medley	254
Potato Salad	171
Potato, Squash Soup	215
Power House Sandwich	276
Preparing Raw Whole Grains	225
Pritikin Apple Pie	324
Pumpkin	304
Quick Mexican Supper	270
Quiona	273
Rainbow Pasta Salad	172
RaspberryLeather	311
Raw Carrot Soup	206
Raw Pumpkin Pie	321
Raw Raisin Chutney	294
Raw Spaghetti	238
Raw Stuffed Peppers	151
Raw Sweet Corn Salad	159
Raw Vegetable Soup	204
Raw Vegetarian Pizza	237
Raw Veggie Stew	242
Raw Whole-Grain Cereal	112
Red Bell Pepper with Bulgar	268
Red Cabbage Slaw	159
Rhonda's No-Oil Salad Dressing	175
Rice-Stuffed Tomatoes	272
Salad Bar Ideas	168
Salsa	288
Sauerkraut	222
Scalloped Potatoes	254
Sea Shell Stew	218
Seasoned Basmati Rice	271
Seed Cheese Pie	236
Shepard's Pie	256
Sloppy Joe Mix	277
Snow Peas with Sesame	163
Soupe au Pistou (Vegetable Soup with Basil)	216
Spaghetti Sauce	291
Spanish Rice	259
Spinach Salad	162
Spinach, Orange Salad	165
Split Pea Soup	208
Spring Garden Salad	158
Stacked Salad	156

Stir-Fry Vegetables 257
Strawberries, Kiwis & More 109
Strawberry & Grape Combo 330
Strawberry Dressing 178
Strawberry Leather 310
Strawberry, Nectarine, Blueberry Salad 148
Stuffed Acorn Squash 258
Stuffed Avocados 238
Stuffed Baked Potatoes 259
Stuffed Cabbage Rolls 261
Stuffed Cucumbers 164
Stuffed Eggplant 260
Stuffed Peppers 232
Stuffed Red Bell Peppers 260
Stuffed Tomatoes 228
Summer Salad 166
Summer Squash Salad 165
Summer Squash, Italian Style .232
Sunflower Loaf 223
Sunshine Carrot Salad 154
Sweet Almond Milk 111
Sweet Potato Casserole 262
Sweet Potato Chips 306
Sweet Potato Delight 269
Sweet Potato Salad 164
Sweet Potato Soup 206
Tabouli 169
Taco Lentil Salad 173
Tacos 231
Tahini 292
Three Bean Salad 172
Three-Day Coleslaw 161
Tofu Cheese Cake 325
Tofu Eggless Salad 295
Tofu Eggless Salad in a Pita Pocket 278
Tofu Ricotta 292
Tomato & Avocado Pita Pocket 278
Tomato Aspic 239
Tomato Basil Dressing 182
Tomato Basil Sauce 293
Tomato Bowls 239
Tomato Bowls with Grain 241
Tomato Chutney 292
Tomato Juice Cocktail 190
Tomato Juice Salad 163
Tomato on a Burger Bun 278
Tomato Paste 287
Tomato Sauce 286
Tomato Soup 203
Tomato, Cucumber, Celery Juice 190
Tomatoes 304
Tostado 240
Two-Potato Casserole 256
Two-Potato Soup 218
Vegetable Aspic 174

Vegetable Chips 306
Vegetable Crisps 305
Vegetable Flakes & Powders 306
Vegetable Leathers 307
Vegetable Lo Mein 263
Vegetable Nut Loaf 226
Vegetable Plate 154
Vegetable Pot Pie 242
Vegetable Seed Cheese 295
Vegetable Soup Broth 307
Vegetable Soup Stock 207
Vegetables & Rice Casserole 262
Vegetarian Chili 271
Vegetarian Lasagna 266
Vegetarian Pizza 267
Vegetarian Spaghetti 264
Vegetarian Taco Salad 264
Veggie / Rice Medley 265
Veggie Combo Sandwich 277
Veggie Stew 219
Watermelon Juice 197
What's for Dinner Loaf 240
White Bean Soup 209
Whole Grain Pie Crust 323
Wild Rice Dressing 265
Wild Rice Pilaf 269
Wild Rice Salad 171
Winter Salad 166
Winter Squash 244
Yam Burger 243
Zucchini Boats 243
Zucchini Chowder 205
Zucchini Salad 162

GLOSSARY OF INGREDIENTS

Hint: All food should be organic, if available.

Agar agar: A natural gelatin and thickening agent made from red algae that is boiled, pressed into a gel and then dried into flakes. It contains no calories and is colorless. Agar agar is 75 percent carbohydrate and is high in a type of fiber that passes through the body undigested, adding bulk to the diet acting as a natural laxative. Flakes dissolve in hot liquids and thicken as they cool to room temperature or below. To prepare 4 tablespoons of flakes to 4 cups fruit juice or stock, boil, reduce heat and simmer 5 minutes or until dissolved.

All Purpose Seasoning: A mixture of herbs used in place of salt and pepper. See Recipe on page 313 or look for bottled herb mixtures without salt at a local health food store.

Almond Butter (raw): A nut butter made from ground almonds. Almond butter is a good alternative to peanut butter and much easier for the body to digest. Can be found in health food stores.

Apple Cider Vinegar: Made from peels and cores of apples, unpasteurized, unheated with no chemicals added.

Arrowroot Powder: A tasteless powder made from West Indian arrowroot plant. Used as a thickener in place of corn starch. Use 1 cup of cold liquid to 1 teaspoon arrowroot powder. Blend with liquid before adding to hot dishes to prevent clumps. Does not have to be heated to thicken. Most thickeners leave sauces white or cloudy, but arrowroot becomes transparent. Arrowroot is easier to digest than flour.

Balsamic Vinegar: A sweetish, aromatic vinegar made from the must of white grapes and aged in wooden barrels. (Transitional; organic raw apple cider vinegar is recommended.)

Basil: An herb that is always preferable fresh, but if fresh is not available, dried can be used. Basil is available in a wide variety of flavors from lemon to purple opal. It has a pungent flavor that has been described as a cross between cloves and licorice. Always store dried herbs in a dark place as sunlight deteriorates their freshness.

Bell Peppers: Are chunky in shape and hollow inside. They are a sweet variety of pepper and come in many colors such as red, yellow, orange, brown, purple and other colors. Green bell peppers are not ripe and not recommended. When ripe, bell peppers provide a wonderful source of vitamin C.

Better Than Milk: A non-dairy milk substitute made with either a rice or tofu base. It is fat free, lactose free, cholesterol free, caseinate free and gluten free. Better Than Milk or another non-dairy milk substitute can be used in any recipe calling for Better Than Milk. The Company that manufactures Better Than Milk states that it should NOT be used as infant formula.

Brewer's Yeast: a yeast used or suitable for brewing, a source of B complex vitamins.

Brown Rice Malt Syrup: A sweetener made from organic brown rice and naturally occurring enzymes from organic malted whole barley and water. Can be used in place of honey or maple syrup.

Caraway Seeds: Store seeds in refrigerator or freezer to prolong life as these seeds lose their flavor quickly.

Cayenne Pepper: An intense seasoning made from grinding small hot cayenne peppers. Caution: Very hot and can burn if too much is used; a little goes a long way.

Celtic Sea Salt: Unrefined, solar evaporated (sun-dried) sea salt; high in natural trace minerals but not sodium chloride. Contains no added chemicals. If using sea salt, choose a reputable source so that you know the salt is pure and unadulterated. Use sparingly. **Hint:** Avoid all table salt. Most table salt is stripped of all of its nutrients and natural minerals that are then chemically added back during processing.

Cilantro: Also called Chinese Parsley (the root of the plant is ground and the spice is called Coriander). Cilantro resembles parsley in appearance except that it is pale in color. Most often used in Mexican and Asian dishes.

Coriander: Is made from the carrot-like root of the Cilantro herb. It has a nutty flavor and delightful aroma. Tastes like lemon peel and sage combined.

Cumin: Member of the parsley family. Cumin is a pungent, strong flavored spice (whole or ground) that aids in digestion. Used in Mexican and Indian cooking. Warm robust flavor; use sparingly.

Curry Powder: A mixture of up to twenty spices, usually including cardamom, coriander, cumin and turmeric. Loses pungency quickly; buy in small amounts.

Dates: The oblong fruit of the date palm. There are many varieties of dates, but three best varieties for food preparation are medjool, khadrawi and honey.

Date Sugar: A natural sweetener from dried ground dates. Can be used in recipes calling for a sweetener. Date sugar has a coarse, brown texture and is not as sweet as refined sugar. Heated during processing; therefore it is not considered raw.

Dulse: A burgundy colored sea vegetable. Wash and soak prior to adding to foods. Can also be washed, dried and ground into flakes or a course powder. Like kelp, dulse can be found in shakers in some health food stores.

Fennel Seeds: These seeds have a licorice-like flavor, are a good seasoning and aid in digestion.

Flax Seeds: Contain high concentrations of beneficial oils. Flax seeds may be ground and used in beverages or sprinkled on salads. May also be used as a thickener.

Garlic: a hardy plant and member of the amaryllis family. The bulb of this plant consists of several small bulbs or cloves. Garlic has a pungent flavor that is distinctive. Fresh garlic is best, far better than powdered or pre-peeled in jars.

Ginger: A reed like plant grown mostly in most tropical countries. The plant's rhizome (root) is dried and ground into a powder or used fresh. Ginger has a pungent spicy flavor (a little goes a long way.) Fresh gingerroot is best stored in the refrigerator or freezer where it will keep several months.

Recipes for Life ... from God's Garden

Herbs: Always use fresh herbs when available. Try basil, oregano, dill, tarragon, chives, mint, thyme, cilantro, fennel, garlic, Italian parsley, marjoram, rosemary, sage, ginger root or your favorite.

Honey (raw unfiltered): A sweet liquid produced by bees from the nectar collected from flowers. Very concentrated sweetener; should not be given to babies as their digestive systems are not developed enough to digest it. Some prefer not to use honey as it comes from an animal source. If using honey, buy raw unfiltered honey from a local beekeeper. Clover and wildflower honey have the mildest flavor.

Kelp: Seaweed also known as Kombu. Can be bought in granules or sheets. Can be used as a salt replacement.

Kudzu or kuzu: A natural gelling and thickening agent. Made from a root that grows wild in Japan.

Lemons: Fresh lemon juice can be used to replace vinegar in most recipes. Buy fresh lemons only. Used to flavor and preserve food.

Maple granules or sprinkles: A granulated sweetener made from pure maple syrup. Because of processing, this is not a raw food.

Nama Shoyu™: Traditional unpasteurized soy sauce from Japan made from wheat. This product is high in sodium and not recommended on the Hallelujah Diet.

Nayonaise™: Natural mayonnaise substitute found in health food stores. Free of egg, dairy and refined sugar. This is a soy product and not recommended on the Hallelujah Diet.

Nutritional yeast: Usually golden or bright yellow in color, but can be a dull brown. Nutritional yeast is 5o percent protein and comes in powder or flakes. Adds a rather cheesy taste to dishes and in hot dishes should be added at the end of cooking. Can be sprinkled on salads, dressings or main course dishes. Good source of B vitamins.

Nutmeg: Hard, aromatic seed of East India. Used in a grated form as a spice with a warm, hardy and sweet aroma.

Oregano: An aromatic herb that is a member of the mint family. The leaves of the plant are used to lend an Italian flavor to dishes. Dried is more pungent than fresh.

Paprika: A red powdery condiment derived from dried, ripe sweet peppers often used to add flavor and color.

Parsley: An herb native to the Mediterranean. Parsley will have either curled leaf clusters (French) or flat compound leaves (Italian). The leaves of this culinary herb are often used as a garnish or to add flavor.

Pine Nuts (pignoli or pignolia): The edible soft white nut or seed from pine cones used primarily for sauces or dressings. Very short shelf life; should be stored in the freezer.

Raisins: Organic Thompson or Monukka varieties are best. "Golden" raisins are those that have usually had the color removed with a bleaching agent.

Scallions: A scallion is any onion that does not form a large bulb; such as green onions, shallots or leeks. Scallions are slightly milder than red, yellow or white onions. Green onions are also sometimes called spring onions.

Sesame Seed, hulled: Sesame seeds whose hulls have been removed.

Sesame Seed, unhulled: Sesame seeds whose hulls have not been removed.

Shallots: Related to the onion and have a similar taste. Shallots consist of a small cluster of bulbs.

Squash: Summer squash: crookneck, zucchini and pattypan have edible skins. Winter squash: acorn, butternut and hubbard have a non-edible hard, thick skin.

Stevia: An herb related to the daisy family that is native to Central America. Stevia extract is 300 times as sweet as table sugar without the harmful side effects of other sugar substitutes. Comes in powder or liquid form.

Tahini, raw: A seed butter made from lightly toasted hulled, sesame seeds. It is light in color and adds flavor to soups, potato salad, spreads or even sweet treats. Tahini is not the same as sesame butter that is thicker, darker and made from unhulled sesame seeds. Can be used instead of nut butters.

Tamari: A wheat-free, unpasteurized soy sauce. Tamari is naturally fermented with no alcohol added.

Tarragon vinegar: Raw unfiltered apple cider vinegar to which tarragon has been added and allowed to sit for several days, allowing the flavors to mingle.

Tofu: Bland cheese-like substance made from soybeans or soy flour; used as a meat replacement. Tofu is very high in protein and should be used sparingly.

Udo's Choice Perfected Oil Blend™: Udo's is a cold-pressed, organic blend of flax seed, sunflower seed and sesame seed oils as well as oils from wheat germ, oat germ and rye germ. Udo's Choice Perfected Oil Blend is not a cooking oil; do not heat.

Vegenaise™: A natural mayonnaise substitute found in the cold case of many health food stores. Vegenaise is free from egg and dairy and contains no refined sweeteners. Since some Vegenaise™ is made with other oils, always check the label to make sure that the product is made from grapeseed oil.

Wakame: A pale green seaweed also called alaria. Comes in sheets and gives soups, salads and other foods a delightful flavor.

Improve Your Health with our Books, Tapes & Videos!

You Don't Have to be Sick: A Christian Health Primer by Dr. George H. Malkmus

George Malkmus put into this small book everything you need to know about The Hallelujah Diet and lifestyle while answering all the Biblical questions regarding diet he's been asked over the years. If you have friends and relatives who still have questions about The Hallelujah Diet, this 52-page booklet will convince them to give it a try. (Paperback, $3.95)

Why Christians Get Sick by Dr. George H. Malkmus

This book is especially helpful in introducing Christians to a natural diet and lifestyle. Letters are received daily from all over the world from people helped by this book, which is now in its 20th printing. *Why Christians Get Sick* is written on a solid Biblical foundation with over 150 Bible verses. (Paperback, $8.95)

God's Way to Ultimate Health by Dr. George H. Malkmus with Michael Dye.

This big book has everything you need to know about how to return to God's original plan for nourishing the human body. Read what the Bible says about diet and how this Biblical wisdom is supported by modern science and hundreds of real-life testimonials. Also an entire section of recipes and tips by Rhonda Malkmus on how to set up your own natural foods kitchen. *God's Way to Ultimate Health* contains 282 $8^1/2$ by 11-inch pages of vital information that has changed the way thousands of people think about what they put into their bodies. Many people say this book has saved their lives. There has never been a book like this put into print. ($18.95)

How to Eliminate Sickness Seminar Video

Unlike all previously videotaped seminars by Dr. Malkmus, this professionally-produced video was shot on-site at Hallelujah Acres. This $2^1/2$ hour tape contains an updated version of the seminar Dr. Malkmus has delivered across the United States and Canada. It covers the basics of why we get sick and how to nourish our bodies to restore our health. *A must-see video!* ($24.95) Two tape audio version ($12.95)

Testimonial Video

Filmed in 1997 at Dr. Charles Pack's annual Bible Prophecy Conference in Tulsa, OK, this moving video features the personal five-minute testimonies of 13 men and women who healed themselves of a remarkable variety of illnesses simply by going on The Hallelujah Diet. This video contains the testimonies by a medical doctor, nurses, preachers, and folks from many walks of life. If you have a friend or loved one who remains resistant to the "You Don't Have to be Sick" message, this amazing tape of true stories should open their hearts and minds to the truth of the power of The Hallelujah Diet. ($14.95)

BarleyMax

Although we're not product-oriented at Hallelujah Acres, we strongly recommend serious health seekers to try at least one bottle of the "super green food" that thousands are using as one of the keystones of The Hallelujah Diet. Combined with juicing and a diet of mainly uncooked fruits and vegetables, BarleyMax will provide your body with a synergistic combination of vitamins, minerals, and phytochemicals that thousands of people just plain wouldn't be without every day of their lives. Comes in a 4.2 oz. bottle ($21.95) or a 8.5 oz. plastic container ($34.95).

Please use order form on page 356 and 357...

The Hallelujah Acres Story

Hallelujah is a Biblical word used to express praise, joy and thanksgiving. It was chosen by Rev. George Malkmus as an expression of gratitude to God after he was healed of not only colon cancer, but *all* physical problems, following his change to a natural diet and lifestyle in 1976. Acres was added to the name of his ministry in 1986 when Rev. Malkmus purchased a 50-acre mountain farm in Eidson, Tennessee. On April 11, 1992, Rev. Malkmus married Rhonda Jean at the farm, and today they operate **Hallelujah Acres.**

Hallelujah Acres actually began as a dream after Rev. Malkmus' research and experience revealed that sickness – including cancer, heart attacks, diabetes, arthritis and most other illnesses – are created by our diet and lifestyle, and are totally unnecessary and avoidable! He also learned that if we will but change our diet and lifestyle, these physical problems will usually go away and stay away!

From his background of 20 years pastoring churches from New York to Florida, Rev. Malkmus felt a compelling need to share this life-saving information with fellow Christians and anyone else who would listen. Much was being discovered in medical and scientific research about the advantages of a vegetarian diet of mainly raw fruits and vegetables. For decades, there has been strong evidence that meat, dairy, eggs, sugar, salt, white flour, processed foods and chemical additives are creating and worsening the diseases that are robbing so many people of their life and health. This evidence has shown a diet that eliminates these harmful substances and nourishes our bodies with living foods can prevent and actually reverse disease.

But this information was not getting out to Christians and other people whose diets and lives were under the firm control of fast food joints, manufacturers of processed foods and junk-food television commercials.

The unique approach of Rev. Malkmus has been to show that this dietary information which has been available to modern medical science for the past few decades only serves to substantiate the wisdom of the original diet of raw fruits and vegetables handed down to mankind by God in Genesis 1:29. So the message of Rev. Malkmus has been to encourage people to return to the diet that God gave us in the first Chapter of Genesis, and to remind Christians that our bodies are "the temple of God."

In an effort to share his knowledge and healing experience with as many people as possible, Rev. Malkmus wrote his first book, *Why Christians Get Sick,* in 1989. It has been very well-received – as letters from all over the world attest – and is now in its 20th printing. Rev. Malkmus also holds seminars in churches and before civic groups all over the United States and into Canada. It has been very exciting in recent years to see Rev. Malkmus' teachings substantiated by new studies in how nutrition and lifestyle relate to our wellness.

But in the early years of Hallelujah Acres, walking into Christian churches with a message encouraging people to give up their meat, junk food, etc., and switch to a vegetarian diet of mainly raw foods was not a popular position. In those early years of the ministry, Rev. Malkmus' message was shunned by most Christians, even those in poor health who so badly needed to make these dietary changes. He won very few converts in those early years.

But those few converts who did listen, change their diet and heal themselves of heart disease, cancer, arthritis, diabetes and other serious diseases soon became powerful testimonials for all around them to see.

Their wellness became contagious. In the small town of Rogersville, Tenn., throughout the country and around the world, wherever people who were sick began sincerely applying the dietary program taught by Hallelujah Acres, they usually regained their health and other people saw their results.

Rogersville (population 5,000) is a good example of how word travels fast in a small town. Rev. Malkmus opened Hallelujah Acres restaurant and health food store in Rogersville on Feb. 12, 1992, first in a small store front, 11 feet wide, that had a seating capacity of 16 people. People came in ever-increasing numbers to obtain better food and to hear his health message. The restaurant and health food store had to be relocated March 1, 1993, into a larger building with a capacity of 56.

The Hallelujah Acres restaurant was successful because it showed people a diet that is healthy can also taste good. In fact, the restaurant was so successful that Rev. Malkmus closed it on March 28, 1994. The problem was that while he was reaching thousands of people by conducting seminars all around the country, writing a new book, and publishing *Back to the Garden,* the enterprise that was taking up the majority of his time was running the restaurant.

After closing the restaurant, Rev. Malkmus and Rhonda relocated Hallelujah Acres back to their 50-acre farm in Eidson, about 12 miles northwest of Rogersville. From there they refocused their goal on reaching the masses through seminars, books, *Back to the Garden* newsletters, video and audio tapes, radio and television appearances, and Back to the Garden Health Ministries. People involved in this exciting ministry came to Tennessee from all over the country to learn more about God's way of eating and healing sickness, and taking that information back to their communities to reach even more people.

Dr. Malkmus' second book, *God's Way to Ultimate Health,* published in 1995, is the most complete compilation of information we have ever seen on how to maintain or regain your health in accordance with God's natural laws. Almost 100,000 copies are in print!

Because of the tremendous growth of his ministry, in November of 1997, Dr. Malkmus and Rhonda relocated Hallelujah Acres to a former Bible college on 17 beautiful acres in Shelby, North Carolina.

The results Rhonda and Rev. Malkmus are seeing in people's lives have been extremely gratifying as they receive daily testimonies from those who have been helped.

The Hallelujah Acres' ministry dreams of reaching the whole world with the knowledge and message, "YOU DON'T HAVE TO BE SICK!!!"

Recipes for Life ... from God's Garden Order Form

Quantity Discounts for *Recipes for Life... from God's Garden*	
Number of Copies	Price
1-3 books	$24.95
4-14 books	$19.96
15-45 books	$17.47
46-over	$14.97

Name _____

Address _____

City _____ State _____ Zip _____

Phone _____ / _____

**If using P.O. Box, please also
provide a physical address for UPS delivery**

If you are not on our mailing list, but would like a free subscription to *Back to the Garden,* please check this box ☐	If you **DO** **NOT** want to continue receiving *Back to the Garden,* please check this box ☐

We appreciate your order. The life-blood of this ministry flows from your purchases of the health-related products and books we offer. Every purchase made helps us to reach more people with the message that "You do not have to be sick!" ... if God's laws of natural health are followed. Together, we are changing the way the world maintains health. Thank you and may God Bless.	Quantity	Item #	Item Name	Price Each	Total

Check   Money Order   Visa   MC   Discover   American Express

Card Number: _____

Signature _____ Card Exp. Date _____

Sub-total	
7% Sales Tax (NC residents only)	
Shipping	
Total	

Shipping Charges

WE SHIP!

Shipping Charges: $5.00 for all orders under $50.00. For orders over $50.00, add 10% for shipping and handling. Outside Continental U.S., call for foreign rates. North Carolina residents, please add 7% sales tax to entire order.

Credit Card Orders
1-800-915-WELL
Questions Call: (704) 481-1700
24-Hour Fax: (704) 481-0345

Visit our Web site
WWW.HACRES.COM

MAIL TO:

Hallelujah Acres
P.O. Box 2388
Shelby, NC 28151

Recipes for Life ... from God's Garden Order Form

Quantity Discounts for *Recipes for Life... from God's Garden*	
Number of Copies	Price
1-3 books	$24.95
4-14 books	$19.96
15-45 books	$17.47
46-over	$14.97

Name _____

Address _____

City _____ State _____ Zip _____

Phone _____ /_____

**If using P.O. Box, please also
provide a physical address for UPS delivery**

If you are not on our mailing list, but would like a free subscription to *Back to the Garden*, please check this box ☐	If you **DO** **NOT** want to continue receiving *Back to the Garden*, please check this box ☐

We appreciate your order. The life-blood of this ministry flows from your purchases of the health-related products and books we offer. Every purchase made helps us to reach more people with the message that "You do not have to be sick!" ... if God's laws of natural health are followed. Together, we are changing the way the world maintains health. Thank you and may God Bless.	Quantity	Item #	Item Name	Price Each	Total
	Check Money Order Visa MC Discover American Express			Sub-total	
	Card Number: _____			7% Sales Tax (NC residents only)	
				Shipping	
	Signature _____ Card Exp. Date _____			Total	

Shipping Charges

WE SHIP!

Shipping Charges: $5.00 for all orders under $50.00. For orders over $50.00, add 10% for shipping and handling. Outside Continental U.S., call for foreign rates. North Carolina residents, please add 7% sales tax to entire order.

**Credit Card Orders
1-800-915-WELL**
Questions Call: (704) 481-1700
24-Hour Fax: (704) 481-0345

Visit our Web site
WWW.HACRES.COM

MAIL TO:

**Hallelujah Acres
P.O. Box 2388
Shelby, NC 28151**